The Sources of Intentionality

PHILOSOPHY OF MIND

Series Editor: David J. Chalmers, Australian National University and New York University

Self Expression
Owen Flanagan

Deconstructing the Mind
Stephen Stitch

The Conscious Mind
David J. Chalmers

Minds and Bodies
Colin McGinn

What's Within?
Fiona Cowie

The Human Animal
Eric T. Olson

Dreaming Souls
Owen Flanagan

Consciousness and Cognition
Michael Thau

Thinking Without Words
José Luis Bermúdez

Identifying the Mind
U. T. Place (author), George Graham,
Elizabeth R. Valentine (editors)

Purple Haze
Joseph Levine

Three Faces of Desire
Timothy Schroeder

A Place for Consciousness
Gregg Rosenberg

Ignorance and Imagination
Daniel Stoljar

Simulating Minds
Alvin I. Goldman

Gut Reactions
Jesse J. Prinz

Phenomenal Concepts and Phenomenal Knowledge
Torin Alter, Sven Walter (editors)

Beyond Reduction
Steven Horst

What Are We?
Eric T. Olson

Supersizing the Mind
Andy Clark

Perception, Hallucination, and Illusion
William Fish

Cognitive Systems and the Extended Mind
Robert D. Rupert

The Character of Consciousness
David J. Chalmers

Perceiving the World
Bence Nanay (editor)

The Contents of Visual Experience
Susanna Siegel

The Senses
Fiona Macpherson (editor)

Attention is Cognitive Unison
Christopher Mole

Consciousness and the Prospects of Physicalism
Derk Pereboom

Introspection and Consciousness
Declan Smithies and Daniel Stoljar (editors)

The Conscious Brain
Jesse J. Prinz

Decomposing the Will
Andy Clark, Julian Kiverstein, and
Tilmann Vierkant (editors)

Phenomenal Intentionality
Uriah Kriegel (editor)

The Peripheral Mind
István Aranyosi

The Sources of Intentionality

Uriah Kriegel

OXFORD
UNIVERSITY PRESS

Oxford University Press is a department of the University of Oxford.
It furthers the University's objective of excellence in research, scholarship,
and education by publishing worldwide.

Oxford   New York
Auckland   Cape Town   Dar es Salaam   Hong Kong   Karachi
Kuala Lumpur   Madrid   Melbourne   Mexico City   Nairobi
New Delhi   Shanghai   Taipei   Toronto

With offices in
Argentina   Austria   Brazil   Chile   Czech Republic   France   Greece
Guatemala   Hungary   Italy   Japan   Poland   Portugal   Singapore
South Korea   Switzerland   Thailand   Turkey   Ukraine   Vietnam

Oxford is a registered trade mark of Oxford University Press
in the UK and certain other countries.

Published in the United States of America by
Oxford University Press
198 Madison Avenue, New York, NY 10016

© Oxford University Press 2011

First issued as an Oxford University Press paperback, 2014.

All rights reserved. No part of this publication may be reproduced, stored in a retrieval system,
or transmitted, in any form or by any means, without the prior permission in writing of Oxford
University Press, or as expressly permitted by law, by license, or under terms agreed with the
appropriate reproduction rights organization. Inquiries concerning reproduction outside the scope of
the above should be sent to the Rights Department, Oxford University Press, at the address above.

You must not circulate this work in any other form
and you must impose this same condition on any acquirer.

Library of Congress Cataloging-in-Publication Data
Kriegel, Uriah.
The sources of intentionality / by Uriah Kriegel.
   p.   cm. — (Philosophy of mind series)
Includes bibliographical references.
ISBN 978-0-19-974297-4 (hardcover : alk. paper); 978-0-19-938031-2 (paperback : alk. paper)
1. Intentionality (Philosophy) I. Title.
B105.I56K75   2011
128—dc22   2010045368

this book is dedicated to Clementine, my daughter, my daughter

Contents

Analytical Table of Contents ix

Introduction 3

1. The Experiential Origins of Intentionality 9
    1.1. The Concept of Intentionality and Anchoring Instances 10
        1.1.1. The Anchoring-Instance Model of Concept Formation 10
        1.1.2. Application to the Concept of Intentionality 19
    1.2. Experiential Intentionality the Anchor 25
        1.2.1. An Asymmetry of Ascription 26
        1.2.2. Explaining the Asymmetry 29
        1.2.3. Objections and Replies 38
    1.3. "Experiential Intentionality" 43
        1.3.1. Definition 43
        1.3.2. Existence 46
        1.3.3. Scope 47

2. The Nature of Experiential Intentionality: I. A Higher-Order Tracking Theory 67
    2.1. A Tracking Theory of Experiential Intentionality? 68
        2.1.1. Background: Tracking Theories of Mental Representation 69
        2.1.2. Representationalist Theories of Conscious Experience 73
        2.1.3. Experiential Tracking 79
    2.2. The HOT Argument 83
        2.2.1. Background: Higher-Order Theories of Conscious Experience 83
        2.2.2. Higher-Order Theory and the Tracking Account of Experiential Intentionality 87

        2.3. Experiential Intentionality and Higher-Order Tracking   94
        2.4. Objections and Replies   100
            2.4.1. "Intentionality," "Representation," "Tracking"   100
            2.4.2. What Do We Want a Theory of Intentionality for?   104

 3. The Nature of Experiential Intentionality: II. An Adverbial Theory   125
        3.1. Background: Intentional Inexistence and
             Intentional Indifference   125
        3.2. The Argument from Intentional Indifference   127
            3.2.1. The Argument   127
            3.2.2. Responses   132
            3.2.3. Brains in Vats   137
        3.3. The Argument from Intentional Inexistence   138
            3.3.1. The Argument   138
            3.3.2. Responses   144
        3.4. Experiential Intentionality as Adverbial Modification   150
        3.5. Objections to Adverbialism   159

 4. The Nature of Non-Experiential Intentionality:
    An Interpretivist Theory   189
        4.1. Potentialism   190
        4.2. Inferentialism   194
        4.3. Eliminativism   198
        4.4. Interpretivism   200
            4.4.1. Interpretivism about Non-Experiential
                   Intentionality   201
            4.4.2. Interpretivism Developed   206
            4.4.3. Objections and Replies   213

 5. Toward a General Theory of Intentionality   229
        5.1. Adverbialism plus Interpretivism   231
        5.2. Higher-Order Tracking Theory plus Interpretivism   240

References   257
Index   269

Analytical Table of Contents

Introduction 3

1. The Experiential Origins of Intentionality 9
Our conception of intentionality is grounded in introspective encounter with mental states that have their intentional content in virtue of their experiential character ("experiential-intentional states").

1.1. The Concept of Intentionality and Anchoring Instances 10
Our conception of certain phenomena, including intentionality, is grounded in observational encounter with certain instances ("anchoring instances").

1.1.1. The Anchoring-Instance Model of Concept Formation 10
There are certain concepts ("observational natural kind concepts") such that an item falls under them just in case it has the same underlying nature as their anchoring instances, which are manifest instances one encountered during their formation.

1.1.2. Application to the Concept of Intentionality 19
The concept of intentionality is an observational natural kind concept. Thus an item falls under it just in case it has the same underlying nature as the anchoring instances of intentionality.

1.2. Experiential Intentionality the Anchor 25
The only instances of intentionality we have observational encounter with are experiential-intentional states. So our conception of intentionality is grounded in observational encounter with experiential-intentional states.

1.2.1. An Asymmetry of Ascription 26
There is a remarkable asymmetry between our ascription of experiential-intentional states to ourselves and all other forms of intentional ascription: the former does not, whereas the latter do, require the deployment of principles of charity.

1.2.2. Explaining the Asymmetry 29
The best explanation of this asymmetry is that we have observational contact, through introspective encounter, with our experiential-intentional states, but with no other intentional states.

1.2.3. Objections and Replies 38
It is possible to object that we do not have observational contact with any experiential-intentional states, or that we have one with other intentional states. But neither kind of objection succeeds.

1.3. "Experiential Intentionality" 43
Some preliminary questions arise with respect to the notion of experiential intentionality: What would it take for there to be experiential intentionality? Is there in fact such intentionality? If so, how much of it is there?

1.3.1. Definition 43
Experiential intentionality is intentionality a mental state has in virtue of its experiential character. This is best understood in terms of a certain counterfactual: the state would not have the intentional content it has if it did not have the experiential character it has.

1.3.2. Existence 46
The existence of experiential intentionality is phenomenologically manifest, but can also be argued for: some conscious experiences are assessable for accuracy purely in virtue of their experiential character.

1.3.3. Scope 47
Perceptual states are clearly endowed with experiential intentionality, but so are many emotional, somatic, conative, and cognitive states.

2. The Nature of Experiential Intentionality: I. A Higher-Order Tracking Theory 67
One promising view is that states have their experiential-intentional content in virtue of being suitably higher-order tracked to track something (i.e., are higher-order tracked in their capacity as trackers of that thing).

2.1. A Tracking Theory of Experiential Intentionality? 68
An account of experiential intentionality in terms of naturalistically kosher tracking relations between physical states of the brain and physical states of the environment would be antecedently attractive.

2.1.1. Background: Tracking Theories of Mental Representation 69
Work on intentionality in the past few decades has centered on the notion of mental representation and on attempts to account for it in terms of tracking relations to the environment.

2.1.2. Representationalist Theories of Conscious Experience 73
According to representational theories of consciousness, a mental state has its experiential character in virtue of representing the environment. Work within this framework offers some options for distinguishing experiential from non-experiential representation of the environment.

2.1.3. Experiential Tracking 79
Superposition of distinctions between experiential and non-experiential representation upon tracking accounts of mental representation produces a number of elegant, though problematic, options for a tracking account of experiential intentionality.

2.2. The HOT Argument 83
Tracking accounts of experiential intentionality face an insurmountable problem: it is not what experiences track that determines their experiential-intentional content, only what they are suitably higher-order represented to track.

2.2.1. Background: Higher-Order Theories of Conscious Experience 83
According to higher-order theories of consciousness, a state has its experiential character not in virtue of representing, but in virtue of being suitably higher-order represented.

2.2.2. Higher-Order Theory and the Tracking Account of Experiential Intentionality 87
Given that what a state tracks and what it is higher-order represented to track may diverge, if the higher-order theory of consciousness is true, then what a state tracks cannot account for the intentional content that state has in virtue of its experiential character.

2.3. Experiential Intentionality and Higher-Order Tracking 94
Experiential intentionality may nonetheless be tracking-based, namely, if higher-order representation is also accounted for in terms of tracking. This would allow a "higher-order tracking theory" of experiential intentionality: a state has its experiential-intentional content in virtue of being suitably higher-order tracked to track something.

2.4. Objections and Replies 100
Higher-order tracking theory withstands the main objections against it.

2.4.1. "Intentionality," "Representation," "Tracking" 100
There is an important distinction between two notions of representation. Once it is drawn, many objections to the higher-order tracking theory are seen to rest on conceptual confusion.

2.4.2. What Do We Want a Theory of Intentionality for? 104
The two notions of representation are the targets of two different philosophical concerns, and only one of those is at the base of the present inquiry.

3. The Nature of Experiential Intentionality: II. An Adverbial Theory 125
An interesting and surprisingly plausible view is that states have their experiential-intentional content not in virtue of bearing any relation of intentional directedness to anything, but rather in virtue of exhibiting a non-relational experiential property of being-intentionally-directed-somehow.

3.1. Background: Intentional Inexistence and Intentional Indifference 125
Intentionality has two essential features: the feature that underlies failure of existential generalization ("intentional inexistence") and the feature that underlies failure of substitution of co-referential terms ("intentional indifference").

3.2. The Argument from Intentional Indifference 127
One argument against tracking-based accounts of experiential intentionality, including higher-order tracking theory, is that they fail to accommodate experiential-intentional states' intentional indifference. The argument is inconclusive.

3.2.1. The Argument 127
We can use thought experiments to construct scenarios in which two subjects are in experiential states that track the same entities, and are suitably tracked to track the same entities, but have different experiential-intentional contents.

3.2.2. Responses 132
The best response is to argue that there is a kind of entities—"response-dependent properties" or "centering features"—such that in the relevant scenarios the subject's experiences are higher-order tracked to track different entities of that kind.

3.2.3. Brains in Vats 137
Brain-in-vat scenarios, which are the converse of intentional-indifference ones, succumb to the same response.

3.3. The Argument from Intentional Inexistence 138
Another argument against tracking-based accounts of experiential intentionality, including higher-order tracking theory, is that they fail to accommodate experiential-intentional states' intentional inexistence. This argument is much more powerful.

3.3.1. The Argument 138
We can use thought experiments to construct scenarios in which a subject is in an experiential-intentional state that fails to track, or be suitably tracked to track, anything.

3.3.2. Responses 144
The conceivability of intentional-inexistence scenarios provides defeasible evidence for their possibility, but the evidence may be defeated by the rebutting consideration that if such scenarios were possible, experiential intentionality could not be naturalized. However, while this rebuts the evidence, it does nothing to undermine it.

3.4. Experiential Intentionality as Adverbial Modification 150
The argument from intentional inexistence paves the way to an adverbial account: experiential intentionality is the non-relational property of being-intentionally-directed-somehow.

3.5. Objections to Adverbialism 159
Many objections to adverbialism suggest themselves. The strongest is that it is incompatible with naturalism about experiential intentionality.

4. The Nature of Non-Experiential Intentionality: An Interpretivist Theory 189

The most plausible view of non-experiential intentionality holds that states have their non-experiential-intentional content in virtue of being consciously interpretable as having it by an ideal interpreter under ideal conditions.

4.1. Potentialism 190

One interesting view is that states have their non-experiential-intentional content in virtue of potentially having experiential-intentional content. However, the view cannot account for the intentionality of certain sub-personal states that are not even potentially experiential.

4.2. Inferentialism 194

Another view is that states have their non-experiential-intentional content in virtue of being inferentially connected to experiential-intentional states. This view cannot account for the intentionality of states of certain simple creatures (as well as sophisticated zombies) that do not have any experiential-intentional states.

4.3. Eliminativism 198

A simple and elegant view is that non-experiential states never have intentionality. This view clearly does not recover the pre-theoretically apparent extent of intentionality, and moreover has no resources to account for linguistic aboutness.

4.4. Interpretivism 200

The view that states have their non-experiential-intentional content in virtue of being consciously interpretable as having it by an ideal interpreter under ideal conditions manages to recover the pre-theoretically apparent extent of intentionality, and moreover in a unified manner.

4.4.1. Interpretivism about Non-Experiential Intentionality 201

An intentional stance theory of all intentionality faces insurmountable difficulties, but a restricted experiential-intentional stance theory of non-experiential intentionality is quite promising.

4.4.2. Interpretivism Developed 206

The view can be developed in a number of directions, depending on one's take on the notions of interpretation, ideal interpreter, and ideal conditions.

4.4.3. Objections and Replies 213

The view withstands the main objections to it, including that it is unduly irrealist about non-experiential intentionality.

5. Toward a General Theory of Intentionality 229

The preceding recommends two general theories of intentionality, generated by combining the adverbial or higher-order tracking theory of experiential intentionality with the interpretivist theory of non-experiential intentionality (against the background of the thesis of the experiential origins of intentionality).

5.1. Adverbialism plus Interpretivism 231
One general theory is that an item has its intentional content in virtue of being either intentionally-directed-somehow or suitably ideally-interpretable-somehow.

5.2. Higher-Order Tracking Theory plus Interpretivism 240
A second and slightly more plausible general theory of intentionality is that an item has its intentional content in virtue of either being suitably tracked to track something or being ideally tracked to be suitably tracked to track something.

References 257
Index 269

The Sources of Intentionality

Introduction

A generation ago, the problem of intentionality was at the center of activity in the philosophy of mind. Indeed, the project of finding a place for intentionality in the natural order—"naturalizing intentionality"—consumed more intellectual energy than virtually any other issue in philosophy. Yet today the naturalizing intentionality research program generates almost no discernible activity. Why the remarkable turnaround?

There appear to be two conflicting explanations. The first is that the exciting part of the research program has been exhausted, and successfully so, with only technical issues remaining to be resolved. The work done a generation ago outlines the solution to the philosophical core of the problem of intentionality: the reason there is intentionality in nature is that some physical items can track others, with the relevant tracking consisting in a scientifically acceptable relation grounded in familiar, unmysterious causal processes. Some issues remain to be addressed: what the best information-theoretic gloss on the tracking relation is; whether the information-theoretic story should be enriched with a teleological dimension; how exactly to account for intentional failure, i.e., misrepresentation; and so on. But these questions are insufficiently titillating to garner the intellectual energy that the research program had enjoyed a generation ago. Hence the felt drop in levels of activity in pursuit of the program.

The other explanation is less sanguine. It is that the naturalizing intentionality research program bears all the hallmarks of a degenerating research program. The program has run up against principled obstacles it seems unable to surmount. Far from being technical, the problems just mentioned are fatal: every information-theoretic gloss offered thus far has turned out to assign counter-intuitive contents in central, non-artificial cases; it is unclear that teleological elements are genuinely explanatory; and tracking relations simply do not provide the resources to accommodate misrepresentation. Instead of addressing these principled difficulties, proponents of the program have chosen to brand them as technical and proceed to effectively ignore them. As a result, no new illumination of intentionality has been offered in years, and whatever work does take place has tended to pad the protective belt of the program more than anything else.

Many critics of the naturalizing intentionality research program see a deep reason for its manifest inadequacy, namely, that it ignores entirely the role of phenomenal consciousness and the first-person perspective in its theorizing about intentionality. In doing so, the program has been in lockstep with philosophy of mind at large. A generation ago, it was not uncommon for philosophers to water down the phenomena so that their more naturalistically recalcitrant aspects—notably, phenomenal and subjective aspects—are defined away. However, now that consciousness and the first-person are recognized again as real and central features of the mind, this is no longer tenable. An understanding of intentionality that takes them into account, and grants them the central place they deserve, is well overdue.

On this diagnosis, the naturalizing intentionality program has suffered from a systemic blindspot. It conceives of intentionality as a theoretical posit of sorts, a property ascribed from the third-person perspective in the context of trying to explain and predict the behavior of persons and other intelligibly-behaving systems. The paradigms of intentionality, so conceived, are the propositional attitudes, especially belief and desire. But this ignores a whole other layer of intentionality that is much closer to home and stands at the heart of any natural conception of our cognitive relationship to the world. Once we adopt a first-person perspective, we can see intentionality as a property we sometimes ascribe to conscious states not because it is theoretically profitable to do so, but simply because they present themselves to us in our personal experience as *directed* in the relevant sense. The paradigms of intentionality so conceived are typically not belief and desire, but manifestly intentional conscious states, such as perceptual experiences and conscious occurrent thoughts. An adequate account of intentionality should, according to these critics, be organized around these conscious experiences, not brute and blind tracking relations between brains and their environments.

While research that focuses on the intentionality of phenomenally conscious states has been taking place at the margins of philosophical activity for at least two decades (as well as, effectively, among Austro-Hungarian philosophers toward the end of the nineteenth century), it is only relatively recently that such research has started to consolidate into a barely discernible competing research program, which we may call the "phenomenal intentionality research program." The foundational insight of this alternative program is that there is a kind of intentionality proper to phenomenally conscious states that is both distinctive and basic. It is distinctive in that it has key features absent from the intentionality exhibited by any items devoid of phenomenal consciousness. It is basic in that the intentionality of non-conscious items is somehow grounded in, or at least dependent upon, the intentionality of conscious ones. A research program for understanding intentionality that was founded on recognition of the basicness and distinctiveness of the intentionality proper to phenomenally conscious states would be more likely to issue in an accurate and honest portrayal of its subject matter, without letting antecedent ideological commitments pervert the phenomena. And the upshot of that portrayal is that the reason there is intentionality in the world is not that certain mental states bear the right kind of tracking relations to the environment, but that certain mental states exhibit the right kind of phenomenal consciousness, that is, have the right kind of phenomenal character.

What we have here, in fact, are two seemingly opposed outlooks on the source of intentionality. One view is that the source of intentionality is the right kind of tracking relation, the other that it is the right kind of phenomenal character. On the first view, intentionality is originally injected into the world, so to speak, with the appearance in nature of a certain kind of tracking relation. It is when the relevant tracking relation occurs between distinct events or states (including brain states and environmental states) that intentionality makes its first appearance on the scene. Once intentionality has been thus injected into the world, it can start being "passed around" to non-tracking items. But the ultimate source of all intentionality is the relevant kind of tracking relation. On the second view, intentionality is originally injected into the world with the appearance of a certain kind of phenomenal character. It is when the relevant phenomenal character shows up that intentionality makes its first appearance. Here too, once this phenomenal character appears, and brings in its train original intentionality, intentionality can be "passed around" to items lacking any phenomenal character. But the ultimate source of all intentionality is the relevant phenomenal character.

Personally, I am attracted to both outlooks, and so am keen to consider in what ways they may be reconciled or even combined. I am interested in finding ways to place phenomenal consciousness at the heart of the theory of intentionality while at the same time priming intentionality for its eventual naturalization and demystification. When a challenger research program is ascendant, in a first stage it is typically confrontational and rejectionist—it is rebellious. But in a second stage, it is often recognized that research programs rarely have no grain of wisdom in them whatsoever, and that the correct approach is to extract the various grains of wisdom, the fundamentally sound insights behind competing research programs, and integrate them within a single stable overarching framework. I am keen to find a framework that gives pride of place to both consciousness and naturalization.

This book presents and defends a framework that attempts to do so. The framework comprises three central elements. First, it argues that all intentionality is grounded—has its origins—in the intentionality proper to conscious experiences (phenomenally conscious states). Secondly, however, it offers a naturalistic account of the intentionality proper to conscious experiences, indeed an account that appeals centrally to tracking relations. Thirdly, it offers a naturalistic account of the manner by which the intentionality proper to conscious experiences grounds all other intentionality, hence a naturalistic account of non-conscious, non-experiential intentionality. The result is a framework where all intentionality is naturalized, but also where the naturalized non-experiential intentionality is seen to be grounded in a naturalized experiential intentionality.

This framework is developed in Chapters 1, 2, and 4 of the book—with each of these chapters handling one of the three central elements of the framework. Chapter 3 examines an alternative, vaguely non-naturalistic account of experiential intentionality, which has obvious disadvantages relative to, but also certain advantages over, the naturalistic account from Chapter 2. Chapter 5 assembles the results of the previous chapters to formulate an overall statement of the emerging picture of intentionality. Let me close with a fuller roadmap to the book.

In Chapter 1, I argue for what I call the "experiential origin thesis." This is the thesis that our very conception of intentionality, or aboutness, is grounded in our grasp of experiential intentionality, the aboutness proper to conscious experiences. The argument proceeds by developing a general model of how we form our conception of certain phenomena, a model which, in combination with the fact that we have a special kind of access to our own experiential-intentional states, casts our access to such states as anchoring our conception of intentionality.

In Chapter 2, I articulate and defend what I call the "higher-order tracking theory" of experiential intentionality. According to the higher-order tracking theory, a mental state's experiential intentionality consists in its being suitably higher-order tracked to track something. After elucidating the notion of tracking, and arguing against first-order tracking accounts of experiential intentionality, I present the case for a higher-order tracking theory, with special attention to a version of it that I call the "naturalized self-tracking account."

In Chapter 3, I examine the case for a very different approach to experiential intentionality, which I call the "adverbial theory." According to this, a mental state's experiential intentionality consists not in any elaborate relation (tracking or otherwise) the state bears to anything, but rather in a certain intrinsic modification of the state's experiential character. A conscious thought or perception of a triangle has its experiential intentionality, on this view, in virtue of being experienced triangle-wise. I motivate the adverbial theory by arguing initially against tracking-based accounts of experiential intentionality, and ultimately against appealing to any relations in such an account. I conclude, however, with skepticism about the naturalistic prospects of the adverbial theory, and end up avowing a degree of credence in it that, while quite high, is not as high as my credence in the higher-order tracking theory.

In Chapter 4, I turn to the task of accounting for non-experiential intentionality. I consider four possible accounts, and endorse one at the expense of the others. According to the endorsed account, which I call "interpretivism" about non-experiential intentionality, an item's non-experiential intentionality consists in its disposition to provoke in an ideal interpreter under ideal conditions an interpretive experience, namely, the experience of assigning intentional content to that state. After elucidating interpretivism, I argue for its superiority over the competing accounts.

Finally, in Chapter 5, I collect the results of the previous chapters and synthesize them into an overarching picture of the nature of intentionality.

In fact, two pictures emerge: one combines the experiential origin thesis, the higher-order tracking theory of experiential intentionality, and interpretivism about non-experiential intentionality; the other combines the experiential origin thesis, the adverbial theory of experiential intentionality, and interpretivism about non-experiential intentionality. Unsurprisingly, I avow greater confidence in the former.

Harlem, U.S.A.
June 2010

1
The Experiential Origins of Intentionality

Introduction/Abstract

The purpose of this book is to develop an account of intentionality that assigns a central theoretical role to a kind of intentionality proper to conscious experience. The purpose of the present chapter is to argue that we *should* have such an account of intentionality; that the intentionality proper to our conscious experience—"experiential intentionality"—*deserves* a central theoretical role in our account of intentionality. I will argue that our conception of intentionality is grounded in our grasp of experiential intentionality, and that to that extent, experiential intentionality is the origin of all intentionality. I call this the *thesis of the experiential origins of intentionality*, or the *experiential origin thesis* for short.

The plan of the chapter is as follows. I start, in §1.1, with a general model of how we form our conceptions of certain phenomena, including the phenomenon of intentionality. In §1.2, I present an argument to the effect that the application of the general model to the case of intentionality generates the result that our conception of intentionality is grounded in our grasp of experiential intentionality. I close, in §1.3, with some elucidations of the central notion of experiential intentionality.

Before starting, a note to the reader: in the course of the discussion, I will often present very precise formulations of central theses and definitions, in the form of indented biconditionals; by and large, these need not be read in order to follow the discussion, and the reader is herewith entreated to skip them if s/he finds no joy in going over them.

1.1. The Concept of Intentionality and Anchoring Instances

On the assumption that intentionality is a natural kind notion, understanding how we form our conception of intentionality requires prior understanding of how we form natural kind concepts in general. This is of course an immense area of research, and we will have to treat it with considerable brevity here.[1] In §1.1.1, I propose a general model of the formation of natural kind concepts—or more accurately, of a certain kind of formation of a certain kind of natural kind concept—that I call the *anchoring-instance model*. In §1.1.2, I suggest an application of this general model to the concept of intentionality that leads to the experiential origin thesis. (The argument for that application will be presented in §1.2.)

1.1.1. The Anchoring-Instance Model of Concept Formation

In this subsection, I discuss three toy models of concept formation, defending the third. All three models are decidedly underdeveloped, as concept formation is a highly rich topic, joined to a vast literature, and there is no hope to discuss it adequately as a mere preliminary to the main subject matter of this book. However, many of the details of how each of the three models could play out do not affect the implications I will be seeking for our conception of intentionality. What I will end up endorsing may thus be better thought of as a family of models of concept formation rather than one specific model; my concern will be with the application of any model from this family to the concept of intentionality.

There is no special reason to expect that a single type of model of concept formation would cover the variety of manners in which we can form concepts. Different types of concept, in particular, may well be formed in different ways. I will focus here on the *non-parasitic* formation of *observational natural* kind concepts. Let me explain what I mean by these specifications.

For present purposes, let a natural kind concept be any concept whose instances all seem to share a "natural similarity," that is, a similarity that is in the nature of things themselves rather than due to our faculties and/or activities.[2] The model I will propose for concept formation might be modified to accommodate other kind concepts, but my concern here is with the formation of *natural* kind concepts.

More specifically, my concern is with *observational* natural kind concepts, where a natural kind concept is observational (relative to a subject S) just in case it is nomologically possible (for S) to observe instances of the concepts. Thus, the concept of a horse is an observational natural kind concept (relative to the normal human subject), because we (normal human subjects) can observe horses; the concept of a lepton is a non-observational natural kind concept, because we cannot observe leptons.[3] The model of concept formation I will propose may or may not be correct for non-observational natural kind concepts, but in any case I am proposing it only for observational ones.

More specifically yet, my concern here is with what might be called "non-parasitic" formation of observational natural kind concepts. Consider our concept of a mammal.[4] As it happens, most of us formed our concept of a mammal by reading (or hearing) about mammals. But this manner of concept formation is parasitic on a more basic manner, namely, that by which those who wrote what we read (or said what we heard) about mammals formed their concept of a mammal.[5] Forming a concept of a mammal on the basis of something like testimony is parasitic on forming it on the basis of perceptual encounter with mammals. It is this sort of non-parasitic concept formation, involving encounter with instances that fall under the concept, that concerns me here.[6]

One traditional model of such concept formation goes something like this. A subject goes out into the world and encounters many particulars, including animals. Among some subsets of those particulars she notices certain systematic and apparently objective similarities, and she therefore groups them together. For example, she notices a similarity among dogs, cats, and horses: they are all furry, four-legged land animals with faces featuring two eyes, a nose, and a mouth similarly spatially arranged. On this basis, she specifies a criterion for membership in a group in terms of observable features of prospective members: being a furry, four-legged land animal with the right kind of face. This criterion, which typically consists in a number of jointly sufficient and severally necessary conditions for membership in the relevant kind, is effectively her concept of a mammal: animals the subject has not encountered qualify as belonging to the group just in case they satisfy the criterion. More generally, and to a first approximation, the model is this:

(C) For any natural kind K and particular x, there is a criterion C, such that x qualifies as a K iff x satisfies C.

We may call this the *criterial model*. Importantly, the "criterion" it adverts to must be specifiable in terms of observable features.[7]

One immediate difficulty with the criterial model, however, is that it cannot explain how we can come to *discover* that whales and bats, for example, are also mammals. On the criterial model, a particular is *discovered* to be a member of a kind by being *discovered* to satisfy the criterion. Thus, although interaction with certain rodents (e.g., the chipmunk) is rare, and the concept of a mammal is not typically formed—not even in part— through interaction with them, one may discover later that they qualify as mammals as well, namely, by discovering that they too are furry four-legged land animals with good faces. However, the whale is none of those things, so it is unclear in what way it could be *discovered* to be a mammal. Perhaps a story could be told about how we might *decide* to count the whale as a mammal, by deciding to *change* our criterion for membership in the mammal kind. But the whale's qualifying as a mammal was never a *decision*—it was a *discovery*. This means that our concept of a mammal was ready to subsume the whale all along, and did not need to be *changed* in order to do so.

The lesson from the criterial model's shortcoming is that the concept of a mammal appeals to certain hidden features of mammals that are taken to go more deeply into what makes them belong together. The manifest similarity between them is always taken to be merely a symptom of a deeper underlying commonality, and our concept of a mammal adverts to this underlying commonality in classifying a given particular as a mammal.[8] In the first instance, the relevant hidden commonality may be still observ*able*, even if not immediately, easily, or typically observ*ed*: being warm-blooded, giving live birth, nursing the young through a mammary gland.[9] But ultimately, there is a deeper unobservable commonality among mammals at the genetic level. We know, for example, that the whale evolved from the hippopotamus, and we know this because whale DNA is extremely similar to hippopotamus DNA. There is, more generally, some underlying genetic commonality among all mammals that makes them mammals (as well as a genetic peculiarity that makes other animals not mammals). This genetic commonality (and peculiarity) is the "underlying nature" of the property of being a mammal.

These observations may inspire a model of natural kind concept formation that makes the concepts appeal solely to such underlying hidden properties. On such a model, acquiring the concept of a mammal fully is a matter of coming to know the underlying nature of mammals. Let G be the underlying genetic commonality among mammals. According to the present model, our concept of a mammal is such that a particular qualifies as a mammal just in case it has G. More generally, and to a first approximation:

(UN) For any natural kind K and particular x, there is an underlying nature N, such that a particular x qualifies as a K iff x has N.[10]

Call this the *underlying-nature model*. Unlike the criterial model, it can readily account for the *discovery* that the whale is a mammal: it is simply the discovery that the whale has the right underlying nature—it has G.

The problem with the underlying-nature model is the opposite of the problem with the criterial model. In the criterial model, too *little* was discoverable. In the underlying-nature model, too *much* is discoverable. Thus, further research could turn up evidence that, initial appearances (and studies) notwithstanding, dogs, cats, and horses do not have G. By the lights of the underlying-nature model, this would effectively be evidence that dogs, cats, and horses do not qualify as mammals. For that matter, it could in principle be discovered that there are no mammals other than the whale and the hippopotamus: all other animals lack G. In fact, it is not clear that the model, as stated above, can rule out the possibility that it be discovered that there are no mammals at all, namely, in case it turns out that no animal has G.[11]

These are absurd consequences. The lesson here seems to be that there are *some* a priori restrictions on what can in principle be discovered regarding the extension of the concept of a mammal, hence some a priori conditions that anything must satisfy in order to qualify as a mammal. In particular, the following seems to be a priori: one's concept of a mammal is such that at least *some* (and probably *most*) of the particulars one encountered during the formation of one's concept of a mammal, and noticed to have the manifest, observable features associated with mammals, must in fact qualify as mammals. That is to say, it is a priori that some (most?) furry, four-legged land animals with good faces encountered during concept formation are mammals. It can in principle be discovered that, surprisingly, dogs do not qualify as mammals. But it *cannot* be discovered that dogs, cats, horses, cows, goats, and every other manifestly similar animal a subject encountered during the formation of her concept of a mammal do not qualify. For the formation of a concept of a mammal requires an early stage in which certain animals are grouped together and used collectively as an anchor for the construction of a kind category. The status of these anchoring instances as mammals may be negotiable individually, but not collectively: each one may turn out not to be a mammal after all, but they cannot *all* turn out not to be mammals.

These observations suggest to me a compromise model that combines the virtues of the criterial and underlying-nature models, a model where *both* observable features and underlying natures are appealed to by natural kind concepts in classifying given particulars as mammals. On a natural model, a subject goes out into the world and encounters many particulars, including many, such as dogs, cats, and horses, that are furry, four-legged land animals with good faces. On this basis alone, she forms the concept of a kind members of which have the same underlying nature as (most of) the furry, four-legged land animals with good faces that she has encountered; this is effectively her concept of a mammal. She may later discover that other animals, such as the chipmunk, are also furry, four-legged, etc. And she may later yet discover that yet other animals, such as the whale, also have the underlying nature that the original encountered animals have, even though they are not furry, four-legged, etc. But her concept of a mammal was always ready to subsume these new instances.

Let us say that the dog, the chipmunk, and the whale are each an *instance* of the concept of a mammal; that the dog and the chipmunk are, but the whale is not, a *manifest instance* of the concept of a mammal; and that the dog is, but the chipmunk and the whale are not, an *anchoring instance* of the concept of a mammal.[12] To a first approximation, an anchoring instance is a manifest instance that the subject encountered in the process of forming the relevant concept; a manifest instance is one that exhibits the relevant observable features.[13] According to the model under consideration, the concept of mammal is such that a particular qualifies just in case it has the same underlying nature as most anchoring mammals. More generally, and to a first approximation:

(AI) For any natural kind K and particular x, there is a nature N, such that x qualifies as a K iff (i) most anchoring instances of K have N, and (ii) x has N.[14]

Call this the *anchoring-instance model*. Unlike the criterial model, it can account for the discovery that the whale is a mammal: it is the discovery that the whale has the same underlying nature as dogs, cats, horses, etc. And unlike the underlying-nature model, it can account for it being undiscoverable that no "manifest mammal" is really a mammal: for that would involve discovering that none of the anchoring instances has the same underlying nature as most of the anchoring instances—a logical contradiction.[15] The anchoring-instance model thus avoids the main pitfalls of its competition.[16]

I close this subsection with ten clarifications of (AI). The first six elucidate central notions in (AI), the last four warn about what is *not* implied by (AI).[17]

First, for something to "qualify" as a K is for it to meet the condition specified in (hence fall in the extension of) the concept of a K. For example, qualifying as a mammal is meeting the condition specified by (thus falling in the extension of) the concept of a mammal. By "the" concept of a mammal, I mean the concept that the normal subject would form under normal conditions. The normality of the subject can be construed either statistically or teleologically: a statistically normal subject is a subject that behaves relevantly similarly to most other subjects; a teleologically normal subject is one whose concept-forming mechanisms function as they are supposed to.[18] The teleological notion of normality is probably the more relevant one here, but presumably the anchoring-instance model itself is neutral on such matters. It may be that an informed-ness condition should be added here: "the" concept of a mammal is the concept that a normal *well-informed* subject would form under normal conditions (here an elucidation of "well-informed" would have to be appended). Also, it is possible that in some areas the normality of the subject would have to be relativized in certain ways (e.g., to a culture or a time); the general shape of the account would not be overly affected.

Secondly, there are far-from-trivial questions surrounding what a "concept" is. Two main approaches treat concepts as abstract entities or alternatively as mental entities. Here I have in mind concepts as mental entities, but it may well be that the anchoring-instance model can operate with concepts as abstract entities as well. In any case, what kind of mental or abstract entity a concept is is something the model is neutral on. One common and congenial approach individuates concepts (construed as mental entities) in terms of their possession conditions (see Peacocke 1992). Of course, what it takes for the subject to possess a concept is no less debatable. Presumably, she needs to have certain discriminatory, recognitional, and classificatory abilities, and probably further facts must hold of her as well. I would insist that, to possess a concept, the subject need not know any associated public-language noun, or be aware of herself as possessing the concept (or for that matter understand the notion of a concept). What exactly is required is an issue that needs to be resolved independently of the anchoring-instance model, and its resolution could be plugged into the model to generate a more explicit account.

Thirdly, the "formation" of a concept is presumably the process that takes the subject from a state of not possessing the concept to a state of possessing it. One natural view is that this process takes as many months or years as the infant or toddler requires before acquiring the relevant abilities (discrimination etc.). A very different view is that there is no clean-cut division between an initial stage of concept formation and a later period of mere concept "maintenance," but rather a single "dynamic," cascading process of ever-evolving, always-live concept formation and maintenance, such that the process of concept formation can never be truly said to have ended. An intermediate view would let the relevant process remain "live" for many years, but still weigh early stages more heavily than later ones (and perhaps let it die out at some point). The anchoring-instance model is neutral on which is the best option here. It should simply recruit whichever view generates the most accurate predictions and retrodictions for the model as a whole.

Fourthly, the notion of "encounter" is fairly straightforward in its application to *tokens*, but has an interesting application to *types* that is less straightforward. One might say that one encountered dragonfruit in one's travels in the East, with the thought that one is now familiar with the *type* dragonfruit thanks to one's seeing and touching *token* dragonfruits. The term "encounter" can be used both for the seeing/touching of the tokens and for the ensuing familiarity with the type. Consequently, when we speak of encounter with dogs, cats, and horses, we may have in mind either token-encounter or type-encounter. Since anchoring instances are manifest instances encountered during concept formation, there are consequently two ways of understanding what counts as an anchoring instance. The stricter view would require token-encounter, counting as anchoring instances of S's concept of a mammal only those individual manifest mammals that S "met" (this particular cat, that particular horse). The more laid-back view would include also individual mammals manifestly belonging to the relevant sub-kind (all cats, all horses), thus requiring only type-encounter of anchoring instances.[19] This second approach strikes me as the most likely to return the right results with respect to who possesses which concepts, but again the anchoring-instance model need not be definitionally tied to this particular take on encounter rather than the other.

A fifth issue concerns what counts as "most" of the anchoring instances. One could require a simple majority, or alternatively require some substantial majority, say 80 percent. Here too, the theoretical choice between the many options should be made by considering which option is such that, when it is plugged into (AI), (AI) returns the right results on concept possession.

Sixthly, (AI) is formulated in terms of "particulars," a notion with straightforward application for natural kind concepts canonically expressed by count nouns (such as "mammal"). The application is less clear when it comes to natural kind concepts canonically expressed by mass nouns, notably substance terms such as "water" and "gold." However, for such natural kind concepts, the thesis can be reformulated in terms of samples, or quantities, or some such type of entity. More conveniently, we may simply allow the term "particular" to range over those types of entity as well. In this (admittedly technical) usage, samples and quantities are particulars.

Seventhly, although the model is tailored to cases in which the underlying nature of anchoring instances is uniform and clear-cut, it can be extended to apply to cases where the situation is murkier. Thus, suppose that some natural kind concept is such that, as it turns out, no majority of its anchoring instances has any underlying commonality. Different minority subsets of the anchoring instances may have local commonalities, perhaps with family-resemblance overlaps, but no majority subset has a commonality. How does the anchoring-instance model treat this case? There are several ways to go here, it seems to me, but the most natural would be to say that there is no natural kind in the area, and that therefore the relevant concept is an empty natural kind concept or a non-natural ("manifest") kind concept.[20] In another scenario, there might be a natural kind concept such that, as it turns out, all of its anchoring instances have two independent (causally and explanatorily insulated) underlying natures N_1 and N_2, but some *non*-anchoring particulars have only N_1 and others only N_2. How does the model handle this scenario? Again, there are several ways to go, but to my mind the most natural are to say either (a) that there are two separate natural kinds here, and thus the concept is ambiguous, or (b) that the concept unambiguously picks out a conjunctive natural kind.[21] There may be other challenging scenarios, but I see no reason to think that any would render the anchoring-instance model predictively impotent.

Eighthly, observe that the model does *not* imply that all anchoring instances are genuine instances—only that most are. For it is true of any anchoring instance that it can turn out not to be an instance at all. This way of putting things may have an initial air of paradox about it, but in fact is perfectly coherent. Consider Twardowski's (1894) distinction between determining and modifying adjectives: whereas a brown car is always a car, and so "brown" functions here as a *determining* adjective, a fake barn is never a barn, and so "fake" functions as a *modifying* adjective. We can introduce a third kind of adjective, the "neutral adjective," which guarantees neither determination nor modification of the predicate it accompanies—sometimes it determines, sometimes it modifies. The adjective "rubber" is a neutral adjective: a rubber tire is a kind of tire, but a rubber duck is not a kind of duck. In the present context, the adjective "anchoring" functions as a neutral adjective in the same sense: some anchoring instances are instances, but some are not. Whether a given anchoring instance is an instance depends on whether its underlying nature is the same as the underlying nature of most of the anchoring instances it is one of. Hence the anchoring-instance model does not prejudge whether a given anchoring instance is indeed an instance. At the same time, it does prejudge that *most* of the anchoring instances are instances (or else that the concept is empty). Observe that this makes the anchoring-instance model non-circular and reductive: it does not account (circularly or non-reductively) for being an F in terms of being a special sort of F (an "anchoring" F), but rather accounts for being an F in terms of being a G (an "anchoring-F").[22]

Ninthly, anchoring instances should not be confused with prototypes—the theoretical role of the former in the present model is quite different from that of the latter in prototype theories of the structure of concepts.[23] There are similarities between the two, but also important differences. The main similarity is that both anchoring and prototypical instances are proper subsets of all instances, set apart from, and in some sense assigned some priority over, other instances.[24] The differences go much deeper, however.

Most notably, some anchors are not prototypes: a bed is an anchoring instance in most subjects' concept of furniture, but appears not to be a prototypical instance.[25] For it appears that beds do not score high on typicality tests (Rosch 1975), even though they are manifest instances of furniture one normally encounters when forming one's concept of furniture. More generally, there are many more anchors than prototypes: whereas chairs and tables are plausibly the only prototypes of furniture, anchors include beds, cabinets, bookcases, and more. The deeper issue here is that anchoring instances enjoy a special *epistemological* status, but no special *metaphysical* status, whereas prototypical instances enjoy a special metaphysical status as well. Thus an anchoring instance of some kind K is in no sense *more of an instance* of K than a non-anchoring instance, whereas a prototypical instance is in some sense more of an instance.[26]

Tenthly, though, it is important to appreciate that the anchoring-instance model of the *formation* of natural kind concepts is consistent with a prototype model of the *structure* of such concepts.[27] In fact, it is consistent with many different theses on the metaphysics of natural kinds and the semantics of natural kind terms and concepts. Perhaps most importantly, it is compatible with the main doctrines currently widely accepted among philosophers about natural kinds and natural kind terms/concepts: that natural kinds are "real" and "objective" (as per realism about natural kinds) that have scientifically discoverable essences (as per scientific essentialism), and that natural kind terms and concepts are rigid designators that allow for a posteriori necessary truths (as per Kripkean semantics).[28]

Hopefully these remarks make the anchoring-instance model sufficiently clear to proceed. The remarks should be taken as *preliminary*, and the model as a *framework* in need of much further elaboration that might enrich it considerably and/or modify aspects of it importantly. As noted at the opening, it is in fact best thought of as a *family* of views. As long as further elaborations and modifications do not undermine certain essential elements of the model, the limited exposition offered here could be used in an application to the concept of intentionality. This is the task of the next subsection.

1.1.2. Application to the Concept of Intentionality

According to the anchoring-instance model, a particular qualifies as an instance of some observational natural kind concept just in case it has the same underlying nature as most anchoring instances of that concept, i.e., has the same underlying nature as most of the manifest instances the subject encountered during the formation of her concept of that kind. This model applies to intentionality on the assumption—highly plausible—that the concept of intentionality is an observational natural kind concept.[29] The application yields that an item qualifies as intentional just in case it has the same underlying nature as most anchoring instances of intentionality. Now: if we add to this that all anchoring instances of the concept of intentionality are experiential-intentional states, we obtain that an item qualifies as intentional just in case it has the same underlying nature as most experiential-intentional states, or more accurately, just in case it has the same underlying nature as most of the experiential-intentional states that serve as anchoring instances of intentionality.

In the next section, I will argue that we should add this extra thesis: all the anchoring instances of (the concept of) intentionality are experiential-intentional states.[30] With this thesis in hand, we will be in a position to use the anchoring-instance model and the claim that the concept of intentionality is an observational natural kind concept to reason as follows:

1. When K is an observational natural kind concept, an item x qualifies as a K iff x has the same underlying nature as most anchoring instances of K;
2. The concept of intentionality is an observational natural kind concept; therefore,
3. An item x qualifies as intentional iff x has the same underlying nature as most anchoring instances of intentionality;
4. There is a subset of experiential-intentional states, such that an item x is an anchoring instance of intentionality iff x is a member of that subset; therefore,
5. There is a subset of experiential-intentional states, such that an item x qualifies as intentional iff x has the same underlying nature as most members of that subset.[31]

Note that this presentation of the reasoning does not commit to whether the subset of experiential-intentional states that serve as anchoring instances of intentionality is a proper or improper subset. For it may well be that although all anchoring instances of intentionality are experiential-intentional states, not all experiential-intentional states are anchoring instances of intentionality.[32]

Recall that an anchoring instance is a manifest instance encountered during the process of the concept's formation. So there are two ways in which some experiential-intentional states might not be anchoring instances of intentionality. One is by failing to exhibit the manifest features of intentional states. This is admittedly not very plausible. The other way is much more plausible, however: it might be that some experiential-intentional states are not *encountered* instances, instances that have been encountered during the (normal subject's non-parasitic) formation of the concept of intentionality.[33] For example, during the formation of my conception of intentionality, I had not yet undergone, hence not yet encountered, gustatory experiences as of snake meat or as of sea urchin sushi.[34] These intentional experiences came relatively late in life, and so are not encountered instances in any relevant sense. Quite plausibly, then, not all experiential-intentional states are anchoring instances of intentionality, but only a *proper* subset thereof, namely, the set of *encountered* experiential-intentional states.[35] If so, we can formulate the above reasoning more precisely, and more pointedly, as follows:

1. For any item x and observational natural kind K, x qualifies as a K iff there is a nature N, such that (i) most of the anchoring instances of K have N and (ii) x has N;
2. The concept of intentionality is an observational natural kind concept; therefore,
3. For any item x, x qualifies as intentional iff there is a nature N, such that (i) most of the anchoring instances of intentionality have N and (ii) x has N;
4. For any item x, x is an anchoring instance of intentionality iff x is an encountered experiential-intentional state; therefore,
5. For any item x, x qualifies as intentional iff there is a nature N, such that (i) most encountered experiential-intentional states have N and (ii) x has N.

As noted, the key premise in this reasoning is 4, and it will be defended in the next section.

The conclusion of this reasoning can be thought of as one possible formulation of the experiential origin (EO) thesis, since it grounds our conception of intentionality in our grasp of experiential intentionality. The formulation is this:

(EO) For any item x, x qualifies as intentional iff there is a nature N, such that (i) most encountered experiential-intentional states have N and (ii) x has N.

There is a straightforward sense in which (EO) captures the *spirit* of the experiential origin thesis, and can thus legitimately serve as its *letter*.

Since (EO) is an application of the anchoring-instance model to the concept of intentionality, the clarifications offered above of the general model apply here as well. First, for an item to qualify as intentional is for it to fall in the extension of the concept of intentionality, where this should be taken as short for "the normally circumstanced (teleologically) normal subject's concept of intentionality." Secondly, different versions of (EO) will have different views on the ontology of the concept of intentionality, and thirdly, different versions will have different views on what is involved in the concept's formation. Fourthly, the set of "encountered" experiential-intentional states can be construed either as the set of encountered tokens or as the set of tokens that belong to the encountered types (and my suspicion is that the latter construal would return the better results).[36] Fifthly, different versions of (EO) will differ on how many encountered experiential-intentional states count as "most." Sixthly, intentional items—items with intentional properties—are all clearly particulars.[37] Seventhly, (EO) does not rule out the possibility that the concept of intentionality is an empty concept or a conjunctive concept. Eighthly, (EO) does not imply that all anchoring instances of intentionality are really instances, only that most are. Ninthly, to say that only experiential-intentional states are anchoring instances of the concept of intentionality is not to say that only experiential-intentional states are *prototypical* intentional states—though these two theses would be somewhat similarly inspired, and the latter thesis may well be independently plausible.[38] Tenthly, (EO) is compatible with any number of rather popular claims about the metaphysics of intentional properties and the semantics of intentional terms, including that the former are "real" and "objective" and that the latter are rigid designators.

In addition, one more central notion must be elucidated in (EO) that was not part of (AI), namely, the notion of an "experiential-intentional" state. I will dwell on this more patiently in §1.3.1, but the general idea is that a mental state is experiential-intentional when it is intentional in virtue of being experiential. It is not self-evident that there are such states (see discussion in §1.3.2), but perceptual experiences are natural candidates: a visual experience as of a pear or a tulip, an auditory experience as of trumpets, and an olfactory experience as of ground coffee are all intentional experiences. Emotional and somatic states, such as joys and itches, are clearly often experiential, though their status as intentional is subject to debate. Conversely, cognitive and conative states, such as thoughts and intentions, are typically intentional, but their status as experiential is uncertain (see discussion in §1.3.3). Depending on how the relevant debates are settled, these may or may not turn out to be potential anchoring instances of intentionality if (EO) is true. The case for (EO) that I will make in §2 is supposed to be insensitive to the scope of experiential intentionality, though obviously the project of grounding all intentionality in experiential intentionality is liable to go more smoothly the more inclusive the prospective grounds.

It will be noted that the experiential origin thesis, as construed here, is in the first instance an *epistemological* thesis: a thesis about the grounding of the *concept* of intentionality, not the *property* of intentionality. It does have a straightforward implication for the property, namely, well, that for an item to instantiate the property picked out by the concept of intentionality, it must have the same underlying nature as most experiential-intentional states. But at its core, the experiential origin thesis is a thesis about our grip on, hence epistemic relation to, the phenomenon of intentionality. A more immediate implication of its is for theory construction: if our grip on intentionality is indeed based upon our grasp of experiential intentionality, then the theory of intentionality ought to be organized, in some sense, around our understanding of the phenomenon of experiential intentionality.

It should also be noted that the experiential origin thesis is not by itself in any tension with the notion that the origin of intentionality is a certain kind of tracking relation. For if the experiential-intentional states that function as anchoring instances of intentionality turn out to have their experiential-intentional content in virtue of tracking the environment, it would be true of the origin of intentionality both that it is experience-based and that it is tracking-based. Indeed, the prospects for such a marriage of experience-first and tracking-first approaches will be taken up in the next chapter.[39]

In the reasoning leading to (EO), Premise 4 is clearly the key: only experiential-intentional states are anchoring instances of intentionality. This will be defended in the next section. Premise 1 is the anchoring-instance model, motivated in the previous subsection, and Premise 2—that intentionality is an observational natural kind concept—is a relatively uncontroversial claim. It could be resisted by denying either the existence of the concept, or its being a natural kind concept, or its being an observational natural kind concept. But none of these options is particularly plausible.

It is certainly hard to imagine that we have no concept of intentionality. Recall that talk of "the" concept of X should be understood as short for "the normally circumstanced normal subject's concept of X." It is implausible that the normal subject has no concept of the intentional. She may not have the *term* "intentionality," but she has a battery of other terms—most notably, "about" and "directed"—with which she can express her concept(ion) of intentionality. Without such a conception, she would be unable, for example, to understand simple traffic signs, which in fact she does understand.[40]

It is not much more plausible to deny that the concept of intentionality is not a natural kind concept or an observational kind concept. Recall that an observational natural kind concept, as understood here, is a kind concept whose instances resemble independently of us but can be observed by us (thus are observable but enjoy an observer-independent similarity). Some intentional items are *perceptually* observed, some are only *introspectively* observed, and some are unobserved (perhaps even unobservable). But for the concept of intentionality to qualify as an observational kind concept, it suffices that it be nomologically possible for us to observe *some* instances of it, in one way or another.[41] Meanwhile, on the face of it, it is clear that the concept of intentionality is also a natural kind concept, since the commonality among its instances—that peculiar directedness one finds in all intentional items—does not appear to be due to our activities or institutions, or to be in any sense "projected" from our thinking on intentionality or our practices of intentional ascription.[42] (Furthermore, if the concept of intentionality is not a natural kind concept, then the role of the anchoring instances is liable to become even greater: in all likelihood, something would qualify as intentional just in case it was manifestly, or superficially, similar to them, instead of just in case it had the same underlying nature as them.[43] Thus there is hardly a danger of *over*playing the role of experiential-intentional states in proceeding as though the concept of intentionality is a natural kind concept.)

To summarize, the purpose of this subsection has been to propose an application of the anchoring-instance model to the concept of intentionality that would pave the way for an anchoring of all intentionality in experiential intentionality. The case for this depends on two additional assumptions. One is that the concept of intentionality is the kind of concept the anchoring-instance model is supposed to cover, which I have just argued. The other is that all anchoring instances of the concept of intentionality are instances of experiential intentionality, which is argued next. If both assumptions are accepted, it follows that an item is intentional just in case it has the same underlying nature as most experiential-intentional states the normally circumstanced normal subject encounters during her formation of her conception of aboutness—and to that extent, that an item is intentional just in case it is appropriately related to experiential-intentional states.

1.2. Experiential Intentionality the Anchor

The anchoring instances of the concept of intentionality are instances encountered during the concept's formation. Given that the concept is observational, presumably encounter here means something like *observational contact* with the encountered. My contention is that the only instances of intentionality with which we have observational contact are experiential-intentional states. We may therefore argue as follows:

1. All the anchoring instances of intentionality are such that we have observational contact with them;
2. The only instances of intentionality with which we have observational contact are experiential-intentional states; therefore,
3. All the anchoring instances of intentionality are experiential-intentional states.

This is effectively a sub-argument for Premise 4 in the argument for (EO) in §1.1.2.[44]

The first premise of this argument falls out of the anchoring-instance model. An objector might protest that, in light of where this seems to lead us, perhaps it was a mistake to put so much weight on encounter with items that fall under a concept. The objection is essentially that there is an undue empiricism creviced in the anchoring-instance model of concept formation. Thus what has to be abandoned is the anchoring-instance model, or perhaps just the part of the model that requires anchoring instances to be encountered.[45]

In response, however, we must keep in mind that the anchoring-instance model is supposed to apply only to observational concepts—concepts whose instances *can* be observed. I would insist that while we may form certain natural kind concepts not on the basis of encounter with instances, this surely characterizes exclusively concepts instances of which we *cannot* observe. It is extremely odd to think that we may (non-parasitically) form the concept of a kind instances of which we can and routinely do encounter but form it independently of our encounter with those instances.

The controversial premise in the sub-argument is the second: why think that experiential-intentional states are the only ones we can have observational contact with? On the one hand, it seems to me entirely natural to suppose that this is so. When an image as of a smiling octopus suddenly and involuntarily pops into my mind, I am aware of my octopus experience, and seem to be aware of it in a direct, non-inferential, and in some admittedly elusive sense observational manner. However, while this seems to me a supposition so natural as to defy doubt, I recognize that others have found it very much doubtful, indeed have found the whole notion of observational contact with conscious experience overly mysterious. The purpose of this section is to provide *an argument* for the claim that we have direct observational contact with some of our experiential-intentional states but with no other intentional states.

The argument is from inference to the best explanation. I will first argue that there is a certain asymmetry in our ascription of experiential-intentional states to ourselves, on the one hand, and our ascription of any other kinds of intentional state, on the other (§1.2.1). I will then argue that the best explanation of this asymmetry is that we have observational contact with our own experiential-intentional states but with no other intentional items (§1.2.2).[46] I will close with discussion of some possible objections (§1.2.3).

1.2.1. An Asymmetry of Ascription

To a first approximation, the asymmetry I have in mind is that while all other intentional ascription requires the deployment of normative principles of charity, ascription of experiential-intentional states to oneself does not.[47] That is, while the ascription of non-experiential-intentional states is *always* governed, and thus mediated, by a normative principle of charity, the ascription of experiential-intentional states is sometimes not.[48] This asymmetry is grounded in a more specific one, which will come out in the discussion to follow.

As our starting point, let us take Davidson's claim that ascription of intentional states to persons is supposed to maximize the intelligibility of these persons' overt behavior, and therefore competent ascription is governed by a cluster of normative principles sometimes loosely referred to as "the principle of charity."[49] These include the principles that (by the interpreter's own lights) persons' beliefs are mostly true and coherent, that their desires are mostly good and mutually satisfiable (and/or suitably prioritized), and that their beliefs and desires mostly conspire to constitute good reasons for action.[50]

The *reason* for claiming that competent intentional ascription is governed by such principles is not always clear in Davidson's writings, but does come through quite nicely in the following passage (Davidson 1974: 18):

If you see a ketch sailing by and your companion says, "Look at that handsome yawl," you may be faced with a problem of interpretation. One natural possibility is that your friend has mistaken a ketch for a yawl, and has formed a false belief. But if his vision is good and his line of sight favorable it is even more plausible that he does not use the word "yawl" quite as you do, and has made no mistake at all about the position of the jigger on the passing yacht.

From which Davidson concludes (Ibid.; italics mine):

[I]f we merely know that someone holds a certain sentence to be true, we know neither what he means by the sentence nor what belief his holding it true represents. His holding the sentence true is thus *the vector of two forces.*

Confronted with a situation in which someone exclaims "Look at this tiger!" while pointing at (what we know is) a pigeon, two coherent interpretations are open to us: (a) that this person believes a tiger is present, and takes the word "tiger" to express the concept of a tiger; (b) that the person believes a pigeon is present, and takes the word "tiger" to express the concept of a pigeon.[51] Two points should be appreciated in this example. First, any competent interpreter would choose the second interpretation. Indeed, we may reasonably consider it a constraint on the competency of an interpreter that s/he choose (b) in a situation such as this. Secondly, there is nothing in the data at the interpreter's disposal (i.e., the exclamation) to favor either interpretation. What favors (b) is only the principle of charity. Thus the reason to hold that intentional ascription is governed by principles of charity—that is, that principles of charity must be operative in competent interpretation—is that without them interpretation is wildly underdetermined.

This observation applies not only to verbal behavior, but to all behavior. As Dennett (1971) notes, if we see a person opening her umbrella when it starts raining, we instantly ascribe to her the desire to stay dry and the belief that opening the umbrella will help. But our data are fully consistent with ascribing to her a desire to get wet and a belief that opening the umbrella will further that cause. What makes us ascribe to her the first belief-desire pair rather than the second has nothing to do with the behavioral data, which are also the vectors of two forces (as Davidson puts it in the passage above). It has to do rather with the fact that (by our lights) the first belief is true and the first desire is good (in the relevant sense), while the second belief is false and the second desire bad.[52] That is to say, what makes us ascribe to her the first belief-desire pair is charity.[53]

In fact, it is natural to treat the case of verbal behavior as just a special case. In the general case, the data for competent intentional ascription—that on the basis of which we ascribe intentional states—are the vectors of two intentional forces, a cognitive force (in the form of a belief or some other doxastic attitude) and a conative force (in the form of a desire or some other pro attitude).[54] The verbal case is one in which the desire is to perform a certain linguistic act (e.g., express or communicate a belief that p) and the belief is that uttering certain words is likely to achieve that (e.g., manage to express the belief that p).[55] Thus, under the interpretation we would naturally adopt, insofar as we are competent interpreters, the person who says "Look at that tiger!" while pointing at a pigeon wants to give voice to her belief that a pigeon is present and believes that uttering "Look at this tiger!" will achieve that.

The reason to take intentional ascription to be inherently normative, then, is what we may call the *vector-of-two-forces observation*. The observation is that the data upon which intentional ascriptions are based cannot typically decide between a number of competing ascriptions. In an ordinary situation calling for the ascription of an intentional state, there is typically one correct (i.e., competent) ascription to make, but a great many alternative ascriptions fully and equally consistent with the data at the interpreter's disposal. That is, many very different intentional states can be ascribed consistently with the data, but typically only one can be so ascribed *competently*.[56] Davidson infers—very reasonably, it seems to me—that principles of charity must be operative in such a situation, and serve to rule out inappropriate ascriptions that are nonetheless consistent with the data.[57]

What I want to argue, however, is that while the Davidsonian insight is cogent, it applies only to the ascription of non-experiential intentionality, as well as the ascription of experiential intentionality to others, but not to the ascription of experiential intentionality to oneself. More precisely, my claim is that although most intentional ascription is indeed based on data that are the vectors of two forces, and thus requires the deployment of principles of charity, ascription of experiential-intentional states to oneself relies on data that are *not* the vectors of two forces, and thus does not involve principles of charity. I further want to argue that the best explanation of this is that ascription of experiential-intentional states to oneself is based on observational contact with the states ascribed, whereas other ascription is not.

To streamline the discussion, let us introduce the terms "exp-intentional" for experiential-intentional and "nexp-intentional" for non-experiential-intentional and distinguish explicitly four kinds of intentional ascription:[58]

a. ascription of non-experiential-intentional states to another ("third-person nexp-intentional ascription")
b. ascription of non-experiential-intentional states to oneself ("first-person nexp-intentional ascription")
c. ascription of experiential-intentional states to another ("third-person exp-intentional ascription")
d. ascription of experiential-intentional states to oneself ("first-person exp-intentional ascription")

My claim can now be put as follows: while (a)-(c) are based on data that are the vectors of two forces, (d) is not. This asymmetry calls for explanation, and I now turn to argue that the best explanation is that (d), and only (d), is based on observational contact with the intentional state ascribed.[59]

1.2.2. Explaining the Asymmetry

In this subsection, I want to examine more closely each of the four types of intentional ascription distinguished above, and argue that the crucial asymmetry I am claiming is best explained in terms of the existence of observational contact with exp-intentional states only. For each type of ascription, I will consider simple examples that bring out particularly crisply the central model for how the relevant type of ascription works.[60] We will see that the mechanics of first-person exp-intentional ascription are crucially different from those of other intentional ascriptions.

Let us start with a prototypical case of third-person ascription. Suppose a person says "It's a nice day" and on that basis you ascribe to her the desire to communicate the belief that it is a nice day, and the belief that just that concatenation of sounds will manage to communicate that belief.[61] In what sense are your data for this ascription the vectors of two forces? The only relevant datum here is the person's utterance, her verbal behavior. The utterance of "It's a nice day" is the vector of two forces in that neither the belief by itself nor the desire by itself could causally explain it. Combined with a different desire, the same belief would cause a different utterance, and combined with a different belief, the same desire would cause a different utterance. For example, combined with the desire to mislead, the same belief might result in uttering "It's an ugly day"; combined with the belief that "day" means night and "night" means day, the same desire would result in uttering "It's a nice night." It is only the conspiracy of a belief and a desire that can cause the utterance, never a belief in isolation from any desire or a desire in isolation from any belief. Accordingly, the datum at your disposal offers no support for ascription of the belief in isolation from the desire or the desire in isolation from the belief.[62] More generally, it is impossible to use the datum at your disposal to ascribe to the person any *single* state; only pairs of complementary states can be ascribed by way of explaining her verbal behavior. It is in this sense that your datum is the vector of two forces.[63,64]

It is clear that a case such as this is one of third-person ascription, but there is an interesting question as to whether it is one of exp- or nexp-intentional ascription. On the one hand, the concepts of belief and desire are the main currency of traditional discussions of intentionality that have tended to disregard the difference between experiential and non-experiential intentionality and treat all intentionality as cut from the same cloth. On the other hand, upon examination of a specific case such as this, it seems to me that when a person exclaims "It's a nice day," she is giving voice to a conscious occurrent thought, and as will be discussed in §1.3.3, there are good reasons to hold that such thoughts have a proprietary experiential character and are thus, in one important sense, *cognitive experiences*. The same is true of this person's conscious desire to share her thought, which conscious desire has an experiential character (a felt quality of pull to action that comes with a distinct and varying dimension of experiential intensity) and may be referred to as a *conative experience*. My own tendency, then, would be to construe the case just discussed as involving third-person *exp*-intentional ascription.[65] In any event, we can consider other cases of third-person intentional ascription that belong more clearly to one category or the other.

Consider first a clearer case of third-person *nexp*-intentional ascription. Suppose that during a departmental meeting one of your colleagues rails with furious fervor ostensibly against a rather meaningless new college procedure. The colleague and you are quite close, and you know that she is in general a fragile, sadly bitter, but fundamentally well-meaning and good-hearted person who is occasionally frequented by free-floating anger energies, a predicament she seems to cope with by seeking vaguely proper objects of indignation and moral outrage to latch her preexisting anger energies onto. This coping mechanism allows her to evince her anger without perturbing her self-conception as a good person, and do so in a socially acceptable manner. All of this, let us suppose, is entirely opaque to the colleague herself, despite years of therapy. Witnessing her latest tirade, you ascribe to her the desire to evince some new anger energies while preserving her favorable self-conception, together with a belief that launching this tirade would accomplish that. In this case, it is clear that you ascribe to your colleague an unconscious belief-desire pair that exhibits only nonexperiential intentionality. It is also clear that the datum at your disposal—her tirade—is the vector of two forces: the desire to evince anger energies without sacrificing a positive self-conception would not lead to the tirade if it were combined, for example, with the belief that the tirade would actually compromise that self-conception; nor would the belief that such a tirade would successfully evince anger energies without compromising the self-conception lead to the tirade if it were combined, say, with the desire to avoid evincing any anger energies.[66]

Consider next a clear case of third-person *exp*-intentional ascription.[67] Suppose you ascribe to *another* a visual experience as of a table. One way you might come to ascribe such an experience is by positing it as cause of table beliefs which, in conspiracy with conversation desires, cause the person's table conversation. In such a case, the ascription behaves essentially as third-person *nexp*-intentional ascription does, and the data are clearly vectors of two forces.[68] Another way you might come to ascribe to her the table experience is by observing the table itself and the position of the person's visual organs, and concluding, perhaps through simulation, that the person must be seeing the table. This kind of ascription may or may not behave completely differently, but in any case it seems to be even more immediately imbued with charity: you assume that the person's perception is *veridical*—and do so without evidence. (You could certainly *produce* evidence, e.g. by probing the person for verbal report, but such evidence would consist in just more behavioral data, which would of course be vectors of two forces.) It appears, then, that third-person exp-intentional ascription is either based on data that are the vectors of two forces or even more immediately governed by principles of charity.

I conclude that all third-person intentional ascription—both exp- and nexp-intentional—is based on data that are the vectors of two forces, or calls even more immediately for charitable interpretation. On a natural model of how such ascription works, this is due to the fact that the beliefs and desires we ascribe to others, whether exp- or nexp-intentional, are posited as behind-the-scene causes of behavior, including verbal behavior. The data at the ascriber's disposal are bits of behavior, which are taken to be the effects of hidden mental (indeed intentional) causes. Thus ascription of intentional states to others is based on *causal inference*: we make inferences about others' intentional states on the basis of observing behavior in the same way we generally make inferences about hidden causes on the basis of observed effects. Just as on the basis of observing smoke you infer that there is unobserved fire, so on the basis of observing the person's utterance you infer that she has certain unobserved intentional states.

Consider, by contrast, a prototypical case of first-person exp-intentional ascription. Suppose you ascribe to yourself a visual experience as of a table. The basis on which you make this ascription, at least in central cases, does not consist in behavioral data of any sort. It is not as though you notice a certain behavior on your part and infer that you must be undergoing a visual experience as of a table. (Perhaps there are cases of first-person exp-intentional ascription that do work like this, but those are surely the pathological or abnormal cases, and in any case not *all* the cases.) It is not immediately clear what should be considered the datum or data of this kind of ascription, but it *is* rather clear that you *can* on the basis of the data at your disposal—whatever they turn out to be—ascribe to yourself an experience as of a table *without at the same time ascribing to yourself any other state*.[69] In particular, there is no desire-like state (a pro attitude) you must ascribe to yourself in tandem with your experience.[70] You can on the basis of your data ascribe to yourself a *single* intentional state; no conspiracy with other intentional states is needed to explain anything.[71]

If this is true, then the mechanics of ascription must be different in this case from the case of third-person (exp- and nexp-)intentional ascription. That is, the ascription cannot based here on causal inference from observed (behavioral) effects to hidden (intentional) causes. The natural model is rather as follows. Insofar as it is appropriate to speak of data for ascription here, the only relevant datum seems to be a certain deliverance of introspection, namely, that it introspectively seems to you that you are having a table experience. Explaining this introspective deliverance does not seem to call for the positing of any intentional state other than the table experience. In fact, no substantive inference at all is needed to ascribe to yourself the state which it introspectively seems to you that you are in. Rather, all that is required is what is sometimes referred to in the case of perception as *endorsement*. Just as you form the perceptual judgment that there is a chair before you because (a) it *perceptually* seems to you that there is and (b) you endorse this perceptual seeming, so you form the introspective judgment that you are having an experience as of a table because (a) it *introspectively* seems to you that you are and (b) you endorse this introspective seeming.[72] In both cases, something seems to be the case and you endorse the seeming. In this kind of intentional ascription, then, your data are certain deliverances of introspection, and once the deliverances are endorsed, you ascribe an exp-intentional state to yourself; or perhaps the endorsing of such deliverances *constitutes* the ascribing.

There is thus a contrast between the mechanics of first-person exp-intentional ascription and third-person (exp-and nexp-)intentional ascription.[73] The former is based on endorsement of introspective seemings, the latter on causal inference from behavior. This is hardly deniable: as noted, when you ascribe to yourself a perceptual experience as of a table, you do not observe putative causal effects of your experience and infer on their basis the existence of a hidden experiential cause. Rather, you seem to make the ascription on the basis of observing, in some (not unproblematic) sense, the experience itself—observing, that is, the very state which you ascribe.[74] And this is *why* your experience of the table *can* yield the relevant deliverance all by itself and in isolation from any other intentional state.[75] More generally, this is why the relevant introspective deliverances are *not* the vectors of two forces. In this way, the "hypothesis" that we have introspective observational contact with our own exp-intentional states *explains* the fact that the data for these states' ascription are not vectors of two forces.[76]

It is important to stress that, in saying this, one need not be indulging in any mystery-mongering about first-person access. Introspection has been claimed sometimes to be infallible, such that if it delivers that p, then p; sometimes to be immune to error of a certain type (e.g., through misidentification), such that if it delivers that p, and further conditions are met, then p; sometimes to be incorrigible, such that if it delivers that p, then the deliverance is incontrovertibly justified; sometimes to be self-intimating, such that if p, then it delivers that p; and so on.[77] None of these claims follows, however, from the assertion that we have introspective observational contact with our intentional experiences. Perceptual observational contact with perceivables is not commonly thought to secure any of these extraordinary epistemic privileges, and introspective observational contact with introspectibles need not be thought to do so either.[78]

In any event, to repeat, all this is supposed to apply to the *central*, not necessarily *universal*, manner in which first-person exp-intentional ascription proceeds. There may well be cases of such ascription that do not fit the observation-cum-endorsement model. But for our present purposes, it is sufficient that *some* exp-intentional ascriptions do—provided that *no* nexp-intentional ascriptions do. For this would suggest that only exp-intentional states can be observed, and therefore that only they can serve as anchoring instances of the concept of intentionality. To complete the case for this, then, we must show that first-person *nexp*-intentional ascription is based on data that are the vectors of two forces and thus requires the employment of a principle of charity.

First-person nexp-intentional ascription involves ascribing to oneself nexp-intentional states, paradigmatically unconscious beliefs and desires.[79] More generally, however, our concern here is with the self-ascription of non-experiential-intentional states. Such states seem to fall into three categories: (i) dispositional or tacit beliefs and desires; (ii) Freudian suppressed or repressed beliefs, desires, and emotions; (iii) occurrent sub-personal states typically posited in the context of cognitive-scientific explanations of behavior. Let us consider the central models for ascription of states in each category.

Consider first the first-person ascription of a dispositional belief, say the belief that Michael Jordan is not a three-headed kangaroo. The central model for how we ascribe such states to ourselves seems to me to be the one presented by Evans. Evans (1982: 225–6) points out that when someone asks you whether you believe that there will be a third world war, you do not start monitoring your internal states in search of an item that fits the description "belief that there will be a third world war"; rather, you start considering whether there will in fact be a third world war. You attend not to psychological facts, but to geopolitical ones. That is, you seek evidence not for your believing the proposition, but for the proposition itself.[80] If you find such evidence, you ascribe to yourself the belief that there will be a third world war, but do not do so on the basis of observing the belief.[81] Thus you charitably ascribe to yourself (non-conscious) beliefs in what you (consciously) take to be true.[82] In a way, this is the most direct application of charity possible: we consciously launch an investigation into the question of a third world war, and when the investigation is completed, that which we consider to be the correct answer is ascribed to ourselves as a content of a belief—even though no belief item was ever sought in the course of the investigation.

In addition, it is not entirely clear that there really *are* dispositional nexp-intentional states. Plausibly, it is not the case that a person *dispositionally believes* that p, but rather that she is *disposed to believe* that p (and likewise for desire). On this view, there are no dispositional intentional states, only dispositions to enter (occurrent) intentional states. The motivation for this view is that any explanatory burden that dispositional intentional states are called forth to meet can be equally met, and more parsimoniously, by dispositions to enter intentional states (Manfredi 1993, Audi 1994).[83] There may be an *intuitive* cost in denying the existence of dispositional states, but there is no *explanatory* cost.[84] This is important, because when we ascribe non-experiential intentional states, the only evidence we can have for their existence is based on the behavioral effects their existence would explain. So lack of explanatory power vis-à-vis those behavioral effects would remove any rationale for positing them in the first place. Thus because no explanatory gain can be found in positing dispositional states generally, there is no reason to suppose that some nexp-intentional states are dispositional.[85] Needless to say, if there are no dispositional intentional states, then *a fortiori* we do not have observational contact with them, and so they cannot be cited to undermine the claim that only exp-intentional states are observable.

Consider now the case of Freudian states. One way we might ascribe to ourselves such states is exactly as we would ascribe them to another. Suppose one day in therapy session your angry colleague reaches an important insight about her relationship to anger. In consequence, immediately after her departmental meeting outburst, she ascribes to herself the same pair of unconscious belief and desire that you ascribe to her: the desire to evince anger energies while preserving her self-conception as a good person along with the belief that lashing out at a meaningless college procedure will serve that purpose. Both belief and desire are unconscious here, but not quite dispositional or "standing"; certainly the belief is occurrent. It is first-person ascription of Freudian suppressed belief and desire. This kind of first-person nexp-intentional ascription obviously works precisely as the corresponding third-person nexp-intentional ascription you were engaged in. Accordingly, the datum for ascription at your colleague's disposal—her outburst behavior—is the vector of two forces: she cannot ascribe to herself the aforementioned belief in isolation from the aforementioned desire, nor the desire in isolation from the belief.

There are other cases of first-person Freudian nexp-intentional ascription that rely on a wider array of indirect behavioral and introspective data. For example, you might infer that you must be sub-consciously expecting bad news in a looming phone conversation from the fact that you have been postponing picking up the phone for a few hours already (a behavioral datum) and have been finding it difficult to concentrate during that time (an introspective datum). Inasmuch as you rely on the behavioral datum (not picking up the phone), the mechanics of ascription are the same as in *third*-person nexp-intentional ascription, so the datum is a vector of two forces. Thus, expecting bad news would explain not picking up the phone only in conspiracy with a desire for *good* news (or at least for there not to be bad news). More interestingly, the same applies to the introspective datum: expecting bad news would explain the difficulty in concentrating only in conspiracy with a desire for good news. If you desired bad news, the expectation of bad news would not explain your concentration problems. Thus even introspective data for first-person Freudian nexp-intentional ascription are vectors of two forces.

It is instructive to consider why it is that the introspective data behave so differently in exp-intentional versus nexp-intentional ascription (i.e., are the vectors of two forces only for the latter). The reason is quite clearly that in the former case, but not in the latter, the data pertain directly to that which is ascribed, in the sense that the relevant deliverances of introspection are that one seems to be in the very intentional state one eventually ascribes to oneself. Because of this, first-person exp-intentional ascription involves nothing but endorsement of seemings, whereas first-person nexp-intentional ascription involves a more substantial inference—essentially, a causal inference from broadly experiential effects to behind-the-scene nexp-intentional causes.[86]

Finally, let us consider first-person ascription of non-experiential sub-personal intentional states. There are many examples of such states posited in cognitive science: Marr's (1982) 2.5D sketches, Milner and Goodale's (1995) dorsal-stream visual representations, blindsight, and subliminal perception would be examples drawn just from vision science. It is worth noting that ascription of such states does not normally take place in the folk, since the folk are typically unaware that such states exist (in contradistinction with Freudian states, which by now are much more folkloresque). In any case, since subjects have no introspective access to such states, they can ascribe such states to themselves only on the basis of behavioral data.[87] If so, the model for first-person ascription of such states would be the same as the model for their third-person ascription: it would be based on inference from observed behavioral effects to unobserved intentional causes. In both cases, the ascription is based on data that are the vectors of two forces.[88]

I conclude that first-person ascription of all three types of nexp-intentional state is based on data that are the vectors of two forces, or else involves a principle of charity even more directly (as in Evans' model for first-person ascription of standing beliefs).[89] Given that the same holds of *third*-person nexp-intentional ascription, I further conclude that *all* nexp-intentional ascription is based on such data, and that therefore there is an important epistemological asymmetry between non-experiential intentionality and experiential intentionality. The asymmetry is that while *all* nexp-intentional ascription is governed by charity, *some* exp-intentional ascription is not.[90]

I have endeavored to show that the best—certainly most natural—explanation for this asymmetry is that we have observational contact with at least some of our exp-intentional states, and none with any nexp-intentional states. Against the background of the anchoring-instance model—in particular, the notion that all anchoring instances of the concept of intentionality are instances with which we have observational contact—it follows that only a subject's own exp-intentional states can serve as anchoring instances of her concept of intentionality. Since this is the key Premise 4 in the argument (presented in §1.1.2) for the experiential origin thesis, we now have a sustained argument for that thesis—the thesis that an item qualifies as intentional just in case it has the same underlying nature as one's (observed, encountered) exp-intentional states. I close this section with consideration of some objections.

1.2.3. Objections and Replies

The argument of the section, recall, is this:

1. All the anchoring instances of intentionality are such that we have observational contact with them;
2. The only instances of intentionality with which we have observational contact are experiential-intentional states; therefore,
3. All the anchoring instances of intentionality are experiential-intentional states.

Objections to this argument can be divided into three groups: objections to the first premise, objections to the second premise, and objections directly targeting the conclusion. Below, I consider examples of each.

Objections to the first premise cannot quite suggest that some anchoring instances of intentionality require no observational contact, since that requirement falls out of the anchoring-instance model of the formation of observational natural kind concepts. However, they *can* simply reject the anchoring-instance model, or its application to the concept of intentionality. I have already defended the model's application to the concept (at the end of §1.1.2), but an objector might insist that the model itself is misguided. For one thing, concept formation is a psychological process, and any account of it is beholden to the vicissitudes of empirical research. Yet my presentation of the model was suspiciously free of empirical encumbrances.

In response, I would point out that although the matter of concept formation is certainly empirical, it may be that while the empirical research needed to establish one model over another at a high level of specificity is quite involved, at a low level of specificity certain relatively mundane observations might suffice. As I noted at the beginning of §1.1.1, my concern is better thought of as with *families* of (underdeveloped) models rather than with specific (well-developed) models. That is, the level of specificity at which the anchoring-instance model is formulated does not call for particularly involved empirical research. Perhaps in putting it forward a philosopher would be wearing her scientist cap, just as scientists oftentimes advance important hypotheses wearing their philosopher caps, but if I am right, the considerations supporting the anchoring-instance model are available to the *unprofessional* scientist.[91]

Most objections to the argument of this section would presumably target its second premise. They would deny either (a) that we have observational contact with exp-intentional states or (b) that we do *not* have observational contact with nexp-intentional items.

The first option is to deny that we have observational contact with exp-intentional states, perhaps on the grounds that introspection is not observational or quasi-perceptual in the way suggested. What is sometimes known as the "perceptual model" of introspection, which construes introspection as crucially analogous to perception, may simply be misguided. Typically, the crucial analogy is understood to be that in both perception and introspection, there is a kind of direct "epistemic contact" with the perceived or introspected. Some philosophers have objected to such a perceptual model from the left, arguing that the relationship between introspection and the introspected is less intimate than between perception and the perceived. Others have objected to it from the right, arguing that the relationship is *more* intimate. My response is different in each case.

One inspiration for the left-wing objection might be the view that introspection is fundamentally directed at the world, rather than at experience, due to the so-called transparency of experience (Harman 1990).[92] Thus, according to Dretske's (1995) "displaced perception" model of introspection, introspective judgments are not generated by endorsing introspective seemings, but rather by *inference* from perceptual experiences. Just as one hears that the postman has arrived by hearing the dog bark, so one introspects that one has a table experience by seeing the table. There is no direct epistemic contact with the postman, and none with the table experience.

In response, it is important to note that regardless of whether ascription is mediated by displaced perception, it is still a fact that one can ascribe the table experience to oneself without at the same time ascribing any other mental state, something one cannot do with one's nexp-intentional states. That is, the asymmetry of ascription that underlies our argument from inference to the best explanation still holds. The proponent of displaced perception is of course allowed to reject our explanation of the asymmetry, but she owes us her own superior explanation. Yet it is not at all clear how the displaced perception model is supposed to explain the asymmetry.[93] Indeed, it is not clear what *resources* the model has for explaining the asymmetry: the asymmetry would be a complete mystery if introspection were nothing but displaced perception.[94]

A different left-wing objector is the philosopher who holds that there is nothing at all like perceptual immediacy in introspection, because introspection is always doxastic or intellectual: introspecting my table experience is simply *thinking* that I am having that experience (see, e.g., Rosenthal 1993).[95] Again, however, this does nothing to either undermine the ascriptive asymmetry pointed out above or offer a better explanation of it. More generally, the left-wing objector cannot simply reject our view of introspection without addressing the argument *for it*.[96]

Consider now the right-wing objector. This is the philosopher who holds that, unlike in perception, the relata of introspection are not "independent existences," i.e., not entities which may persist in the other's absence (see, e.g., Shoemaker 1994).[97] The term "acquaintance" is sometimes used to denote such an epistemic relation. The objection before us is that introspection involves acquaintance not observation. This objection strikes me as an *ignoratio elenchi*: what matters for the ability of exp-intentional states to serve as anchoring instances is that normal subjects have some kind of direct epistemic contact with them. Whether that epistemic contact is "observation," because the contacted is numerically distinct from one's introspective judgment, or "acquaintance," because it is not, is beside the point.[98]

So much for the first option for rejecting the second premise of the argument—arguing that we do not have observational contact with exp-intentional states. The second option is to concede that we do but insist that we also have observational contact with some *nexp*-intentional items. This again may be divided into two kinds of objection: one suggesting that we have observational contact with non-experiential mental intentional states, and one suggesting that we have such contact with altogether non-mental intentional items.

The first kind of objection may be mounted by appeal to cases in which we seem to directly perceive the intentional states of others. Thus, it has sometimes been claimed that just by attending to facial expressions, one can *see* that a friend is nervous or distressed, say about an upcoming meeting with a romantic prospect. It is natural to interpret such ascription as involving nothing but endorsement of a *perceptual* seeming: it seems to one perceptually that one's friend is distressed or nervous about *p*, and one endorses that seeming. This in turn might render the relevant data of ascription "single-forced."

My response is that although this kind of intentional ascription is immediate in a way that may tempt us to assimilate it to first-person exp-intentional ascription, the temptation trades on an equivocation in the notion of immediacy. When we see that a friend is in distress, our ascription of distress to her is immediate in the sense of not being mediated by conscious inference, instead being rather "automatic." However, it is clearly not immediate in the sense that we observe *the distress itself*. For we do not observe the distress itself, only its facial manifestation. Accordingly, the facial manifestation is the vector of two forces: it indicates distress only against the background of attribution to the friend of a strong desire that the meeting with the romantic prospect be successful. If one knew for a fact that the friend was utterly uninterested in the person she is about to meet, one would not be in a position to (competently) ascribe distress or nervousness to the friend on the basis of the relevant facial expression.[99]

The second kind of objection under consideration is that we have some perceptual observational contact with non-mental intentional items, such as paintings and road signs. Assuming that "observational contact" can come in both introspective and perceptual forms, one might suggest that we form our concept of intentionality through both introspective encounter with exp-intentional states and perceptual encounter with paintings, road signs, and so on. According to Siegel (2006), for example, we not only *understand*, but can also *see*, that some words on a page mean that the basketball game has been canceled. This would involve perceptual contact with a nexp-intentional item.

Note, however, that the intentionality of language and road signs, certainly, and arguably also that of paintings and photographs, is partly conventional and depends on interpretation. This means that a subject needs to understand the role and nature of the interpretive conventions before seeing such items *as intentional*. In effect, it means that the subject needs to already have a conception of intentionality before seeing such items as intentional. Thus inked or mouthed words do not present themselves as contentful to a subject who has no conception of intentionality whatsoever.[100] Given this, such items cannot serve as anchoring instances of our conception of intentionality. By contrast, exp-intentional states do present themselves to introspection as directed, as possessed of aboutness or ofness, before we have any conception of intentionality.[101]

The last kind of objection to the argument of this section simply rejects its conclusion, leaving it unspecified what exactly might have gone wrong in the argument. One reason for which one might reject the argument's conclusion is the suspicion that the resulting account of intentionality will fail to capture all intentionality. The objector suggests that we have a pre-theoretic conception of which things are intentional and which are not, and any account of intentionality must capture this pre-theoretic extension of intentionality more or less correctly. However, if we accept the conclusion of this section's argument, she claims, we will fail to do so, because much of what seems pre-theoretically intentional does not share an underlying nature with exp-intentional states. Indeed, the cases of language and pictures are in point: it is unlikely that linguistic occurrences of "table" have the same underlying nature as table experiences.

In response, one could insist that linguistic expressions may turn out to share a deep feature with exp-intentional states in virtue of which both are intentional. More plausibly, however, I am tempted to suggest that the intentionality of linguistic expressions, even if it fails to share an underlying nature with exp-intentional states, may nonetheless be somehow *accountable for in terms of* the intentionality of items that do share an underlying nature with exp-intentional states. If so, there is no need to posit further intentionality to account for the domain of phenomena in need of accounting for. All that is required is the identification of the general relation R that obtains between intentional items that do not exhibit the same underlying nature as encountered exp-intentional states and intentional items that do when, and only when, we account for the intentionality of the former in terms of that of the latter. Once this is done, we can offer the following augmented formulation of the experiential origin thesis:

(EO★) There is a relation R and a nature N, such that (i) most encountered exp-intentional states have N and (ii) for any item x, x qualifies as intentional iff either (a) x has N, or (b) there is an item y, such that (b-i) y has N and (b-ii) x bears R to y.

The strategy is to argue that (EO*) recovers the instances of intentionality that (EO) may fail to. All this depends, of course, on the feasibility of somehow accounting for all intentionality in terms of intentional items that have the same underlying nature as encountered exp-intentional states. I undertake to outline a way of doing this in Chapter 4.

There are probably other objections that could be raised to the argument of this section, and which have not occurred to me. But it strikes me that the argument ultimately rests on a relatively straightforward observation, namely, that there is an asymmetry between first-person exp-intentional ascription and other kinds of intentional ascription, inasmuch as the data for intentional ascription are crucially different, and differently culled. Fundamentally, the difference is that whereas ascription of all nexp-intentional states is based on observation of those states' *causal traces*, ascription of at least some exp-intentional states is based on observation of those states *themselves*, not their traces. If we accept this basic claim about intentional ascription, it becomes plausible that only exp-intentional states can serve as anchoring instances of intentionality. This in turn makes it plausible that any item qualifies as intentional only if it shares an underlying nature with exp-intentional states.

1.3. "Experiential Intentionality"

I have discussed the experiential origin thesis, and the central role it gives to experiential intentionality in our conception of intentionality, without clarifying exactly what is meant by the notion of experiential intentionality. The purpose of this final section is to fix ideas with respect to this notion of experiential intentionality. I take up the following three questions (§1.3.1–1.3.3, respectively): What would it take for there to be experiential intentionality? *Is there*, in fact, any experiential intentionality? And if so, *how much* experiential intentionality is there? I do not discuss these matters with the goal of settling them once and for all. Rather, the goal is to give the notion of experiential intentionality sufficient texture to bring through the meaning and significance of the experiential origin thesis.

1.3.1. Definition

By "experiential intentionality," I mean the intentionality that conscious experiences have in virtue of being conscious experiences.[102,103] Conscious experiences have many properties, only some of which they have in virtue of being conscious experiences. Thus, my visual experience of the blue sky has the property of occurring on a Wednesday, but it does not have this property in virtue of being a conscious experience. It would have this property even if it were an unconscious, subliminal perception (or a blindsighted one).[104] Its being conscious is irrelevant to its occurring on a Wednesday. But my experience does have its bluish qualitative character in virtue of being a conscious experience. It would not have this qualitative character if it were not a conscious experience. Thus its being conscious/experiential is crucial to its having a qualitative character.

Let us say that every conscious experience has an *experiential character*, and that a conscious experience is the conscious experience it is, and is a conscious experience at all, because it has the experiential character it does, and has one at all. Then to say that some conscious experience x has an intentional property P in virtue of being a conscious experience is the same as to say that x has P in virtue of x's experiential character. We may thus define being an exp-intentional property through the following biconditional:

> A priori, for any intentional property P and state x, P is an exp-intentional property of x iff there is an experiential character E, such that (i) x has E, (ii) x is P, and (iii) x is P in virtue of x having E.[105]

With this definition of an exp-intentional property in hand, we can define *experiential intentionality* as the determinable, or genus, of all (and only) exp-intentional properties.[106] And we can define an *exp-intentional state* as either (a) the exemplification of an exp-intentional property at a time or (b) a bare particular of the right kind that instantiates an exp-intentional property.[107]

The above definition of an exp-intentional property can be read in two ways, however, depending on how we understand "in virtue of." On the first reading, x's being P is somehow *grounded* in its having E, in a way that gives E metaphysical primacy over P.[108] The second is neutral on matters of grounding and primacy, and implies merely that x has its intentional property *in its capacity as*, or *qua*, a conscious experience, in the sense that a certain counterfactual is true of it: if it did not have E, it would not be P. Call the former reading *doctrinal* and the latter *neutral*.[109] The doctrinal definition of experiential intentionality is this:

> A priori, for any intentional property P and state x, P is an exp-intentional property of x iff there is an experiential character E, such that (i) x has E, (ii) x is P, and (iii) x's being P is grounded in x's having E.

The neutral definition is this:

> A priori, for any intentional property P and state x, P is an exp-intentional property of x iff there is an experiential character E, such that (i) x has E, (ii) x is P, and (iii) if x did not have E, x would not be P.

In order to avoid prejudging certain issues, I will work here with the neutral definition of "exp-intentional," and hence of "experiential intentionality."[110]

This is also the main reason I have chosen to conduct the discussion in this book using the term "experiential intentionality" rather than the more entrenched "phenomenal intentionality." The latter seems to me to have implicitly acquired the doctrinal definition, perhaps due to the substantive commitments of the first philosophers to use it (Loar 2003, Horgan and Tienson 2002).[111] Thus, many today already hear the term "phenomenal intentionality" as implying the primacy of the phenomenal to the intentional.[112] However, my concern in this book is not to argue for the primacy of the experiential over the intentional, merely for the primacy of the experiential-intentional over the non-experiential-intentional. Whether the experiential is in some sense prior to the intentional within the realm of the experiential-intentional, or conversely the intentional prior to the experiential, or neither—say, because they are one and the same—is something I wish to remain silent on.[113]

Another reason to prefer "experiential intentionality" is that to many philosophers the term "phenomenal" connotes the presence of sensuous qualities: a phenomenal state, to them, must be a sensory (or somatic) state.[114] Since I am keen to insist that there are non-sensuous, purely intellectual (cognitive) experiences, such as the experience of suddenly grasping a mathematical proof, or of realizing the solution to a philosophical problem, but am not at all keen to quarrel about whether the term "phenomenal" should apply to such experiences, I choose to work with the term "experiential."[115,116]

One last issue left open is how to define "experiential character." One approach to this question is to understand "experience" intuitively, as whatever it means in its everyday sense.[117] Another is to pin our hopes on the phrase "what it is like for the subject" capturing uniquely experiential character.[118] Here I am going to take a more involved approach, which is to understand experiential character as that for which there is, or appears to be, an *explanatory gap* (Levine 1983).[119] More precisely, to a first approximation we may use the following rigidified definite description to fix the reference of "experiential": a property P is experiential iff in the actual world, there is (or appears to be) an explanatory gap between P and physical properties.[120] We can then define the experiential character of a mental state x at a time t as the sum (or conjunction) of all experiential properties instantiated by x at t.[121]

1.3.2. Existence

With the definition of experiential intentionality in place, two substantive questions present themselves: is there in fact any experiential intentionality, and if so how much of it is there? That is, are there any mental states endowed with experiential intentionality, and if so how many kinds of mental state are so endowed? This subsection and the next offer brief discussions of these matters, mostly by way of reportage on others' work.

Against the background of our definition of experiential intentionality, the claim that there *exists* such a thing amounts to the thesis that there is at least one instance of an exp-intentional property. Call this the *experiential intentionality thesis*: For some mental state x and intentional property P, P is an exp-intentional property of x.[122] Note that the thesis does not require *every* intentional property to be experiential, nor every experiential property to be intentional. It is merely an existential thesis.

There are several sources, and grades, of potential resistance to the experiential intentionality thesis. One relatively radical view is that experiences are never intentional (Travis 2004). A more common view is that experiences are often intentional, but never intentional *qua* experiences: they have intentional properties, and they have experiential properties, but they could have the very same intentional properties even if they had very different experiential properties (see, e.g., Block 1990, 1996).[123] In the literature, there appear to be two main reasons for accepting the experiential intentionality thesis in the face of such resistance.

One reason—unlikely to win converts but central in motivating sympathizers—is the claim that experiential intentionality is simply *introspectively manifest*: attending to one's stream of consciousness in the right way brings out that some conscious episodes are intentional, and intentional because experiential.[124] Horgan and Tienson's (2002) descriptions of certain conscious episodes are naturally understood as attempts to bring out something like that.

An argument with a more neutral starting point is due to Siewert (1998 Ch.6). He observes that some conscious experiences are assessable for accuracy purely in virtue of what it is like for the subject to be in them, and without need of interpretation. They thus have accuracy conditions—an intentional property—in virtue of their experiential character. Suppose you undergo an experience with a reddish experiential character. If nothing around you is red, then your experience is assessable as inaccurate. If something *is* red, then your experience may be assessable as accurate (under the right conditions). Thus experiential character brings in its train accuracy conditions. Since having accuracy conditions is an intentional property, and experiential character is (trivially) an experiential property, these accuracy conditions constitute an exp-intentional property.

In this book, I am going to take for granted the existence of experiential intentionality. I do so not because—at least not primarily because—I think this is self-evident or otherwise not in need of justification; rather because I have nothing substantially new to say in its defense, and I want to focus on other issues.[125] The next question I want to consider concerns the *scope* of experiential intentionality.

1.3.3. Scope

Work on the scope of experiential intentionality has tended to fall into two categories, concerned with experiential intentionality *within* and *without* the sphere of perceptual experience.

Within that sphere, there are elements in perceptual experience that outrun sensory phenomenology narrowly construed but are claimed to nonetheless involve experiential intentionality. Perhaps the most systematic contribution to this kind of research is probably due to Siegel (2005, 2006), who argues that high-level properties are represented in perception. These include causation, meaning, and kind properties, among others.[126]

Outside the sphere of perceptual experience, four potential types of experiential intentionality are debated, instantiated by somatic, emotional, conative, and cognitive states. Somatic states, such as pains and pleasures, have historically often been treated as experiential but not intentional. More recently, it has been argued that such somatic states do have directedness: a toothache is an experience intentionally directed at a tooth and an armpit tickle is an experience intentionally directed at an armpit (see Armstrong 1962, Tye 1997). Ditto for emotions and moods: a disappointment with the New England Patriots' season is intentionally directed at their season, while a general, "undirected" depression is in reality a quiet, prolonged experience intentionally directed at the world as a whole and presenting it as dull and pointless (see Seager 1999 Ch.8).[127] With conative and cognitive states, historically it has been more common to conceive of them as intentional but not experiential, but again their experiential character has been stressed in more recent work. It is, in truth, hard to understand how desires, intentions, and other conative states could have been denied an experiential dimension, given that there is clearly a varying degree of experiential intensity or vivacity involved in them: one can want an ice cream very much or only mildly, where the difference is not only functional but also experiential.[128]

The liveliest area of debate here is the question of whether there are purely intellectual or cognitive experiences. Among views that accept such experiences, a further distinction can be made between those that allow similar cognitive experiences to have different intentional contents and those that insist that cognitive-experiential character determines intentional content.[129] In the literature, three main argumentative strategies have been wielded by way of defending the existence of (content-determining) cognitive experience: arguments from experiential overwhelm, arguments from experiential contrast, and arguments from first-person knowability.[130]

Arguments from experiential overwhelm attempt to identify specific, rather unusual cognitive states whose experiential character is supposed to be overwhelming in a way that approximates the experiential overwhelm involved in, say, visual and somatic experiences. Perhaps the best known instance of this argument is based on the sudden and acute onset of an experience of grasping something. Consider the following passage (Mangan 2001, Chudnoff forthcoming-a):[131]

A newspaper is better than a magazine. A seashore is a better place than the street. At first it is better to run than to walk. You may have to try several times. It takes some skill but it is easy to learn. Even young children can enjoy it. Once successful, complications are minimal. Birds seldom get too close. Rain, however, soaks in very fast. Too many people doing the same thing can also cause problems. One needs lots of room. If there are no complications it can be very peaceful. A rock will serve as an anchor. If things break loose from it, however, you will not get a second chance.

This passage elicits mostly puzzlement, until one is told that it is about *kites*. Once informed, one typically undergoes the acute onset of the grasp experience of which I speak.[132] Arguments of this sort are particularly effective dialectically, but suffer from the limitation that they do not obviously establish the stronger kind of claim one might make about cognitive-experiential character, namely, that they determine intentional content. Yet it is this stronger claim that is of interest if we are interested in the existence of cognitive experiential intentionality.

In arguments from experiential contrast, two overall conscious episodes of a subject are presented, such that (i) it is intuitively clear that there is an experiential difference between the two, and (ii) the best explanation of this overall experiential difference is that one instantiates a cognitive experiential character but the other does not. Thus, Strawson (1994 Ch.1) argues for the existence of "understanding experience" by contrasting the overall experiences of a French speaker and a non-French-speaker listening to the news in French (see also Moore 1953). Strawson argues that there is an experiential difference between their overall conscious episodes, and that the difference is best accounted for in terms of an element of understanding-experience present only in the French speaker's stream of consciousness.[133] As it stands, the argument does not clearly establish that different cognitive-experiential characters go along with different intentional contents, but it can be tweaked to do so. Consider that p a i n refers to an unpleasant sensation in English and to bread in French. Imagine a world where two languages are so similar graphically and phonetically that the very same passage can express a news report about a faraway war in one of them and a children's bedtime story in the other. We can envisage two subjects listening to a reading of the passage and each understanding it in a different language. Here there would be an overall experiential difference that is best explained by supposing that one subject's cognitive experience had one intentional content while the other's had another intentional content.

In arguments from first-person knowability, it is pointed out that the knowledge we have of our occurrent thoughts is the kind of knowledge we have only of our conscious experiences, from which it is inferred that these thoughts must be conscious experiences (*qua* thoughts, that is, not only in virtue of their accompanying imagery).[134] Thus, Pitt (2004) argues that we have an immediate, non-inferential knowledge of some cognitive states, and that only conscious experiences are knowable in this way, which suggests that the cognitive states have a proprietary experiential character.[135] Pitt further argues that whenever cognitive states differ in intentional content, we can know the difference between them in this non-inferential way peculiar to experience, wherefore he concludes that cognitive experiential characters determine intentional content.

For my part, I am persuaded of the existence of cognitive experience by all three lines of reasoning, but perhaps most vividly by something like everyday experiential overwhelm: it simply seems that my inner life is much more interesting to me than it would be if my conscious experience consisted merely in perceptual experiences. Thus, when I contemplate the problem of determinism and free will, it is not the accompanying imagery that fascinates.[136] In addition, however, I develop a more theoretical argument for it in Kriegel forthcoming. Working with the conception of experiential properties as suitably explanatory-gap-able properties, I argue that we can conceive of a world in which subjects have no perceptual, somatic, or emotional experience, but where the philosophical anxiety captured by the explanatory gap nonetheless appropriately arises. This suggests that the suitably explanatory-gap-able property is instantiated in that world, even though perceptual, somatic, and emotional experiential characters are not—which in turn suggests that the explanatory-gap-able properties of the subjects there are cognitive properties.[137]

Much more can be (and has been) said about the scope of experiential intentionality. As noted, in this book I will assume rather dogmatically that there *is* such a thing as experiential intentionality. In the same vein, I will also assume that experiential intentionality extends beyond purely sensory experience to high-level perceptual experience and cognitive experience. Although I recognize that these assumptions are not beyond rational doubt, it so happens that I personally do not doubt them. My concern here, in any event, is to consider what sort of overall understanding of intentionality we may obtain if we assume the existence of experiential (including cognitive-experiential) intentionality and accept the experiential origin thesis argued for earlier in the chapter. The purpose of the present section has been merely to elucidate (and give texture to) the notion of experiential intentionality.

Conclusion: The Experiential Origin Thesis and the Case for It

The purpose of the chapter has been to argue for the experiential origin thesis. In spirit, this is the thesis that our conception of intentionality is grounded in our grasp of experiential intentionality. I proposed a precisification of the thesis that would provide its letter: an item qualifies as intentional by the lights of one's concept of intentionality if, and only if, it has the same underlying nature as exp-intentional states encountered during the formation of one's concept of intentionality, where a state is exp-intentional just in case it has an intentional content and an experiential character such that it would not have the content if it did not have the character.

The argument I offered proceeded essentially as follows. First, for certain kinds of concept, an item falls under the concept just in case it has the same underlying nature as most manifest instances encountered during the concept's formation. Secondly, the concept of intentionality is of the relevant kind. Thirdly, the manifest instances of intentionality we encounter during the formation of our concept of intentionality are exclusively exp-intentional states (because these are the only instances of intentionality we have observational contact with). It follows that an item falls under our concept of intentionality just in case it has the same underlying nature as most encountered exp-intentional states.

If we do accept the experiential origin thesis, the theory of intentionality assumes a certain structure, dividing into two main parts: an account of experiential intentionality and an account of non-experiential intentionality. Chapters 2 and 3 are devoted to experiential intentionality, each proposing one account that I find reasonably plausible (and eventually comparing those two accounts). Chapter 4 is devoted to non-experiential intentionality, considering several possible accounts thereof and arguing for the superiority of one among them. Chapter 5 revisits the general theory of intentionality in light of the proposals made in the chapters leading up to it.[138]

Notes

1. There are familiar semantic, epistemological, and metaphysical questions surrounding natural kinds. These concern the determination of reference and extension of natural kind terms and concepts, the formation and acquisition of natural kind concepts, and the identity, existence, and membership conditions of the kinds themselves. Typically, accounts of natural kinds and natural kind terms/concepts come in comprehensive package deals driven by insights either from the semantic or from the metaphysical angle. Here I will focus, atypically, on the epistemological angle. The question I want to concentrate on concerns how we form natural kind concepts.

2. There are three contrast classes here. First, there are concepts of kinds whose similarity is due to our activities. Thus, artifactual kind concepts are not natural kind concepts, as the similarity among

their instances is due to human activity: tables are similar because they were built *by us* with a purpose in mind. Likewise, social kinds are due to our legal or social institutions: the similarity among bachelors is only relative to the institution of marriage. Secondly, there might be concepts whose instances resemble only mind-dependently. This would be the case, according to subjectivists about value, or color, with our value or color concepts. Thirdly, there could also be concepts whose instances are such that there is *no* similarity of any kind among their instances (this may be a far-fetched possibility if we are liberal about what counts as similarity, but need not be ruled out a priori).

3. It is not immediately obvious how to draw the observation/not observation distinction. One option is to pattern the *prima facie* distinction between observational and non-observational (natural kind) concepts on the traditional distinction between observational and theoretical terms (e.g., an observational concept would be thought of as a concept expressed by an observational term, and a theoretical concept as a concept expressed by a theoretical term), but I am not keen to do so, given the doctrinal baggage that has tended to come with the distinction in the hands of logical positivists.

4. Arguably, mammals form a natural kind, and our conception thereof is as of a natural kind. That is, our concept of a mammal is a natural kind concept.

5. This is of course an oversimplification: those who wrote what we read probably read about mammals in other sources. But at the end of the chain is someone who formed a concept of a mammal not by reading about mammals but by interacting with them.

6. Certain non-observational natural kind concepts are such that *nobody* forms them on the basis of encounter with instances. Thus, nobody has ever encountered a lepton, yet our concept of a lepton is a natural kind concept. The models discussed in the text of this subsection therefore do not apply to such concepts.

7. The criterial model is very natural for certain kind concepts, such as the concept of a bachelor. To qualify as a bachelor is clearly to satisfy the conditions of being a man and being unmarried. In a way, the criterial model takes the formation of the concept of a bachelor to be paradigmatic and suggests that other concept formations should be understood along the same lines.

8. This is supported by empirical work in developmental psychology that demonstrates young children's appeal to hidden natures in classifying objects (Gelman and Markman 1986).

9. Linnaeus classified whales as mammals, in the mid-eighteenth century, on the basis of such in-principle-manifest, observable-but-typically-unobserved features as having hollow ears and a warm heart. I trust it is clear that although such features are in principle observable, they are not observed during the (non-parasitic) formation of normal persons' conception of a whale.

10. Note that in this formulation the underlying nature is said to be possessed by particulars. If this sounds clunky to our ears, and we think that underlying natures are of properties not particulars, then the formulation would have to be changed to refer to underlying common features rather than underlying natures, or perhaps better yet, to the underlying nature of commonalities. Here I will continue to refer to natures as had by particulars.

11. One could mean something else by the "underlying-nature model of natural kind concept formation," and on this alternative understanding these consequences may not follow. But here I understand by the "underlying-nature model of natural kind concept formation" exactly what (UN) states— no more and no less.

12. Notice that I am using the term "instance" to denote any item that falls under the concept. The term "instance" is sometimes used to denote only items that instantiate the corresponding property, but this is not how I use the term.

13. This will be refined and modified when the model assumes more shape below.

14. This could be made more explicit by introducing the anchoring instances with an operator and plugging in the explication of "anchoring instance" as a relevantly encountered manifest instance.

The result would be this: For any natural kind K and particular x, there are particulars $k_1, \ldots, k_n$ and a nature N, such that x qualifies as a K iff (i) all of $k_1, \ldots, k_n$ are encountered manifest instances of K, (ii) most of $k_1, \ldots, k_n$ have N, and (iii) x has N.

15. There is the empirically quite unlikely possibility that every single anchoring instance turns out to have a different underlying nature. In this case, the concept is either (a) an empty natural kind concept or (b) a non-natural kind concept (this I find more plausible). If (a), then it will be discoverable that there is no such thing as mammal-ness, which is not quite the same discovery as that there are no mammals. If (b), then in the scenario envisaged all the anchoring instances would qualify as mammals.

16. With the exact formulation of the anchoring-instance model in place, we can formulate a precise explication of the notion of an anchoring instance, based on its theoretical role in the model: A priori, for any particular x and natural kind K, there are items $k_1, \ldots, k_n$ and a nature N, such that x is an anchoring instance of K iff (i) for any y, y qualifies as a K iff (i-a) y has N and (i-b) most of $k_1, \ldots, k_n$ have N, and (ii) $x \in k_1, \ldots, k_n$.

17. The six notions are: "qualify as," "concept," "formation," "encounter," "most," and "particulars."

18. Ditto for the normality of conditions: there are statistically normal conditions and teleologically normal conditions, the latter being the conditions that allow the subject's concept-forming mechanisms to perform their function(s) as they are supposed to.

19. Note that it is still required here that the unperceived individuals be manifest, or observably, similar to the perceived one. On this view, if there are very unusual cats or horses, which do not look sufficiently like the individual cats and horses the subject token-encountered during the formation of her concept of a mammal, these unusual cats and horses—non-manifest cats and horses—do not qualify as anchoring instances of her concept of a mammal. But other cats and horses do.

20. I am enamored of the thought that in such circumstances the concept defaults into manifest kind concept status. But clearly this is not the only option for the model. Other options are to construe the concept as an empty natural kind concept, or perhaps as a concept that refers to a disjunctive kind or a concept that has divided reference.

21. Two further comments are in order. First, the conjunctive line would make the non-anchoring instances that have only one of the two natures not instances at all (since they would not share the conjunctive underlying nature exhibited by the anchoring instances). Secondly, this line requires there to *be* conjunctive natural kinds. Presumably, some of Armstrong's (1978 Ch.15) arguments for the existence of conjunctive universals could be adapted to make the case that there are conjunctive natural kinds. In particular, the argument that universals are posited to explain objective similarity relations among particulars, and that conjunctive universals, such as the red square, are thus needed to explain the objective similarity among certain particulars, such as all red squares, would transfer straightforwardly to natural kinds.

22. As is common in philosophical practice, here and elsewhere I use hyphens to indicate that the parts of the expression are morphological parts but not syntactic parts (in the way "apple" is a morphological but not syntactic part of "pineapple").

23. For a classic on prototype theory, see Rosch 1973.

24. More accurately, given the eighth clarification, we should say that the anchoring instances that are genuine instances are a proper subset of the genuine instances. Also, perhaps a qualification such as "typically" should be introduced for anchoring instances, since there is no reason to rule out a priori the possibility of a concept all of whose instances turn out to be anchoring instances.

25. There might in principle also be prototypical instances that are not anchoring instances, in case highly prototypical instances of some concept are rarely encountered and thus do not play an anchoring role in the formation of that concept. I cannot think of a concrete example of this, but see no reason to exclude the possibility.

26. How to make sense of the notion of being "more of an instance" is of course not a trivial matter. Presumably different approaches to vagueness could be applied here in different ways, or fuzzy logic could be used to regiment talk of degrees of "instance-hood."

27. It is not entirely clear to me what theories of the "structure" of concepts target—what notion of structure they have in mind and what phenomenon they hope the notion denotes. I do note, however, first, that typically prototype theorists present their theories as about the structure of concepts, and second, that in their mouths the notion seems to be metaphysical rather than epistemological.

28. It is less clear whether the model is compatible with a direct reference account of natural kind concepts. More likely, the model requires concepts to refer via a description such as "has the same underlying nature as most anchoring instances." Correspondingly, the model is probably also incompatible with a pure causal theory of natural kind terms/concepts' reference (Kripke 1972). This doctrine is much more controversial, however, and in my view faces systemic problems that have been pointed out more or less immediately after its inception. I will not discuss these issues here, as they would take us too far afield, but see Zemach 1976 and Kim 1977 for incisive criticism.

29. I will consider objections to this later on. These will take two forms: denying that the concept of intentionality is a natural kind concept, and accepting that it is a natural kind concept but denying that it is an observational one.

30. In what follows, I will often drop the parenthetical reference to concepts for smoothness of exposition. This is not intended to lure the reader into forgetting that my thesis concerns concepts rather than properties—I am quite explicit that the thesis is primarily epistemological.

31. A more precise formulation is this: 1) For any item x and natural kind K, x qualifies as a K iff there is a nature N, such that (i) most of the anchoring instances of K have N and (ii) x has N; 2) The concept of intentionality is a natural kind concept; therefore, 3) For any item x, x qualifies as intentional iff there is a nature N, such that (i) most of the anchoring instances of intentionality have N and (ii) x has N; 4) For any item x, x is an anchoring instance of intentionality iff x is an encountered experiential-intentional state; therefore, 5) For any item x, x qualifies as intentional iff there is a nature N, such that (i) most encountered experiential-intentional states have N and (ii) x has N.

32. Keep in mind, in any case, that to ground our conception of intentionality in our grasp of experiential intentionality, all that is required is that *only* experiential-intentional states be anchoring instances of our conception of intentionality; it is not required that *all* be.

33. It may be objected that some—many—normal subjects do not undergo non-parasitic formation of most of their concepts. This is true, but a *non-sequitur*. The claims I am making are only about concept formation in normal subjects when they form the concepts they do non-parasitically. I take it that parasitically formed concepts inherit their structure from non-parasitically formed ones.

34. As I will mention more explicitly soon, the kind of encounter at play here is more plausibly construed as (what I called in §1.1.1) type-encounter, that is, the encounter a subject has with a type of entity on the basis of directly perceiving (i.e., token-encountering) individual tokens.

35. The qualification "probably" is needed since it could still turn out that some encountered experiential-intentional states do not exhibit the relevant manifest features. As noted, this is not very probable, but is a coherent possibility.

36. This means that the set of encountered experiential-intentional states probably includes all the experiential-intentional states that have the same manifest properties as the token experiential-intentional states that have actually been "met." So, for example, if a subject has "met" (had a "direct" awareness of, in some duly explained sense of "direct") a visual experience as of a table, then all visual experiences as of tables (or at least all experientially type-identical visual experiences as of tables) count as "encountered."

37. I am assuming here that *states* in general are particulars. This does not necessarily mean that they are *bare* particulars, as opposed to, say, property instantiations or tropes. For the latter are widely regarded to be abstract particulars (see Williams 1953), thus *a fortiori* particulars. Certainly, in any case, intentional states are not *quantities* or *samples* in the way units of water and gold are. Furthermore, propositions are likewise particulars: there is one of each (at most!). The fact that they are abstract entities does not affect their status as particulars.

38. It strikes me as quite plausible that the prototypes of intentionality are exclusively experiential-intentional states. However, this is an empirical thesis and the empirical confirmation for it would be difficult to generate (though I suspect an empirical disconfirmation would be even harder). Elsewhere, Terry Horgan and I have suggested a somewhat similar thesis, according to which all the prototypical *mental* states are phenomenally intentional states (Horgan and Kriegel 2008).

39. It is clear, nonetheless, that there is a temperamental difference—a difference in animating sensibilities—between the two approaches (see Montague 2010, Kriegel and Horgan forthcoming). More on this later.

40. Traffic signs are about something: a sign on Interstate 95 that says "New York, next exit" is *about* the sorts of actions that have to be taken in order to reach New York from where the reader is at.

41. This thin existential claim is highly plausible *prima facie*, but will also be argued for, in effect, in §1.2.

42. On some views, such as Dennett's (1971, 1987) "intentional stance" theory, intentionality *is* observer-dependent in this way. We will, in fact, discuss some relevant ideas in §1.2 and §4.4. However, while the view has insightful things to say about the practice of intentional ascription, the inference from those things to the anti-realist, observer-dependent view of intentionality is somewhat mysterious, and to my mind has been soundly refuted by Fodor and LePore (1993), who comment (1993: 76): "It's mysterious . . . either how you could make facts out of stances, or how stances could make facts disappear."

43. I suspect that every concept we have we treat initially as potentially picking out a natural kind. We approach the kind open to the possibility that it has a deep underlying nature. If and when we realize that it does not, the manifest features of the anchoring instances become the kind's "essential" feature, that is, the individuating features.

44. This is a rather informal sub-argument. Its conclusion is not exactly the same as Premise 4 above. The more precise formulation would be as follows: 1) For any item x, x is an anchoring instance of intentionality iff x is an encountered intentional item; [anchoring-instance model] 2) For any item x, x is an encountered intentional item iff the (normal) subject has observational contact with x; [plausible assumption] 3) For any item x, the (normal) subject has observational contact with x only if x is an experiential-intentional state; [to be argued for] therefore, 4) For any item x, x is an anchoring instance of intentionality only if x is an experiential-intentional state; [from 1,2,3] 5) For any item x, x is an anchoring instance of intentionality if x is an encountered intentional item; [from 1] 6) For any item x, x is an encountered intentional item if x is an encountered experiential-intentional state; [logical truism] therefore, 7) For any item x, x is an anchoring instance of intentionality if x is an encountered experiential-intentional state; [from 5,6] therefore, 8) For any item x, x is an anchoring instance of intentionality iff x is an encountered experiential-intentional state. [from 4,7]

45. The objector might point out that many natural kind concepts involve no encounter with instances; the concept of a lepton is a case in point, as are many other concepts of "theoretical entities."

46. This provides a non-demonstrative argument for the second premise of the argument with which I opened this section, which in turn is a demonstrative argument for Premise 4 of the previous section's argument for the experiential origin thesis.

47. Note, however, that there are many different senses in which intentionality is sometimes said to be normative. Sometimes it is said to be normative in aiming at truth, sometimes in connection with

rule following, sometimes in other senses. The only sense that will concern us here, however, is the Davidsonian claim that principles of charity are needed for competent ascription.

48. The expression "non-experiential-intentional" is ambiguous, and I mean by it anything that has non-experiential intentionality, not anything that does not have experiential intentionality. (Obviously, experiential intentionality is not prior in any sense to everything else!)

49. I use the term "overt behavior" to refer to publicly observable, third-personally accessible behavior, i.e., bodily behavior. There is a sense of "behavior" in which many mental acts, e.g. calculating, count as behavior, namely, the sense in which calculating is something one does, not something that happens to one. It is these mental acts that are supposed to be excluded by the notion of *overt* behavior. We may think of them as *covert* behavior.

50. As Davidson (1970: 97) puts it, in constructing a theory of someone's behavior, "we will try for a theory that finds him consistent, a believer of truths, and a lover of the good (all by our own lights, it goes without saying)."

51. By saying that the person takes the word "tiger" to express the concepts of a tiger (or pigeon), I mean that she takes the word to express the concept *we* take the words "tiger" (or "pigeon") to express.

52. A quick comment on the goodness of the desire: the desire is good not in the moral sense, but in the *prudential* sense. In that sense, a desire is good when it is a desire for something that is genuinely good *for the desirer*. Consider the robber's desire to get out of the bank as quickly as possible. This is a prudentially good but not morally good desire.

53. There are also descriptive principles of ascription at play here, which favor both these options over, say, ascribing to the person the belief that the moons of Jupiter are nice and the desire to fly backwards. Descriptive principles ensure that this assignment is inferior, on this occasion, to the options considered in the text. But the options in the text are discriminated by normative principles, not descriptive ones.

54. We might say, using terminology from Searle (1983 Ch.1) among others, that it involves one force that is an attitude with a mind-to-world direction of fit and one with a world-to-mind direction of fit.

55. Here too I follow Davidson (1963), now in his account of a reason for Φ-ing as a combination of a desire that p obtain and a belief that Φ-ing would make the obtaining of p more likely.

56. There may certainly be cases where there are several possible ascriptions that a competent interpreter might choose among while remaining competent. But my concern here is with other cases.

57. Davidson's reasoning here may be represented as an argument by inference to the best explanation. What needs explaining is that competent interpreters manage, *qua* competent interpreters, to converge on a single interpretation (and can recognize that that is the correct interpretation) in most typical situations, even though the data at their disposal grossly underdetermine interpretation. The best explanation of this is that competent interpreters, *qua* competent interpreters, employ principles of charity that rule out possible interpretations otherwise consistent with the data. Alternative explanations would cite some other device(s) competent interpreters might employ, in their capacity as competent interpreters, to rule out those interpretations. But it is not clear what other device(s) there might be, so no plausible alternatives present themselves to the Davidsonian explanation that competent interpretation must employ, and is to that extent governed by, principles of charity. (Needless to say, all this applies only to *competent* interpretation. Faced with the pigeon-pointer who exclaims "This is a tiger," we can, if we want, interpret her as believing that she is looking at a tiger. We can also interpret her, if we very much want, as believing that she is looking at a three-headed kangaroo. What we cannot do, however, is interpret her in this way *competently*.)

58. We obtain the four-way distinction by crossing two simpler distinctions, one between ascription of experiential-intentional states ("exp-intentional ascription") and non-experiential-intentional

states ("nexp-intentional ascription") and the other between ascription of an intentional state to oneself (first-person ascription) and ascription of an intentional state to another (third-person ascription).

59. In this respect, my argument will use Davidson's own vector-of-two-forces observation to argue for a very non-Davidsonian approach to first-person ascription, and thus self-knowledge. For Davidson's own views on the matter, see Davidson 1987.

60. There certainly exist much more complex instances of intentional ascription. But my contention is that the complexity in those cases does not change the basic mechanics of ascription, though it may well serve to becloud those mechanics. This is a reason to focus on simple examples in which the mechanics come through clearly.

61. Recall that, as we saw in the previous subsection, these are the sorts of belief and desire that we need to ascribe in this case to subsume the case of verbal behavior under the more general case of behavior.

62. In other words, there are different desires that could be ascribed together with the same belief, and different beliefs that could be ascribed together with the same desire, but it is impossible to ascribe the belief in isolation from *any* desire or the desire in isolation from *any* belief.

63. A non-mental analogy may be useful. Suppose you are presented with a color patch projected on a window pane. You are told that the color is produced by projection from two different light sources, one from the left and one from the right. You can see the patch, but not the light sources. Thus, when you see a purple patch on the pane, your data are compatible with at least three hypotheses: that the left light is blue and the right one red; that the left light is red and the right one blue; that both are purple. Since the color of the patch is the vector of two forces, and you do not have direct access to those forces themselves, ascribing colors to the light sources must involve an element of *decision*. (In the present case, that the decision must be arbitrary; in the case of nexp-intentional ascription, it is based on charity.) Compare now a case in which you *can* see not only the patch, but also the light sources—at least *sometimes*. Here you do have direct access to the lights, and so ascribing colors to them is not the vector of two forces. This is what happens, I will argue below, in the central case of exp-intentional ascription.

64. There are places where Dennett seems to suggest that in many of our intentional ascriptions, we are simply ascribing to others beliefs in whatever we happen to think is true (see especially Dennett 1971). Thus, we may ascribe to someone a belief that *p* not on the basis of their behavior, but on the basis of it being the case that *p*. Such ascription would certainly not be based on data that are the vectors of two forces, but I hope it is clear that it would be imbued with charity in an even more straightforward way.

65. The notions of cognitive experience will be discussed more fully in §1.3.3. See also Kriegel forthcoming.

66. We may stipulate, since this is a thought experiment, that your colleague does not in addition have a conflicting desire to evince anger etc. There is no internal division inside her will. Her will is one, so to speak.

67. It should be stressed that, given that what we have been concerned to establish is that some exp-intentional ascription is based on data that are not the vectors of two forces, without committing on the question of whether *all* such ascription is, there is no need for us to worry overmuch about third-person exp-intentional ascription. For our existential claim can be established simply by examination of first-person exp-intentional ascription, and regardless of how third-person exp-intentional ascription turns out to work. Nonetheless, for the sake of completeness, let me consider briefly this kind of ascription.

68. The causal structure of the hidden mechanism is a little different when the ascribed state is not a belief, but the kind of perceptual state that causes belief. In the former case, the envisaged mechanism involves two states, the belief and the desire. In the latter, it involves three states, the belief, the

desire, and the perceptual state that causes the belief. In both cases, however, it is impossible to ascribe a single, non-conspiratory state.

69. One might object as follows. To ascribe to oneself an experience as of a table, one would have to possess the concept of a table, but possession of the concept of a table requires the possession of many other concepts, for example those that combine with one's concept of a table to constitute one's beliefs about tables. This seems to me a *non sequitur*. First, a concept is not a mental state, but a constituent of a mental state, so the symmetry between attributions holds even if first-person exp-intentional attribution requires the attribution of certain concepts. Secondly, and even more importantly, the fact—if it is a fact—that first-person exp-intentional attributions require the existence of certain *concepts* does not entail that it requires the *attribution* of those concepts. So again this would not undermine the asymmetry with other forms of intentional ascription (which do not require *attribution* of more than one mental state).

70. Thus although the experience, being perceptual, has a mind-to-world direction of fit, its ascription need not be accompanied by the ascription of any intentional state with a world-to-mind direction of fit.

71. This may invite the misguided objection that a perceptual experience is itself a combination of two states, say a sensation and a belief, and so first-person exp-intentional ascription also ascribes only two states at once. Clearly, however, even if we accept this view of perceptual experiences as combinations of two states, there are differences between the reason we can only ascribe two states at once in this case and the reason in other kinds of intentional ascription. The fact (if it were a fact) that we can only ascribe two states at once in first-person exp-intentional ascription would not entail that there are competing interpretations fully consistent with the data, as is the case with the other kinds of intentional ascription, and therefore it would not entail that principles of charity must be operative in choosing among these ascriptions.

72. I use the term "endorsement" to cover not only conscious acts, but also automatic sub-conscious processes that involve ratification of the content of one's experience. I am thus not wedded to a model according to which one consciously and deliberately goes through two distinct steps in performing a perceptual judgment. It may feel immediate to the subject when the subject judges that there is a table before her. Nonetheless, the cognitive processes involved in the production of such a judgment divide into different steps, one of which can be described as endorsement.

73. I will discuss first-person nexp-intentional ascription momentarily.

74. It is not a straightforward matter to elucidate the sense in which the epistemic relation you bear to your experience can be described as "observation." What I have in mind is the thought that there is an epistemic relation we sometimes bear to our own mental states that is analogous in some respects to perception of external entities. There is a difference between believing that it is raining on the basis of the weather report and believing this on the basis of *seeing* the rain. The latter case involves a kind of direct contact with the state of affairs believed to obtain that the former case does not. In an analogous way, there is a difference between the way you know that what you are visualizing right now is a smiling octopus and the way I know this. I know it on the basis of testimony, you know it on the basis of direct contact with the believed state of affairs. It is this kind of contact that I think would not be misleadingly described as "observation." As I will argue in §1.2.3, however, this perceptual model of introspection is not necessary (but only useful) for the claims I am making using it.

75. I use the term "yields" in a way that is neutral between a causal and a constitutive reading, to accommodate different views of the nature of introspection. I will discuss some of these views more explicitly in §1.2.3.

76. I put "hypothesis" in quotation marks because, as I mentioned earlier, the view that we have such observational contact strikes me as phenomenologically obvious in a way that makes calling it a

hypothesis sound funny. To me, it is almost a datum. As noted, however, I am offering an argument for those who see things differently, and in the context of the argument treat the claim as a hypothesis.

77. This statement of self-intimation is sloppy. What is claimed to be self-intimating is not introspection, actually, but that which is introspected. Also, it is not for *every p* that a doctrine of self-intimation counts as self-intimating; only *mental* propositions are relevant.

78. As it happens, I happen to believe that a strong kind of epistemic privilege does attach to the deliverances of introspection, and have argued so elsewhere (Horgan and Kriegel 2007), but that view is logically independent of the claims made here.

79. Importantly, conscious occurrent beliefs and desires do not qualify as nexp-intentional states, but as exp-intentional ones. As will be discussed in §1.3.3, I hold that beliefs can constitute conscious experiences—"cognitive experiences"—so I am assuming here that exp-intentional ascription is not restricted to states with a specifically *sensory* experiential character. It has sometimes been claimed that beliefs cannot be conscious and occurrent (Crane 2001). I am somewhat sympathetic to this claim, understood as a claim about how the English word "belief" is normally used, but it is clear that there is no substantive issue at stake here, inasmuch as a tacit belief could still transform into a conscious, experiential intentional state; it is just that that state would not qualify as a belief the way the word is normally used. A natural term to pick out the kind of state a tacit belief transforms into when it becomes conscious is "thought."

80. To be sure, sometimes the evidence is so overwhelming that no process of "seeking" is needed. This seems to be the case with the belief that Michael Jordan is not a three-headed kangaroo. But even in this case the evidence for ascribing the belief is nothing but the evidence for the proposition believed.

81. It is true that just as when I ask you whether you are having a table experience, you reply immediately that you do, so when I ask you whether you believe that there are more than four countries in Africa, you reply immediately that you do; and the immediacy of reply might suggest direct observation in both cases. But given Evans' model, the immediacy of reply is not to be explained by the fact that you observe your belief, but in some other way. My guess is that the right explanation of the immediacy is that when the proposition you are asked whether you believe is obviously true, in that the evidence you have for it is overwhelming and readily available, you will answer the question immediately because the question is so easy. The explanation for this immediacy is therefore not that you have observed the believing, but rather that the proposition believed is obvious (again, in the sense that the evidence for it is overwhelming and readily available). Thus there is no argument from immediacy-of-reply to direct observation.

82. There is a sense in which the word "charity" is a little strained for this kind of case, but this seems to do with the pragmatics of normative talk when self-applied. At bottom the cases are of the same general kind. Thus just as we often ascribe to others beliefs in whatever we realize is true, by way of charity, so we ascribe to ourselves dispositional beliefs in whatever we realize is true—also a form of charity.

83. Another possible motivation might be that there is something incoherent about the notion of a dispositional state—any respectable ontological assay of states would cast them as occurrent entities. To say that a *state* is dispositional is really a confusion. This kind of argument may be harder to prosecute, but my hunch is that it is fundamentally sound.

84. It is a fair question whether there is indeed an intuitive cost. On the one hand, it does sound counter-intuitive to deny that most people want (right now) to stay alive. But on the other hand, it is not counter-intuitive to deny, and is in fact counter-intuitive to assert, that most Americans believe (right now) that Michael Jordan is not a three-headed kangaroo. Overall, I do think there is an intuitive cost here, and recognize this cost to be a liability on the view that there are no dispositional states. Nonetheless, I think the cost is worth paying for the sake of the economy in states posited.

85. I take this eliminativism about dispositional states to cover both tacit beliefs that were never occurrent and those that were once occurrent and then were stored in long-term memory. It may seem that with the latter type of state there is more reason to be realist. But again there is no explanatory gain in preferring stored dispositional states over stored dispositions to enter states. (The only new pressure presented by stored states is that the intuitive cost of denying their existence seems greater.) In the case of beliefs stored in *short*-term memory, there seems to be genuine explanatory gain in admitting their existence, but this is mainly because such states are most certainly occurrent (short-term memory being what it is).

86. I use "broadly experiential" because I hold that only experiential states, in the sense of "experiential" I am working with here (to do with having a warranted sense of an explanatory gap), are introspectible. But if one insisted that there are introspectible states that are not experiential in the sense of warranting explanatory gap worries, then there is surely some broadened sense of "experiential" such that in *it* only experiential states are introspectible.

87. It is possible that, as with the attribution to oneself of Freudian nexp-intentional states, there could be indirect introspective evidence for the existence of such sub-personal nexp-intentional states. But the remarks I made above about the case of Freudian nexp-intentional states would apply here too: since there is no direct observation of the state being ascribed, the vector-of-two-forces observation would still hold.

88. Block (1995, 2007) has argued that some sub-personal state may be, and probably are, phenomenally conscious. Since Block means by "phenomenal" what we mean here by "experiential" (see Block 1995: 382 in the 1997 reprint), if he is right there would be exp-intentional states that are sub-personal and thus introspectively inaccessible. There would therefore be some first-person exp-intentional ascription that would behave just as this form of first-person nexp-intentional ascription does. As before, this would not undermine the epistemological asymmetry between exp- and nexp-intentional states, since the asymmetry requires only that *some* exp-intentional state be ascribed in the special way mentioned in the text.

89. Either so, or else they are imbued even more directly with charity and normativity, as we have seen in some cases of third-person exp-intentional ascription.

90. Interestingly, this reaction to claims that all intentional ascription is governed by principles of charity is structurally similar to an early reaction due to McGinn (1977). McGinn's discussion is complex, but let me crush the subtleties and present what I take to be its upshot: ascription of *de dicto* intentionality may be based on data that are the vectors of two forces, but ascription of *de re* intentionality is not. Consider the person who utters the words "This balloon is yellow" while pointing at a yellow refrigerator. As interpreters, we may be concerned to ascribe to her either beliefs *de dicto* or beliefs *de re*. Suppose we wish to ascribe beliefs *de dicto*. Our data are consistent with two interpretations: (i) she believes that the refrigerator is yellow and by "balloon" she means refrigerator; (ii) she believes that a balloon is yellow and uses words as we do. But now suppose we wish to ascribe to this person beliefs *de re*. While the data are consistent with saying that the person believes, of a refrigerator, that it is yellow, they are *inconsistent* with saying that the person believes, of a balloon, that it is yellow. If there is no balloon, it is false that the person believes anything of a balloon. This reaction is structurally similar to ours, in that it indicts the normativist about intentional ascription with failure to make certain distinctions, and subsequently failure to appreciate that the vector-of-two-forces observation applies only to some kinds of intentional ascription and not others. It is worth noting, however, that *de re* intentional ascription is extensional (Quine 1956), whereas exp-intentional ascription is intensional (i.e., features substitution failure and failure of existential generalization). So even if McGinn is right (as I think he is), I would still maintain that exp-intentional ascription provides the only case of intensional intentional ascription that is non-normative.

91. It is an interesting question how much of philosophical research can be cast in these terms, that is, as involving empirical claims supported by considerations that do not require very involved empirical research but are available, in some sense, to the casual observer. In any case, it should be noted that the various clarifications of the anchoring-instance model in §1.1.1, in presenting a number of ways the model could go, make it clear that the level of specificity at which the model is presented is indeed very low, and thus susceptible to understanding in these terms.

92. The notion of transparency of experience will be discussed in greater detail in §2.1.2.

93. How to do justice to the transparency observation (which I accept) given this fact is a good question, but the displaced perception model cannot be right. For my part, I am persuaded that experience is transparent in the sense that its vehicular properties are not available to direct introspection. But it seems to me not to follow that experience is itself unavailable to direct introspection. On the contrary, an experience is directly introspectible due to the fact that its content properties are directly introspectible. For further discussion, see Kriegel 2009 Ch.5.

94. Furthermore, it is hard for me to believe that the model can be successfully applied across the board. Even if made to work for perceptual experiences, it faces severe difficulties as a model of our introspective access to certain *imaginative* experiences. When a visual image of a smiling octopus pops up in my mind arbitrarily and involuntarily, I can introspect it, but no displaced perception can take place. It is not as though I become aware that I am having an experience as of a smiling octopus on the basis of being perceptually aware (or seemingly-aware) of an octopus. It might be claimed that I *pretend* to be perceptually aware of an octopus, but of course pretending is itself an imaginative exercise, so this account would be circular and vacuous.

95. Presumably, this would have to be conjoined with the claim that thoughts, or intellectual states more generally, do not involve a kind of epistemic contact with their objects. This second claim is denied by some (e.g., Chudnoff forthcoming-b).

96. It might be objected that this intellectualist view of introspection can explain the asymmetry by noting that, even if introspecting an experience is just thinking about it, the relevant thought would be formed on the basis of data that are not vectors of two forces: it is possible to think that I am having a table experience *without* at the same time thinking that I am in any other intentional state. However, this is to confuse the *explanandum* for an *explanans*: it is precisely this asymmetry that is in need of explanation!

97. This is in fact my own view—see Kriegel 2009 Ch.5 and Horgan and Kriegel 2007.

98. Furthermore, it is not clear to me that acquaintance cannot be thought of as a form of observation: that the numerical identity of the state of acquaintance and the state acquainted rules out the appropriate describability of the latter as "observed." This is an entirely verbal matter, however, that we need not go into. The substantive issue, as stressed in the text, is that of direct epistemic contact.

99. This may be an instance of the more general fallacy of confusing *causal immediacy*, which is a matter of lack of intervening causal links, and *temporal immediacy*, which is a matter of lack of temporal lag (or, more accurately, *noticeable* temporal lag). The above ascription of distress to one's friend may be immediate in the temporal sense, but not in the causal one. To show this, however, we would need an individuation of causal links and temporal interval to support this, making it the case that seeing the facial expression is a mediating causal link in the case of ascription of distress to the friend.

100. This does not require denying that a mature subject, possessed of a concept of intentionality, can be perceptually aware of nexp-intentional item *as intentional*, as per Siegel's (2006) claim. It is only to deny that a subject *lacking* the concept of intentionality can.

101. It may be objected that the intentionality of paintings and photographs is not convention-based in the way that of language is. However, while it is not entirely clear to me whether the resemblance between a portrait and its sitter is conventional, for resemblance to amount to intentionality

certain further conditions must be met, and those are likely to involve convention. Indeed, as we will see in Chapter 4, one quite plausible view is that the intentionality of pictures is structurally the same as the intentionality of language and the kind of Gricean basis required for linguistic intentionality is also required for pictorial intentionality (Abell 2005, Blumson 2006).

102. It is a separate question whether there *is* an intentionality conscious experiences have in virtue of being conscious experiences. If there is not, then there is no experiential intentionality. But what it takes for there to be experiential intentionality is for conscious experiences to have a kind of intentionality they have purely in virtue of being conscious experiences. The question of existence is taken up in §1.3.2.

103. I should clarify that I use "conscious experience" so that every experience is conscious and every conscious state is an experience. I prefer this term over "phenomenally conscious state" because it is less technical, and for other reasons that will come out later in this subsection.

104. By "blindsighted perception" I mean a perceptual state of the sort that occurs in blindsight (a condition that issues in subjects being able to navigate the environment on the basis of visual processing of information about the environment but do not undergo corresponding visual experiences—see Weiskrantz 1986).

105. Another possible formulation of the same idea would be this: A priori, for any intentional property P and state x, P is and exp-intentional property of x iff there is an experiential character E, such that (i) x is P, (ii) x has E and (iii) it is the case that (i) because it is the case that (ii). Note well, however: the "because" in (iii) should be read not causally but constitutively, that is, not in the sense in which I might say "I am a bachelor because I never met the right woman," but in the sense in which I might say "I am a bachelor because I am an unmarried man." For a well-behaved gloss on aprioricity, which might help in this particular context, we could appeal to the notion of epistemic possibility (see Chalmers forthcoming, Huemer 2007).

106. This is akin to defining color as the determinable of which green, yellow, black, etc. are determinates. The claim that there is such a thing as experiential intentionality then becomes the thesis that there is at least one exp-intentional property.

107. Which definition we go with depends on our metaphysics of states in general. Option (a) works with an account of states as dated property exemplifications, akin to the way events are understood in Kim's (1976) account of events. Option (b) works with an account of states as bare particulars that *have* properties, rather than being partially *constituted* by properties, akin to Davidson's (1969) account of events.

108. I have in mind here a notion of grounding with the kind of robust primacy content, along the lines developed by Kit Fine (2001).

109. We may say that where the doctrinal definition of experiential intentionality requires *metaphysical* dependence of the intentional on the experiential, the neutral one requires only *counterfactual* dependence.

110. The main issue not to prejudge is whether the experience is more basic than intentionality. While I am seeking an account of intentionality that gives pride of place to experiential intentionality, it is not part of my project to establish the primacy of experience over intentionality within experiential intentionality. More on this momentarily.

111. A term I am much fonder of is "subjective intentionality." However, Loar (1987) used this term early on, and I do not wish to acquire the baggage he associated with it. I also prefer "experiential intentionality" to "conscious intentionality"—a term used by McGinn (1988), Searle (1992), Kriegel (2003a), and Georgalis (2006)—because the literature on consciousness these days features a variety of concepts of consciousness, some of which (e.g., "access consciousness") have no recognizable experiential, or phenomenal, or first-personal dimension (see Block 1995).

112. Relatedly, the term "phenomenal intentionality" is sometimes heard as definitionally non-reductive, so that asserting the existence of phenomenal intentionality implies the existence of physically irreducible intentionality. Some also hear it as denying the divisibility of the mind into two broad categories, the sensory and the cognitive. And so on and so forth. By contrast, the term "experiential intentionality" does not come with any doctrinal baggage.

113. If we want to give an experiential property E metaphysical primacy over an intentional property P within experiential intentionality, we must keep the two properties distinct and posit some intimate relation between them, such as logical supervenience, constitution, or realization. If we do not want to give any primacy to the experiential property, we are free to claim that the experiential property and the intentional property are one and the same (Pautz 2008, Mendelovici 2010). I must say that I find myself most attracted to this view of the matter. There may be a way to adopt this identity view while giving the intentional some *explanatory* or *conceptual* primacy, however. For example, one might hold that there is an experiential concept and an intentional concept that pick out one and the same (exp-intentional) property, but that the former concept is in some sense prior to the latter (e.g., in that the former can be used in explaining the latter more easily than the converse). There are some obvious difficulties presented by these notions of conceptual and explanatory priority, but a full discussion will take us too far afield anyway.

114. Thus, Georgalis (2006) argues against the notion of phenomenal intentionality, even though his view of intentionality is very much in line with the one I wish to defend here (as we will see momentarily, as well as in Chapter 4). This seems to be due to his understanding "phenomenal" as "sensory."

115. I suppose one could also claim that the mental states of understanding and realizing I just described do not qualify as experiences. But here we can appeal to the everyday usage of the term "experience" to reveal the implausibility of this claim, something we cannot do with a technical term such as "phenomenal," since the latter has no everyday use.

116. I will say more about cognitive experiences in §1.3.3. Their existence is somewhat controversial, but is defended in Goldman 1993, Strawson 1994 Ch.1, Peacocke 1998, Siewert 1998 Ch.8, Horgan and Tienson 2002, Kriegel 2003b, Pitt 2004, Klausen 2008, and Tennant 2009. See also Bayne and Montague 2011. My fullest defense of it is in Kriegel forthcoming.

117. This sense may be revealed by conceptual analysis, perhaps through the Ramsey sentence for "experience."

118. This seems to me overly optimistic, insofar as intuitions about what is such that there is something it is like to have it seem to align miraculously with philosophers' theoretical commitment about what is such that there is something it is like to have it, and thus raise the suspicion that the intuitions lie downstream of theory.

119. In Kriegel 2009 Ch.1, I propose—following a cue from Block (1995)—to define "phenomenal" in terms of the explanatory gap, as suggested here for "experiential." If this proposal is adopted, the two terms become equivalent of course. (But, also of course, some philosophers do not adopt this proposal, and instead hear "phenomenal" as having to do with the sensory/somatic.) Chalmers (1995, 1996 Ch.1) uses the term "experience" for whatever feature of conscious states presents the Hard Problem of consciousness. If the Hard Problem is the same as the explanatory gap, this would be exactly the definition proposed in the text. I happen to think they are slightly different (Kriegel 2009 Ch.8), but very close. It is possible to hold, of course, that the understandings of "experiential character" in terms of the everyday notion of experience and in terms of the explanatory gap are equivalent: plausibly, at least in one of its uses, the mundane notion of experience coextends with the explanatory-gap-based notion.

120. This requires a number of qualifications and clarifications, which I provide elsewhere (Kriegel forthcoming). The reference-fixing description I end up with there is this: For any property P, P is an experiential property iff in the actual world, there is at least an appearance of a non-derivative empirical

explanatory gap, relative to the human intellect, between P and physical properties. The qualification of "empirical" explanatory gap is supposed to rule out potential explanatory gaps between normative properties and physical properties. The qualification of "non-derivative" explanatory gap is supposed to rule out potential explanatory gaps parasitic on the explanatory gap between conscious experience and physical matter; thus, it has sometimes been claimed that there is an explanatory gap between color and physical matter, but also that this latter explanatory gap exists only insofar as color is tied up with color consciousness in such a way that an explanatory gap arises. As for the relativization to the human intellect, it is mandated by the fact that the availability of explanations depends partly on the cognitive abilities of the explanation-seeking subjects. For fuller discussion, see Kriegel forthcoming.

121. This elucidation of "experiential character" allows us to formulate an even more explicit statement of the neutral definition of an exp-intentional property: A priori, an intentional property P is exp-intentional iff there is a mental state x and a property E, such that (i) x is P, (ii) x has E, (iii) in the actual world, there is (or appears to be) an explanatory gap between E and physical properties, and (iv) if x were not E, x would not be P.

122. A more explicit way to formulate the thesis, given the neutral definition of an exp-intentional property, would be this: (EI) There is a state x, an intentional property P, and an experiential character E, such that (i) x is P, (ii) x has E, and (iii) if x did not have E, x would not be P.

123. Typically, the thought is that the experiential character of a conscious experience is the *medium* of intentionality rather than *message*. This is what McGinn (1988) calls the "medium conception" of experience's intentional role.

124. Certainly introspection suggests that some mental states have both intentionality and experiential character. Whether introspection reveals that sometimes the former counterfactually depends on the latter is a harder question. Admittedly, it is implausible that introspection presents any counterfactual dependence *as* counterfactual dependence. But it is much more plausible that it presents what is in fact counterfactual dependence under a simpler guise, but in such a way that a sufficiently sophisticated theoretician could justifiably conceptualize what is presented as counterfactual dependence.

125. One thought-experiment that convinces me of the existence of experiential intentionality is this. One can conceive of a disembodied soul in an otherwise empty world who is experientially indistinguishable from oneself. Intuitively, portions of the soul's inner life are also *intentionally* indistinguishable from corresponding portions of one's own inner life. The fact that some experiential duplication secures intentional duplication provides evidence (and according to some, may even entail) that some experiential properties are sufficient for intentional properties. This brings us very close to counterfactual dependence of the latter upon the former.

126. I have already mentioned Siegel's claim that we can perceive the meaning of linguistic expressions, but she makes similar claims about causation (e.g., we can see that one billiard ball causes the motion of another) and belonging to a kind (e.g., we can see that something colorful and shapely is a parrot—see also Siewert 1998 Ch.7). A related and quite central debate concerns the presentation of perspectival properties in conscious experience. Suppose you look at a tilted coin. Does your perceptual experience present the coin as (having the non-perspectival property of being) circular or as (having the perspectival property of being) elliptical? Kelly (2004) argues that only the (non-perspectival) circularity is presented in experience, whereas Noë (2004 Ch.5) claims that both the (non-perspectival) circularity and (perspectival) ellipticality are presented.

127. It is sometimes argued that there is an experiential residue in emotion that is better understood in terms of intentional directedness at bodily states (see, e.g., Armstrong Ch.8). Thus, disappointment with anything may be accompanied by a feeling of "sinking heart," and that feeling is best understood as nothing but intentional directedness toward the internal bodily event in the vicinity of the heart. This view strikes me as wrongheaded, insofar as the bodily experiences in question are not

part of the *proprietary* emotional experiential character, instead being contingent accompaniments more accurately classified as self-standing somatic experiences.

128. Associated with this is the experiential character of agency (trying and/or doing). This is argued for most thoroughly by Horgan and collaborators (see Horgan, Tienson, and Graham 2003 for agentive experience in general, and Horgan and Timmons 2008 for moral experience more specifically). For my part, I accept the existence of agentive experience not only on introspective grounds, but also due to an argument from Merleau-Ponty (1944: 93). Merleau-Ponty notes that when we rub our hands together, we can experience, more or less voluntarily, first the right hand doing the rubbing and the left hand being rubbed and then the left hand doing the rubbing and the right hand being passively rubbed. The strictly tactile experience in those two moments is the same, but there is a residue in the *overall* experience that is *not* the same. That residue concerns which hand is agent and which is patient, so to speak.

129. Perhaps the strongest thesis of the second kind is Pitt's (2004) claim that thoughts and beliefs have an experiential character which is both *proprietary* and *individuative*, that is, an experiential character that both is different from all other types of experiential character and varies whenever the content varies. Weaker theses might suggest that there is an individuative but non-proprietary cognitive phenomenology (say, because every belief is accompanied by imagery, and the imagery varies with the belief's content); or that there is a proprietary but non-individuative phenomenology (say, because although beliefs in general feel different from hopes, suppositions, and other propositional attitudes, it is not the case that a belief that p feels different from a belief that q for any p and q). In Kriegel 2003b, I consider a number of theses in decreasing order of ambition.

130. Most existing arguments for cognitive phenomenology fall under one of these three categories. Nonetheless, some arguments do not fit comfortably into these. They include arguments by Lurz (2006), Klausen (2008), Tennant (2009), and Mendelovici (2010).

131. The passage is taken from Klein 1981: 83.

132. Similar arguments are presented in Goldman's (1993) and Mangan's (2001) discussion of tip-of-the-tongue phenomenology, Siewert's (1998 Ch.8, 2011) and Horgan and Potrč's (2010) discussion of delayed understanding, and Siewert's (2011) and Chudnoff's (forthcoming-a) discussion of intellectual Gestalt shifts. The tip-of-the-tongue experience is familiar to most of us and is claimed by Goldman and Mangan to involve a distinctively cognitive phenomenology. Siewert's delayed understanding concerns experiences in which we suddenly understand a piece of text we have been rereading and trying to understand for a while (imagine suddenly thinking of kites on your own when reading the above passage). Intellectual Gestalt shifts, meanwhile, concern experiences in which a phenomenon is construed one way but is suddenly reinterpreted another way; Siewert (forthcoming) illustrates this with an entertaining exchange he overheard in Miami on an unbearably hot day, in which one woman said to the other "I am so hot" and the other responded "You don't have to brag about it."

133. For other arguments of this form, see Peacocke 1998, Siewert 1998 Ch.8, Horgan and Tienson 2002, Kriegel 2003b, Pitt 2004, and Chudnoff forthcoming-a.

134. Schematically, the argument proceeds as follows: we have a special, immediate access to our cognitive states (and their intentional contents); only to conscious experiences (and their contents) can we have this kind of special access; therefore, our cognitive states (and their contents) are conscious experiences (and exp-intentional).

135. An earlier argument of a similar form is developed in Goldman 1993 and recently endorsed in Lycan 2008.

136. I would like to thank Galen Strawson and Angela Mendelovici for openly sharing this sentiment. Strawson once put things to me very succinctly: we know that there is cognitive experience because without it life would be boring. Mendelovici once wondered aloud whether opponents of cognitive experience do philosophy because they enjoy the accompanying imagery so much.

137. For details, see Kriegel forthcoming.

138. For comments on a previous draft of this chapter, I thank Ned Block, Brian Fiala, Jesse Prinz, anonymous referees for Oxford University Press, and especially Angela Mendelovici, Stephen Pearce, and Lee-Anna Sangster. For comments on material from this chapter, I thank Michael Bruno, David Chalmers, and Farid Masrour. I have also benefited from conversations with David Bourget, Jordi Fernández, Lizzie Graf, Iris Oved, Declan Smithies, and especially Farid Masrour, as well as audiences at La Trobe University, New York University, University of Arizona, University of California—Riverside, University of Western Ontario, and a workshop on phenomenology and intentionality at the University of Modena e Reggio Emilia (I thank in particular Gillian Barker, John Bigelow, Frank Jackson, Marc Johansen, Benji Kozuch, Michelle Montague, Jack Reynolds, Eric Schwitzgebel, Charles Siewert, Alberto Voltolini, Meghan Winsby, and probably a number of other people I am forgetting).

2

The Nature of Experiential Intentionality
I. A Higher-Order Tracking Theory

Introduction/Abstract

Experiential intentionality is the intentionality a conscious experience has in virtue of being a conscious experience. In the previous chapter, I argued that our pre-theoretic grasp of experiential intentionality anchors our conception of all intentionality. My next task is to develop a *theoretic* grasp of experiential intentionality, that is, a theory of experiential intentionality. My problem is that there are two accounts, more or less incompatible with each other, that I find almost equally appealing. Unfortunately, neither is free from difficulties or liabilities. But each also has important strengths and assets. I develop one of them in this chapter and the other in the next.

Developing a philosophical account of experiential intentionality requires answering the following question: what are the identity and existence conditions of experiential intentionality? That is:

(EIQ) For any experiential-intentional state x, what makes x the experiential-intentional state it is (rather than another, different exp-intentional state) and an experiential-intentional state at all (rather than a state devoid of experiential intentionality)?[1]

Let us assume that the intentional content of an intentional state is what makes it the intentional state it is, and an intentional state at all.[2] Then the question is:

(EIQ★) For any mental state x and property F, what would make it the case that F figures in the experiential-intentional content of x?[3]

In what follows, I discuss *tracking accounts* of experiential intentionality (§2.1), go on to argue against such accounts (§2.2), and then formulate and defend a *higher-order tracking theory* (§2.3), before closing with some objections to it and replies (§2.4). According to the higher-order tracking theory, a property F figures in the experiential-intentional content of a state *x* just in case *x* is suitably higher-order tracked to track F. What this exactly means will become clearer in due course. The overall thesis of this chapter is that although the standard tracking theory is rather implausible, the higher-order tracking theory is quite plausible. As in the previous chapter (and the next, for that matter), I will often offer indented precise formulations of central theses, but by and large these can be safely skipped.

2.1. A Tracking Theory of Experiential Intentionality?

Research on intentionality since the seventies has been dominated by what I will refer to as the "tracking approach."[4] As we will see in more detail momentarily, the main goal has been to *naturalize* intentionality, by reducing it to tracking relations holding between physical items.[5] This line of research has also been dominated, if more subliminally, by the assumption that experiential intentionality is nowise special, and whatever account is true of intentionality in general is also fully adequate for specifically experiential intentionality. In this section, I want to consider the possibility of embracing the tracking approach even in the context of rejecting this more subliminal assumption. The purpose of the present section is thus to explore the options for a *tracking account of experiential intentionality*. The idea is to seek a special kind of tracking distinctive of conscious experiences, and identify experiential intentionality therewith. This would have the advantage of generating an account of experiential intentionality on the basis of a dominant and widely popular approach to intentionality, which moreover holds the promise for eventual naturalization of experiential intentionality.

A natural way to devise a tracking account of experiential intentionality proceeds in two phases: first a tracking account of intentionality in general is adopted, then a way of distinguishing experiential from non-experiential tracking is offered. Accordingly, §2.1.1 presents a number of tracking accounts of intentionality in general, §2.1.2 presents a number of options for distinguishing the experiential from the non-experiential, and §2.1.3 combines the two to generate a number of possible tracking accounts of experiential intentionality. Note well: the purpose of the present section is primarily exploratory and expository. Although I will remark in passing on certain possible disadvantages of some of the views discussed, the main purpose of the section is not critical. A blanket argument against all tracking accounts of experiential intentionality will be presented in §2.2.

Before starting, a final word on motivation. Exploring a tracking account of experiential intentionality may seem odd against the background of the experiential origin thesis from Chapter 1. Proponents of the notion that experiential aboutness ought to be more central to our theory of intentionality are often hostile to tracking approaches to intentionality, sometimes hostile to the very goal of naturalizing intentionality.[6] Conversely, proponents of the tracking approach are typically ill-disposed to grant experiential intentionality a special place in the theory of intentionality. However, it is important to realize that there is no incoherence in combining the two—no incoherence in the view that experiential intentionality is a kind of tracking and all other intentionality is somehow grounded in that kind of tracking. The tension between the two is more temperamental than logical. Proponents of experiential origins tend to be philosophers who think that conscious experience has not been accorded the central role it deserves in our theorizing about many phenomena, intentionality included, and that this is in large part due to an ideologically driven fear that focus on conscious experience would spoil naturalization projects (since conscious experience is widely regarded as harder to naturalize than other phenomena). Advocates of naturalizing intentionality, meanwhile, have felt that intentionality is ubiquitous in nature, far outstripping the sphere of the conscious, and that focus on conscious experience is often driven by gratuitous mystery-mongering. These sentiments on both sides may be well-founded, as far as we are concerned here. It remains that the thesis of experiential origins and a tracking account of experiential intentionality are perfectly consistent. Indeed, combining them could be thought of as the best of both worlds, paving the way to naturalizing intentionality without downplaying the role of conscious experience.[7]

2.1.1. Background: Tracking Theories of Mental Representation

Research on naturalizing intentionality has tended to focus on the notion of *mental representation*, where the terms "intentionality" and "representation" are sometimes treated as strictly synonymous and sometimes not.[8]

Within this research area, the most popular approach has attempted to account for mental representation in terms of tracking relations between states of the brain and states of the physical environment. In this subsection, I provide some background on tracking accounts of mental representation.[9]

The notion of tracking was introduced to philosophy in the context of epistemological discussions of the difference between knowledge and true belief (Nozick 1981), but was quickly adapted as, or extended to, an approach to mental representation and intentionality (Dretske 1981).[10] Nozick claimed that a true belief qualifies as knowledge just in case the belief tracks the truth, and unpacked this in terms of the idea that the belief would not occur if it were not true (and would occur if it were true).[11] Intuitively, the general idea is that A tracks B if the state in which A is somehow depends systemically upon the state in which B is.[12]

There are, however, many different ways in which one system's state can depend systematically upon another's. To that extent, there are many different tracking relations. Much of the discussion in philosophy of mind between the late seventies and early nineties was premised on the notion that there is some specific tracking relation T, such that mental representation is nothing but T; and that the task of the philosopher is to correctly identify T. Different theories of mental representation thus offered different tracking relations as capturing mental representation and hence intentionality. The shared assumption was what we may call the *tracking account of mental representation*. To a first approximation, the thesis can be captured through the following biconditional:

> There is a tracking relation T, such that for any mental state x and property F, F figures in the representational content of x iff x bears T to F.[13]

The tracking account clearly has a modal dimension, however, which should be reflected in its ultimate formulation. The exact modal commitment of the account is a non-trivial matter. In the first instance, we might want to require that it hold with metaphysical necessity. It is a fixture of modern naturalization projects, however, that some phenomena are multiply realizable (Putnam 1967), and could be realized super-naturally in some possible worlds consistently with naturalism, provided that in the *actual* world they are realized naturally. Thus it seems that the modal profile of naturalization theses is rather subtle, and makes a distinction between the sufficient-condition and necessary-condition parts of the biconditional: the sufficient-condition part must hold with metaphysical necessity, but the necessary-condition part need not be more than contingently true, or perhaps nomologically necessary.[14] Applying this to the above biconditional, we obtain the following thesis:

> There is a tracking relation T, such that (a) metaphysically-necessarily, for any mental representation x and any property F, F figures in the representational content of x if x bears T to F, and (b) nomologically-necessarily, for any mental representation x and property F, F figures in the representational content of x only if x bears T to F.[15]

For convenience of exposition, let us introduce the operator "necessarily★," which combines metaphysically necessary sufficient-condition and nomologically necessary necessary-condition. We can now formulate the tracking account of mental representation as follows:

> (TMR) Necessarily★, there is a tracking relation T, such that for any mental state x and property F, F figures in the representational content of x iff x bears T to F.

Against the background of the assumption that a mental representation is the representation it is (and a representation at all) in virtue of having the representational content it has (and having one at all), (TMR) can be understood as stating that the identity and existence conditions of a mental representation are determined by the right tracking relation.[16]

To illustrate this approach, let us briefly consider some salient versions of (TMR).[17] Dretske's (1981) original account of mental representation is couched in informational terms. Suppose a person has a belief about trees. For Dretske, this means that the property of being a tree figures in the representational content of the belief, i.e., that the belief represents that property. On Dretske's informational account, this means that the belief carries information about the property of being a tree, where this amounts to the belief nomically depending upon the property of being a tree: as a matter of the laws of nature, the belief does not occur unless the property is instantiated.[18]

Later, Dretske (1986, 1988) introduced a teleological component into this account (for the purposes of accommodating the possibility of error, or *misrepresentation*). According to the updated account, x represents F iff it is the *function* of x to carry information about F, where this means that x has been recruited to play a certain functional role in virtue of nomically depending upon F. More formally:

> (TMR1) Necessarily★, for any mental state x and property F, there is a functional role R, such that F figures in the representational content of x iff (i) x plays R, (ii) x nomically depends upon F, and (iii) it is the case that (i) because it is the case that (ii).[19]

Call this *teleo-informational semantics*. (TMR1) is a version of (TMR) if, as is certainly the case, the relation of having-the-function-of-nomically-depending-upon is a tracking relation.[20]

Another central version of (TMR) is Fodor's (1990) "asymmetric dependence" account. The basic idea here is that a property x represents F just in case instances of F cause occurrences of x lawfully and asymmetric-dependently, where this latter condition means that the causing of x by any non-Fs depends on the causing of x by Fs but not conversely. (This asymmetric-dependence condition is Fodor's attempt to accommodate misrepresentation.[21]) More precisely:

> (TMR2) Necessarily★, for any mental state x and property F, F figures in the representational content of x iff (i) it is a law of nature that instances of F cause occurrences of x, (ii) some instances of F actually cause occurrences of x, and (iii) if any non-Fs (i.e., things that are not instances of F) cause occurrences of x, the fact that they do is asymmetrically dependent upon the fact that Fs (i.e., instances of F) cause occurrences of x.

Call this *Fodorian semantics*. (TMR2) is a version of (TMR) if, again very plausibly, the relation of being-caused-lawfully-and-asymmetric-dependently-by is a tracking relation.

It is an open question whether more purely teleological accounts, such as Millikan's (1984, 1993) "biosemantics," should be regarded as a variety of (TMR).[22] Millikan's account is quite complex and not easily summarizable in a single intellectually surveyable biconditional, but the main idea is this: a state represents a property when the correspondence, or covariance, between the two enables some sub-system that "consumes" the state to perform its natural biological function. Crushing some subtleties, let us offer the following biconditional as an approximation of the view:

> (TMR3) Necessarily★, for any mental state x and property F, there is a consumer system S, such that F figures in the representational

content of x iff (i) S consumes present tokens of x, (ii) past tokens of x nomically depended upon past instances of F, and (iii) S can perform its biological proper function because (i) and (ii) are the case.[23]

That is, x represents F just in case x bears the relation of consumer-system's-proper-functioning-enabling-nomic-dependence-upon to F. A full understanding of (TMR3) would require elucidation of the notions of consuming system and biological proper function. Millikan (1984, 1993) and Papineau (1993) have their views on this. Whether (TMR3) is a version of (TMR) depends on whether we are willing to consider the relation of consumer-system's-proper-functioning-enabling-nomic-dependence a tracking relation. This is mostly a verbal matter, but the relation certainly strikes one as continuous with the relation Dretske, for example, appeals to.

It is not immensely important for our present purposes which of these versions of (TMR) is best, or why. For my part, I think I favor (TMR1).[24] What matters more for our present purposes is not what *distinguishes* versions of (TMR), but what *unifies* them: the notion that mental representation is at bottom a certain kind of tracking. This notion holds the promise of a naturalization of mental representation, and eventually intentionality, since tracking is a natural relation that takes natural relata.[25] There are well-known difficulties for this tracking approach to representation, but I postpone discussion of relevant ones.

2.1.2. Representationalist Theories of Conscious Experience

The naturalization of mental representation would be doubly satisfying if it paved the way to a naturalization of conscious experience. And indeed some philosophers have thought that conscious experience can be reduced to a certain kind of mental representation—that the experiential properties of conscious episodes are ultimately determined by, perhaps are nothing but, those episodes' representational properties. Not any kind of representational property would do, since some non-experiential states have representational properties as well. But there is *some* determinable (or genus) representational property, such that every conscious experience must have some determinate (or species) of it.[26]

Still treating the "experiential character" of a conscious experience as that which makes it the experience it is and an experience at all, we may formulate *representationalism about conscious experience*, or *representationalism* for short, as follows:

> (RCE) Necessarily★, for any mental state x and experiential character E, there is a representational property R, such that x has E iff x is R.

In the literature, one finds other ways of formulating representationalism, but the present formulation will serve our purposes fine. The basic idea is that the identity and existence conditions of conscious experiences are determined by their representational properties.[27]

There are, of course, different kinds of representational properties. Different versions of representationalism issue from different characterizations of the representational properties relevant to fixing experiential character. I will now review what I take to be the central options, remarking in passing on some difficulties they face.[28] My main concern here is not, however, to assess the plausibility of these versions of representationalism, but to lay the foundations for discussion of a tracking account of experiential intentionality in the next subsection.

To start, we may distinguish between *pure* and *impure* representational properties, and correspondingly between pure and impure representationalism (Chalmers 2004). The former characterizes the experience-determining content in terms of *what* is represented, the latter in terms of *how* it is represented. According to pure representationalism, there is a class of worldly properties such that when one of them is represented by a mental state, that state has experiential character.[29] Furthermore, token conscious experiences are experientially type-different just in case they represent the same properties of that class; type-identical otherwise. Thus the identity and existence conditions of a conscious experience are determined by the properties it represents:

> (RCE1) Necessarily★, for any mental state x and experiential character E, there is a property F, such that x has E iff x represents F.[30]

It is important to appreciate how radical pure representationalism is. On the face of it, every property that can be represented consciously can also be represented non-consciously. Pure representationalism must deny this. To adopt pure representationalism is to posit properties that lend themselves only to experiential representation, properties it is impossible to represent non-experientially. Representing them guarantees conscious experience.

Moreover, a world where none of the relevant properties are instantiated is *ipso facto* a zombie world. Thus in some sense a world can be a zombie world regardless of the nature of the subjects inhabiting it.[31]

I trust it is evident how implausible all these consequences are. Impure representationalism, appealing instead to the impure representational properties of mental states, is on its face more plausible: what gives a conscious experience its experiential character is not *what* it represents, but *how* it represents what it does. For example, Dretske's (1995 Ch.1) version of impure representationalism appeals to having *non-conceptual* content as the crucial kind of representational property.[32] On this view, what makes a representational state conscious is that it represents what it does non-conceptually (and type-identical conscious experiences have the same non-conceptual contents, while type-different ones have different non-conceptual contents).[33] Call this *non-conceptual representationalism*:

> (RCE2) Necessarily*, for any mental state x and experiential character E, there is a property F, such that x has E iff x represents F non-conceptually.[34]

As I mentioned, I do not wish to spend much time here evaluating versions of (RCE). But we should note that (RCE2) appears to get the extension of experience wrong.[35] On the one hand, it is too broad: unconscious perception, such as is involved in (e.g.) blindsight and subliminal perception, can carry non-conceptual content as well. So non-conceptual content is not *sufficient* for experiential character. At the same time, non-conceptual representationalism is too narrow: if there is such a thing as purely intellectual or cognitive experiences, as I claimed in §1.3.3, and if (as is plausible) such experiences have conceptual content, then non-conceptual content is also not *necessary* for experiential character.[36] These observations suggest to me that while the distinction between conceptual and non-conceptual content may be diagnostic of an important difference, it is not the difference between *the experiential and the non-experiential* but between *the perceptual and the non-perceptual* (or perhaps between *the sensory and the non-sensory*).[37] Since some experiences are non-perceptual and some perceptions are non-experiential, the appeal to non-conceptual content gets the extension of experience wrong.[38]

Bourget (2010) argues that while the representational content of non-experiential states is holistic, in that the content of individual non-experiential states depends partly on the content of other states, the representational content of individual experiential states is atomistic and independent of any others'.³⁹ Call this *atomistic representationalism*:

> (RCE3) Necessarily★, for any mental state x and experiential character E, there is a property F, such that x has E iff x represents F atomistically.⁴⁰

Whether atomistic representationalism gets the extension of experience right will of course be quite controversial. Some philosophers deny that holism is true of any representational content, experiential or not (Fodor and Lepore 1992). But short of such a sweeping claim, it would certainly be odd if a perceptual experience of a square, say, had its content atomistically, while a subliminal or blindsighted perception of the same square did not. This suggests that having atomistic content is not a sufficient condition for being experiential, but at most for being *perceptual*. Conversely, the existence of cognitive experiences would again pose a problem. The case for content holism relies typically on the thought that propositional attitudes have concepts as their constituents and that the content of those concepts is determined partly by their conceptual role within the subject's overall conceptual scheme. However, cognitive experiences, being in effect conscious propositional attitude tokens, have conceptual content as well. If having conceptual content indeed leads to content holism, then content holism is true of cognitive experiences, and having atomistic content is not even a *necessary* condition for being experiential.⁴¹ As with non-conceptual representationalism, my sense is that atomistic representation coextends with perceptual rather than experiential representation.⁴²

Perhaps the best-known version of representationalism is Tye's (1995, 2000) PANIC theory, according to which the crucial content is PANIC: poised, abstract, non-conceptual, intentional content. On this view, x has E just in case x represents F poisedly, abstractly, and non-conceptually.⁴³ As Tye himself notes, however, the key feature here is poise.⁴⁴ Poise is a functional-role property of conscious experiences: the latter are claimed to be poised for impact on beliefs and desires in a way non-experiential states are not. The upshot is a view whereby what gives a conscious experience its experiential character (rather than another) is the fact that it carries the poised representational content that it does (rather than another), and what gives it an experiential character at all is that it carries a poised representational content at all.⁴⁵

Once we appeal to functional role, however, there are functional roles that are clearly more closely associated with conscious experience than Tye's "poise." These could be used in a more promising account of the difference between experiential and non-experiential representation. In particular, it is often thought that conscious experiences are functionally distinctive in their *global availability*: the representational content of a conscious experience is broadcast to a vast array of downstream modules or subsystems throughout the cognitive system (Baars 1988). We may call this *global-availability representationalism*:

> (RCE4) Necessarily★, for any mental state *x* and experiential character E, there is a property F, such that *x* has E iff *x* represents F globally-availably.⁴⁶

Both (RCE4) and Tye's PANIC theory are versions of what we may call *functionalist representationalism*, of which other versions could be formulated by focusing on other functional roles. It seems to me, however, that (RCE4) is the most plausible version of functionalist representationalism. In any event, to my mind there is something fundamentally wrongheaded about *any* functionalist representationalism. For functionalist representationalism, an essential part of what gives a conscious experience its experiential character is the functional role the experience plays. But playing a certain functional role is a *dispositional* property of conscious experiences, whereas having a certain experiential character is surely an *occurrent* or *categorical* property. Accounting for an occurrent/categorical property in terms of a dispositional one seems to put the cart before the horse: it is more plausible that a mental state is globally available because it is experiential than that it is experiential because it is globally available.⁴⁷

The versions of representationalism we have considered thus far are *reductive*: they attempt to characterize the kind of representational content distinctive of (and peculiar to) conscious experience in entirely non-experiential terms. Some philosophers have suggested a *non-reductive representationalism* according to which there is an irreducibly experiential kind of representational content, such that the identity and existence conditions of a conscious experience are determined by the content it carries of that kind (Levine 2003, Chalmers 2004, Thomasson 2008, Pautz 2010):

(RCE5) Necessarily*, for any mental state x and experiential character E, there is a property F, such that x has E iff x represents F experientially.[48]

The obvious price of going non-reductive is the loss of the naturalizing force of representationalism.[49] But more deeply, in giving up on an account of the experiential in non-experiential terms, a non-reductive treatment leaves something unaccounted for. In a way, it does not so much account for experience as comments on it.[50]

I have briefly considered a number of versions of representationalism. They differ in how they characterize the kind of representational content that, according to (RCE), is constitutive of experiential character. Although my main purpose has been expository and not critical, I did mention in passing some outstanding difficulties facing these versions of representationalism. My conclusions are as follows: (a) pure representationalism can work only if there are properties which can be represented only experientially; (b) non-conceptual representationalism and atomistic representationalism can work only if the experiential and the perceptual are necessarily coextensive; (c) functionalist representationalism can work only if experiential character is a dispositional property; (d) non-reductive representationalism is crucially unsatisfying in leaving something unaccounted for (and giving up on naturalization). Thus all these accounts involve significant liabilities.

My primary goal in this subsection, however, has not been to evaluate the plausibility of representationalism about conscious experience, but rather to lay the foundations for seeking a tracking account of experiential representation in the next subsection. Before doing so, let me comment briefly on what motivates all versions of representationalism, since the issue will become relevant later in the chapter. The central motivation is what has come to be known as the *transparency of experience* (Harman 1990). There are a number of different ways to characterize the idea of transparency. I will focus on the thought that introspecting one's current conscious experiences reveals nothing but representational properties of those experiences. Thus the only aspect of a conscious experience manifest to introspection is its representational content.[51] An economical statement of this idea would be: "all introspectible experiential properties are representational properties." More precisely:

(TE) For any property P, if (i) P is an experiential property and (ii) P is an introspectible property, then P is a representational property.[52]

So formulated, I think the transparency thesis is true (Kriegel 2009 Ch.3, Ch.5).

It should be fairly clear how (TE) supports (RCE). If introspection reveals only the representational properties of conscious experience, then pending some special story that would recommend positing non-introspectible experiential properties, there is no motivation to posit non-representational aspects of experiential character. (TE) does leave it open that there might be *non-introspectible* experiential properties that are non-representational, but it is unclear what is supposed to compel us to posit such properties (or *any* non-introspectible experiential properties, really). Thus (TE) provides strong *prima facie* evidence for (RCE). The reasoning could be stated as the following argument:

1. For any property P, if (i) P is an experiential property and (ii) P is an introspectible property, then P is a representational property; so,
2. For any mental state *x* and experiential character E, if E is introspectible, then there is a representational property R, such that *x* has E iff *x* is R;
3. Pending a special story, for any experiential character E, E is introspectible; therefore,
4. Pending a special story, for any mental state *x* and experiential property E, there is a representational property R, such that *x* has E iff *x* is R.

Call this the *transparency argument* for representationalism.[53]

There are, of course, arguments *against* representationalism as well. The literature is awash with purported counter-examples to it (see Peacocke 1983 Ch.1, Block 1990 and 1996, Lopes 2000, *inter alia*). Full discussion of the matter is unnecessary for our present purposes.[54] Our purpose in this subsection has been to review the major options for a representationalist account of conscious experience, so that we may consider, in the next subsection, how these options can be married with the tracking account of mental representation to produce a tracking account of specifically *experiential* representation. I also remarked in passing on some of the liabilities each view incurs, but a full assessment of the views' merits was not my central aim.

2.1.3. Experiential Tracking

Let us consider, then, how to marry (TMR), the tracking account of mental representation, with (RCE), the representational theory of conscious experience. Recall that according to (TMR), there is a tracking relation that determines the representational content of a representational state. On its own, (TMR) does not tell us what distinguishes experiential from non-experiential representational states, and thus does not offer any clues to the nature of experiential intentionality (which is what we are seeking). This is where the various versions of representationalism come in. We have formulated five versions, each offering a different characterization of the representational content allegedly distinctive of experience.[55] By marrying each with (TMR), we obtain tracking-based accounts of experiential representation, thence experiential intentionality. In this subsection, I present a number of such possible accounts. Here too, I will comment on some of the liabilities of these accounts, but my central aim will be more exploratory than critical. The main argument against tracking accounts of experiential intentionality will be presented in the next section.

Consider first the combination of (TMR) and (RCE1), pure representationalism. This generates an account according to which a mental state has experiential-representational content just in case it tracks the right environmental properties. Call this the *pure tracking account of experiential representation*:

(PTER) Necessarily★, there is a tracking relation T, such that for any mental state x and property F, F figures in x's experiential-representational content iff x bears T to F.[56]

Using as a lemma what we may call the "representational account of intentionality,"[57] we obtain the following *pure tracking account of experiential intentionality*:

(PTEI) Necessarily★, there is a tracking relation T, such that for any mental state x and property F, F figures in x's exp-intentional content iff x bears T to F.[58]

According to this pure tracking account, experiential intentionality is just a matter of bearing the right tracking relation to the right properties. Whenever an item x bears the right relation to the right properties, x has experiential intentionality.

There are as many different versions of (PTEI) as there are accounts of the "right" tracking relation T. In §2.1.1, we reviewed three such accounts of T: Dretske's teleo-informational semantics, Fodorian semantics, and Millikan's biosemantics. Corresponding to those are three versions of (PTEI). I will not go through all three, but for the sake of illustration, consider the version of (PTEI) based on (TMR1), Dretske's teleo-informational semantics:

> (PTEI1) Necessarily*, for any mental state x and property F, there is a functional role R, such that F figures in x's exp-intentional content iff (i) x plays R, (ii) x nomically depends upon F, and (iii) it is the case that (i) because it is the case that (ii).

On this view, exp-intentional content, and hence the identity and existence conditions of an exp-intentional state, are determined by that state's function of nomically depending upon the right properties.

(PTEI) and (PTEI1) are attractive in their elegance and straightforward naturalism. However, they inherit—indeed exacerbate—the oddities associated with pure representationalism. There are, in fact, two ways to think of the pure tracking account: as an a priori, conceptual thesis, or as an a posteriori, substantive thesis.[59] As a conceptual thesis, the pure tracking account seems incredible: surely it is not conceptual analysis of the concept of experiential directedness, or of felt aboutness, or any related notion, that instructs us of the pure-tracking nature of the property it is a concept of. As a kind of Kripkean a posteriori necessity, the pure-tracking account does not come across as so blatantly unbelievable. Perhaps it is in the underlying nature of things that tracking certain properties results in, or rather constitutes, experiential directedness. Thus the hidden essence of experiential intentionality might be such tracking. Still, for such a substantive pure tracking account to work, there would have to exist properties that can only be tracked experientially. The tracking of those properties would have to somehow bestow experiential character on the state doing the tracking—and do so even though the tracking of other properties does not. It is hard to wrap one's mind around the notion that the tracking of some properties, but not others, could spark conscious experience in this way.[60] In any event, the main argument against (PTEI) will be presented in the next section.

So much for the combination of (TMR) with (RCE1). Recall that (RCE1) was the only *pure* version of representationalism we considered. (RCE2-5) were impure, distinguishing the experiential from the non-experiential in terms of *how* properties are represented, not *what* properties are represented. An *impure tracking account of experiential intentionality* would distinguish the experiential from the non-experiential not in terms of the tracking itself, but in terms of the *manner* of tracking. Consider, by way of illustration, the combination of (TMR) and (RCE4), global-availability representationalism. This combination generates the thesis that a mental state has experiential-representational content just in case it tracks certain properties in a globally available manner. Against the background of the representational construal of intentionality, this leads to the following version of the impure tracking account of experiential intentionality:

> (ITEI4) Necessarily*, there is a tracking relation T, such that for any mental state x and property F, F figures in the exp-intentional content of x iff x bears T to F globally-availably.[61]

Again, (ITEI4) inherits the problems of (RCE4): having a certain exp-intentional content is an occurrent or categorical property, whereas tracking something while playing a global-availability functional role is a dispositional property.[62]

I will not go through the combination of (TMR) with other versions of impure representationalism.[63] The generic impure-tracking view of experiential intentionality is that there is a special "manner," such that a state acquires exp-intentional content when it tracks something in that manner. More precisely:

> (ITEI) Necessarily*, there is a tracking relation T and a 'manner' M, such that for any mental state x and property F, F figures in the exp-intentional content of x iff x bears T to F in M.

Every instance of this would cast the difference between exp-intentional and nexp-intentional states in terms of how the tracking of certain properties is done. As before, the different versions of (ITEI) will inherit the problems of the corresponding versions of (RCE), but again, the main argument against (ITEI) will be presented in the next section.

One difference between pure and impure tracking accounts is in which relatum of the tracking relation they focus on in distinguishing experiential from non-experiential intentionality. Pure accounts focus on that which is being tracked, impure accounts on that which does the tracking. Another option for a tracking account, however, is to focus neither on the tracked nor on the tracker, but on the tracking relation between them. Thus, one might hold that while one tracking relation, T_1, relates non-experiential states with the properties they are intentionally directed at, a different tracking relation, T_2, relates *experiential* states with the properties *they* are intentionally directed at. Call this, doubtless sub-optimally, the *neutral tracking account* of experiential intentionality. A neutral theorist could hold, for example, that the relation of having-the-function-of-nomically-depending-upon relates experiential states to the properties they are directed at, while the relation of being-caused-lawfully-and-asymmetric-dependently relates *non-* experiential states to what *they* are directed at.

I am not familiar with any actual neutral account of experiential intentionality, and there is something *prima facie* implausible about the idea that what distinguishes experiential from non-experiential intentional states comes down to the specific tracking relation they bear to the world.[64] The implausibility here is somewhat akin to that of the pure tracking account.[65] Why would one tracking relation to some properties spark experience when another, quite similar tracking relations to the very same properties fail to?[66] A proponent might answer that it just does ("it is a brute fact"), but although that is a coherent position, it is not a particularly illuminating one. Something remains unclear.

In conclusion: by combining tracking accounts of mental representation with representationalist attempts at distinguishing conscious experiences from non-conscious states, and assuming a representational construal of intentionality, we can obtain elegant tracking accounts of experiential intentionality. These are quite attractive, insofar as they offer a way to naturalize experiential intentionality. Each seems to face significant difficulties, as we have noted in passing. However, it is only now that I present my main argument against this type of account—a single blanket argument against all tracking accounts of experiential intentionality (pure, impure, and neutral).

2.2. The HOT Argument

The mandate of this section is both destructive and constructive. After laying out relevant background (§2.2.1), I present an argument against tracking accounts of experiential intentionality (§2.2.2). In the next section, I will use the main consideration behind this argument as a launching pad for an alternative account of experiential intentionality.

2.2.1. Background: Higher-Order Theories of Conscious Experience

On the face of it, it should not be surprising that one's theory of conscious experience in general is relevant to one's account of experiential intentionality in particular. But it is not often noticed that the motivation for tracking-style accounts of experiential intentionality is based on, and beholden to, a particular approach to experience in general, namely, the representational theory from §2.1.2. In the next subsection, I am going to present an argument to the effect that tracking accounts do not survive a shift to a different (equally motivated and quite popular) theory of conscious experience, namely, the *higher-order theory* of consciousness (sometimes "higher-order representationalism"). In this subsection, I provide some of the background on the higher-order theory and its motivation. I offer a full defense of one particular version of the theory, one I call *self-representationalism*, in Kriegel 2009.

According to higher-order theory, a mental state is conscious just in case it is represented in the right way by a higher-order state of the right kind. More precisely, a mental state x of a subject S becomes a conscious experience—acquires experiential character—when, and only when, S has some suitable mental state y that represents x. In most versions of higher-order theory, not only the *existence* of an experiential character is determined by suitable higher-order representation, the *identity* of the experiential character is so determined as well: what specific experiential character a conscious experience has is determined by the properties it is higher-order represented to have.[67]

Presumably, not every feature of a first-order state suitably represented by a higher-order state contributes to its experiential character. For example, if a suitable higher-order state represents an experience as occurring on a Wednesday, while another, otherwise indistinguishable, suitable higher-order state represents another experience as occurring on a Thursday, the two experiences would not be experientially distinct for that. So there must be a class of properties P, such that the experiential character of an experience is determined by the subset of P that the experience is suitably higher-order represented to have. Assuming that the experiential character of an experience is given by the set of all experiential properties the experience instantiates, this means that every experiential property is constituted by the suitable higher-order representation of a member of P. That is, for any experiential property E, there is a (non-experiential) property P_i, such that (i) P_i is a member of P and (ii) the property of being E is identical to the property of being suitably higher-order represented to be P_i.

With these clarifications as background, we may formulate the higher-order theory of consciousness as follows:[68]

> (HOT) Necessarily★, for any mental state x and experiential character E, there is a property F, such that x has E iff there is a suitable mental state y, such that y represents x to be F.[69]

Different versions of (HOT) are obtained by different ways of unpacking "suitably." According to Rosenthal (1990, 2002, 2005), for example, a higher-order state is suitable just if it is a (i) non-inferential (ii) occurrent (iii) *de se* (iv) thought.[70] Other versions of (HOT) are obtained by other understandings of "suitable."[71]

A closely related account of consciousness is the so-called self-representational theory, according to which a mental state is conscious in virtue of *representing itself* in the right way. Call this *self-representationalism*:

> (SR) Necessarily★, for any mental state x and experiential character E, there is a property F, such that x has E iff x suitably represents itself to be F.[72]

Again, different versions of (SR) are obtained by different ways of unpacking "suitably."[73]

That (SR) is "closely related" to (HOT) can be seen from the fact that, given the above formulations, strictly speaking (SR) is a *version* of (HOT); namely, the version where x is represented by y, but $y = x$. Perhaps for this reason, self-representationalism is sometimes referred to as "intrinsic higher-order theory" (Rosenthal 2004).[74] The complementary, and more standard, version of (HOT) is what we may call *extrinsic higher-order theory*, which is just (HOT) with the stipulation that $x \neq y$.[75] What extrinsic higher-order theory and self-representationalism share is the idea that conscious states are *represented*. The difference is that according to extrinsic higher-order theory, they are represented by *numerically distinct* states, whereas according to self-representationalism, they are represented by *themselves*.

In Kriegel 2009, I develop and defend a version of (SR).[76] To me, what motivates (SR), and more generally (HOT), is a certain conception of the structure of experiential character. As I look at the blue sky, I undergo a conscious experience, and there is a bluish way it is like for me to undergo this experience. This "bluish way it is like for me" is the experience's experiential character, what makes it the experience it is and an experience at all. According to Levine (2001), there is a conceptual distinction to be made between two components of this "bluish way it is like for me": (i) the bluish component and (ii) the for-me component. I call the former *qualitative character* and the latter *subjective character* (Kriegel 2005, 2009 Ch.1). To a first approximation, the experience's bluish qualitative character is what gives it the specific experiential character it has, while its for-me-ness is what gives it an experiential character at all. A better, if initially less clear, approximation is this: my experience has the experiential character it does because it is bluish-for-me, and has an experiential character at all because it is someway-for-me (or qualitatively-for-me).[77] Thus qualitative character is what varies among conscious experiences, while subjective character is what is common to them (as well as peculiar to them).

Many philosophers, especially representationalists of the sort encountered in §2.1.2, have assumed that the core of the problem of consciousness is qualitative character. But an interesting result of the above conception of the structure of experiential character is that it is actually subjective character that is more central (Levine 2001, Kriegel 2009). For although it is important to understand what accounts for experiential differences among conscious episodes, it is more central to the philosophical problem of consciousness to understand what accounts for some mental states (and not others) having experiential character to begin with. Thus according to Levine and me, the deeply mystifying feature of consciousness is that when I have a conscious experience, the experience does not only take place *in me*, but is also *for me*. There is some sort of (admittedly elusive) direct presence, a subjective significance, of the experience to the subject, and this is what *makes* it an experience. This claim is of course controversial, but I will not argue for it here.[78] What I want to focus on is how it motivates (HOT).

(HOT) accounts—whether extrinsic or intrinsic—are essentially accounts of subjective character. They claim that a conscious experience has subjective character, or for-me-ness, because it is (suitably) higher-order represented. The argument for this is fairly straightforward.[79] The key idea is that for a conscious experience to be not only *in* me, but also *for* me, I have to be aware of it in the right way. This claim, with the support of two relatively uncontroversial lemmas, leads to (HOT). The first lemma is that being aware of something is a matter of suitably representing it. The second is that representing something is a matter of being in a mental state that represents it.⁸⁰ It follows that for a conscious experience to be for me, there must be a mental state that represents it. The argument can be formalized as follows:

1. For any mental state x and subject S, such that S is in x, x has subjective character (is *for* S) iff S is suitably aware of x;
2. For any entity X and subject S, S is suitably aware of X iff S suitably represents X;
3. For any entity X and subject S, S suitably represents X iff there is a mental state y, such that (i) S is in y and (ii) y suitably represents X; Therefore,
4. For any mental state x and subject S, such that S is in x, x has subjective character (is *for* S) iff there is a mental state y, such that (i) S is in y and (ii) y suitably represents x.⁸¹

Call the first premise of this argument the *awareness principle*.⁸² The awareness principle is directly motivated by the conception of the structure of experiential character presented above. Conjoined with the two lemmas, it *entails* (HOT).

In Kriegel 2009 Ch.4, I argue that certain additional considerations support specifically self-representationalism, making it preferable over extrinsic higher-order theory. But the choice between self-representationalism and extrinsic higher-order theory need not concern us here. The purpose of this subsection has been to introduce higher-order theory in its general form, and at least one motivation for it. In the next subsection, I present an argument against the tracking account of experiential intentionality that relies on higher-order theory. As already noted, it should not be surprising that a theory of conscious experience that rivals representationalism would lead to an account of experiential intentionality that rivals the tracking account. Yet it is worthwhile to see exactly how the tracking account is undermined once representationalism is relinquished.

2.2.2. Higher-Order Theory and the Tracking Account of Experiential Intentionality

According to (HOT), the experiential character of a conscious experience is determined by the higher-order representation of that experience. Rosenthal (1990) provides an acute illustration of this by comparing the wine-tasting experiences of a wine connoisseur and a novice. The two may degust the same wine and yet undergo different gustatory experiences. We can stipulate that they go through the same gustatory (and olfactory) processing, and consequently enter the same *sensory* state, in a relevant sense of "sensory" to be explicated shortly. We can further stipulate that their emotional attitudes and somatic responses to that state (and the wine) are the same. And yet, claims Rosenthal, their wine experiences may be different. What explains the difference is the fact that the connoisseur has a richer, more fine-grained conceptual scheme with which to conceptualize and categorize her winey sensory states. Presumably she has discriminatory, recognitional, and classificatory capacities with respect to her winey sensory states that the novice lacks, with the result that the two produce different higher-order representations of their sensory states and thus undergo different winey experiences.[83]

We can describe the situation more precisely in terms of the class of properties P representation of which constitutes, according to (HOT), experiential properties. Although the connoisseur's and the novice's experiences instantiate the same members of P, they are higher-order represented to instantiate *different* members of P. Interestingly, neither need misrepresent her sensory state. Typically, what happens is that the sensory state instantiates both a determinable coarse-grain gustatory property and a determinate fine-grained gustatory property, and while the connoisseur higher-order represents the fine-grained property (either in addition to, or instead of, the coarse-grained one), the novice higher-order represents only the coarse-grained one. In other words, within the class of relevant properties P, there are properties P_i and P_j, such that P_i is a determinable of P_j, and while both the connoisseur's and the novice's sensory state instantiates both P_i and P_j, the connoisseur higher-order represents her state as P_j, whereas the novice represents her only as P_i. As a result, the connoisseur has a p_j-ish experience whereas the novice has a P_i-ish one.

The case of the wine-tasting experiences is presented as involving mental states that are in one way type-different and in another type-identical. There is a dimension along which they are different—the experiential dimension. But there is also a dimension along which they are the same—to do purely with sensory processing, and as a result with the subsets of P they instantiate. Let us put this by saying that it is a case of two token first-order states which are *sensorily* indistinguishable but *experientially* distinct: they are type-identical sensory states but type-different conscious experiences.[84] This gap between sensory and experiential individuation is due, according to (HOT), to the experiential (but not sensory) individuation being sensitive to second-order discriminatory capacities.

It is a fair question whether Rosenthal's diagnosis of the situation is the right one. I am not so sure that it is: an alternative explanation of the difference between the connoisseur's experience and the novice's is that the two represent *the wine* to have different properties.[85] But I do think that the gap between sensory and experiential individuation is real. In Rosenthal's scenario, it is claimed to arise due to differences in second-order discriminatory abilities. But it may also arise for other reasons: in particular, due to second-order *misrepresentation*. We can readily imagine a situation in which a subject's visual processing is intact but her higher-order processing malfunctions. Suppose that upon exposure to the right surface under the right conditions, LeShane enters a sensory state that tracks the reflection property characteristic of blue surfaces (and/or volumes). (According to some objectivists about color, this reflection property *is* blueness. According to other philosophers, it is not. We need not take a stance on this here.) Let us call the property of tracking the reflection property characteristic of blue surfaces "bluishness★." So in the above situation, LeShane enters a bluish★ sensory state. However, due to malfunction in subsequent processing, he enters a higher-order state that misrepresents the first-order sensory state as greenish★. That is, the higher-order state "mis-categorizes" the first-order state. This situation is not only *logically* possible, there is every reason to suppose it *nomologically* possible, indeed actual. For there is no reason to suppose that processing leading to the formation of higher-order representations is somehow immune to malfunction.

What does LeShane experience when this is how things are with him? Does he experience blue or green? Using the terms "bluish" and "greenish" to denote the relevant experiential properties, and assuming that bluishness★ and greenishness★ are members of P, we can put the question as follows: when a subject S has a bluish★ sensory state but higher-order represents her state as greenish★, does S undergo a bluish experience or a greenish experience? The (HOT) answer is that S has a *greenish* experience (she "experiences green").[86] Philosophers who reject (HOT), however, can answer differently. For example, representationalists who embrace a tracking account (Dretske 1995, Tye 1995, and others) will claim that S has a *bluish* experience (she "experiences blue"), since S's state tracks (the reflection property associated with) blueness.

The general point is this. If experiential character is determined by what an internal state tracks, as these representationalists claim, then an internal state that tracks (the reflection property associated with) blueness has a bluish experiential character, regardless of how the subject is aware of that state. But if experiential character is determined rather by how the subject is aware of her internal state, as higher-order theorists hold, then an internal state of which the subject is aware as greenish★ has a greenish experiential character, regardless of what that state tracks.

In line with previous work, I will be assuming here that (HOT) is the right theory of consciousness, and representationalism is false.[87] It follows that a suitable higher-order misrepresentation of a bluish★ sensory state as greenish★ would result in (or rather constitute) a greenish, not bluish, experiential character.[88] Once we adopt (HOT), it is clear that we should reject the tracking account of experiential intentionality: as we have just seen, the latter predicts that LeShane's experience is bluish, whereas the former predicts that it is greenish. Since the experience's greenishness is plausibly an exp-intentional property, but according to (HOT) not a tracking property, we must admit that at least some exp-intentional properties are not tracking properties—contrary to the tracking account of experiential intentionality. The reasoning can be formalized as follows:

1. LeShane's experience's greenishness is an exp-intentional property;
2. If the higher-order theory of consciousness is true, then LeShane's experience's greenishness is not a tracking property; therefore,
3. If the higher-order theory of consciousness is true, then some exp-intentional properties are not tracking properties.

We can then add:

4. According to the tracking account of experiential intentionality, all exp-intentional properties are tracking properties; therefore,
5. If the higher-order theory of consciousness is true, then the tracking account of experiential intentionality is false.[89]

Call this the *HOT Argument*. I will later suggest that the reasoning behind it extends to show that *no* exp-intentional property is a tracking property.

It may be objected to the first premise that while LeShane's experience's greenishness is clearly an experiential property, it is not at all obvious that it is an *intentional* property. However, this greenishness is clearly an *introspectible* property: when I have a greenish visual experience of grass, I can introspect that my experience is greenish. As a general rule, we can introspect the experiential properties of our conscious experiences, including our color experiences. By this I do not mean that we can introspect them to be intrinsic qualities of experience. I simply mean that when we have a conscious experience, we can use introspection to become aware of its experiential character. When a certain experiential property is claimed to be non-introspectible, some special story must be offered as explanation or justification. Pending such a story, we should hold that subjects can introspect the greenishness of their experience.[90] So it would seem that LeShane's experience's greenishness is both an experiential property and an introspectible property. Recall, now, that according to the thesis of the transparency of experience, (TE), every introspectible experiential property is an intentional property. It follows that LeShane's experience's greenishness is an intentional property. Since it is both experiential and intentional, it is exp-intentional.[91]

It may strike the reader as "surprising" to use the transparency of experience in the context of employing (HOT) to undermine the tracking account of experiential intentionality, since transparency is typically used to motivate representationalism, a competitor of (HOT). In other words, representationalism and higher-order theory cannot *both* be true of conscious experience, so if the transparency thesis supports representationalism (as discussed in §2.1.2), then it must to that extent militate against higher-order theory. My response, however, is that representationalism and higher-order theory are *sub-personal* stories about greenishness: whether greenish experiential character is fixed by tracking, or by higher-order representation of tracking, is not something accessible from the first-person perspective. By contrast, the observation of transparency *is* a first-person observation: it is the observation that, when one attends to one's greenish experience, the greenishness presents itself to one as an intentional feature of one's experience. This first-person impression of one's conscious experience's greenishness would be the same regardless of whether that greenishness was constituted by what the experience tracks or by what it is higher-order represented to track.[92] Thus the greenishness presents itself to the first-person perspective as intentional regardless of whether representationalism or (HOT) is the correct sub-personal story.[93]

An objection to Premise 2 of the HOT Argument is that although (HOT) construes LeShane's experience's greenishness differently from the tracking account, the way it construes it can be developed in a tracking way as well. The idea behind Premise 2 is that if (HOT) is true, then this greenishness is the property of being suitably higher-order represented to be greenish★, and the property of being suitably higher-order represented to be greenish★ is *not* a tracking property. The reason to say that it is *not* a tracking property is that, as LeShane's case shows, a state can be higher-order represented to track F without actually tracking F. However, the objector might insist that higher-order representation, like *first*-order representation, should be accounted for in terms of tracking relations, with the result that the property of being higher-order represented to track something is just the property of being higher-order tracked to track something. This property, she might insist, is a tracking property. This is a complicated objection featuring an admixture of substantive and verbal issue, and I will address it at the beginning of the next section.

I conclude provisionally that both Premises 1 and 2 of the HOT Argument are well justified. Premise 4 is true by stipulation. The argument goes through, and its conclusion is the conditional I have stated above: if we adopt (HOT), we must reject the tracking account of experiential intentionality.[94]

Once we have accepted that *some* exp-intentional properties are not tracking properties, it is very plausible to hold that *no* exp-intentional properties are. This stronger conclusion can be reached through two generalizations: from greenish experiences involving higher-order misrepresentations to all greenish experiences, then from greenish experiences to all experiences.[95]

First, note that although LeShane's experience involves higher-order misrepresentation, once we appreciate its lesson we can see that it applies equally to greenish experiences involving veridical higher-order representation. A person may have a first-order sensory state that tracks greenness and a higher-order state that represents the first-order state to track greenness. This person has a conscious experience that is both greenish★ and greenish. Here there is no divergence between the sensory and experiential properties of the state. Nevertheless, according to (HOT) they are *numerically distinct* properties: what makes the experience greenish is not the same as what makes it greenish★. So although the difference between the exp-intentional properties of a greenish experience and its sensory tracking properties is brought out more vividly when we consider greenish experiences involving higher-order *mis*representation, the difference applies to all greenish experiences.

Secondly, although I have used *color* experience to establish the divergence of exp-intentional properties and tracking properties, the point could be made for any other type of conscious experience.[96] An auditory experience may exhibit the sensory property of tracking trumpet sound, but the sound of trumpet does not figure in its exp-intentional content, according to higher-order theorists, unless the experience is suitably higher-order represented to track trumpet sound. If instead it is higher-order represented to track xylophone sound, it will have a xylophonish experiential character, and so it is the sound of xylophone that will figure in its exp-intentional content. Likewise for an olfactory experience that tracks rose petal odor, gustatory experience that tracks sea urchin flavor, etc. Furthermore, the point applies to altogether non-perceptual experiences. It is a matter of some debate whether all non-perceptual experiences are intentional—perhaps certain somatic, emotional, and/or mood experiences are non-intentional.[97] But for those that *are* intentional, their experiential intentionality is always distinct from their tracking properties (for the same reasons). As long as (HOT) is true of *all* experiential properties, as I claim, the HOT argument against a tracking account of experiential intentionality will apply to *all* exp-intentional properties.

Interestingly, this applies also to cognitive experiences, which are clearly intentional. According to (HOT) as formulated above, if a subject thinks that *a* is F, but is suitably higher-order misrepresented as thinking that *b* is G, then the experiential character of her cognitive experience is the that-*b*-is-G-ish character. This may seem strange, but is in fact no stranger than the parallel case of perceptual experiences. The intuition of strangeness in both cases can be explained as an artifact of the illusion, as (HOT) must hold it is, that the first-order representation is introspectively accessible. If (HOT) is right, we cannot introspect the property of representing something, but only property of being suitably represented to represent something. For the property of representing something is never a constituent of an experience's experiential character. Only the property of being suitably represented to represent something is. In the case under consideration, then, the subject cannot be introspectively aware of her property of representing that *a* is F; she can only introspect her property of being represented to represent that *b* is G.

I conclude that, in all likelihood, no exp-intentional property is constituted by tracking, and that therefore the tracking account of experiential intentionality is wrong across the board. This is only the subsidiary thesis of this section, however. The main thesis is that at least *some* exp-intentional properties are not constituted by tracking, i.e., are not tracking properties. I have argued that this is entrained by (HOT). Although I have not argued here for (HOT) itself, it is already important to know that proponents of (HOT) cannot adopt the tracking account of experiential intentionality. It is especially important to me, since I *am* a proponent of (HOT) and have argued for it elsewhere (Kriegel 2009).[98]

2.3. Experiential Intentionality and Higher-Order Tracking

An objector might concede all of the foregoing but claim that experiential intentionality is nonetheless based on tracking, on the grounds that higher-order representations are themselves constituted by tracking relations, just as first-order representations are. They are higher-order trackers. According to this objector, although the exp-intentional content of a conscious experience is not determined by what the experience tracks, it *is* determined by what the experience is higher-order tracked to track. This could well be thought of as a sophisticated tracking account of experiential intentionality.

There is a substantive issue here and a verbal issue. The substantive issue is whether exp-intentional properties can be accounted for in terms of what a state is suitably higher-order tracked to track. The verbal issue is whether such an account should be considered a "tracking account." I take it the verbal issue is uninteresting. There is one usage of "tracking account" that makes the objector's proposed account qualify, and another that makes it disqualify. Here I will work with the latter, narrower usage, and so consider the objector's proposed account *not* to be a tracking account.[99]

The important issue is the substantive one: is the objector's proposed account viable? Can exp-intentional content be accounted for in terms of what a state is suitably higher-order tracked to track? An immediate challenge concerns the intelligibility of the locution "(higher-order) tracked to track," which has an ungrammatical ring to it. This challenge may have only superficial appeal, however. The locution is arrived at by adopting a tracking account of representation, and the locutions "(higher-order) represented to represent" is clearly grammatical and fully intelligible. Thus to say that *x* is higher-order tracked to track F is just an awkward way of saying that *x* is higher-order represented to track F and that the higher-order representation is correctly accounted for in terms of tracking relations. Perhaps better than "tracked to track F," from a grammatical point of view, would be "tracked in its capacity as an F-tracker" or "tracked *qua* F-tracker." Whatever the expression we end up using, whether continuous with mundane speak or somewhat technical, the notion the expression is supposed to connote is certainly coherent. The notion is that of *x* being higher-order represented to track F (or as an F-tracker) where the higher-order representation is accounted for in terms of tracking.

With this initial challenge set aside, the account of experiential intentionality in terms of higher-order tracking seems to me quite promising. The account is less simple than the tracking accounts from §2.1.3, but if we accept (HOT) as a theory of conscious experience, it has the advantage of conforming better to the data. In particular, while the tracking accounts from §2.1.3 cannot accommodate LeShane's blueness-tracking greenish experience, this kind of *higher-order tracking theory* of experiential intentionality can.

To a first approximation, we might formulate the higher-order tracking theory simply in terms of the combination of two occurrences of tracking: a first-order state's tracking of an environmental feature and a second-order state's tracking of that first-order state.[100] However, a better approximation would require not only that the second-order state track the first-order one, but that it track more specifically the first-order one's *tracking of the relevant environmental feature*. What is tracked is not just the state, but a certain property of the state, a tracking property. In other words, we want the first-order state to be tracked precisely in its capacity as a tracker of F. Otherwise we only have two tracking facts coming together in an entirely accidental way that there is no reason to suppose constitutes experiential intentionality. With this in mind, we may formulate the higher-order tracking theory as follows:

(HOTT) Necessarily★, there is a tracking relation T, such that for any mental state *x* and property F, F figures in *x*'s exp-intentional content iff there is a suitable mental state *y*, such that *y* bears T to *x*'s bearing T to F.[101]

Some clarificatory remarks are in order.[102]

First, so far we have discussed the tracking of properties, but here y is said to track x's tracking of F. What is unclear is whether "x's tracking of F" denotes a *property*, or an entity of some other ontological category.[103] If it denotes a property, then y is tracking a property, but if it is not, we have here an expansion of the domain of entities that the tracking relation can take as relata. The looming worry can be put as a dilemma: either "x's tracking of F" denotes a property, or it does not; if it does denote a property, then some explanation is called for of why x's-tracking-of-F is a property; if it does not denotes a property, then some explanation is called for of why tracking can take a non-property as a relatum. One natural view is that "x's tracking of F" denotes not a property but a *state of affairs*. After all, "x's tracking of F" is an imperfect nominal, and imperfect nominals typically denote states of affairs (see Bennett 1988 Ch.8). States of affairs are traditionally conceived of as constituted by a particular and a property, or a plurality of particulars and a relation.[104] So the view might be that x is a particular and the tracking of F is a relational property instantiated by that particular—and that the resulting state of affairs is what y tracks.[105] Another view might be that "x's tracking of F" denotes not a token state of affairs, but a state-of-affair *type*. What y tracks, on this interpretation, is the presence of a state of the kind that tracks F. It tracks the presence of an F-tracker.[106] Arguably, being an F-tracker is a property, and more generally state-of-affair *types* are properties. This is plausible because state-of-affair types are wholly present at different places at the same time, hence are universals. So on this interpretation, y tracks a property after all. This interpretation is probably the more convenient one, being the more conservative.[107]

Secondly, the notion of tracking at play must be one that allows for *mistracking*: it must be possible on a dated occasion for x to "track" F even though F is not instantiated, and likewise on a certain occasion for y to track the property of being an F-tracker even though that property is not instantiated.[108] In LeShane's greenish experience, for example, the higher-order state tracks the presence of a greenness-tracker even though no greenness-tracker is present. It *mistracks* the presence of a greenness-tracker. How to account for such mistracking is a matter of considerable debate. Proponents of the tracking approach to mental representation have been concerned with this issue and have offered a number of accounts (e.g., Dretske 1986, Fodor 1990 Ch.3). For now, let us assume that it is possible to account for mistracking. Obviously, if this assumption is incorrect, then both the tracking accounts and the higher-order tracking theory are unviable as accounts of experiential intentionality. This issue will be taken up more fully in §3.3.

Thirdly, as before, there are as many versions of (HOTT) as there are accounts of the relevant tracking relation. By way of illustration, consider the version obtained by plugging into (HOTT) Dretske's teleo-informational semantics, that is, by using the function of nomically depending upon something as a substitution instance of T. According to the resulting view, a property figures in a state's exp-intentional content just in case there is a higher-order state that bears the having-the-function-of-nomically-depending-upon relation to the first-order state's bearing of the same relation to the property in question. More precisely:

(HOTT1) Necessarily*, for any mental state x and property F, F figures in x's exp-intentional content iff there is a functional role R and a suitable mental state y, such that (i) y plays R, (ii) y nomically depends upon x bearing the relation of having-the-function-of-nomically-depending-upon to F, and (iii) it is the case that (i) because it is the case that (ii).[109]

This does not read very smoothly, but the way the world is if it is true is not particularly complicated for that.

The advantages of the higher-order tracking theory of experiential intentionality should be clear. Unlike tracking accounts of experiential intentionality, it is compatible with the higher-order theory of consciousness, and thus returns (what I consider to be) the right result in the case of LeShane's experience (and cases like it).[110] At the same time, it is just as naturalistically kosher as the tracking accounts, since it adverts to nothing but tracking relations. This combination—of naturalistic credentials and compatibility with the approach to conscious experience that I find independently plausible—makes me very sympathetic to (HOTT). Nonetheless, I recognize some disadvantages of the view. The most important will be discussed in the next chapter.[111]

I mentioned that my sympathy for (HOTT) is partially grounded in prior commitment to (HOT).[112] But as noted above, my prior commitment is more specifically to the self-representational version of (HOT). This might lead, initially at least, to a *self-tracking account* of experiential intentionality, according to which a property figures in a state's exp-intentional content just in case the state tracks itself to track that property. We might formulate this as follows:

> (STA) Necessarily*, there is a tracking relation T, such that for any mental state x and property F, F figures in x's exp-intentional content iff x bears T to x's own bearing of T to F.[113]

And again there would be as many versions of (STA) as there are accounts of the relevant tracking relation.[114]

One problem with (STA) concerns its naturalistic credentials: no known tracking theory of mental representation can make sense of self-tracking; I argue for this in some detail in Kriegel 2009 Ch.6. For some, this is a reason to reject the tracking approach to representation (Buras 2009). However, another approach is to refine one's account of self-representation. In Kriegel 2009 Ch.6, I propose a refinement that appeals crucially to a distinction between *direct* and *indirect* representation, as well as to the notion of a mental state *part*.[115] To a first approximation, the story is this. First, for x to self-represent is for x to have two parts, x_1 and x_2, such that one of them represents (i) the other part *directly* and (ii) the whole of which they are both parts *indirectly*. Secondly, the tracking approach to representation applies only to *direct* representation, and *indirect* representation is accounted for in terms of the combination of the direct-representation relation and some relation R, which we may call the *representation-transmission* relation, that holds between what is represented directly and what is represented indirectly. For example, if I represent a house by representing its façade, I represent the façade directly in virtue of tracking it and represent the house indirectly in virtue of (i) my directly representing the façade and (ii) the façade bearing the representation-transmission relation to the house.[116] Consider now a state that has two parts, such that one part tracks the second part and the second part bears the representation-transmission relation R to the whole of which both are parts. Such a state could be considered self-representing, insofar as a part of it represents the whole of it.[117] On the emerging proposal, x represents itself iff there are states x_1 and x_2, such that (i) x_1 is a proper part of x, (ii) x_2 is a proper part of x, (iii) x_1 tracks x_2, and (iv) x_2 bears R to x. In Kriegel 2009 Ch.6, I go on to argue that conscious experiences fit this bill.[118]

If we apply the same model to (STA), we can salvage the notion of self-tracking, albeit in a modified form. The result would be a *naturalized self-tracking account* according to which a property F figures in some state's exp-intentional content just in case the state has two parts, such that one part tracks the other part to track F, and the other part bears the representation-transmission relation R to the whole of which they are both parts. That is:

> (NSTA) Necessarily*, there is a tracking relation T and a representation-transmission relation R, such that for any mental state x and property F, F figures in x's exp-intentional content iff there are states x_1 and x_2, such that (i) x_1 is a proper part of x, (ii) x_2 is a proper part of x, (iii) x_1 bears T to x_2's bearing T to F, and (iv) x_2 bears R to x.[119]

Interestingly, there is a certain similarity between (NSTA) and the more standard (HOTT), inasmuch as in both cases the core of the account involves a higher-order item tracking a first-order item. The difference is that in (NSTA), but not in the standard (HOTT), the two items are required to be part of a single mental state. How significant this extra requirement is depends on what we demand from two items in order for them to qualify as parts of a single overall mental state. The more demanding the requirement, the more significant the difference between (NSTA) and the standard (HOTT). For my part, I require that fairly substantive conditions be met, involving the obtaining of psychologically real relations of cognitive unification between the two (Kriegel 2009 Chs. 6–7).[120]

As before, there are as many versions of (NSTA) as there are accounts of T. The teleo-informational version would look like this:

> (NSTA1) Necessarily*, there is a representation-transmission relation R, such that for any mental state x and property F, F figures in x's exp-intentional content iff there are states x_1 and x_2 and a functional role K, such that (i) x_1 is a proper part of x, (ii) x_2 is a proper part of x, (iii) x_1 plays K, (iv) x_1 nomically depends upon x_2's bearing of the relation of having-the-function-of-nomically-depending-upon to F, and (v) x_2 bears R to x.[121]

What I can report at this stage is this: my credence in (NSTA1) is higher than my credence in any other account of experiential intentionality at the same level of specificity.[122] However, my primary concern in this section has been to articulate and defend (HOTT) in general, not any more specific version of it.

The lesson of this section and the last is that although naturalistic approaches to intentionality, including experiential intentionality, have attempted naturalization exclusively in terms of first-order tracking, there is a whole family of options for naturalizing (experiential) intentionality that advert instead to higher-order tracking. This is particularly plausible against the background of certain approaches to conscious experience in general (namely, approaches that cast experience as involving both awareness of the world and awareness of that awareness). This family of higher-order tracking accounts remains a virtually unexplored area of research among philosophers of naturalist bent interested in intentionality.

2.4. Objections and Replies

I close with discussion of some objections and confusions that may arise in connection with (HOTT). These orbit round the same general theme, but I divide them into ones that can be handled by conceptual clarifications (§2.4.1) and a surviving substantive core (§2.4.2).

2.4.1. "Intentionality," "Representation," "Tracking"

Suppose (HOTT) is the truth about experiential intentionality: the expintentional content of a conscious experience is identical to what the experience is suitably tracked to track. If we combine this with the experiential origin thesis from Chapter 1, it follows that our conception of intentionality is grounded in our grasp of a kind of intentionality that is constituted by conscious experiences' being suitably tracked to track something. If this is right, then *first*-order tracking either does not qualify as intentional at all or qualifies only in virtue of bearing some relation to higher-order tracking. This might be taken by some to be an unbelievable consequence. For it is natural to think that, whatever else is the case, tracking something is a way of representing it. But if tracking is a kind of representing, then given the representational construal of intentionality, tracking is also a kind of intentionality. Yet surely intentionality constituted by first-order tracking is not grounded in intentionality constituted by higher-order tracking—that seems to put the cart before the horse.

My response is that first-order tracking is not a form of intentionality at all, and the air of plausibility in the contrary claim is due to an equivocation in the term "representation." While it is true that there is *a* notion of representation that makes representation the same as intentionality, and there is also *a* notion of representation that makes tracking a kind of representation, these are not the *same* notion. In other words, the term "representation" is ambiguous: in one sense it means the same as "intentionality," but in another it is looser and may apply to phenomena that do not qualify as intentionality, including first-order tracking. The ambiguity tempts us to infer that there is a kind of intentionality constituted by first-order tracking, but such an inference would rest on a fallacy of equivocation.

We can appreciate the equivocation by considering representation talk in the context of brain-in-vat scenarios. There is a possible world in which a brain neurophysiologically, neuroanatomically, and neurogenetically indistinguishable from mine is placed in a vat and fed random sensory stimulations by a machine suitably hooked to it. In fact, there are many, many such worlds—as many as there are random sequences of stimulations. In one of them, the influx of sensory stimulation to the envatted brain happens to be identical to the one my brain has enjoyed since its formation (in the actual world).[123] Consequently, let us suppose, whenever the machine stimulating that brain is in state S_1, the envatted brain undergoes an experience that is experientially indistinguishable from my visual experience of an apple; when the machine is in state S_2, the brain undergoes an experience indistinguishable from my visual experience of a banana; when the machine is in S_3, the brain undergoes an experience like my experience of a cherry; and so on and so forth.[124] We may then be tempted to ask the following question: what is it that the envatted brain's S_1-caused apple-ish experience *represents*? Is it an apple, as traditionally supposed, or S_1, as (e.g.) Putnam (1981 Ch.1) argued? The correct answer, it seems to me, is "both"—but in different senses of "represents." It seems a little silly to argue that one of these answers is correct and the other incorrect. Much more plausibly, there are simply two notions of representation, one on which the experience represents an apple and one on which it represents S_1.[125] We may say that the experience represents$_1$ an apple and represents$_2$ S_1.[126]

With this distinction in place, we can see that it is natural to hold that intentionality goes with representation$_1$ but tracking goes with representation$_2$. The envatted brain's relevant internal state represents$_2$ S_1

in virtue of tracking S1, but represents₁ an apple in virtue of having an apple-y exp-intentional content.¹²⁷ Since representation₁ and representation₂ are distinct notions, and what a mental state represents₁ can be different from what it represents₂, the fact that tracking is certainly a way of representing₂ does not entail that tracking is a kind of intentionality.¹²⁸ Importantly, while conscious experiences do track, and therefore do represent₂, they do not do so *qua* conscious experiences, or *in virtue of* their experiential character. Rather it is representation₁ that conscious experiences exhibit in virtue of their experiential character.

(What prevents an objector from deciding to use the term "intentionality" so as to make it identical to, or at least cover, representation₂? After all, "intentionality" is a technical term that one can use any way one likes. This is of course possible, but as we all know, stipulations alone can never change the dialectic, they can only force rewording. In this case, I would reword my claims by distinguishing two notions of intentionality, intentionality₁ and intentionality₂, and put forward higher-order tracking theory and the experiential origin thesis as theses specifically about intentionality₁. No substance will be compromised: obviously, I make my claims about intentionality in one sense of the term "intentionality," not in *every possible sense* of that term. If the objector decided to use "intentionality" as a name for New York City, I would certainly not advance a higher-order tracking theory of intentionality in *that* sense of "intentionality"! Instead, my claims are about intentionality in the sense in which our envatted brain is intentionally directed at an apple.)

I conclude that the objection before us fails to undermine the picture of intentionality that emerges from the combination of higher-order tracking theory and the experiential origin thesis. It does instruct us, however, of something quite important, namely, that there is a notion of representation for which it is most natural to embrace a tracking account. More deeply, the lesson is that there are two notions of representation, one of which is conceptually tied to intentionality, the other (contingently) tied to tracking. This is an important lesson, not least because it reveals the fact that recognizing a close connection between tracking and representation, in one sense of the latter term, can cohabit peaceably with the conjunction of higher-order tracking theory and the experiential origin thesis.¹²⁹

The distinction between two notions of representation can also help illuminate another fact otherwise somewhat bewildering, namely, that (HOTT) appears to use higher-order representation to account for first-order intentionality. If we use the terms "representation" and "intentionality" as synonyms, this makes no sense: representation of order n must go with intentionality of order n, not intentionality of order n-1. We make sense of this, however, by recalling that "intentionality" is synonymous at most only with "representation$_1$." Thus it would be nonsensical to account for first-order intentionality in terms of higher-order representation$_1$. But it makes perfect sense to account for first-order intentionality in terms of higher-order representation$_2$. And indeed this is what (HOTT) does, since (HOTT) attempts to account for first-order intentionality in terms of higher-order representation only in the sense of "representation" that ties it to tracking—hence higher-order *tracking* theory.

This is also why the picture of intentionality presented here, in which intentionality is in some sense grounded in consciousness, is consistent with the self-representational theory of consciousness I defend in Kriegel 2009. Of course, if "representational" is synonymous with "intentional," then accounting for intentionality in terms of consciousness and then for consciousness in terms of (self-)representation would be circular. In other words, the picture of intentionality we get from combining (HOTT) with the experiential origin thesis does not go well with self-representationalism$_1$ about consciousness. However, it goes perfectly well with self-representationalism$_2$ about consciousness. It is not circular to account for intentionality in terms of consciousness and for consciousness in terms of (self-)tracking.[130]

Finally, the distinction between two notions of representation also illuminates why the transparency of experience can, as we saw in §2.2.2, be used to motivate an account of experiential intentionality inspired by a competitor of representationalism. As a personal-level observation, transparency really supports only representationalism$_1$, the thesis that every experiential property is a representational$_1$ property, that is, an intentional property. But it has often been advanced as supporting representationalism$_2$, the thesis that every experiential property is a representational$_2$ property, that is, a tracking property. As we saw, however, this involves sub-personal commitments that the transparency thesis is silent on. When the envatted brain introspects its S1-caused apple-ish experience, what it becomes aware of is that the experience has an apple-y content—not that the experience tracks S1. Thus it is only representational$_1$ properties that introspection reveals and that transparency recommends accounting for intentionality in terms of, not representational$_2$ properties. Now, while higher-order theory is a competitor of representationalism$_2$, it is fully compatible with representationalism$_1$—and representationalism$_1$ is fully compatible with higher-order representationalism$_2$: even if experiential character is determined by suitable higher-order representation$_2$, i.e. higher-order tracking, it may still be identical with first-order representation$_1$, i.e. first-order intentionality.¹³¹ (I should state, however, that nothing I have said in this chapter commits me to representationalism$_1$. I have attempted to account for what it takes for a mental state to be exp-intentional. I have *not* suggested that every experiential state *is* exp-intentional, as representationalism$_1$ would require.)

2.4.2. What Do We Want a Theory of Intentionality for?

In many areas of philosophy, it is possible to deal with an apparently substantive dispute about the nature of some phenomenon by simply distinguishing two notions of the phenomenon and suggesting that one party to the dispute is right about one notion and the other about the other. After this move is made, however, it is rarely felt that the original philosophical concern has been disposed of—that the original philosophic anxiety is no longer warranted. Rather, something else happens—the concern takes a new form. Typically, what happens is that it becomes a more elusive concern about *value*. The substantive core of the question becomes: which of the two notions of the phenomenon is the more *important*?¹³²

I suggested that there are two notions of representation, one for which a tracking theory is appropriate (representation$_2$) and one for which only a higher-order tracking theory is (representation$_1$). This has the appearance of dissolving a dispute about the nature of representation along the above lines. Accordingly, the philosophical concern that fuels the dispute also undergoes a transformation along the above lines: it becomes a dispute about value. The question becomes: which of the two notions of representation is more important?

Which notion is more important depends on what our goal is, what intellectual itch we are trying to scratch through reflection on the nature of representation. This brings up the question of what we as philosophers want when we seek a theory of representation. This is of course a very deep question, to which full justice cannot be done here, but I want to suggest that distinctively philosophical interest in representation—at least mental representation—is motivated by two very different concerns, and that each is spoken to by a different notion of representation.

I will do so by engaging in some broad-brushed and speculative historiography (consider yourself warned). My contention is that in reconstructing the historical sources of philosophical interest in mental representation, we find two distinct storylines. I want to suggest that one storyline is grounded in a concern that motivates interest in representation$_2$, the other in one that motivates interest in representation$_1$.

One story starts with the positivists and their concern for the philosophical foundations of science. Very little has survived from the positivist agenda in current philosophy, but the thought that "philosophy of science is philosophy enough," as Quine (1953) once put it, is still very influential, especially in the philosophy of mind. For Quine, many philosophical questions were to be settled in the context of such concern with the foundations of science. Thus he identified what there is with what ultimate science will quantify over (Quine 1948). Although Quine himself, being a behaviorist and an "intensional-entity" antagonist, thought that ultimate science will not quantify over representations (Quine 1975), later philosophers adopted his conception of philosophy of science as philosophy enough without his eliminativism about representation. Behaviorism had gone on the retreat and the new best science of the mind operated with a cognitivist paradigm, understanding mental life in terms of symbol manipulation, information processing, etc. What this new science of the mind quantified over most centrally were representations and computational transformations thereof (Fodor 1975).[133] It therefore became imperative to develop philosophical accounts of the nature of mental representation, understood as a cognitive-scientific posit. This is one route through which mental representation became a central object of study in the philosophy of mind.

The second storyline starts much earlier—no later than with Descartes. Concerned with a potential systematic gap between appearance and reality, between how we take things to be and how they are in themselves, modern philosophers from Descartes through Kant and onwards were interested in the nature of our cognitive relation to the world. The matter was treated primarily through an epistemological prism in early modern philosophy, but was distilled into semantic terms in early analytic philosophy, most conspicuously in Russell's philosophy of language (see, e.g., Russell 1910). There are many reasons why the philosophy of language was so central in twentieth-century philosophy, but one of them, it seems to me, has to do with this foundational interest in the relationship between representation and reality. Importantly, however, once Grice (1957, 1969) argued that linguistic meaning is grounded in speaker intentions, hence that *linguistic* representation derives from *mental* representation, it had become natural to study the relationship between representation and reality primarily from the angle of the philosophy of mind not language.[134] This is another route through which mental representation became a central concern, where it is studied in the context of investigating the connection between mind and reality, the threat of a systematic gap between how things are and how we represent them to be.

To be sure, in practice most philosophical work on mental representation has been fueled by an impure admixture of these two fundamental concerns. But the concerns are distinct all the same. My suspicion is that the positivistically rooted, philosophy-of-science-oriented concern with the theoretical posits of cognitive science leads more naturally to interest in representation$_2$, while the early-modern-rooted, metaphysically oriented concern with the connection between mind and reality leads more naturally to interest in representation$_1$. If this is right, then the fact that the theories of mental representation pursued most vigorously over the past half-century are geared toward representation$_2$, where tracking theories are appropriate, may be merely a reflection of a sociological fact about the periodically predominant concern.

Note well, in any case, that although the narrative I have just sketched, mostly seriously, provides a way of disentangling the two concerns, the fundamental point does not rely on the narrative's historical accuracy. The fundamental point is this: there are two distinct concerns that fuel philosophical interest in mental representation, one to do with the nature of the scientific posits of cognitive science and one to do with the nature of the cognitive connection between mind and reality; while the former motivates interest in representation$_2$, the latter motivates interest in representation$_1$. The broader issue into which the former interest plugs is the debate over physicalism and dualism: how to integrate psychology into the physical sciences. The broader issue into which the latter interest plugs is the debate over metaphysical realism and anti-realism: the extent of mind-independent reality.

My suggestion, then, is this. When philosophers are concerned to regiment the ultimate scientific picture of reality, it is natural for them to conceive of mental representations as internal items that track external conditions. That is, it is natural to take interest in representation$_2$ (where a tracking theory is plausible). But when, reflecting on their own place in the world, they are concerned with the specter of a systematic difference between how things seem to them from the inside and how things are on the outside, it is more natural for them to focus on how their own conscious states present the world to them, that is, on representation$_1$ (where tracking theories seem much less plausible).

To appreciate this, consider that the problem arising from our inability to rule out a systematic difference between how the world is and how we represent it to be ("the problem of skepticism") arises only when representation$_1$ is concerned. As long as we are dealing with representation$_2$, we can readily rule out such a gap, precisely as Putnam (1981 Ch.1) showed: the envatted brain's apple-ish experience represents$_2$ a state of the vat-controlling machine, or a state of the evil demon, or a state of the Matrix, or what have you, and the world indeed contains the represented$_2$ state. The skeptical challenge arises only when we work with the notion of representation$_1$: the envatted brain's apple-ish experience represents$_1$ an apple, but the world may not contain an apple.

Note also that the broadly causal relation underlying tracking is the typical currency of scientific theorizing. It is thus natural for work designed to firm up the foundations of cognitive science to appeal to something like it. The picture of the mind that arises from understanding mental representations as lawfully manipulable internal trackers is intellectually pleasing in this context, being continuous with the mechanistic paradigm of scientific theorizing. Concordantly, observe that the approach to mental representation one is led to from this direction is entirely third-personal. It concerns, in the first instance, not oneself but something else—science.

Things are very different when one's concern is with the issue of one's own cognitive connection to reality. Here the concern is more personal, familiar to many of us from adolescence. There is no complicated theoretical background the relevant issues *require*, no literature they *presuppose*.[135] They arise through unprompted and unsophisticated reflection on such scenarios as popularized in "The Matrix" but already present in Descartes' evil-demon thought experiment. Such reflection concerns oneself in the first instance—as everything outside oneself is put into question—and is thus fundamentally first-personal. Here one's subjective take on what one's experience presents to one seems to be of much greater relevance than what one's internal states happen to covary with or track.

To sum up: I opened this subsection by noting that distinguishing two notions of mental representation does not settle which is the more important, more valuable to study; I remarked that which notion it is valuable to study depends on what philosophical anxiety we are trying to quell through the studying; I suggested that there are in fact two distinct philosophical anxieties, or concerns, surrounding the notion of representation, and that studying representation$_1$ speaks to one of them while studying representation$_2$ speaks to the other.[136]

The upshot is this. I have no objection to saying that tracking something is a way of representing it, but in that sense of "representing," representing something does not amount to being intentionally directed at it. This impoverished notion of representation may nonetheless be the only notion called for when one's goal is to account for the nature of explanatory posits in cognitive science. When, however, one's goal is to understand the relationship between mind and reality as it presents itself in our personal experience, a more robust notion of representation is needed, one which does amount to intentional directedness. At that point, (first-order) tracking falls out of the picture as constitutively irrelevant. Still, the a higher-order tracking theory is plausible for (conscious) representation in this robust sense—or so I have attempted to argue in this chapter.

It may be objected that even if there are two distinct sources of philosophical interest in representation, this merely postpones the substantive core of the issue before us, with the issue now becoming which of two concerns is *really* deeper, or more genuinely troubling, or more warranted—in short, more important. Should we be worried more about the nature of the scientific posits of cognitive science or about the connection between mind and reality? My own inclination, however, is to say that philosophical reason is the slave of the philosophical passions: there is no objective fact of the matter as to which concern is more important, there are only variations in psychological (and phenomenological!) strengths of concern. All I can report is that my own philosophical passions are geared toward the concerns that motivate interest in representation$_1$, that is, representation in the sense in which the aforementioned envatted brain represents an apple, not in the sense in which it represents S1; the sense in which representation reveals itself to the subject from the first-person perspective; the sense in which a distinctively philosophical anxiety looms concerning a potential systematic gap between representation and reality; the sense in which representation amounts to intentionality.

Conclusion

The thesis of this chapter is that although tracking accounts of experiential intentionality are implausible, a higher-order tracking theory is quite plausible. Since the only materials such a theory uses are tracking relations, it retains the naturalistic credentials of tracking accounts. At the same time, it may well get the extension of experiential intentionality right, whereas tracking accounts fail to do so at least in cases of higher-order misrepresentation.[137] This makes the higher-order tracking theory of experiential intentionality very attractive. Personally, independent commitments make me attracted to one specific version, which I called the naturalized self-tracking account. In the next chapter, however, I consider—fairly favorably, all told—an argument that threatens both first- and higher-order tracking accounts of experiential intentionality, and instead motivates an account of experiential intentionality that does not appeal to tracking relations at all and is most naturally developed as non-reductive. I will not subscribe to that account, but I will avow high credence in it—almost as high as in the higher-order tracking theory.[138]

Notes

1. My discussion will assume that identity and existence conditions are generally closely tied, in that the property which determines existence conditions is always a genus or determinable of the property which determines identity conditions: what makes a K the K it is (and not another K) is always a species or determinate of what makes a K a K (at all). For example, if we hold that what makes fish F the fish it is (and not another fish) is that F is blue, then we should hold that what makes F a fish at all (rather than a non-fish) must be a genus or determinable of which blue is a species or determinate—color, or color of a certain kind, or some such. There is, perhaps, no a priori necessity that identity and existence conditions be intimately connected in this way, but accounts of any phenomenon that divorce the two tend to come across as leaving an inexplicable incohesion in the essence of the phenomenon they target.

2. This assumption can be thought of either as stipulative or as substantive-but-virtually-certain.

3. Two comments. First, this formulation requires adverting specifically to experiential-intentional content, and not just intentional content, because for all that has been said thus far, it can be that experiential-intentional states have both an intentional content they have in virtue of being experiential-intentional

states and an intentional content they have independently of the fact that they are experiential-intentional states, and it is only in the former that we are interested. Secondly, I use the locution "figures in the content," here and in what follows, in a non-technical way. The most natural account of what it means for an entity to figure in a content is that the entity is a *constituent* of the content. This does require that content be conceived of as itself an entity, and one that has constituents. The first part of this *will* become problematic in Chapter 3, but is fine to work with for now.

4. One natural point to regard as the starting point of this research program is Stampe 1977. But the effect of Kripke's (1972) causal theory of reference cannot be overstated, since causation provides the "material" from which tracking relations are "made," as we will see momentarily.

5. What it means in the general case to "naturalize" a given phenomenon is something there is no philosophical consensus on, but philosophers do seem to know a naturalizing account when they see one. Two general points seem clear, however: (a) a necessary condition for naturalizing something is showing that it need not be thought of in super-natural terms; (b) showing that something is a *physical* phenomenon is a sufficient condition for naturalizing it. I will revisit the issue of naturalization and what it involves in §3.5.

6. One exception is Brandl (2009), who argues that neither "phenomenological semantics" nor informational semantics is deeply flawed, and allows that there may be "a deeper level of explanation at which [they] might be reconciled with each other" (2009: 10). See also Kriegel 2003a.

7. For a more systematic discussion of the surface tension between the two approaches, see Kriegel and Horgan forthcoming (as well as Montague 2010).

8. Using the second understanding of "representation," where it is not *definitionally* the same as intentionality, makes the "representational account of intentionality" a substantive thesis (see, e.g., Cummins 1989 Ch.1). I will discuss the different uses of "representation," and how they relate to "intentionality," in §2.4.

9. In the section overall, I explore the prospects for devising an account of specifically *experiential* intentionality along these lines. As noted, to do so one would need some way of distinguishing experiential from non-experiential mental representations. Some options can be gleaned from recent discussions of so-called representational theories of consciousness, which require a distinction between conscious and non-conscious representation. This task will be undertaken in the next subsection. Once we have a tracking account of mental representation, and a way of distinguishing experiential from non-experiential mental representation, we will be able to devise an account of experiential tracking. That will be undertaken in the third and final subsection of this section.

10. It should be noted that Nozick's truth-tracking account of the difference between knowledge and true belief is itself inspired by an earlier account of knowledge due to Dretske himself (Dretske 1971). So it may be misleading to say that Dretske adapted an idea from Nozick.

11. Nozick's original account of tracking faces a number of counter-examples (see, e.g., Goldman 1983, DeRose 1995), but its fundamental idea—of responsiveness to the way the world is (Roush 2005)—can and is used to guide appropriate modifications.

12. Thus, as Dwayne Wade drives to the hoop through heavy traffic, my visual system is tracking him insofar as the direction of my gaze (hence the state of my visual system) depends systematically on his location (hence his state).

13. Here, and in what follows, I focus on the tracking of properties. I realize that there is much to be said about the tracking of particulars (and other entities from ontological categories different from the category of properties). I focus on properties mostly as a harmless simplification. Whether the simplification is indeed harmless will depend, ultimately, on two things: (a) whether particulars can be constituents of intentional contents we might want to capture in terms of tracking, and (b) whether there is anything about the tracking of properties that would not transfer readily to the tracking of

particulars. I do not believe that the answer to (b) is "yes," so I am unworried about the simplification. In §3.5, however, the issue raised by (a) will become relevant, and will be revisited.

14. Perhaps it is justified to require that the necessary condition hold with *nomological* necessity, that is, in every possible world in which the laws of nature are the same as those of the actual world, in order to rule out the thesis coming out true accidentally (by luck). This would require construing nomological possibility so as to include a "that's all" clause ruling out additional laws of nature or para-legal activity.

15. I insert reference to nomological necessity to be on the safe side: consistently with the previous endnote, it is not entirely clear to me whether the modal force of naturalizing biconditionals should be construed as requiring nomologically necessary or merely contingently true necessary conditions, but it is safer to impose the stronger requirement.

16. Thus consider the following inference, whose first premise is (TMR): 1) Necessarily*, there is a tracking relation T, such that for any mental representation x and any property F, F figures in the representational content of x iff x bears T to F; 2) Necessarily, for any mental representation x, x is the mental representation it is (and not another) because x has the representational content it does (and not another), and x is a mental representation (at all) because x has a representational content (at all); therefore, 3) Necessarily*, there is a tracking relation T, such that for any mental representation x and property F, if F figures in the representational content of x, then x is the mental representation it is (and not another) at least partially because x bears T to F (and not to something else), and x is a mental representation (at all) at least partially because x bears T to something (at all).

17. Note to the reader: in each case I will present at some point a very explicit biconditional that is supposed to capture the relevant version, but it is not necessary to read the biconditional to follow the discussion.

18. It is worth noting that Dretske's Wisconsin colleague Dennis Stampe developed an earlier version of a tracking account, though he applied it to *linguistic* representation. On Stampe's (1977) account, roughly, a property F figures in the representational content of a linguistic item iff in normal conditions instantiations of F cause occurrences of x.

19. As in Chapter 1, the "because" in this formulation is to be understood as denoting an in-virtue-of relation, that is, understood as constitutive rather than causal (the "because" of "I am a bachelor because I never married," not of "I am a bachelor because I never met the right woman").

20. Recall that the intuitive idea is that A tracks B if the state in which A is depends systemically on the state in which B is. When A is in a state that has the function of nomically depending upon the state B is in, it would seem that the state A is in depends systematically on the state B is in. So tracking occurs.

21. Although if Fodor's account manages to accommodate misrepresentation there is no need to introduce a teleological component to it for that purpose, there may be independent motivations to introduce such a component. Maloney (1994) offers a modified Fodorian account with a teleological component. In rough outlines, his account appears to be this: F figures in the representational content of x iff (i) it is a law of nature that instances of F cause occurrences of x, (ii) some instances of F actually cause occurrences of x, (iii) if any non-Fs (i.e., things that are not instances of F) cause occurrences of x, the fact that they do is asymmetrically dependent on the fact that Fs (i.e., instances of F) cause occurrences of x, (iv) there is a motor response R, such that x causes R, and (v) it is the case that (iv) because it is the case that (i), (ii), and (iii).

22. There are many other varieties of teleological semantics—see Papineau 1984, McGinn 1989, Whyte 1990. My discussion of Millikan's variety has obvious parallel moves for these other varieties. I focus on Millikan's simply because it is better known.

23. As before, the "because" here is constitutive rather than causal. Perhaps a more explicit formulation would be this: F figures in the representational content of x just in case there is a system S, such

that (i) S consumes present tokens of *x*'s type, (ii) past tokens of *x*'s type occurred mostly when instances of F occurred, and (iii) S can perform its biological proper function because (i) and (ii) are the case. This explains better the reference to tokens and type. It does call on us to clarify, however, what kind of type is relevant for the assessment of the thesis. Presumably something like a neuro-anatomical type is what is relevant.

24. I expand on it in Kriegel 2009 Ch.3. It is worth remembering, however, that there may be deep compatibilities between these various seemingly competing accounts. Thus, being consumable by a consumer system, as Millikan requires, could be exactly the kind of functional role R that Dretske appeals to; having the function of nomically depending may be precisely the *reason why* asymmetric dependence holds; and so on and so forth.

25. As noted above, it is not immediately clear what naturalization amounts to, but there appears to be consensus among philosophers that reducing something to a tracking relation does amount to naturalizing it. More on the general issue of what naturalization is in §3.5.

26. Furthermore, different experiences have different determinates (or species) of it while similar experiences have similar ones. Thus there is a determinable (or genus) representational property R, such that for any conscious experience x, x has the experiential properties it does (and not others) because x has the determinate (or species) R_i—R_j that it does (and not others) and x has experiential properties (at all) because x has some determinate (or species) of R (at all). The determinable/determinate (or genus/species) apparatus is useful, in particular, in getting clear that there is a specific *kind* of representational property that is relevant for consciousness according to representationalists, and that the identity and existence conditions of experiences are determined by the representational properties they have *of that kind*.

27. Thus consider the following inference, whose first premise is (RCE): 1) Necessarily*, for any mental state x and experiential character E, there is a representational property R, such that x has E iff x is R; 2) Necessarily, for any mental state x and experiential character E, if x has E, then x is the conscious experience it is (and not another) because x has E (and not some other experiential character), and x is a conscious experience (at all) because x has an experiential character (at all); therefore, 3) Necessarily*, for any mental state x and experiential character E, if x has E, then there is a representational property R, such that x is the conscious experience it is (and not another) because x has R (and not to some other representational property), and x is a conscious experience (at all) because x has a representational property (at all).

28. As in the previous subsection, I will offer some explicit biconditionals along the way, but they will not play an indispensable role in the discussion. They are provided merely for the sake of precision, that is, to ensure that there are no incoherencies hidden in the details.

29. I am not familiar with an explicit subscription to pure intentionalism, so construed, in print. Thau (2002) comes closest.

30. A somewhat more explicit, but also more cluttered, formulation is possible in terms of a set of properties the representation of which constitutes experiential character. On way to put this would be: Necessarily*, there is a class of properties P, such that for any mental state x and experiential character E, x has E iff some P_i, P_j ∈ P, figures in the representational content of x.

31. I develop these considerations in Kriegel 2002b. See also Chalmers 2004.

32. Having non-conceptual representational content, or representing non-conceptually, is a matter of representing a property without possessing a concept for it (a concept that picks it out). How exactly to cash out the difference between conceptual and non-conceptual content is something Dretske himself seems to have changed his mind about, drawing the distinction in terms of analog and digital information earlier (Dretske 1981) and in terms of a distinction between "systemic" and "acquired" representations later (Dretske 1995). There are, of course, any number of other potential construals of the distinction. For

present purposes, we can incorporate into Dretske's representationalism whatever turns out to be the best construal.

33. Presumably, any property that can be represented non-conceptually can also be represented conceptually, namely if the subject acquires the concept for it. What is involved in acquiring concepts, or in concepts at all, is a complicated question we need not get into here. What matters is only the fact that nobody believes that there are properties which can be represented but in principle cannot be conceptualized. However, if someone did believe that, they could conjoin appeal to non-conceptual content with pure representationalism.

34. As before, against the background of familiar assumptions, we can deduce the following: Necessarily*, for any conscious experience x, x has the experiential character it does (and not another) because x carries non-conceptually the representational content it does (and not another), and x has experiential character (at all) because x carries non-conceptually a representational content (at all).

35. Here and elsewhere, I take it that not only predicates have extensions, but properties do too: the extension of a property is the set of all its instantiations. If the reader prefers to think of extensions as of predicates only, s/he should read me as saying "the extension of 'experience.'"

36. It may be thought that this should not be worrisome, since for naturalization projects it is only the sufficient condition that matters. However, this is inaccurate: naturalization projects require only the sufficient condition to hold with (typically metaphysical) necessity, but they do require the necessary condition to hold in the actual world. More specifically: naturalization of intentionality does not require that any possible kind of intentionality be natural, but it does require that any actual instance of intentionality be natural. Since the counter-examples I am offering to the necessary-condition part of the biconditional are actual, this is a real worry for the proponent of the biconditional.

37. Even this more modest claim can be challenged, however. For it suggests that a creature who enjoyed a perceptual or sensory state because they represented the right feature non-conceptually would *lose* the ability to enjoy that state as soon as they acquired the concept for that feature (see Kriegel 2002b).

38. I should mention that Dretske is more likely to embrace the coextension of experience and perception. For starters, he is skeptical about the notion of unconscious perception (Dretske 2006). In addition, although he nowhere discusses this explicitly, some of his remarks suggest that he would be skeptical of cognitive experience too (see Dretske 1995 Ch.1). So Dretske may not himself be moved by the considerations raised in the text. However, since to me it is obvious that there are both unconscious perception and cognitive experience, I am persuaded that these considerations undermine non-conceptual representationalism.

39. Bourget himself puts this in other terms, saying that the intentionality of experiential states only is "underived." But what his view comes down to is the kind of atomistic representationalism I am describing in the text. In Chapter 4, I will use the term "derived intentionality" for purposes that are mine, and in a way that does not accord with Bourget's use in one central respect. For this reason, I do not use the term here.

40. Against the background of familiar assumptions (regarding experiential character providing the identity and existence conditions of conscious experiences), we can obtain the following: Necessarily*, for any conscious experience x, x has the experiential character it does (and not another) because x carries non-conceptually the representational content it does (and not another), and x has experiential character (at all) because x carries non-conceptually a representational content (at all).

41. Bourget (2010) allows that there may be cognitive experiences ("phenomenal attitudes," in his terminology), but insists that if there are such, their content must be atomistic as well. This would require motivating holism in some other way, not relying on the dependence of conceptual content on conceptual role. It should be noted, though, that at least for non-experiential cognitive states, Bourget's own way of motivating holism does rely on something like what I describe in the text.

42. This may suggest that having non-conceptual content and having atomistic content are closely tied. And indeed they seem to be, if we consider the reasons for adopting content holism and their reliance on conceptual role. This suggests to me that an atomistic and non-conceptual representationalism would be quite plausible adopted as an account of perception, or at least an aspect of perception, but not of experience.

43. We might formulate the view, more fully, as follows: Necessarily*, for any conscious experience x and experiential character E, there is a property F, such that x has E iff x represents F PAN-ly (i.e., poisedly, abstractly, and non-conceptually).

44. Tye (2000: 62–3) claims that the difference between blindsight and conscious sight is that the former is not poised. As we have already seen, non-conceptuality cannot by itself account for the difference between conscious and unconscious intentional states. Abstractness is likewise irrelevant: it has to do with the properties figuring in the content being "abstract" in the sense that they do not need to be instantiated. (Perhaps the thought is that it is properties-as-universals rather than properties-as-tropes that figure in the intentional content of conscious experiences.) Thus poise seems to be the crucial feature. It is possible, of course, that it is the conspiracy of non-conceptuality and poise that gets the extension right, but my argument in the text will not turn on whether the extension is gotten right or not. For fuller discussion, see Kriegel 2009 Ch.3.

45. It is important to realize, however, that the phrase "poised content" is somewhat misleading, inasmuch as what plays a certain functional role is in the first place not a *content* but a *vehicle* (or *state*). We could, of course, *define* a functional-role property of contents, as follows: the property P, such that for any content C, C is P iff there is a vehicle V and a functional role R, such that (i) V plays R and (ii) V carries C. In other words, contents can have the property of being carried by a vehicle with a certain functional role. This is, in some sense, a functional-role property of contents. However, it is clear that this notion of content functional role is entirely parasitic: we have no grasp of it independently of our grasp of vehicular functional role.

46. As before, against the background of familiar assumptions, we obtain: Necessarily*, for any conscious experience x, x has the experiential character it does (and not another) because x carries in a globally available manner the representational content it does (and not another), and x has experiential character (at all) because x carries in a globally available manner a representational content (at all).

47. I argue for this in Kriegel 2009 Ch.2, Ch.4, and Ch.6.

48. As before, we can obtain the following: Necessarily*, for any conscious experience x, x has the experiential character it does (and not another) because x carries in an irreducibly experiential manner the representational content it does (and not another), and x has experiential character (at all) because x carries in an irreducibly experiential manner a representational content (at all).

49. This is not to say that (RCE5) is *inconsistent* with naturalism; merely that it does not *deliver* naturalism (that is, that it is not inconsistent with non-naturalism). Thus, it is possible to hold that the irreducibly experiential representational properties are nomologically supervenient upon physical properties and are instantiated by physical particulars, and that this is sufficient for naturalism. Indeed, this is probably Chalmers' position, given the combination of his non-reductive representationalism (Chalmers 2004) and his "naturalistic dualism" (Chalmers 1996).

50. By saying that it just comments on it, I mean to suggest that it merely expresses a contingent proposition about the phenomenon it targets, rather than attempting to capture its deep essence or underlying nature. There are further implausibilities involved in going non-reductive, but I postpone fuller discussion of the matter till the next chapter.

51. Thus experiential properties present themselves to introspection as representational properties. In other words, the only properties that figure in the content of introspective states about conscious experiences are representational properties—representational properties of those experiences. Or rather, they are properties presented in the content of the introspective state as representational properties

belonging to the conscious experiences. If introspective states can misrepresent (as most philosophers, myself included, believe), then the properties they ascribe to the conscious experiences they are about may not actually be instantiated by those experiences.

52. A more *explicit* formulation would be: For any conscious experience x, introspective state y, and property P, if y represents x as P, then P is a representational property. Note well, however: P here is (represented to be) a property of x, the conscious experience, not y, the introspecting thereof.

53. This is a non-deductive argument *for representationalism*, even though it is a deductive argument for a thesis of the form "pending a special story, a contingent variant on representationalism is true." Two further things must be added to reach representationalism from it: that there is no relevant "special story" and that there is good reason to move from contingency to necessity. As it happens, I do believe there is a special story, and that representationalism is false, even though the transparency thesis is true. For details, see Kriegel 2009 Ch.5.

54. I discuss the matter in some detail in Kriegel 2009 Ch.3. There I argue that none of the counter-examples work, that experience is indeed transparent, but that representationalism is nonetheless false.

55. The five versions are pure, non-conceptual, atomistic, functionalist, and non-reductive representationalism.

56. The complete derivation might go something like this: (TMR) Necessarily★, there is a tracking relation T, such that for any mental state x and property F, F figures in the representational content of x iff x bears T to F; (RCE1) Necessarily★, for any mental state x and experiential character E, there is a property F, such that x has E iff F figures in the representational content of x; therefore, (PTER-) Necessarily★, there is a tracking relation T, such that for any mental state x and experiential character E, there is a property F, such that x has E iff x bears T to F; (BridgePrinciple) Necessarily★, for any mental state x, experiential character E, property F, and factor X, if F figures in x's representational content due to X and x has E due to X, then F figures in x's representational-experiential content; therefore, (PTER) Necessarily★, there is a tracking relation T, such that for any mental state x and property F, F figures in x's experiential-representational content iff x bears T to F.

57. I mentioned that the terms "representation" and "intentionality" are sometimes treated as synonyms and sometimes not. Insofar as they are, intentionality could trivially be accounted for in terms of representation. If they are not, then we would have to adopt the account as a substantive claim. The claim could be formulated, to a first approximation, as follows: For any intentional property I, there is a representational property R, such that I=R.

58. Two comments. First, recall that "exp-intentional" is short for "experiential-intentional." Secondly, to obtain (PTEI), we would need the further lemma that if F figures in the experiential-representational content of a mental state which qualifies both as representational and as intentional, then F figures in the experiential-intentional content of that state. Thirdly, as noted before, I focus on properties as the constituents of intentional content, to the exclusion of entities from other ontological categories (notably particulars) as a harmless simplification; when the prospects of the simplification being harmful will arise, in the next chapter, I will address the issue explicitly.

59. More accurately, the former construal of the pure tracking account would *entail* (PTEI) rather than be a *version* of (PTEI), since in that construal the pure tracking account is conceptually necessary, whereas (PTEI) is just metaphysically necessary (recall that metaphysical necessity is all that is required by "necessity★").

60. Furthermore, as far as (PTEI) and (PTEI1) are concerned, there could be two intrinsically (and functionally) indistinguishable internal states, but one of them would be experiential and the other not, because one is suitably related to some properties and the other to others. This is something that "phenomenal externalists" (Dretske 1996, Davies 1997, Lycan 2001) are willing to accept, but it does not

become less *prima facie* implausible because they are, and anyway their willingness typically lies downstream of theory: they are typically driven to externalism about conscious experience by their prior commitment to representationalism about conscious experience and externalism about representational content. As far as I can tell, there is no independent, theory-free attraction in going externalist with respect to experience. In addition, we should keep in mind that another challenge to a posteriori pure tracking would be general skepticism about Kripkean a posteriori necessity.

61. We may call (ITEI4) the *global-availability tracking account* of experiential intentionality. We obtain it with something like the following reasoning: (TMR) Necessarily★, there is a tracking relation T, such that for any mental state x and any property F, F figures in the representational content of x iff x bears T to F; (RCE4) Necessarily★, for any mental state x and experiential character E, there is a property F, such that x has E iff F figures in the representational content of x globally-availably; therefore, (ITER4-) Necessarily★, there is a tracking relation T, such that for any mental state x and experiential character E, there is a property F, such that x has E iff x bears T to F globally availably; (BridgePrinciple) Necessarily★, for any mental state x, experiential character E, property F, and factor X, if F figures in x's representational content due to X and x has E due to X, then F figures in x's representational-experiential content; therefore, (ITER4) Necessarily★, there is a tracking relation T, such that for any mental state x and property F, F figures in x's experiential-representational content iff x bears T to F; (Lemma) Necessarily, for any mental state x and property F, if F figures in the experiential-representational content of x, then F figures in the experiential-intentional content of x; therefore, (ITEI4) Necessarily★, there is a tracking relation T, such that for any mental state x and property F, F figures in the exp-intentional content of x iff x bears T to F globally-availably.

62. In order to instantiate this property, a particular would have to both track F and be globally available. While the tracking of F is occurrent, the global availability is merely dispositional. So there is a dispositional element in the instantiation conditions of the property—a particular must be disposed a certain way in order to instantiate the property. This makes the property dispositional.

63. Combining (TMR) with these other versions of impure representationalism would result in what we may call the *non-conceptual tracking* account, the *atomistic tracking account*, and the *non-reductive tracking* account, of experiential intentionality. I leave their formulation as an exercise for the reader.

64. It would seem that a neutral tracking account would be marginally more plausible if there was a strong commonality between T_1 and T_2, so that they were both determinates, or species, of some reasonably homogeneous determinable, or genus, tracking relation. If there were two kinds of nomic dependence, for example, such that one characterized the relation exp-intentional states bear to the properties that figure in their characteristic content and the other characterized the relation nexp-intentional states do, the result would be a quite elegant tracking account of experiential intentionality. One would still need to make the case for that account: show that it gets the extension right, is "theoretically virtuous," etc. And as noted, I am not familiar with any attempt to do so.

65. In fact, note that neutral accounts would fall under the letter of (PTEI), and thus qualify as versions of pure tracking accounts as formally stated here.

66. The neutral tracking account allows for the possibility of two intrinsically and functionally indistinguishable states, bearing (moreover) the same determinable relation to the same properties, such that one of the states is experiential and the other is not, because the determinate tracking relation one bears is different from the determinate tracking relation the other does. This is slightly odd. Thus part of the problem with both pure and neutral tracking accounts is that, fundamentally, the difference between experiential and non-experiential states, including experiential and non-experiential intentional states, seems more appropriately located in the states themselves, not in what they are related to or what relations they bear to what they are related to. Pure and neutral accounts locate the difference outside the conscious experiences. Phenomenal externalists such as Dretske (1996) and Lycan (2001)

may be comfortable with this consequence, but it still strikes me as rather a liability on an account of experience (and hence of experiential intentionality).

67. Recall that the experiential character of a conscious experience is what determines what it is like for the subject to have it (and *that* there is something it is like for the subject to have it) and is thus what makes the experience the experience it is (and an experience at all) in the relevant sense.

68. The acronym HOT is often used not for "higher-order theory" but for "higher-order thought." As it happens, some philosophers' higher-order theory is also a higher-order thought theory (Rosenthal 1990, 2002, 2005), but here I use the acronym to stand for "higher-order theory." Other versions of higher-order theory, according to which the higher-order representation is not a thought, such as Lycan's (1996) "higher-order perception" theory, also qualify as versions of HOT as I use the acronym here.

69. Naturally, F would be a member of a privileged class of properties P the representation of which can constitute experiential character. A much more explicit statement of higher-order theory would be this: There is a class of properties P, such that for any conscious experience x and subject S, where S is in x, there is a suitable mental state y, where S is in y, such that x is the conscious experience it is because y represents x to have the member(s) of P that y does (rather than representing x to have other members) and x is a conscious experience (at all) because y represents x to have some member(s) of P (at all). Note that this thesis states that higher-order theory makes claims not only about the existence conditions, but also about the identity conditions, of conscious experiences. Some versions of higher-order theory may not make such a further claim. I ignore them here, simply because they will not be useful in developing my argument against the tracking account of experiential intentionality and devising an alternative account.

70. That is, it is an occurrent cognitive state (rather than a quasi-perceptual or conative state, or a standing cognitive state) that was not formed through conscious inference and represents x as a state *of oneself*. More precisely, we might formulate the view as follows: (HOT1) Necessarily★, for any experiential character E, mental state x, and subject S, where S is in x, there is a property F, such that x has E iff there is a mental state y, such that (i) S is in y, (ii) y is an occurrent non-inferential *de se* thought, and (iii) y represents x to be F.

71. Some higher-order theorists deny that the higher-order representation is occurrent, claiming it is instead dispositional (Carruthers 2000, Wilberg 2009). Others deny that it is a cognitive state, claiming instead either that it is a quasi-perceptual state (Lycan 1996) or that it is a conative state (Kobes 1995).

72. Again, F would be a member of P. Also again, a more explicit statement would be this: There is a class of properties P, such that for any conscious experience x, x has the experiential character it does because x represents itself suitably to have the member(s) of P that x does represents itself to have (rather than other members) and x has experiential character (at all) because x represents itself suitably to have some member(s) of P (at all).

73. I consider some options in Kriegel 2009 Ch.4 and Ch.6.

74. Essentially, self-representationalism is similar to standard higher-order theories in positing higher-order contents, but dissimilar in not positing higher-order states (or vehicles). Whether we should describe this as positing higher-order representations depends on whether we want to characterize the order of a representation in terms of the order of its vehicle or in terms of the order of its content. I think it is more natural to do so in terms of the content, so I consider self-representing states to be higher-order representations of themselves. But nothing of substance rides on this.

75. We might formulate the view as follows: (eHOT) Necessarily★, for any mental state x and experiential character E, there is a property F, such that x has E iff there is a suitable mental state y, such that (i) y represents x to be F and (ii) $x \neq y$. Note that (SR) is equivalent to (iHOT): Necessarily★, for any mental state x and experiential character E, there is a property F, such that x has E iff there is a suitable mental state y, such that (i) y represents x to be F and (ii) $x = y$.

76. As noted above, different versions are obtained by different ways of unpacking "suitably." In Kriegel 2009 Ch.4, I unpack "suitably" as meaning (i) non-derivatively, (ii) specifically, and (iii) essentially. This is not the place to recapitulate what these conditions amount to. The result, in any case, is the following thesis: (SR1) Necessarily*, for any mental state x and experiential character E, there is a property F, such that x has E iff x non-derivatively, specifically, and essentially represents itself to be F. Against the background of assumptions we have already encountered above, we can further obtain the following thesis: There is a class of properties P, such that for any conscious experience x, x has the experiential character it does because x represents itself non-derivatively, specifically, and essentially to have the member(s) of P that x does represent itself to have (rather than other members) and x has experiential character (at all) because x represents itself non-derivatively, specifically, and essentially to have some member(s) of P (at all).

77. The latter is a determinable, or genus, of which the former is a determinate, or species. As is common, and as already discussed here, I take what makes a K the K it is to be a determinate, or species, of what makes a K a K at all. See Kriegel 2009 Ch.2 for details.

78. For that, see Kriegel 2009, especially Ch.2, Ch.5, and Appendix.

79. Something like this straightforward argument is offered by Lycan (2001), who seems to present it, however, as an argument specifically for what I call here extrinsic higher-order theory. That the argument cannot be used in this way, and supports only higher-order theory in general, understood to cover self-representationalism, is argued by Gerken (2008). What I present in the text is not Lycan's argument, in any case, but mine.

80. Both these lemmas (that a person being aware of something requires the person representing that thing and that a person representing something requires that the person be in a mental state that represents that thing) can be contested. The former is denied by Levine (2001, 2006) and Hellie (2007), for example, and the latter by Masrour (in conversation). Nonetheless, I take it the lemmas are *prima facie* plausible. I *argue* against Levine and Hellie in Kriegel 2009 Ch.4.

81. Observe that this conclusion does not comment on whether x and y are numerically distinct or not. It is thus neutral between extrinsic higher-order theory and self-representationalism. Also, the conclusion of the argument is not *verbatim* the same as (HOT), but I trust it is evident that it is essentially the same thesis.

82. Rosenthal motivates (HOT) by appeal to a similar principle he calls the *transitivity principle* (Rosenthal 1993). He often puts the principle as "conscious states are states we are conscious of," but sometimes more neutrally as "conscious states are states we are aware of." How to formulate the transitivity principle more precisely is an important question. Certainly one legitimate formulation is precisely as Premise 1 in the above argument, that is, as the awareness principle.

83. My concern right now is not to evaluate the plausibility of this argument. As it happens, I think that it is problematic, but that other considerations support the same conclusion (see Kriegel 2009 Ch.4).

84. There is, of course, a way of using the term "sensory" so that it implies "experiential," with the result that a non-experiential sensory state is impossible. I will not use the term in this way. Rather, I use the term so that there are sensory non-experiential states, such as blindsight, and correspondingly, there are sensorily type-identical but experientially type-different states. Basically, sensory properties are properties that potentially belong to P, that is, are properties the (suitable) higher-order representation of which constitutes experiential properties. (Note, however, that not *all* members of P need be sensory properties.)

85. On this view, what matters here are not higher-order discriminatory powers but first-order ones. I discuss this in more detail in Kriegel 2009 Ch.4.

86. Some philosophers have argued that the possibility of higher-order misrepresentations of the kind just considered presents a grave problem for higher-order theory (Neander 1998), and some have

attempted to devise a version of higher-order theory that relieves higher-order misrepresentations of relevance to experiential character (Wilberg 2009, 2010). But I am going to assume that all these reactions are misguided and S's experience is greenish—has greenish experiential character. I do think that the possibility of certain more radical higher-order misrepresentations—in which a higher-order state misrepresents not only the *properties* but also the *existence* of a first-order state—presents an insurmountable difficulty for standard versions of (HOT) (Byrne 1997, Levine 2001). However, they present no difficulty for (SR): a self-representing state may misrepresent its own properties, but cannot misrepresent its own existence, since without existing it cannot represent itself at all (Caston 2002, Kriegel 2003c, 2009 Ch.4). This is, in fact, one of the major reasons to adopt (SR).

87. For the case against representationalism, see Kriegel 2009 Ch.3.

88. The term "result" is to some extent infelicitous, as it implies a causal process whereby the higher-order representation alters the conscious experience, when in fact the connection between the higher-order representation and the conscious experience is claimed here to be constitutive rather than causal.

89. To repeat, this is not particularly surprising, but nor is it trivial. It is not trivial because the higher-order theory of consciousness and the tracking theory of experiential intentionality are not theories of the same thing. The former is a theory of experience in general, whether intentional or not, whereas the latter is a theory of a specific type of intentionality, namely experiential.

90. The fact that the experiential character of this experience is determined by a higher-order *mis*representation does not provide such a story: whether the higher-order representation is veridical or not has no relevance to the introspectibility of a color experience's qualitative character. Indeed, if the proponent of (HOT) is right, we probably cannot tell from the first-person perspective which of our experiences are based on a higher-order misrepresentation. Certainly nobody has ever argued that the veridicality value of higher-order representations is relevant to the introspectibility of the corresponding experiential properties—and it is not clear how such an argument would go.

91. It may be thought that this step is not so trivial. Recall that experiential intentionality is an intentional property that a conscious experience has in virtue of being a conscious experience. So perhaps the fact that a property is both experiential and intentional does not guarantee that it is exp-intentional. However, if a property is both experiential and intentional, then it is experiential, and every experiential property is a property a conscious experience has in virtue of being a conscious experience. So it is a property that the conscious experience has in virtue of being a conscious experience. Since it is an intentional property, it appears now to be a property which is both an intentional property and a property the conscious experience has in virtue of being a conscious experience. That is, it is an exp-intentional property. Thus every property that is both experiential and intentional is exp-intentional.

92. This is precisely why the argument from transparency discussed in §2.1.2 is, as we saw, a non-deductive argument. The result is that although (TE) *militates* against (HOT), it is not *incompatible* with (HOT). In a way, it *suggests* representationalism, in that it requires nothing more than (first-order) representational properties to account for the greenish experiential character. But if there are independent reasons to posit something else, that is consistent with (TE). In Kriegel 2009 Ch.5, I argue in some detail that self-representationalism—which, recall, is a version of (HOT)—is compatible with, and in fact predicts, the transparency of experience. It is possible, of course, to defend (HOT) by arguing that the inner awareness (HOT) built into experiential character is a counter-example to transparency (Lesson Ms). But personally, I do not take that route, and instead I embrace transparency (understood, as here, as a claim about introspectible experiential properties). So it is open to me to use the idea of transparency in the present context.

93. In conclusion, we should accept that LeShane's experience's greenishness is an exp-intentional property (as per Premise 1 of the HOT argument) because it is supported by the following argument: 1)

The experience's greenishness is an experiential property (by definition of "greenishness"); 2) The experience's greenishness is an introspectible property (pending a special story to the contrary); 3) All introspectible experiential properties are intentional properties (as per the transparency thesis); therefore, 4) The experience's greenishness is an intentional property (from 1–3); and therefore, 5) The experience's greenishness is an exp-intentional property (from 1 and 4).

94. We can take the sub-arguments for Premises 1 and 2, as they emerge from the discussion of objections, and use them to produce a formulation of the overall argument for my conditional: 1) LeShane's experience's greenishness is an experiential property; 2) The experience's greenishness is an introspectible property; 3) All introspectible experiential properties are intentional properties; therefore, 4) LeShane's experience's greenishness is an intentional property; therefore, 5) LeShane's experience's greenishness is an exp-intentional property; 6) If (HOT) is true, then LeShane's experience's greenishness is the property of being suitably higher-order represented to be greenish★; 7) the property of being suitably higher-order represented to be greenish★ is not a tracking property; therefore, 8) If (HOT) is true, then LeShane's experience's greenishness is not a tracking property; therefore 9) Some exp-intentional properties are not tracking properties; but, 10) According to the tracking account of experiential intentionality, all exp-intentional properties are tracking properties; therefore, 11) If (HOT) is true, then the tracking account of experiential intentionality is false. (It is possible also to run the argument slightly differently, arguing first that if (HOT) is true, then the property of being suitably higher-order represented to be greenish★ is an exp-intentional property, and then that the property of being suitably higher-order represented to be greenish★ is not a tracking property. The considerations brought will be the same, but the argument will be logically reorganized. The overall argument would look like this: 1) If (HOT) is true, then LeShane's experience's property of being suitably higher-order represented to be greenish★ is an exp-intentional property; 2) The property of being higher-order represented to be greenish★ is not a tracking property; therefore, 3) Some exp-intentional properties are not tracking properties; but, 4) according to the tracking account of experiential intentionality, all exp-intentional properties are tracking properties; therefore, 5) The tracking account of experiential intentionality is false.)

95. The upshot of these two extensions is that not only the universal thesis that all exp-intentional properties are tracking properties is false, so is the *existential* thesis that some exp-intentional properties are tracking properties.

96. I use the case of color experience mostly, I suppose, because color experience is paradigmatic among conscious experiences.

97. See discussion in §1.3.3. For my part, I hold that all experiences are intentional, and moreover that all qualitative characters are intentional properties (Kriegel 2009 Ch.3). But such a view is irrelevant to our present concern. Our present concern is with the nature of exp-intentional properties, not experiential properties as such. If there are experiential properties that are not exp-intentional properties (that is, that are not intentional), then we can simply disregard them.

98. I remind the reader, however, that here I use the acronym HOT non-standardly, to include varieties of higher-order theory that appeal not only to higher-order *thoughts* but also to other kinds of higher-order representations, and also to include both extrinsic and intrinsic varieties of higher-order theory. This is not how I used the acronym in Kriegel 2009.

99. There are several reasons for this (not that this is particularly important). For one thing, we have already formulated tracking accounts, in §2.1.3, in the narrow way exclusive of the objector's proposed account. For another, the difference between an account that characterizes a state's experiential-intentional properties in terms of what that state tracks and an account that characterizes them in terms of what the state is higher-order tracked to track is a deep and significant difference, a difference of spirit and not only letter; it is therefore useful to have two distinct labels for them. Since we have already designated "tracking account" for the former, we should use a different label for the latter.

100. This would yield the following thesis: Necessarily*, there is a tracking relation T, such that for any mental state x and property F, F figures in x's exp-intentional content iff there is a suitable mental state y, such that (i) y bears T to x and (ii) x bears T to F.

101. Against the background of familiar assumptions, we can obtain from this the following: There is a tracking relation T, such that for any mental state x, x has the exp-intentional content it does (and not another) because there is a suitable mental state y, such that y bears T to x's bearing of T to what y does bear T to x's bearing of T to (and not to anything else), and x has an exp-intentional content (at all) because there is a suitable mental state y, such that y bears T to x's bearing of T to something (at all).

102. A very basic clarification is that even though the acronyms HOT and HOTT are very similar, this is not to be confused for intimating a particularly close relationship between the two (such as that of a genus to a species, say). In fact, (HOT) and (HOTT) are theories of *different things*. The former is a theory of consciousness, or conscious experience, whereas the latter is a theory of experiential intentionality. The two phenomena would be coextensive only on the assumption, which I am not making (or rejecting) here, that all conscious experience is intentional.

103. In somewhat archaic terminology, we might put the question as follows: what ontological category (or categories) does the formal object (or do the formal objects) of tracking fall under?

104. For a relatively recent discussion, see Armstrong 1997. There is some debate over whether another constituent of a state of affairs is the instantiation relation between the particular and the property (or the plurality of particulars and the relation). The discussion often centers on so-called Bradley's Regress. According to Bradley (1893), the "metaphysical glue" that joins a particular and a property when they together compose a state of affairs cannot be a relation between the particular and the property because that would require something to glue the object, the property, and the relation, and appealing to a second-order to glue would launch us on a regress—Bradley's Regress.

105. This treats x, a state, as a particular. Some philosophers take states to be properties, understood to be different from particulars, but I never managed to appreciate the pull of this view. Certainly being-in-a-state is a property, but the state itself seems to me to belong in the same ontological category as events and facts, which nobody thinks of as properties—at least not universal properties. Some philosophers do take events and facts to be tropes (Lombard 1986), which are particularized properties, but tropes are of course particulars, since they are abstract particulars (Williams 1953). So even on this view assimilating states to events and facts would cast states as particulars.

106. Note well: to say that y tracks an F-tracker need not be to say that y tracks x *as* an F-tracker. One view is that no tracking is tracking-as. There is such a thing as seeing an MX-5, but in addition, there is also such a thing as seeing an MX-5 *as* an MX-5. The same does not hold, however, for tracking: there is such a thing as tracking an MX-5, but there is not, additionally, such a thing as tracking an MX-5 *as* an MX-5. (This would make the locution "tracks x to track F" a little forced, as it is hard to hear this locution, in ordinary English, as not implying that x is tracked *as* an F-tracker.) How a state that tracks MX-5 "conceptualizes" the MX-5 is not a matter of a kind of tracking involved, but is rather a matter of downstream processing. Thus (HOTT) is silent on how y "conceptualizes" the F-tracker it tracks. It just tracks an F-tracker. Whether the result is a representation of the F-tracker *as* an F-tracker depends on y's functional role, on which (HOTT) may have nothing to say.

107. I do not think that there is much riding on how these ontological issues are resolved. Unlike some, I think the ontological issues are genuine. But I doubt that the nature of experiential intentionality is sensitive to how these issues are resolved. Here I will assume the interpretation that assigns state-of-affair types as the objects of the higher-order tracking we are interested in mainly because, as I said, it is more conservative, in that it is more continuous with natural assignment of properties as the formal objects of tracking.

108. It may be that this does not sit well with how the word "tracking" behaves in ordinary English. But if so, this just means that we have to introduce some technical term T, such that T-ing behaves just

like "tracking" behaves in ordinary English *except* that it tolerates mis-T-ing. This is not just a hypothetical worry: it seems to me that describing A as tracking F implies that A is a type, whereas typically it is tokens that are said to misrepresent. If it is inappropriate, in ordinary English, to describe a token as tracking, then it is also inappropriate to describe a token as mistracking. Thus we would have to say more accurately that the token was mis-T-ing.

109. More explicitly: Necessarily★, for any mental state x and property F, F figures in x's exp-intentional content iff there are functional roles R and R★, and a suitable mental state y, such that (i) y plays R, (ii) y nomically depends upon the putative fact that (ii-a) x plays R★, (ii-b) x nomically depends upon F, and (ii-c) it is the case that (ii-a) because it is the case that (ii-b), and (iii) it is the case that (i) because it is the case that (ii).

110. What makes tracking accounts incompatible with (HOT), remember, is that the latter makes it possible that some experience be greenish but track blueness rather than greenness. This would be impossible if tracking accounts were correct.

111. Some of these will be inherited from the general problems of the tracking approach to mental representation. For example, a typical problem for tracking theories is to find a way to extend the account from simple cases (perceiving red, for example) to sophisticated abstract thoughts (e.g., that virtue is its own reward). Since this is not a tract on tracking approaches to mental representation as such, I will not discuss such problems here.

112. Recall, again, that (HOTT) is a theory of experiential intentionality whereas (HOT) is a theory of conscious experience in general, and thus they are different theories nonetheless, one with a broader mandate, as it were, than the other.

113. As before, against the background of familiar assumptions, we obtain from this the following: For any mental state x, x has the exp-intentional content it does (rather than another) because x tracks itself to track what x does track itself to track (rather than tracking itself to track something else), and x has exp-intentional content (at all) because x tracks itself to track something (at all). And more precisely: There is a class of properties P and a tracking relation T, such that for any mental state x, x has the exp-intentional content it does (rather than another) because x bears T to x's own bearing T to the member(s) of P that x does bear T to its bearing of T to (rather than other member(s)), and x has exp-intentional content (at all) because x bears T to x's own bearing T to some member(s) of P (at all).

114. The Dretskean version, for example, would be this: (STA1) Necessarily★, for any mental state x and property F, F figures in x's exp-intentional content iff there is a functional role R, such that (i) x plays R, (ii) x nomically depends upon x's own bearing of the relation of having-the-function-of-nomically-depending-upon to F, and (iii) it is the case that (i) because it is the case that (ii).

115. Both the distinction and the notion require some defense, of course—and are provided one.

116. What this comes down to will depend partly on one's account of the representation-transmission relation. One view, which I consider in Kriegel 2009 Ch.6, is that a *sufficient condition* for x bearing that relation to y is that y be a complex of which x is a part, where a complex is a whole in which the parts are essentially interconnected in a certain way. Thus, a mere sum can only be destroyed by destroying one of its parts, whereas a complex can be destroyed even if none of its parts are destroyed (namely, if the interconnection between them is destroyed).

117. This is admittedly different from the way we instinctively think of a self-representing state, namely, as a state the whole of which represents the whole of which. But this difference does not seem to run deep, especially given that the whole state is represented by something that does not have an existence independently of the state.

118. Let me stress that this is only a first approximation of how this naturalistic challenge is handled; for further details, see Kriegel 2009 Ch.6.

119. Here too, against the background of familiar assumptions we can formulate something more precise: There is a class of properties P and a tracking relation T, such that for any mental state x, there are states x_1 and x_2 and a representation-transmission relation R, where (i) x_1 is a proper part of x, (ii) x_2 is a proper part of x, and (iii) x_2 bears R to x, such that x has the exp-intentional content it does (rather than another) because x_1 bears T to x_2's bearing T to the member(s) of P that x_1 does bear T to x_2's bearing T to (and not other member(s)), and x has exp-intentional content (at all) because (i)-(iii) hold and x_1 bears T to x_2's bearing T to some member(s) of P (at all).

120. The obtaining of these relations entails, among other things, that the functional role of the sum of x_1 and x_2 is different from the sum of the functional roles of x_1 and x_2. In any case, one way to formulate the emerging view is as follows: necessarily*, there is a tracking relation T, a representation-transmission relation R, and a cognitive unification relation U, such that for any mental state x and property F, F figures in x's exp-intentional content iff there are states x_1 and x_2, such that (i) x_1 is a proper part of x, (ii) x_2 is a proper part of x, (iii) U holds between x_1 and x_2, (iv) x_1 bears T to x_2's bearing T to F, and (v) x_2 bears R to x.

121. As before, against the background of familiar assumptions we can obtain something like this: There is a class of properties P, such that for any exp-intentional state x, there are states x_1 and x_2 and a representation-transmission relation R, where (i) x_1 is a proper part of x, (ii) x_2 is a proper part of x, and (iii) x_2 bears R to x, such that x has the exp-intentional content it does (rather than another) because x_1 has the function of nomically depending upon x_2's having the function of nomically depending upon the member(s) of P that x_1 does have the function of nomically depending upon x_2's having the function of nomically depending upon (and not other member(s)), and x has exp-intentional content (at all) because (i)-(iii) hold and x_1 has the function of nomically depending upon x_2's having the function of nomically depending upon some member(s) of P (at all).

122. This only applies to accounts at the same level of specificity, or abstraction, because obviously my credence in (NSTA) can only be higher than my credence in (NSTA1), given that my credence in the teleo-informational account of tracking is lower than 1. Thus to say that my credence in (NSTA1) is the highest is just to say what I have said already, namely, that I am most sympathetic to the self-representational account of conscious experience and to the teleo-informational account of tracking.

123. Note that on this way of telling the story, we need not posit an "evil neuroscientist" intentionally replicating a certain stream of consciousness. The replication of my stream of consciousness is entirely accidental.

124. I say "let us suppose" because I recognize that one reaction to this scenario is simply to deny the metaphysical possibility of what I have just described, at least *as* described. I discuss this matter more fully in §3.2. For now, let us treat this thought experiment merely as an expository device.

125. This is the true moral of the brain-in-vat thought experiment, in my opinion: that a distinction must be drawn between two notions of representation, or two senses of the word "representation." The experiment is needed because in ordinary circumstances it is hard to distinguish the two notions. With my own apple experiences, for example, what the experiences present to me and what they track is typically one and the same: an apple. It is only in the fantastic circumstances of the thought experiment that an experience can be envisaged which consistently presents to the subject one thing but tracks another.

126. A more descriptive terminology might be to say that there are two notions of representation, *objective representation* and *subjective representation*, and that the experience subjectively represents an apple and objectively represents S1. I employ this terminology elsewhere, in the context of making the case more fully for the distinction between these two notions of mental representation (Kriegel Ms).

127. Recall that exp-intentional content is the intentional content a mental state has in virtue of its phenomenal character. Since the envatted brain's experience is apple-ish rather than S1-ish, it is the apple, not S1, that shows up in its exp-intentional content.

128. So, while it is plausible that tracking something is a way of representing$_2$ it, it may not be a way of representing$_1$ it, and while intentionality may well be one and the same as representation$_1$, it is unlikely to be one and the same as representation$_2$. This means that the "representational theory of intentionality" is plausible only if it is a *representational$_1$* theory of intentionality.

129. None of which is to say that (HOTT) can actually accommodate brain-in-vat scenarios, that is, assign to envatted brain the exp-intentional states we intuitively think they have. In §3.2, however, I will argue that it actually does.

130. And indeed, in Kriegel 2009 (see especially Ch.6) what I attempt to do is account for consciousness in terms of higher-order tracking. That is consistent with the project of the present book, which is to account (in some sense) for intentionality in terms of consciousness.

131. That is, experiential character can be determined by how the experience is higher-order tracked, and at the same time the experiential character can be nothing but intentional content, since according to (HOTT) that comes down to what the experience is higher-order tracked as well.

132. It might be thought surprising that the substantive core of many philosophical disputes (perhaps all!) turns out to be normative rather than descriptive. It is indeed surprising, but I stand by it.

133. In general, Fodor's influential work from the seventies and eighties fit the mold of philosophy of mind as philosophy of science applied to cognitive science. Thus, in arguing for both the Language of Thought Hypothesis (Fodor 1975) and the modularity of mind (Fodor 1983), Fodor always followed the general argumentative strategy of claiming that the best cognitive science we have appears to presuppose a Language of Thought and a massively modular mind.

134. Philosophers who directly and self-consciously followed Grice on this point include Cummins (1979, 1989 Ch.1), Dretske (1988 Ch.3), and Searle (1983 Ch.1, 1992 Ch.7).

135. Of course, one *can* be acquainted with them on the basis of the literature, and certainly one's thinking about them benefits from the literature. But the literature is not a *prerequisite* for the issues arising. For example, there is no need to understand the Quinean approach to ontological commitment or be concerned for the foundational soundness of science. Those concerns do require a theoretical background normally unavailable in adolescence!

136. There are systematic differences, then, between the concerns that motivate interest in each notion of representation. On the side of representation$_2$, we find the following keywords: philosophy of science, physicalism, positivism, third-person perspective, theoretical, scientific posits in cognitive science. On the side of representation$_1$, we find: metaphysics, metaphysical realism, early modern philosophy, first-person perspective, personal, connection between mind and world.

137. We may thus say that (HOTT) is both extensionally adequate and theoretically satisfying. We can think of this in terms of something akin to empirical and theoretical virtues in scientific theories. Extensional adequacy in a philosophical theory is akin to empirical virtue in a scientific theory: it is a matter of accommodating the "data" (even when the data are such only if some other theories are true, as is the case here). Theoretical satisfaction is a kind of theoretical virtue: having naturalistic credentials is something we want out of a philosophical theory in the same sense in which we want simplicity, parsimony, conservativeness, etc. from a scientific (and for that matter philosophical) theory. I will discuss this perspective on philosophical theories more fully in Chapter 4.

138. For comments on a previous draft of this chapter, I would like to thank David Chalmers, Victor Kumar, and an anonymous referee for OUP. For comments on material from this chapter, I would like to thank Stephen Biggs, Ben Blumson, Allan Hazlett, and Farid Masrour. I also benefited from presenting parts of this chapter at NYU's Consciousness Project. I would like to thank the audience there, in particular David Chalmers, Jennifer Corns, Robert Howell, Farid Masrour, David Pereplyotchik, Jim Pryor, David Rosenthal, Dan Shargel, Jon Simon, and Sebastian Watzl.

3

The Nature of Experiential Intentionality
II. An Adverbial Theory

Introduction/Abstract

The purpose of this chapter is twofold. After laying out some relevant background (§3.1), I consider two arguments (§§3.2–3.3) against tracking-based accounts of experiential intentionality, including higher-order tracking theories. I then use the main considerations behind them as a launching pad for an alternative account (§3.4) and discuss some objections to that account (§3.5). In the conclusion, I compare the relative merits and demerits of this account and the higher-order tracking theory.

3.1. Background: Intentional Inexistence and Intentional Indifference

Since Chisholm's (1957) seminal analysis of these notions, *intensionality* (with an *s*) has been standardly taken as the criterion for *intentionality* (with a *t*). In this section, I introduce the notion of intensionality (with an *s*). Later, I will discuss a line of argument according to which no tracking-based account of experiential intentionality, whether first- or higher-order, can recover the intensionality of experiential intentionality.[1]

We may put the main point of Chisholm's analysis as follows: a property is intentional just in case it is picked out by a predicate that is intensional, and a predicate is intensional just in case it fails to support certain inferences. Chisholm himself lists four types of inference failure, but standard discussions focus on two: failure of existential generalization and failure of substitution of co-referential terms.

Existential generalization is inference of the form "*a* is F, therefore, there is an *x*, such that *x* is F" (F*a* |–∃*x*F*x*), or "*a* bears R to *b*, therefore there is an *x*, such that *a* bears R to *x*" (R*ab* |–∃*x*R*ax*). This is generally a valid inference: "Jimmy is cruel, therefore there is something that is cruel" is valid (the premises cannot be true unless the conclusion is), as is "Jimmy kicked a parrot, therefore there is something that Jimmy kicked." However, certain predicates do not support such inference. Consider "Jimmy is thinking of a parrot, therefore there is something that Jimmy is thinking of." This is clearly invalid, as the premise can very well be true without the conclusion being true, e.g. if Jimmy lives in a parrot-less world and is the victim of a grand parrot illusion.[2]

Substitution of co-referential terms is inference of the form "*a* is F and *a* = *b*, therefore *b* is F" (F*a* & *a*=*b* |–F*b*), or "*a* bears R to *b* and *b* = *c*, therefore *a* bears R to *c*" (R*ab* & *b*=*c* |–R*ac*).[3] Again, this is generally valid but some predicates are exceptional: "Tim is shaking hands with the fastest man in Harlem, Tom is the fastest man in Harlem, therefore Tim is shaking hands with Tom" is valid, but "Tim is thinking about the fastest man in Harlem, Tom is the fastest man in Harlem, therefore Tim is thinking about Tom" is not (Tim may be unaware that Tom is the fastest man in Harlem).[4]

Chisholm's intensional criterion of intentionality is satisfyingly precise, and appears to be extensionally adequate, but it is somewhat dismaying that the criterion is formulated in the formal mode of speech, given that the phenomena themselves are certainly not linguistic.[5] If certain verb phrases exhibit the logical features just described, it is surely because there is something about the properties they pick out that makes them do so. It is implausible to suppose that the property of thinking inherits its special attributes from the logical attributes of the verb "to think." More plausibly, "to think" inherits its relevant attributes from thinking. The logical features of intensional predicates are thus best thought of as *symptoms* of two special attributes that certain properties have and others do not: the attribute that underwrites failure of existential generalization and the attribute that underwrites substitution failure. The former is sometimes referred to as *intentional inexistence*. For the sake of esthetic uniformity, I will refer to the latter as *intentional indifference*.[6] (Impressionistic rationale: just as intentional inexistence involves an object that does not exist in reality but does "exist" *qua* intentional, so intentional indifference involves objects that do not differ in reality but do "differ" *qua* intentional.)

In the next two sections, I will consider arguments to the effect that neither first-nor higher-order tracking accounts of experiential intentionality can accommodate the intentional indifference (§3.2) and intentional inexistence (§3.3) exhibited by exp-intentional states. My discussion will find the argument from intentional indifference inconclusive, so the burden of the case against tracking-based approaches will rest on the argument from intentional inexistence. To that extent, the next section can be skipped without loss to the main thread of argument in this chapter.

3.2. The Argument from Intentional Indifference

The first argument is that experiential intentionality exhibits intentional indifference, but neither first- nor higher-order tracking can account for this. This is the argument I develop and consider, without quite endorsing, in this section. I develop the argument in §3.2.1, then consider some responses, including one I am sympathetic to, in §3.2.2. I close, in §3.2.3, with a related discussion of brain-in-vat scenarios.

3.2.1. The Argument

Let us start with the (first-order) tracking account from §2.1. Consider Tassandra, a subject unaware of the fact that Phosphorus is Hesperus, and compare the overall, global, visual-cum-cognitive experience she undergoes when (a) knowingly looking at Phosphorus (i.e., looking at Phosphorus while being aware that she is looking at Phosphorus) and when (b) knowingly looking at Hesperus. We can stipulate that illumination conditions are identical, the position of Venus in the sky is identical, Tassandra's visual apparatus on the two occasions is identical, etc. And, of course, we can also stipulate that Tassandra is unaware of whether it is morning or evening, despite being aware of which star she is looking at. This is possible, because—we stipulate further—she is unaware that Phosphorus is visible in the morning and Hesperus in the evening, but has a strong gut feeling that she is looking at one star rather than the other.[7] Here are two claims about Tassandra's two experiences: (1) they have different exp-intentional contents; (2) they are indistinguishable in terms of tracking. The first would establish that exp-intentional content exhibits intentional indifference, the second that tracking accounts of experiential intentionality cannot accommodate intentional indifference. It would follow that tracking accounts of experiential intentionality cannot account for a feature exhibited by exp-intentional content. I now turn to present the case for each of the two claims. After that, I will extend the argument to higher-order tracking theory.

The first claim is that Tassandra's overall experiences have different exp-intentional content. We can appreciate this in two steps: (1a) the two experiences have different experiential characters, and (1b) the difference in experiential character is an (exp-)intentional difference.

It certainly seems that the two experiences have different experiential characters, as per (1a), since Tassandra is aware of looking at Phosphorus and at Hesperus, but unaware that they are one and the same. Given the specifications of the case, with the indistinguishable perceptual conditions, it is plausible perhaps that the purely *sensory* component of the experiential character is the same. But the *overall* experiential character is different. For there is an element—a non-sensory element—in the overall experiential character that corresponds to *identifying the object*. Thus there is likely an experiential difference between looking at Phosphorus and *recognizing* it and looking at Phosphorus *without* recognizing it. If so, there should also be an experiential difference between looking at an object and recognizing it to be Phosphorus, on the one hand, and looking at it and recognizing it to be Hesperus, on the other (without recognizing that it is one and the same object). This means that there is an experiential property instantiated by Tassandra's Phosphorus experience but not by her Hesperus experience and conversely. The experiential characters of her two experiences are thus different. We might say that one of her experiences has a Phosphorescent experiential character while the other has a Hesperescent experiential character, and that these are different characters.

The key claim supporting an experiential difference here is the claim that there is an experiential element corresponding to *identifying* or *recognizing* an object. The plausibility of this can be appreciated from the following considerations. Compare the experiences of a normal subject seeing her mother's face and that of a prosopagnostic or visual agnostic.[8] There appears to be an experiential contrast between the two. The most natural explanation of this contrast is that there is an experiential property instantiated by the normal subject's conscious episode but not by the prospoganostic's or visual agnostic's. What the normal subject enjoys, but the prosopagnostic and visual agnostic lack, is the experiential dimension of *recognizing* one's mother's face, that is, *identifying* the object they are looking at (Siewert 1998 Ch.7, Masrour forthcoming-a).⁹ If this experiential dimension cannot be accounted for in terms of purely sensory experiential character (as I suspect is the case), then some sort of non-sensory (perhaps cognitive) experiential character must be involved. Either way, some experiential character must be associated with recognizing/identifying an object. This experience of identifying an object is present in Tassandra's experiences of Phosphorus and Hesperus.¹⁰ She experiences the former *as* Phosphorus and the latter *as* Hesperus—while being unaware that they are the same object—with the result that she undergoes experientially distinct conscious episodes.

The experiential difference here is akin to the difference between knowingly seeing one of two identical twins and knowingly seeing the other. When I knowingly look at my friend Mike, I have a different overall conscious experience from when I knowingly look at his twin brother, even though the two impinge identically on my sensorium.¹¹ This is because I *take* them to be two different men. Likewise, when Tassandra knowingly looks at Phosphorus, she has a different overall conscious experience from when she knowingly looks at Hesperus, even if conditions are such that her sensorium is impinged upon identically on both occasions. Again this is because she *takes* them to be two different objects. The *experiential* situation is the same in my case and Tassandra's.¹² Thus there is nothing particularly suspect about the experiential difference between a Phosphorescent and a Hesperescent experiential character.

Turning now to (1b), it is clear that this experiential difference between Tassandra's two conscious episodes is an *intentional* difference. Not only does the Phosphorescent experience have an experiential dimension of identifying Phosphorus, this experiential dimension is one in virtue of which the experience is *assessable for accuracy*. If Tassandra is not even facing Venus, but rather Neptune, or for that matter a chair, and is undergoing a radical illusion in having an experience as of Phosphorus, then her experience is non-veridical. Thus the experiential dimension of identifying Phosphorus, which is a component of the overall experience's experiential character, contributes to or modulates the veridicality conditions of the experience. That is, it is an exp-intentional property of the experience.

We can see this further by noting that the experiential property of identifying Phosphorus is an *introspectible* property of the experience. According to the transparency thesis from §2.1.2, an introspectible experiential property is always an intentional property. So assuming transparency, the property of identifying Phosphorus is not only experiential, but exp-intentional. The same goes for the property of identifying Hesperus, of course. Since the properties of identifying Phosphorus and identifying Hesperus are different experiential properties, and are exp-intentional properties, they are different exp-intentional properties.[13]

This concludes the case for the first claim about Tassandra's two experiences: they have distinct exp-intentional contents. The second claim is that the two experiences are indistinguishable in terms of tracking (they are type-identical trackers). This can be appreciated through a dilemma. In §2.1.3, we distinguished pure and impure tracking. But, I want to argue, the two experiences are indistinguishable in terms of either. In other words, neither (PTEI) nor (ITEI)—neither the pure nor the impure tracking account of experiential intentionality—can account for the exp-intentional difference between Tassandra's two experiences.

For (PTEI), any exp-intentional difference comes down to a difference in properties being tracked. But Phosphorus and Hesperus have all the same properties in the scenario envisaged, and more pertinently, there is no pair of properties of Venus, F and G, such that Tassandra's Phosphorescent experience tracks F but not G and/or her Hesperescent experience tracks G but not F. Since (as stipulated) Tassandra is unaware of whether it is morning or evening, and of whether Phosphorus is visible in the morning or evening, there is no property she can ascribe to Phosphorus but not Hesperus, and accordingly no property her experience might be tracking in one case but not the other. To be sure, she ascribes only to Phosphorus the property of being Phosphorus, and only to Hesperus the property of being Hesperus, but by most accounts of property individuation these are one and the same property.[14]

According to (ITEI), exp-intentional differences are due to different *manners* in which properties are tracked. These "manners" are most naturally understood in terms of functional role (as in the functionalist representationalism discussed in §2.1.2). The idea would be that one item can track Venus and play a Phosphorus-appropriate functional role while another tracks Venus and plays a Hesperus-appropriate functional role (McGinn 1982).[15] This suggestion has an initial air of plausibility but does not withstand scrutiny. The functional role of a mental state is a matter of its (typical) causes and effects. If two states are to have different functional roles, they must have different causes and/or different effects. One might suggest that the functional-role difference is that (typically) Phosphorus experiences cause Phosphorus beliefs (and/or actions) while Hesperus experiences cause Hesperus beliefs (and/or actions). But that presupposes that we can account for the intentional indifference exhibited by Phosphorus and Hesperus *beliefs* (and/or actions). Alternatively, one might suggest that Phosphorus experiences cause thoughts about *this* star while Hesperus experiences cause thoughts about *that* star, but this presupposes that we can account for the intentional indifference exhibited by *demonstrative* thoughts. Thus finding an individuation of causes and effects that will account for intentional indifference without presupposing it appears hopeless.[16]

This may well be a symptom of the deeper point, made by Searle (1992 Ch.9) and convincingly argued by Shagrir (2001), that there is no way to understand functional role, or syntax, independently of intentional content, or semantics. The point is most obvious when functional role is understood as *inferential* role (Field 1977, Brandom 1994b), since the notion of inference presupposes the notion of content.[17] But it should apply to any relevant understanding of functional role—though I will not pursue this line of thought here.[18]

This concludes the case for saying that Tassandra's Phosphorus and Hesperus experiences exhibit intentional indifference, and that this intentional indifference cannot be accommodated by tracking accounts of experiential intentionality. I now turn to argue for the following conditional: if tracking accounts cannot accommodate intentional indifference, then the higher-order tracking theory cannot either. The argument is straightforward. Given that functional role cannot help (as we have just seen), the failure of (first-order) tracking accounts is due to the simple fact that whenever the tracked is the same, so is the tracking. Trackers individuate by trackees, if you will. This is why the tracking of Phosphorus is the same as the tracking of Hesperus. But if the tracking of Phosphorus is the same as the tracking of Hesperus, and whenever the tracked is the same so is the tracking, then the tracking of the tracking of Phosphorus must be the same as the tracking of the tracking of Hesperus. Thus higher-order tracking cannot bring intentional indifference into the picture: either first-order tracking can do it, or no tracking can.

This concludes my presentation of the argument that neither first- nor higher-order tracking can account for intentional indifference.[19] Call this the *argument from intentional indifference*. I will now consider three possible responses, in increasing order of plausibility.

3.2.2. Responses

The first response is to deny that there is an experiential difference between Tassandra's Phosphorus and Hesperus experiences, presumably on the grounds that there is no such thing as non-sensory experiential character, and in any case no such thing as an experiential character to do with *identifying an object*.

It is hard for me to take this response seriously.[20] We already noted above that there seems to be an experiential difference between seeing one's mother with and without recognizing her to be one's mother. At the same time, there seems to be an experiential overlap, or commonality, between recognizing one's mother when *seeing* her and recognizing one's mother when *hearing* her. The experiential commonality is presumably due to an experiential property shared by the two experiences and corresponding to identification of one's mother. All this creates at least a presumption in favor of admitting an experiential character associated with identifying an object, a presumption I see no way to controvert.[21]

The second response is that pure tracking does exhibit intentional indifference, on the grounds that tracking relations are broadly causal relations, and causal attributions are themselves intensional (see Dretske 1980). If Smith dies after eating a poisoned fish in Cardiff's westernmost pub, it may be true that Smith's death was caused by eating a poisoned fish but false that it was caused by eating in Cardiff's westernmost pub, even though the culinary event is one and the same.[22] By the same token, the thought goes, it may be true that one of Tassandra's visual experiences was caused by Phosphorus but false that it was caused by Hesperus, even though the planetary object is one and the same. It then becomes plausible, given the causal basis of tracking, that "this experience tracks Phosphorus" could be true even when "this experience tracks Hesperus" is false. If so, conscious experiences exhibit intentional indifference purely in virtue of their broadly causal relations to the external world, which underlie tracking.

This approach is quite ingenuous at first glance, but does not withstand scrutiny either. What calls for scrutiny here are the interrelations among (a) causal relations, (b) linguistic attributions of causal relations, and (c) thoughts about causal relations. The question is where in all this the intensional phenomenon appears originally. This question leads to a trilemma argument against the suggestion.

The first option is to claim that causal relations themselves are "intensional relations." On this view, it is possible for x to cause (or be caused by) y but not z even where $y = z$, and it is because this is possible that causal attributions in thought and language are intensional. This seems incredible. The only way it could be the case, it seems to me, is if there were something deeply observer-dependent about causal relations. Only then could causal relations obtain between two entities under one description but not under another. Now, there are certainly irrealist views of causation that cast it as observer-dependent (e.g., Menzies and Price 1998). However, if causal relations are "intensional relations" in virtue of being observer-dependent, one must wonder what it is about the observer, or the observing, that bestows the intensionality on the relations. One naturally imagines it has something to do with thoughts about causation exhibiting intentional indifference. But this means that the story about causal relations being "intensional" cannot be used to account for the intentional indifference exhibited by thoughts, on pain of circularity.[23]

The second option is that intensionality occurs originally in linguistic attributions of causal relations. Antecedently, it is not particularly plausible to ground the intensionality of all intentionality in the properties of inked or mouthed physical marks, but the implausibility is specially acute against the background of the experiential origin thesis argued for in Chapter 1. For this reason, I will disregard this option as unviable in light of what has already been argued for in this book.

The third and most plausible option is that it is because thoughts about causal relations exhibit intentional indifference that (i) causal relations are "intensional" and (ii) linguistic causal attributions are intensional. But as already noted, this could not be used by anyone who hopes to use the "intensionality" of causal and tracking relations to account for the intentional indifference of mental states. It casts intentional indifference as occurring originally in thought. I conclude that the intensionality of causal attributions cannot help tracking accounts of experiential intentionality accommodate the intentional indifference exhibited by exp-intentional states.

It remains to explain the fact that "Smith's death was caused by eating a poisoned fish" is true but "Smith's death was caused by eating in Cardiff's westernmost pub" is false. There seem to be two possible explanations for this. One is that the corresponding *thoughts* exhibit intentional indifference, and the sentences somehow inherit this intentional indifference from them. The other is that the sentences do not exhibit intentional indifference at all, because "Smith's eating a poisoned fish" and "Smith's eating in Cardiff's westernmost pub" are actually *not* co-referential: they pick out distinct events or facts, albeit spatiotemporally coincident ones.[24]

The third response to the argument from intentional indifference is to deny that Tassandra's Phosphorus and Hesperus experiences track the same entities (are type-identical trackers), on the grounds that they track different *appearance properties* of Venus. The key idea here is that although Phosphorus and Hesperus are one and the same object, and although the property of being Phosphorus and the property of being Hesperus are one and the same property, the property of appearing-to-be-Phosphorus and the property of appearing-to-be-Hesperus are numerically distinct. If so, then although it is impossible to track Phosphorus without tracking Hesperus, or to track the property of being Phosphorus without tracking the property of being Hesperus, it is very much possible to track the property of appearing-to-be-Phosphorus without tracking the property of appearing-to-be-Hesperus. In arguing above that pure tracking cannot account for intentional indifference, I wrote "there is no pair of properties of Venus, F and G, such that Tassandra's Phosphorescent experience tracks F but not G and/or her Hesperescent experience tracks G but not F." This claim is denied here: the properties of appearing-to-be-Phosphorus and appearing-to-be-Hesperus are such that the Phosphorescent experience tracks the former but not the latter and the Hesperescent one the latter but not the former.

I think this response has quite a bit of merit to it, but it does come with a cost. To appreciate the cost, let me develop the response somewhat. Full development of the suggestion would probably deserve its own volume, but a limited discussion may be helpful.

There are various ways to construe appearance properties (see Egan 2006). My own is to construe them as *response-dependent* properties (Kriegel 2008b, 2009 Ch.3). These are properties defined in terms of the eliciting of certain responses in certain respondents. More precisely, a property F is response-dependent just in case for any x, it is a priori that x is F iff there is a type of response R, a type of subject S, and a type of circumstance C, such that x is such as to elicit R in S under C (Johnston 1989).[25] Thus in specifying an appearance property, one must specify the relevant kinds of response, subject, and circumstance, for there are as many appearance properties as there are combinations of those.

To obtain the result that appearing-to-be-Phosphorus and appearing-to-be-Hesperus are different properties, we must find combinations of values for R, S, and C for them that differ. I propose that we focus on normal conditions (for C), subjects in a predicament relevantly similar to Tassandra's (for S), and whatever distinct internal states occur in these subjects when they are aware, respectively, of Phosphorus and of Hesperus (for R).[26] While the conditions and subjects are certainly the same here, the responses might be different. Plausibly, there are some (distinct) responses R_1 and R_2, such that Venus is such as to elicit R_1 in Tassandra when she knowingly looks at Phosphorus but not when she knowingly looks at Hesperus and elicit R_2 in her when she knowingly looks at Hesperus but not Phosphorus.[27] The result is that the property of appearing-to-be-Phosphorus-to-the-relevantly-ignorant-subject-in-normal-conditions and the property of appearing-to-be-Hesperus-to-the-relevantly-ignorant-subject-in-normal-conditions are different properties.[28] If Tassandra's Phosphorescent experience tracks the former and her Hesperescent experience tracks the latter, then her experiences can have different exp-intentional contents purely in virtue of what they track.[29]

There are some challenges for this approach, to be sure. In particular, a characterization is needed of the responses the eliciting of which is constitutive of the relevant appearance properties, a characterization that is at once non-circular and plugs into an overall account that returns the right results in a wide range of cases; I offer my own characterization in Kriegel 2009 Ch.3.[30] In addition, Egan (2006) has argued convincingly that there are important advantages to appealing, in contexts such as this, not to response-dependent properties but to what he calls *centering features*, which are universals associated with a function from *centered* worlds to extensions.[31] This need not matter for present purposes: even if Tassandra's experiences track different centering features, rather than different response-dependent properties, we still have here the makings of a *prima facie* viable response to the argument from intentional indifference.

Once first-order tracking is shown to accommodate intentional indifference, higher-order tracking does so as well. It may be that Tassandra's Phosphorescent experience is (higher-order) tracked to track to the property of appearing-to-be-Phosphorus, while her Hesperescent experience is (higher-order) tracked to track the property of appearing-to-be-Hesperus. To make this transparent, we might modify (HOTT) so as to advert explicitly to response-dependent properties (or centering features). Thus:

(HOTT*) Necessarily*, there is a tracking relation T, such that for any mental state x and property F, F figures in x's exp-intentional content iff (i) F is response-dependent and (ii) there is a suitable mental state y, such that y bears T to x's bearing T to F.[32]

Strictly speaking, (i) is redundant, as it is guaranteed by (ii) if the present response to the argument from intentional indifference is correct. Adding (i) is thus just an expository device. We can employ the same device with the "naturalized self-tracking" version of (HOTT):

(NSTA*) Necessarily*, there is a tracking relation T and a representation-transmission relation R, such that for any mental state x and property F, F figures in x's exp-intentional content iff there are states x_1 and x_2, such that (i) x_1 is a proper part of x, (ii) x_2 is a proper part of x, (iii) F is response-dependent, (iv) x_1 bears T to x_2's bearing T to F, and (v) x_2 bears R to x.[33]

In these formulations, I focus on response-dependent properties for illustrative purposes, but we could of course formulate corresponding theses that advert instead to Egan's centering features.

Some care is needed in describing this as an *accommodation* of intentional indifference. Strictly speaking, what is suggested here is that, contrary to initial appearances, conscious experiences do not exhibit intentional indifference: when their exp-intentional contents are different, the entities they are intentionally directed at are different as well. It is just that the entities exp-intentional states are directed at are of a very specific kind (response-dependent properties or centering features), and we should be careful to specify correctly what figures in exp-intentional content.[34] However, the phenomena that lead to the characterization of exp-intentional states as exhibiting intentional indifference are accounted for. It is only in this sense that the proposal "accommodates" intentional difference.

In any case, this response to the argument from intentional indifference is to recognize that only appearance properties can be constituents of exp-intentional content.[35] Once this is accepted, we can appreciate that exp-intentional states do not actually exhibit intentional indifference. Clearly, this response to the argument from intentional indifference is quite radical and would require much more development and examination.[36] I leave the discussion here, because it seems to me that the phenomenon of intentional *inexistence* is ultimately more troubling for tracking-based accounts of experiential intentionality. This is the topic of the next section.

3.2.3. Brains in Vats

Before moving to the next section, however, let me close with some remarks concerning brain-in-vat scenarios. In discussing the argument from intentional indifference against tracking accounts of experiential intentionality, I presented a pair of conscious experiences that seemed to have different exp-intentional contents but track the same aspect of the world. Thompson (2010) develops two thought-experiments that present the converse situation: a pair of conscious experiences with the same exp-intentional content that track different features of the environment.[37] One involves Doubled Earth, an earth just like ours but everywhere doubled in size. Perceptual experiences of the Meter in Paris and in Doubled Paris are experientially indistinguishable but the former track the property of being one meter long whereas the latter that of being two meters long. The second thought-experiment involves El Greco World, a world where everything is stretched, somewhat in the manner of objects in El Greco's paintings, but where visual processing is different from actual-world processing in a way that cancels out the stretch, with the result that perceptual phenomenology is exactly the same as in the actual world.[38] Here too, the two experiences have the same exp-intentional content but track different properties.[39]

Thompson's thought-experiments provide particularly realistic scenarios that present a situation crucially similar to the one presented by brain-in-vat thought-experiments. An envatted brain can be made to have conscious experiences with the same experiential character as yours but tracking entirely different environmental features. Moreover, the relevant experiential character carries with it accuracy conditions. This presents the same difficulty for tracking accounts of experiential intentionality, as Horgan et al. (2004) argue. The brain-in-vat scenario is less realistic than the El Greco scenario, but it is clearly nomologically possible—everything we know about the laws of neuropsychology suggests that a lifelong envatted brain with the same sensory-stimulation history as my brain's would undergo the same experiential life as mine.[40] Regardless of which scenario we prefer, this kind of case—the converse of the one involving intentional indifference—presents a problem for tracking accounts of experiential intentionality. Furthermore, the problem spreads to higher-order tracking theories by the same reasoning we encountered in developing the argument from intentional indifference.

However, this new problem succumbs to the same solution as its converse. My experiences and my lifelong envatted duplicate's track the same *appearance properties*—construed as either centering features or response-dependent properties. When my duplicate and I both have an experience as of a yellow butterfly, the property of being disposed to elicit sensory stimulation characteristic of a yellow butterfly (say) is presented in both experiences. Likewise, experientially indistinguishable perceptual experiences on earth and on Doubled Earth, or in the actual world and El Greco World, track dispositions to elicit the same sensory stimulation.[41]

3.3. The Argument from Intentional Inexistence

The phenomenon of intentional inexistence, too, can be the basis of an argument against first-and higher-order tracking accounts of intentionality. The argument will have the same structure as the argument from intentional indifference: a conscious experience is presented that exhibits intentional inexistence, and tracking-based accounts are shown to be incapable of accommodating this feature. As before, I will proceed by showing first that first-order tracking cannot accommodate intentional inexistence, then that if so higher-order tracking cannot either. The argument is presented in §3.3.1, with possible responses considered in §3.3.2.

3.3.1. The Argument

Discussions of intentional inexistence typically focus on cases of intentional directedness toward non-existent *objects*—or rather, putative objects that do not exist—such as Santa Claus or Bigfoot.[42] So far I have discussed exp-intentional content purely in terms of the *properties* that figure in it, skirting the difficult question of whether *particulars* figure in it as well. For now, I wish to continue doing so; I will discuss intentional directedness at particulars in §3.5. At present, I focus on cases of intentional directedness toward non-existent *properties*—or rather, putative properties that do not exist—instead of non-existent *objects*. Note well: by "non-existent property," I do not mean just an *uninstantiated* property. Rather, what I mean are putative properties that we have no reason to make ontological commitment to—putative properties that never make it into our ontology.[43] What would qualify as such a putative property depends on one's views on the ontology of properties. But on virtually every view of properties, there are such properties, and they are experienceable.

This is clearest with sparse ontologies of properties. Lewis (1983), for example, argues that only properties instantiated by particulars at the fundamental level of reality exist (spin, charm, etc.). If this is right, then a conscious experience as of something being a butterfly exhibits intentional inexistence, since its content features a non-existent property (a putative property that does not exist), the property of being a butterfly. A more lenient but still sparse ontology admits properties from non-fundamental levels of reality, but requires that they be instantiated in the actual world (Armstrong 1978 Ch.13, Schaffer 2004). If we adopt this view of properties, then a perceptual experience as of a dragon, and a cognitive experience (a conscious thought) as of phlogiston, exhibit intentional inexistence.

Even latitudinarian ontologies of properties likely concede that some putative properties do not exist. For example, *logically-necessarily uninstantiated* properties—properties that no logically possible particular can instantiate—are unlikely to be countenanced. Thus, the notion that there exists a property of being a square circle seems scandalous. Now, for the putative property of being a square circle, it may be plausible to deny the possibility of a corresponding perceptual experience (though it is a more interesting question whether the same could be said of a corresponding *cognitive* experience). However, for other necessarily uninstantiated (putative) properties, such as the putative property of being an Escher triangle, the same cannot plausibly be said: it certainly seems we can have experiences—both perceptual and cognitive—as of Escher triangles.[44]

For this reason, I will focus below on such an experience. To neutralize a number of possible distracting features, I am going to focus on the following case. Suppose Emorie undergoes an hallucination as of an Escher triangle. Consider a world in which there happens to be a lifelong brain in a vat who is an accidental lifelong experiential duplicate of Emorie.[45] This brain, Twin-Emorie, undergoes a conscious experience that is experientially indistinguishable from Emorie's Escher-triangle hallucination. Here are two claims about Twin-Emorie's experience: (1) The putative property of being an Escher triangle figures in its exp-intentional content; (2) The putative property of being an Escher triangle is *not* tracked by it. The first would establish that exp-intentional content exhibits intentional inexistence, the second that tracking accounts of experiential intentionality cannot accommodate intentional inexistence. It would follow that tracking accounts of experiential intentionality cannot account for a feature exhibited by exp-intentional content.

The case for (1) should be familiar by now. Twin-Emorie's experience has an Escher-triangle-ish experiential character, and seems assessable for accuracy in virtue of it. So part of the accuracy conditions, hence content, of Twin-Emorie's experience has to do with the putative property of being an Escher triangle. Since this aspect of its content the experience has in virtue of its experiential character, this is an aspect of its exp-intentional content.[46]

The case for (2)—the claim that Twin-Emorie's experience does not track the putative property of being an Escher triangle—is also relatively straightforward. A standard tracking account of experiential intentionality, of the sort discussed in §2.1, would account for Twin-Emorie's experience's content in terms of the experience bearing the right tracking relation T to the putative property of being an Escher triangle. But there are at least five reasons Twin-Emorie's experience could not bear T to being an Escher triangle. These form a dilemma, with the first reason handling one horn and the rest handling the other.

The first reason is simply that, as noted, there is probably no such property as being an Escher triangle (just as there is no such property as being a square triangle). If there is no property of being an Escher triangle, then it is impossible to bear any relation to it, tracking or other. It is sometimes claimed that there is a class of special relations, "intentional relations," that do not require the existence of the relata. Strictly speaking, however, this is nonsense. The only way it could make sense is if a two-place relation could be instantiated even when there are not two relata. Yet nobody thinks it remotely plausible that a *monadic* property could be instantiated even when there is no entity that instantiates it, e.g., that squareness could be instantiated even if there are no squares. That is clearly absurd. The same absurdity attaches, I contend, to the parallel claim about relations: just as a monadic property cannot be instantiated in the absence of an instantiator, so a relation (including the "x tracks y" relation) cannot be instantiated in the absence of relata.[47]

Secondly, although ontological commitment to logically-necessarily uninstantiated properties ("incoherent properties," if you will) is unwholesome, in a way what I find most objectionable about it is not so much the commitment itself, as the notion that such a commitment should be incurred in the context of accounting for the facts of conscious experience. The only properties we should have to admit into our ontology to account for the facts of conscious experience are *mental* properties. It is strange to expect non-mental entities, such as of being a certain triangle, to enter our ontology because—and only because!—certain conscious experiences are possible.

Thirdly, and relatedly, I find it hard to believe, more generally, that the facts of concrete conscious experience require us to posit abstract entities we might otherwise not need to posit.[48] This is probably grounded in a more general suspicion of the tendency to adduce abstract entities in the context of accounting for phenomena entirely internal to the realm of concreta (or in the context of solving metaphysical problems that arise entirely within that realm).[49] This vague sentiment may be captured more precisely by a certain principle of the *explanatory closure of the realm of concreta*. To a first approximation, the principle is this: every aspect of the realm of concreta can be fully explained exclusively by appeal to what goes on inside the realm of concreta. On the assumption that concreta are characterized by their spatio-temporal existence (by their existing within space-time), the principle might be put more precisely as follows: every spatio-temporal fact can be fully explained by spatio-temporal facts.[50] The kind of explanation at issue here is not—at least not in the first instance—*causal* explanation; rather it is something like *constitutive* explanation (the kind of explanation offered in philosophy rather than in science).[51] This principle of the (constitutive-)explanatory closure of the spatio-temporal realm is perhaps not as antecedently plausible as the celebrated principle of the (causal-)explanatory closure of the physical realm, but it is really only a pair of tweaks removed from that principle: it changes the domain from the physical realm to the concrete/spatio-temporal realm, and it covers primarily constitutive rather than causal explanation. These changes should not result in a major loss of plausibility.

(It might be objected that these changes do result in a meaningful loss of plausibility. In particular, the switch to constitutive explanation makes a big difference. For example, it puts the principle in tension with Armstrong's

(1978) celebrated argument for positing universals. According to Armstrong, universals are needed to explain similarities between concrete particulars—where the explanation in question is constitutive rather than causal. The similar particulars are concreta, but the universals are abstracta. So the argument, although apparently cogent, appears to violate the principle of the (constitutive-)explanatory closure of the realm of concreta. However, Armstrong's argument is intended to establish only the existence of universals *in re*, which exist in the concrete things that instantiate them and are thus spatio-temporal in the relevant sense. To that extent, Armstrong's universals are part of the realm of concreta in the sense relevant to the principle. In fact, this may well be (partly?) why Armstrong does *not* countenance the existence of *uninstantiated* properties: uninstantiated properties would have to exist "outside" space-time, since they cannot exist *in re*, and no justification can be found within the realm of space-time (the realm of concreta) for positing something "outside" that realm.)

Fourthly, if someone decided to be so latitudinarian as to admit necessarily uninstantiated properties, they could at most admit one such, at least by the lights of the highly plausible principle that properties individuate in terms of functions they generate from possible worlds to extensions.[52] Since all necessarily uninstantiated properties generate the same function—namely, the function that assigns the null set to any possible world—it would follow that all necessarily uninstantiated properties are the same, or in other words, that there is only one necessarily uninstantiated property. That would mean that the property of being an Escher triangle and the property of being a square triangle would be one and the same. But then a tracking account would have no resources for distinguishing an experience as of an Escher triangle from any other experience as of an impossible figure, much less any resources for explaining why an experience as of an Escher triangle is possible but one as of a square triangle is not.[53,54] In any case, note that all necessarily uninstantiated properties are *ipso facto* necessarily co-extensive—and it is not clear how a property might be tracked without all the properties necessarily co-extensive therewith being also tracked.

Fifthly, even if the ontology of necessarily uninstantiated properties is set aside, it is highly doubtful that such (putative) properties could be tracked. Consider the teleo-informational take on tracking, as the relation of having-the-function-of-nomically-depending-upon, and recall that x nomically depends upon F just in case it is a matter of the laws of nature that x

cannot occur unless F is instantiated. Surely there are no laws of nature that govern the behavior of necessarily uninstantiated properties. Nature does not include laws that say that such-and-such events would take place if Escher triangles were present under such-and-such conditions. Therefore, there is no law of nature according to which certain experiences can occur only if the property of being an Escher triangle is instantiated. That means that the property of being an Escher triangle is untrackable by the lights of the teleo-informational gloss on tracking. Similar results are sure to apply to other glosses.

The discussion has focused thus far on *pure* tracking, but the point applies to *impure* tracking as well. Recall that according to the impure tracking account of experiential intentionality, there is a tracking relation T and a "manner" M, such that any exp-intentional state has its exp-intentional content in virtue of bearing T in M to something. However, Twin-Emorie's Escher-triangle-ish experience has an exp-intentional content, but does not bear T to anything, in M or otherwise.

This concludes the case for saying that some exp-intentional states exhibit intentional inexistence and that this intentional inexistence cannot be accommodated by the tracking account of experiential intentionality. I now turn to argue for the following conditional: if the tracking account cannot accommodate intentional inexistence, neither can the higher-order tracking theory. The argument is this. The basic idea behind the reasoning thus far is that when a putative property F is necessarily uninstantiated, then it is impossible to bear a tracking relation to F. But if it is impossible to bear a tracking relation to F, then the putative property of being an F-tracker is necessarily uninstantiated as well. If so, it is impossible to bear a tracking relation to the putative property of being an F-tracker. Thus there can be no higher-order tracking of trackers of impossible objects. As before, if the tracking account of experiential intentionality cannot accommodate intentional inexistence, neither can higher-order tracking theory.

It may be thought that since tracking theorists of mental representation have been keen to accommodate the possibility of misrepresentation, they must have *some* story or other about intentional inexistence. However, intentional inexistence involves a particularly acute kind of misrepresentation, and we can readily see that stories such as Dretske's and Fodor's do not have the resources to accommodate Twin-Emorie's experience.[55] Dretske's (1986) story is that misrepresentation of F occurs when an internal state fails to fulfill its function of nomically depending upon F and instead is triggered by (or in the presence of) an instance of G. However, Twin-Emorie's Escher triangle experience is not at all an internal state whose function is to nomically depend on Escher triangles but instead is caused by a state of the stimulating machine. Depending on one's view of functions, it rather has either the function of nomically depending on states of the machine or no function at all. Likewise, Fodor's (1990 Ch.3) story is that misrepresentation of F occurs when a token internal state is caused by a G but the G's causing it is asymmetrically dependent upon Fs causing other tokens of the same internal-state type. However, Twin-Emorie's Escher triangle experience does *not* asymmetrically depend upon Escher triangles causing this type of experience. Similar remarks apply to other accounts in the same vein.[56] It would seem, then, that standard discussions of the problem of misrepresentation within the tracking theory literature do not really address the problem of intentional inexistence.

This concludes my presentation of the argument that neither first- nor higher-order tracking can accommodate intentional inexistence. Call it the *argument from intentional inexistence*.

3.3.2. Responses

There are two ways to object to the argument from intentional inexistence: deny that Twin-Emorie's experience fails to track the putative property of being an Escher triangle, or deny that Twin-Emorie can really have an experience as of an Escher triangle. I presented five considerations against the former option, so will focus on the second one.[57]

Recall that the tracking-based accounts from the previous chapter have a peculiar modal force, which I called "necessarily★." This requires that the right kind of (first- or higher-order) tracking be necessary for experiential intentionality contingently, or perhaps with nomological necessity. It does not require that such tracking be necessary for experiential intentionality in every *metaphysically* possible world. So the objector only needs to show that it is *nomologically* impossible for Twin-Emorie (or anybody else) to have an experience as of an Escher triangle.[58] The problem for the objector is that it is not clear why that would be. Twin-Emorie's experience is certainly conceivable, which provides defeasible evidence for its metaphysical possibility. Moreover, however, the conceiving of it does not involve supposing that certain laws of nature do not obtain, or that non-actual laws (or unlawful activity) do obtain, so the conceiving provides defeasible evidence for the experience's *nomological* possibility as well.

To deny the experience's nomological possibility, the objector would have to proffer actual defeaters of this defeasible evidence. These would be either *undercutting* defeaters, suggesting that the conceivability of Twin-Emorie's experience does not support its nomological possibility after all, or *rebutting* defeaters, suggesting that there is counter-evidence against the nomological possibility of Twin-Emorie's experience that outweighs the evidence provided by the experience's conceivability.[59]

The most brazen version of the undercutting-defeater response would be to deny that conceivability can ever provide any evidence for possibility. This is not the place to delve overdeep into modal epistemology, but this strikes me as a non-starter. Arguably, conceivability is just apparent possibility, at least in one sense of "apparent": to say that S conceives p is to say that p appears possible to S.[60] To say that Twin-Emorie's experience is conceivable is therefore to say that the experience appears possible. And to say that the experience can be conceived without envisaging different laws of nature is to say that the experience appears to be possible consistently with the laws of nature, that is, appears nomologically possible. Now, in the relevant sense of "appears," in general appearance is evidence of reality: it appearing that p provides *prima facie*, defeasible evidence for it being p.[61] So this sweeping version of the undercutting-defeater response is unpromising.

A more sensible version would hold that although conceivability is sometimes evidence of possibility, it must first meet certain conditions. In particular, while *ideal* conceivability does provide evidence for possibility, *superficial* conceivability does not.[62] The objector could then maintain that Twin-Emorie's experience is perhaps superficially conceivable, in that a fleeting act of contemplating it does not expose any overt incoherence in the notion of having it, but it is not *ideally* conceivable, in that careful examination of what having it is supposed to involve brings to light more subtle incoherencies.[63] This examination would effectively undercut, and thus defeat, the evidence for the experience's possibility.

One thought along these lines might be that careful phenomenological examination reveals that we never really have a visual experience as of an entire Escher triangle. We can visually trace the triangle along its sides, from angle to angle, and in the process undergo experiences as of individual angles and sides. But we never experience the entire triangle at once. The properties of having those sides and angles, however, are not at all necessarily uninstantiated. In fact, they are *actually* instantiated—and are thus trackable.

There are three problems with this response, however. First, it creates the following dilemma: either (a) it is impossible to experience all triangles in their entirety (every triangle is such that we only experience its different angles and sides in succession), or (b) it is possible to experience certain triangles in their entirety but not Escher triangles. If (a), then a regular triangle, say a Yield sign in the American system of traffic signs, cannot be experienced in its entirety. This is phenomenologically hard to swallow. If (b), the objector owes us an explanation of why it should be that certain triangles can be experienced as a whole but others cannot.[64] Moreover, if the suggestion were right, there would have to be deep phenomenological dissimilarity between experiencing a Yield sign and experiencing an Escher Yield (if you will)—the former would have to feature a spatial phenomenal unity that the latter would not. Yet there seems to me to be no deep dissimilarity of this sort when I imagine first a Yield sign and then an Escher Yield.

Secondly, for this response to work across the board, it would have to apply not only to *perceptual* experiences of Escher triangles, but also to *cognitive* experiences of them. That is, it would have to be claimed that consciously thinking of an Escher triangle is impossible—an extraordinary claim.[65] As long as we accept the existence of cognitive experiences, and recognize that they have an intentional content in virtue of being the experiences they are, it is hard to see how we could deny the existence of mental states with an Escher-triangle-ish cognitive-experiential character that have an appropriate intentional content there-in-virtue.

Thirdly, the claim that the conceivability here is merely superficial, even if it has some traction vis-à-vis experiences as of *logically*-necessarily uninstantiated properties, has none when it comes to experiences as of *nomologically*-necessarily uninstantiated properties or even merely-*actually* uninstantiated properties. For example, there are certain so-called chimerical colors that we can experience but which are nomologically impossible (Churchland 2005).[66] The ideal conceivability of such experiences is hardly deniable, given their actuality. Yet the case against their amenability to a tracking-based accommodation is extremely strong. In the previous subsection, I presented five problems for tracking of *logically*-necessarily uninstantiated properties; most apply with equal force to the tracking of *nomologically*-necessarily uninstantiated properties, as I will now try to show.

The first problem pertained to the very existence of logically-necessarily uninstantiated properties, ontological commitment to which seems outrageous. This problem is admittedly considerably less acute for nomologically-necessarily uninstantiated properties. As noted already, some philosophers deny the existence of any uninstantiated properties (Armstrong 1978). But surely many more philosophers would find ontological commitment to such putative properties much more palatable than to "incoherent properties." However, the other problems are still pressing.

The second problem had to do with the oddity of positing abstracta in the context of accounting for the fact that certain hallucinations are possible. This problem would apply to any posit that must be construed as abstract in the relevant sense, namely, the sense of being a-spatial. Any such posit would be odd when introduced to account for the facts of concrete experience. Now, nomologically impossible properties, and in fact to all actually uninstantiated properties, must be construed as abstract in the relevant sense. Instantiated properties, construed either as tropes/individual accidents or as universals *in re*, exist within space-time, and are to that extent part of the realm of concreta.[67] But uninstantiated properties can be construed neither as tropes nor as universals *in re*—they must be construed as Platonic universals, universals *ante rem*, which do not exist in space-time.

Relatedly, the third problem pertained to the principle of the explanatory closure of the realm of concreta, or the spatio-temporal realm. This problem applies to nomologically-necessarily and even actually uninstantiated properties, since as we have just seen they too must be construed as abstract. If the spatio-temporal realm is explanatorily closed, then no aspect of it should be explained by appeal to any universals *ante rem*. Thus we can generally say, along with Mackie (1975), that there is something offensive about appealing to uninstantiated properties in the context of explaining a pattern of instantiated properties. Yet this is precisely what the tracking-based accounts of experiential intentionality must do to accommodate intentional inexistence.[68,69]

To bring out the point, consider, if only for illustrative purposes, the view that some abstracta exist contingently, i.e., exist in some worlds and not others. Colyvan (2001) argues that Platonism in the philosophy of mathematics is true contingently, that is, that there are Platonic numbers in the actual world but in other possible worlds there are none. This is a somewhat strange view, but appears perfectly coherent.[70] A similar view could be formulated regarding (some) uninstantiated properties: they exist in some possible worlds but not others. For my part, I tend to think such a view implausible. But let us suppose it hypothetically, as an expository device. Under this supposition, positing uninstantiated properties to account for instantiated experiential properties would have the consequence that two spatio-temporally indistinguishable worlds could be distinct in terms of the experiences taking place in them, because in one of them the right abstract entity exists and in the other it does not. That is, it is a consequence that experiential properties do not supervene on spatio-temporal properties. For the addition or removal of certain abstracta would bring in its train the addition or removal of conscious experiences, even without any direct intervention in the lives of conscious creatures. This is because what hallucinations a conscious creature can undergo depends partly on what abstracta happen to exist in her world. In a way, it is sheer luck that we can have conscious experiences as of dragons—we are lucky to live in a world where the uninstantiated property of being a dragon exists. Parachuted into another possible world, indistinguishable from the actual one as far as space-time is concerned but lacking some of the actual world's abstracta, including the property of being a dragon, we would lose our capacity to visualize dragons. This strikes me as absurd, and absurd in a way that is not fully inherited from the absurdity of contingent abstracta. There is added absurdity that flows directly from the outlook that makes concrete conscious experiences constitutively dependent upon abstracta.

The fourth problem pertained to the individuation of logically-necessarily uninstantiated properties, which seems to lead to the view that there is at most one such. This problem, too, appears to be blunted when we move to nomologically-necessarily uninstantiated properties. Some dispositional essentialists, who maintain that properties individuate by their nomic causal powers (e.g., Bird 2007), might claim that there could be only one nomologically-necessarily uninstantiated property as well.[71] But of course, many philosophers reject dispositional essentialism, allowing properties to individuate in terms of underlying "quiddities," and for them individuation of nomologically-necessarily uninstantiated properties would be straightforward.

The fifth problem pertained to the untrackability of logically-necessarily uninstantiated properties, due to the lack of natural laws governing them. This problem may not apply to merely-actually uninstantiated properties, but it does to nomologically-necessarily uninstantiated ones. For certainly there are no laws of nature governing such (putative) properties, so they would be untrackable by Dretskean and Fodorian lights (which involves laws of nature in the account of tracking). Thus, there is no law of nature dictating that chimerical-color-ish experiences do not occur unless the chimerical color properties are instantiated.[72]

It might be objected that even though existing accounts of the tracking relation problematically rule out the tracking of nomologically-necessarily uninstantiated properties, mindful of this issue one might devise a more permissive account of tracking that would rule *in* the tracking of such properties. The immediate rejoinder is to point out that no such account actually exists. But more deeply, there may be a reason to suspect that any account that would be permissive enough to allow the tracking of nomologically-necessarily uninstantiated properties would lose the main attraction of tracking-based accounts of intentionality, namely, their naturalistic credentials: their proclaimed capacity to make intelligible how something like intentionality can occur in the natural world. If nomologically-necessarily uninstantiated properties can be tracked, then tracking cannot be grounded in the laws of nature. It then becomes less clear how intentionality, even understood in terms of tracking, can be cast as part of the web of nature.[73] The naturalistic promise of tracking-based theories is lost, or at least jeopardized.

This leads me to the other possible response to the argument from intentional inexistence, appealing to rebutting rather than undercutting defeaters. Here the strategy is to grant that the case of Twin-Emorie's experience provides evidence for the experience's nomological possibility, but insist that there is counter-evidence that overrides this evidence. The counter-evidence cannot be simply the truth of the tracking-based approach to experiential intentionality—that would beg the question. But it *can* be the truth of a certain doctrine of "philosophical naturalism," combined with the claim that there is no naturalistically kosher way to accommodate Twin-Emorie's experience. In fact, there may well be no naturalistically kosher way to accommodate any experience as of nomologically-necessarily uninstantiated properties (and perhaps none to accommodate any experience as of merely-actually uninstantiated properties). Consistently with the discussion above, tracking-based naturalization is unworkable. Plausibly, no other naturalization is more workable. If so, the plausibility of philosophical naturalism generates concordant counter-evidence against the possibility of relevantly recalcitrant experiences.

Pursuing this line of reasoning, proponents of tracking-based accounts of experiential intentionality, both first- and higher-order, might argue that although their account accrues certain liabilities, inasmuch as it must rule out as impossible (nomologically) certain conscious experiences that *appear* perfectly possible (nomologically), these liabilities are an inevitable cost of naturalizing experiential intentionality. Assessing this move would require addressing the question of how to weigh the costs and the benefits here— the costs of ruling out seemingly possible experiences and the benefits of naturalization. This is a complicated question with many methodological facets. How should we weigh bottom-up, pre-theoretic evidence against top-down, theoretically driven considerations? How much should we value naturalization? How exactly to analyze the notion of the natural, hence what to require for bonafide naturalization? Such questions call for their own focused treatment, so for now I will conclude simply by noting the dialectical state of affairs the above discussion seems to lead to, and postpone further discussion until the end of the chapter.

The dialectical state of affairs is this. On the one hand, the argument from intentional inexistence seems cogent, in that certain apparently (nomologically) possible exp-intentional states exhibit intentional inexistence but do not track anything relevant, nor are higher-order tracked to track anything relevant. There are certain putative properties that figure in their exp-intentional content but are not tracked by them, nor higher-order tracked to be tracked by them. On the other hand, it is open to proponents of first- and higher-order tracking accounts to simply deny the genuine (nomological) possibility of the relevant exp-intentional states, on the grounds that their possibility is inconsistent with the doctrine of naturalism. Such a denial certainly represents a liability for those accounts, but may or may not be deemed a worthwhile liability to accrue for the sake of naturalizing experiential intentionality.[74] This, it seems to me, is the dialectical state of affairs.

3.4. Experiential Intentionality as Adverbial Modification

The basic idea behind the argument from intentional inexistence is that exp-intentional content can feature putative entities which do not exist, and which therefore the exp-intentional state cannot bear a (first- or higher-order) tracking relation to. This is an argument against understanding experiential intentionality in terms of tracking relations. Interestingly, however, the argument generalizes to *all* relations. For any relation R, arguably it is impossible for R to hold between an experience and the putative property of being an Escher triangle, or any other putative entity that does not exist. For as noted in §3.3.1, it is nonsense to suppose that there are relations whose instantiation does not require the existence of all relata. Given this, the phenomenon of intentional inexistence suggests something quite a bit more radical than that exp-intentional states do not constitutively involve (first- or higher-order) tracking relations to what they are about. It suggests that exp-intentional states do not constitutively involve *any* relation to what they are about.[75] This is what I want to argue for in this section: that a feature F figuring in the exp-intentional content of a state x does not require x bearing a relation—any relation—to F.

Consider, for example, the view that experiential intentionality is a matter of bearing a relation to properties, not a tracking or any other naturalistically recognized relation however, but an irreducibly experiential relation of "experiential entertaining" (Chalmers 2004, Pautz 2010); call this view *primitivism*.[76] Primitivism does not deliver naturalization in the way tracking-based accounts do, and accordingly is not vulnerable to the worry associated with the fact that putative properties that do not exist cannot be tracked. However, it *is* vulnerable to the worry associated with the fact that putative properties that do not exist cannot be *relata*. The only way to assuage that worry is to insist that all experienceable putative properties exist, including necessarily uninstantiated putative properties—something I have already rejected. In addition, primitivism too violates the explanatory closure of the concrete, spatio-temporal realm.[77] Thus primitivism cannot accommodate intentional inexistence any more than tracking-based accounts can. *No* account that requires an experience to bear a relation to F in order for F to figure in its exp-intentional content can.

This way of putting things invites confusion, however. For the term "content" is ambiguous: it is used to refer sometimes to whatever it is that makes an intentional state the intentional state it is, but sometimes more specifically to an entity that an intentional state is related to. These two understandings are taken to go hand in hand.[78] But it is only the second that invites ontological talk, where a property might be said to be a "constituent of" a content, "figure in" a content, "enter" a content, or be "featured by" a content. The first understanding does not invite such talk. Yet it is this first understanding that plays the more minimal theoretical role of the notion of content in the theory of intentionality. On the view I will develop in this section, the two understandings come apart, because there is no entity intentional states are the intentional states they are in virtue of being related to. For this reason, here I will use the term "content" in its more minimal sense, to denote whatever makes an intentional state the intentional state it is.

In many ways, under these conditions it may be preferable to replace talk of intentional *content* with talk of intentional *types*. Instead of saying that a certain state has some intentional content, we would say that the state betokens some intentional type. Although this would be the theoretically better way to speak, for the sake of terminological continuity I will continue to speak of intentional contents. The reader should keep in mind, however, that talk of intentional contents is henceforth ellipsis for talk of intentional types. Correspondingly, speaking of (putative) properties "figuring in" content can no longer be understood to mean that those properties are constituents of a certain entity. It is to be understood as an elliptical way of describing the kind of intentional type an intentional state falls under. Thus, when I say that a putative property F figures in the intentional content of a state x, this is to be understood as ellipsis for saying that there is an F-ly intentional type that x betokens. What talk of an "F-ly intentional type" exactly means will emerge later. For now, consider that it is often remarked that the folk naturally describe the qualitative properties of their color experiences by elliptically using color terms, terms describing the properties of surfaces and volumes. We can understand "F-ly intentional type" as a generalization of that from the case of color experiences to the case of all intentional experiences.

Speaking in terms of intentional types, I would put as follows what I claim is the real lesson of the argument from intentional inexistence: when an experience falls under an F-ly exp-intentional type, it is not in virtue of standing in any relation to F that it does (the reason being that for some values of F, experiences fall under F-ly exp-intentional types even though the putative property F does not exist, hence cannot serve as a relatum). Speaking in terms of intentional content, the lesson would be put as follows: when an experience's exp-intentional content features F, it is not in virtue of standing in any relation to F that it does (because for some values of F, experiences' exp-intentional content feature F even though the putative property F does not exist). The first way of speaking is the more accurate; the second is better interpreted elliptically.

What kind of positive account can we give for experiential intentionality, if it involves no relation to what it is about? Elsewhere, I develop an *adverbial theory* of experiential intentionality that I take to be the only stable account consistent with this anti-relational idea (Kriegel 2007, 2008a).[79] According to this adverbial theory, having a conscious thought about chocolate, say, does not involve (constitutively) bearing a thinking-about relation to the property of being chocolate, but rather engaging in the activity of thinking in a certain *way*—chocolate-wise. Just as in "Omar is moving quietly" the adverb "quietly" denotes a modification of Omar's moving, and not a relation between Omar and quiet, so in "Omar is thinking chocolate-wise" the adverb "chocolate-wise" denotes a modification of Omar's thinking, not a relation between Omar and chocolate.[80] More generally, for any putative property F, for F to figure in the exp-intentional content of a state x is not for x to bear a relation of intentional directedness toward F; rather, it is for x to exhibit the property of intentional directedness F-wise.[81]

The question is what it means for a state to be intentionally directed F-wise. I will return to this momentarily. But first let us state more precisely the *adverbialist theory of experiential intentionality*:

(ATEI) Necessarily★, for any mental state x and putative property F, there is an experiential property E, E = being-intentionally-directed-F-wise, such that F figures in x's exp-intentional content iff x is E.

Here the adverbialist thesis is stated in terms of intentional *content*. The formulation in terms of intentional types would be this:

(ATEI★) Necessarily★, for any mental state x and exp-intentional type I, there is an experiential property E, E = being-intentionally-directed-I-wise, such that x betokens I iff x is E.[82]

Although the "type"-based (ATEI★) is in many ways the superior formulation, I will discuss adverbialism primarily in terms of the "content"-based (ATEI), which I will take to be just an elliptical way of saying the same thing as (ATEI★).

Note that in the content formulation, F figuring in the content of x is accounted for in terms of x being directed F-wise. This requires us to have an independent grasp of what property being directed F-wise is. We cannot explicate F-wise directedness in terms of the putative property F, if for no other reason than that doing so would violate the principle of the explanatory closure of the concrete realm. Nonetheless, we can draw an illuminating connection between F and F-wise directedness that could indirectly shed light on the latter. The connection is as follows: (a) whenever the state directed F-wise is veridical, it bears the appropriate relation to F; (b) whenever the state directed F-wise is *non*-veridical, a certain counterfactual is still true of it, namely, that if x *were* veridical, x *would* bear the appropriate relation to F.[83] Thus, when the property of being a dragon figures in the content of some experience, it must be the case that if the experience *were* veridical, it *would* bear the appropriate relation to being a dragon. The appropriate relation may be the primitive relation of experiential entertaining, a tracking relation, or whatever. Given the argument of the previous chapter, I would personally adopt a higher-order tracking gloss on the appropriate relation. The result is the following connection between bearing a directedness relation to F and being directed F-wise: (a) whenever the state directed F-wise is veridical, it is suitably tracked to track F; (b) whenever the state directed F-wise is non-veridical, it is still true of it that if it *were* veridical, it *would* be suitably tracked to track F. It is important to appreciate, however, that on the adverbialist view the truth of the counterfactual is not the *grounds* for the state's F-wise directedness. On the contrary, the *reason* the counterfactual is true is that the property of being directed F-wise has the nature it does.[84] In a way, the counterfactual ascribes a certain dispositional property to x, and the categorical basis of this dispositional property is the occurrent adverbial property of being intentionally directed F-wise. Nonetheless, the connection between the two serves to shed indirect light on the nature of F-wise directedness.

Similar remarks may be made regarding the connection between adverbial intentional talk and *aboutness* talk. A preliminary question, however, concerns how we hear the term "aboutness" when it comes to imagination, hallucination, etc. When I hallucinate a dragon, is my hallucination *about* a dragon? There is a way of hearing "about" in which it is, and another way in which the experience is rather about nothing. In the former hearing, an exp-intentional state is about F iff it is directed F-wise, and therefore (a) whenever the state that is about F is veridical, it bears the appropriate relation to F, and (b) whenever the state that is about F is non-veridical, a certain counterfactual is still true of it, namely, that if it *were* veridical, it *would* bear the appropriate relation to F. In the second hearing of "about," the connection between adverbial talk and aboutness talk is rather like the connection between adverbial talk and relational intentional talk: (a) whenever the state directed F-wise is veridical, it is about F, and (b) whenever the state directed F-wise is non-veridical, it is still true of it that if it *were* veridical, it *would* be about F.[85] In any case, as before these conjunctions should not be taken as an *account*, or *explication*, of F-wise directedness in terms of F-aboutness. The order of (constitutive) explanation is opposite: within the adverbialist framework, we understand aboutness talk in terms of adverbial talk. The above conjunctions serve to illuminate F-wise directedness only indirectly, by mapping out its conceptual connections to neighboring notions in the theory of intentionality.

The question that remains open, then, is how to understand the notion of being intentionally directed F-wise independently of its connections to other notions we understand in terms of it. What does it mean for my current visual experience to be intentionally directed laptop-wise, or for my current thought to be intentionally directed dragon-wise? Without an answer to this question, the very *intelligibility* of the view is in question. The first thing to note, however, is that experiential properties are amenable to grasping simply by ostension though something like direct introspective encounter. So given that the relevant adverbial properties are experiential, they may be grasped in this way. And indeed, when I reflect on why adverbialism seems *to me* perfectly intelligible, and how *I* get a sense of grasping the property of being directed dragon-wise, it seems to me that it is simply introspective encounter with the property that affords me this grasp.[86] By this I do not mean that introspection instructs me of the adverbial nature of exp-intentional properties; merely that it instructs me of what are in fact adverbial exp-intentional properties. Thus, just now I stopped writing and visualized a smallish (about a foot long) green dragon hovering motionless about a yard away from me directly in front of my eyes. When I attended introspectively to this visualizing experience, I encountered a certain property of the experience, a property we have theoretical reasons for construing as visualizing smallish-green-hovering-dragon-wise.[87] This property is a determinate (or species) of the determinable (or genus) property of being directed dragon-wise. My sense of grasping the determinable (genus) is based on my sense of being able to grasp (m)any of its determinates (species). Moreover, my sense of grasping the property of being intentionally directed some*how*—the highest-genus intentional property, as construed by adverbialism—is likewise based on my sense of grasping *its* many species.

156 THE SOURCES OF INTENTIONALITY

Introspective encounter, then, offers us a grasp of adverbial intentional properties. But it does not advance a *theoretical* account of what they are. Such a theoretical account calls for phenomenological analysis, or description, of the property of being directed some*how*. This property is, in a sense, the phenomenological signature of intentionality: it is the generic feeling of directing the mind onto something, a feeling of aboutness, if you will, that is present in all and only exp-intentional states. To elucidate the key notion of being intentionally directed somehow, we must therefore examine the nature of this phenomenological signature of intentionality, this generic felt aboutness. I now turn to consider four phenomenological accounts of it.[88]

One view about this feeling of aboutness—a view which seems to be suggested by Loar (2003)—is that it is a sort of *sui generis* phenomenal feature, a feature that cannot be explained in terms of any other, simpler type of experience. On this view, there is a *sui generis phenomenal directedness* that characterizes some mental states and not others, and when (and only when) a mental state exhibits this phenomenal directedness, it is endowed with experiential intentionality. There is a question as to whether *all*, or only *some*, conscious experiences are exp-intentional, but that question is orthogonal to the view under consideration. If all conscious experiences are exp-intentional, the view would have to be that all conscious experiences exhibit the *sui generis* phenomenal directedness. If only some are, the view would be that only those do.[89]

This is an intriguing view, but it has the disadvantage of being relatively uninformative, in the way all appeals to the *sui generis* are. A somewhat more informative suggestion might be culled from Strawson (2008). In the course of criticizing tracking accounts of intentionality, Strawson claims that tracking is indeterminate between different links in the causal chain leading up to the intentional state. For example, a laptop experience tracks not only the presence of a laptop, according to him, but also the presence of laptop-distinctive imprint on one's sensorium, standard causes of laptop presence, etc.[90] Strawson claims, on this basis, that tracking accounts cannot produce determinate content for conscious experiences. Yet conscious experiences do have determinate (exp-intentional) content. What gives them this determinate content, he suggests, is a certain aspect of their experiential character, an aspect he calls *taking*. There is a subtle experiential feature, cognitive rather than sensory in nature, whereby a conscious experience *takes* something to be thus-and-so.[91] My laptop experience involves an experiential element of *taking something to be a laptop*. More generally, every exp-intentional state has an experiential character that involves this *experiential taking* (if you will) as a component, and it is in virtue of this experiential-taking component that the state is intentionally directed some*how*.[92]

A fuller account of the nature of experiential taking would clearly be helpful, if what we want is an informative account of the property of being experientially directed somehow. Another, still more informative suggestion is due to Masrour (2008 Ch.2), who claims that it is only when a conscious experience exhibits an experiential feature he calls *objectual unity structure* that it becomes intentionally directed.[93] Two experiential items are objectually unified in a perceptual experience, according to Masrour, just in case the experience presents them as belonging to the same object. Consider R.C. James' Dalmatian (Figure 3.1). Upon first looking at the picture, normal subjects only experience an array of unrelated black spots against a white background. This initial experience, according to Masrour, is non-intentional. But after staring at the picture for a while and/or hearing instructions as to where to find the Dalmatian therein, subjects typically undergo an experiential Gestalt shift and see the Dalmatian. That is, they

FIGURE 3.1. R.C. James' Dalmatian.

come to enjoy a visual experience as of a Dalmatian. The way this occurs, phenomenologically speaking, is that certain black spots in one's visual experience become objectually unified that previously were not.[94] Thus one's experience comes to exhibit objectual unity structure.[95] We may suggest, then, that in acquiring this objectual unity structure, the experiential character of one's visual experience acquires the dimension of being intentionally directed Dalmatian-wise.[96]

My favorite account of the phenomenological signature of intentionality is due to Frey (forthcoming), who focuses on a subtle kind of "phenomenal otherness" in intentional experiences. An exp-intentional state may present something to the subject in any number of ways, but the minimal way in which it must present what it does is precisely as *other than the subject*.[97] Talk of otherness may be more suited to describing directedness at particulars, and slightly strained when describing directedness at properties. To cover directedness at (putative) properties, we may speak of *foreignness*: an exp-intentional experience must present a property as foreign, that is, as instantiated by something other than oneself.[98] I will therefore refer to this feature of experiences as *phenomenal foreignness*.[99]

All four views on the phenomenological signature of intentionality—as *sui generis* phenomenal directedness, as experiential taking, as objectual unity structure, and as phenomenal foreignness—strike me as interesting, viable, and worth pursuing.[100] Each can be used to generate a different version of (ATEI), by offering a precisification of the experiential property of being intentionally directed F-wise. For example, by adopting the experiential-taking account, we can construe being-intentionally-directed-F-wise as experientially taking-something-to-be-F (or experientially taking-F-to-be-instantiated-by-something). My own inclination is to adopt the phenomenal-foreignness account, which casts being-intentionally-directed-F-wise as phenomenally presenting-an-other-to-be-F (or phenomenally presenting-F-to-be-instantiated-by-an-other). This produces the following version of (ATEI):

(ATEI1) Necessarily★, for any mental state x and putative property F, there is an experiential property E, E = phenomenally presenting-an-other-to-be-F, such that F figures in x's exp-intentional content iff x is E.[101]

Other versions would be generated by the *sui generis* phenomenal directedness account and the objectual unity structure account. My main hope is that our brief tour of options has given the reader some confidence that being-intentionally-directed-somehow need not be an ultimately mysterious notion—that some intelligible and informative account of its phenomenological nature should be possible to devise, and that rational debate of the relative merits of these different accounts could be sensible.[102]

In any version, the adverbial theory is certainly a very radical view. And indeed it faces a number of serious difficulties, both technical and principled. I will address the more extraordinary ones in the next section. But fundamentally, what motivates (ATEI) is the notion that, however radical, it is the only account of experiential intentionality consistent with the fact that exp-intentional states exhibit intentional inexistence. In other words, there is a simple argument for adverbialism: F can figure in the exp-intentional content of x even if F does not exist, but x cannot bear a relation to F if F does not exist, so F can figure in the exp-intentional content of x even if x bears no relation to F. More precisely:

1. For some state x and some putative property F, (i) F figures in the exp-intentional content of x and (ii) F does not exist;[103]
2. For no state x, putative property F, and relation R, (i) x bears R to F and (ii) F does not exist; therefore,
3. For no state x, putative property F, and relation R, F's figuring in the exp-intentional content of x = x's bearing R to F.[104]

Call this *the master argument for adverbialism*.[105] To undermine it, one would have to deny one of the two premises. But both the claim that either we cannot think of Escher triangles or there is such a property as being an Escher triangle (i.e., rejecting Premise 1), and the claim that relations do not require relata (i.e., rejecting Premise 2), are even more radical than adverbialism.

3.5. Objections to Adverbialism

I end this chapter with discussion of what I take to be the deepest objections to the adverbial theory of experiential intentionality, one of which I take to be truly damaging.

The first objection I would like to consider is that adverbialism is an overreaction to the problem of intentional inexistence. There are two versions of this objection, both offering strategies for resisting Premise 1 of the master argument above. I call them the *peculiar entity strategy* and the *compositionalist strategy*.

The peculiar entity strategy is to claim that, although when Worel hallucinates a butterfly, there is no actual concrete physical butterfly Worel is related to, there is nonetheless a *non-actual* butterfly (Parsons 1980, Priest 2005), or an actual *abstract* butterfly (Salmon 1988), or an actual concrete *mental* butterfly (Jackson 1977), that Worel is related to.

My response takes the form of a destructive dilemma. The question is: when Worel has an experientially indistinguishable *veridical* experience of a butterfly, is he related to (a) an actual concrete physical butterfly, or (b) whatever peculiar entity he is related to when hallucinating? If (a), then the veridical and hallucinatory experiences are intentionally type-different. Although I realize that capable philosophers have maintained this—disjunctivists—I cannot bring myself to take the view seriously. In addition, since we stipulate that the two experiences are experientially indistinguishable, this means that the intentional type they betoken is not fixed by their experiential character. If so, the intentional type cannot be an exp-intentional type, so the view cannot address that of which we seek an account.[106] If (b), then there are familiar phenomenological, epistemological, and ontological problems for the resulting view. Phenomenologically, it seems to be in tension with the transparency of experience. Epistemologically, it seems to erect a veil of appearances between us and the realm of actual concrete physical entities (the realm of unpeculiar entities, if you will).[107] Ontologically, it commits to the existence of *entia non grata*.[108]

The compositionalist strategy is to offer a bifurcated account of experiential intentionality, where exp-intentional states are divided into two classes: those whose exp-intentional content is given by some relational story (e.g., tracking-based or primitivist), and those whose exp-intentional content is inherited from the previous class through some compositional mechanism. The former are in some sense the "foundational" intentional states, the latter composites thereof. Thus, when Razz hallucinates a unicorn, the exp-intentional content of his experience is inherited via a compositional story from the exp-intentional content of experiences as of horses and as of horns. More strongly, whenever a necessarily uninstantiated property figures in the exp-intentional content of some state, the state inherits its content from other states that are suitably related to properties that are *not* necessarily uninstantiated.

This view is tempting whenever we *start* reflecting on the problem of intentional inexistence, but it seems to me that the temptation is founded entirely on confusing a genealogical/psychological story about content for a constitutive/philosophical one. It is a promising story about how our experiences *come to have* their contents, but not a plausible story about *what it is* for our experiences to have their contents. Considered as a constitutive/philosophical story, it suffers from obvious difficulties. First of all, in a variety of brain-in-vat scenarios the story would not yield the right results, since we can stipulate that the envatted brain is not suitably related to *any* relevant property, even as its "foundational" exp-intentional states are concerned. More deeply, it is odd to think that an experience as of a horse and an experience as of a unicorn have a different *kind* of property when they have their intentional contents: the having of an intentional content is one kind of property in the former (a relation to the property of being a horse) and another kind of property in the latter (essentially, a relation to other experiences). What is plausible is only that there are two different ways they acquire the same kind of property.

A second objection to the adverbial theory of experiential intentionality starts from the observation that few philosophers today seem to take seriously the original adverbial theory of perception (Ducasse 1942, Chisholm 1957). If the theory is so obviously implausible for perception, how come we can apply it plausibly to experiential intentionality?

I think there are two main reasons adverbialism about perception has been considered so obviously implausible, one technical and one non-technical. The non-technical reason is that, at bottom, the adverbial theory of perception was felt to miss the fact that perception is intentional. It was thought that if we accepted an account of perceptual qualities in terms of adverbial modifications, we would lose the intentional directedness of perception. Clearly, however, once we embrace adverbialism as an account of intentionality itself, this reason for rejecting adverbialism about perception evaporates. For the adoption of an adverbial account of perception is seen to be consistent with construing perception as intentional.

The technical reason for rejecting *perceptual* adverbialism had to do with a particular objection, due to Jackson (1977), which does threaten to carry over to *intentional* adverbialism. In its adapted form, the objection would be that while "I am thinking about green dragons and purple butterflies" is not equivalent to "I am thinking about purple dragons and green butterflies," both would have to be paraphrased by the adverbialist into the same sentence, "I am thinking green-wise and purple-wise and dragon-wise and butterfly-wise." The natural move for the adverbialist here is to propose the following distinguishable paraphrases: "I am thinking green-dragon-wise and purple-butterfly-wise" for the first sentence and "I am thinking purple-dragon-wise and green-butterfly-wise" for the second. But Jackson argues that these newer paraphrases lose a level of compositionality present in the original sentences. This may be problematic in a number of ways, but the main one is that the compositionality of the original sentences enabled certain inferences which may be disabled in the paraphrase.[109] In particular, the claim is that while from "I am thinking about a green dragon" one can infer "I am thinking about a dragon," from "I am thinking green-dragon-wise" one cannot infer "I am thinking dragon-wise," because "dragon-wise" is only a morphological component, not a syntactic component, of "green-dragon-wise" ("green-dragon-wise" being syntactically simple). If this is right, then the adverbial paraphrases, despite purporting to be equivalent to the original sentences, would actually fail to preserve the inferential connections of the latter to surrounding sentences in the logical neighborhood.

It seems to me, however, that while the lack of compositionality blocks one way of making the above inference, other ways remain unblocked. One way to reason from "I am thinking about green dragons" to "I am thinking about dragons" is through something like conjunction elimination: I am thinking about green dragons; therefore, I am thinking about green and I am thinking about dragons; therefore, I am thinking about dragons. This mode of reasoning is unavailable on the adverbialist story, since one cannot reason as follows: I am thinking green-dragon-wise; therefore, I am thinking green-wise and I am thinking dragon-wise; therefore, I am thinking dragon-wise. Note, however, that the same fallacy would attach to the following reasoning: I am kicking a strawberry; therefore, I am kicking a straw and I am kicking a berry; therefore, I am kicking a berry. And yet the inference from "I am kicking a strawberry" to "I am kicking a berry" seems acceptable. So the question is what makes it acceptable, and whether the adverbialist cannot co-opt this way of making it acceptable. To me, it seems that what makes the last inference acceptable is some tacit principle to the effect that the property of being a berry is a genus, or determinable, of which the property of being a strawberry is a species, or determinate. So the full reasoning is something like this: I am kicking a strawberry; whatever is a strawberry is a berry; therefore, I am kicking a berry. This form of reasoning is valid, and I contend that it is available to the adverbialist as well, because another principle our reasoner could appeal to is that the property of thinking dragon-wise is a genus, or determinable, of which the property of thinking green-dragon-wise is a species, or determinate. So we can reason as follows: I am thinking green-dragon-wise; whatever is green-dragon-wise thinking is dragon-wise thinking; therefore, I am thinking dragon-wise.[110]

A third objection is that adverbialism cannot account for the fact that exp-intentional content is (at least sometimes) singular, in the sense of being object-involving. My visual experience of the laptop before me is an experience not just as of a collection of *properties*, not even as of a collection of co-instantiated properties (or compresent property instances), but as of a *concrete particular*. This means that exp-intentional content must be singular rather than existentially quantified. That is, when I experience the laptop as silver, my experience's content is not of the form "there is an x, such that x is $F_1, F_2, \ldots, F_n$, and x is silver," but rather of the form "a is silver." The only way this could be, claims the objector, is if exp-intentional content involved a relation to what the experience is intentionally directed at. But adverbialism denies such a relation.

My response to this objection has two parts. First, I deny that exp-intentional content is singular in the relevant sense. Secondly, I attempt to recover the sense in which conscious experience is often as of concrete particulars, and not just properties, within a framework that rejects singular exp-intentional content.

To see why it is plausible to deny the singularity of exp-intentional content, it is important to appreciate that such singularity requires that exp-intentional contents be different even when the experiences that carry them are directed at fully indistinguishable particulars. By "fully indistinguishable," I mean indistinguishable not only with respect to their intrinsic properties, but also with respect to their relational properties, spatio-temporal locations, etc. What we have to envisage is the following situation. Let Twin-World be a possible world indistinguishable from the actual world in every detail but one: the laptop I am looking at right now in that world is a numerically distinct individual from the one I am looking at in the actual world.[111] Although qualitatively indistinguishable from my actual laptop, it is *another* laptop (perhaps because it has a different *haecceity*, perhaps for some other reason—depending on one's view of what makes a concrete particular the concrete particular it is).¹¹² According to the objector, the exp-intentional content of my experience in the actual world and in Twin-World is different. This verdict strikes me, however, as obviously counterintuitive. It is much more intuitive that the exp-intentional contents are the same—that the two experiences are exp-intentionally type-identical.¹¹³

It is true, of course, that what the experiences *refer to* is different.¹¹⁴ But this in itself does not entail that they have different contents. Compare the semantics of definite descriptions. The description "the first black US president" denotes Barack Obama in the actual world and Mike Tyson in some counterfactual world, and are thus about different particulars in those two worlds. But it does not follow that the description's content in the two worlds is different. Indeed, it is widely agreed to be the same.¹¹⁵ The present suggestion—originally due to Farkas (2008)—is that the contents of exp-intentional states should be thought of on the model of the contents of definite descriptions. Both are existentially quantified rather than singular.¹¹⁶

Although I deny that exp-intentional content is characterized by *singularity*, I recognize that it is characterized by *particularity*, in the sense that its bearers often have the experiential character of presenting concrete particulars. This can be accommodated by claiming that such experiential character exhibits what Montague (2011) calls an *object-positing phenomenology*, which is the phenomenology of particularity, and then offering an adverbial gloss on this phenomenology. The adverbial gloss construes the phenomenology of particularity as the experiential character of being intentionally directed concrete-particular-wise. One way to think of this object-positing phenomenology is as enriching the existentially quantified content of exp-intentional states by incorporating into it attribution of particularity. Thus, the content of my silver-laptop experience is more fully specified as "there is an x, such that x is F_1, . . ., a concrete particular, . . ., F_n, and x is silver." This object-positing dimension of experiential character is the same in every exp-intentional state directed at a concrete particular, and does not vary among exp-intentional states directed at numerically distinct particulars. So it cannot deliver content singularity. But it does deliver content particularity, that is, the sense that some conscious experiences are directed at concrete particulars.¹¹⁷

A related objection, which may in fact capture the deep worry animating the previous one (perhaps the previous two), is that it is unclear how experiential intentionality, as construed by the adverbialist, could "connect us to world." The objector claims that the whole point of intentionality is that it puts us in "cognitive contact" with reality. Her worry is that while bearing the relation of being intentionally directed at some*thing* may accomplish this, the adverbial property of being intentionally directed some*how* certainly does not. In sum, intentionality involves referential connections to the world, and cannot be identified with an adverbial property.

There may be some technical responses to this objection. For example, one could embrace a deflationary theory of reference (Field 1944, Brandom 1994a Ch.5). According to such a theory, a schema of the form "'N_1' refers to N_1, 'N_2' refers to N_2, . . ." accounts for everything a theory of reference needs to account for. Concomitantly, there is no substantive reference relation of which something more illuminating can be said. Marrying such a deflationary theory of referential connections to the world with adverbialism about intentional content may speak to the worry that something central has been left out by the adverbialist.

My favored response is different, however, and has several aspects. First, I want to agree that intentionality connects us to the world, but suggest that it does so *contingently* rather than *constitutively*. Adverbialism can very well allow that many of our exp-intentional states bear an appropriate relation to the world—namely, the veridical ones. All adverbialism denies is that *non-veridical* ones do as well, and therefore that it is not constitutive of exp-intentional states that they bear such a relation.[118] Given that the relevant relation does manage to connect us to the world, it follows that many of our exp-intentional states do connect us to the world. It is just that what makes them exp-intentional states and what makes them connect us to the world are two different properties.

The deeper point here is that there is a confusion lurking in the way the "cognitive contact" requirement is often wielded. The requirement need not be satisfied by intentionality as such, only by *successful* intentionality. A *true* thought connects us to the world; but it does so in virtue of being true, not in virtue of being a thought. An accurate auditory experience as of trumpets connects us to trumpets, not in virtue of being an experience as of trumpets however, but in virtue of being accurate. Admittedly, there must be a bridge between intentional states and reality. But intentionality is the bridged, not the bridging. The bridging is provided by such notions as truth, accuracy, veridicality, and the like.[119] What is true of non-veridical experiences is not that they connect us to the world, but that they *would* connect us to the world if they *were* veridical. This is why it is true of a non-veridical trumpet experience, on my view, that if it were veridical it would be suitably tracked to track trumpets.

What intentionality *per se* must do is *make possible* our cognitive contact with the world. I realize that it is a little opaque what "making possible" means in this context, but then again "cognitive contact" itself is not the most transparent of notions. One way to think of this is that intentionality provides truth *conditions*, or accuracy *conditions*, which then may or may not be satisfied, depending on the world's cooperation. When the conditions are satisfied, cognitive contact with the world will have been established. The role of intentionality is only to make such contact possible by *laying the conditions* whose satisfaction would constitute the establishment of contact. If this is right, then in order to identify experiential intentionality with the relevant adverbial property, all that must be shown is that the adverbial property sets conditions whose satisfaction would establish contact with the world, not that the adverbial property itself establishes contact with the world.[120] I conclude that when the connection-to-the-world requirement is properly understood, there is reason to expect adverbialism to meet it.

So far I have considered objections that I think the adverbialist can overcome. I end with discussion of an objection that I think saddles adverbialism with a genuine and major liability. The objection is that adverbialism precludes, or at least puts in question the prospects for, the naturalization of experiential intentionality. Whereas tracking accounts and higher-order tracking theories not only do not preclude such naturalization, but *deliver* it, adverbialism certainly fails to deliver naturalization, and moreover appears to preclude it. It does not deliver naturalization in that it does not offer any account of the experiential property E, in virtue of which an experience is intentionally directed somehow, in non-experiential terms. It appears to *preclude* naturalization, in that it casts E as an adverbial property distinct from the naturalistic properties typically adduced in the context of naturalizing intentionality.[121] There might, of course, be some other naturalistic property E might be reductively explained in terms of, but it is unclear at present what that other property might be.

One response to this objection is to deny that naturalization is so valuable and simply assert that experiential intentionality is a super-natural, or just non-natural, phenomenon.

THE NATURE OF EXPERIENTIAL INTENTIONALITY   167

My instinct is to dismiss this response without argument. It may turn out that we *cannot* naturalize intentionality. But surely naturalization *is* valuable, and its achievement should be greatly valued. It is, of course, not entirely clear exactly what it is that makes naturalization so intellectually valuable. My sense is that naturalizing a phenomenon is a reliable way of rendering it intelligible in a pertinent sense. More on this momentarily.[122]

A second response is to offer naturalization of the relevant adverbial properties through brute identity claims. The adverbialist may conjoin (ATEI) with the thesis that for any determinate experiential property E_i, of being intentionally directed F_i-wise, there is a neural property N_i, such that $E_i = N_i$. These identities can be proffered as brute and inexplicable, perhaps on the grounds that *no* identities admit of explanation (there is no explaining why something is identical to itself). This response can be patterned after Block and Stalnaker's (1999) approach to the reduction of conscious experience generally. According to them, psycho-physical (including neuro-experiential) identities are not explicable, and they cannot be deduced from any other propositions. Rather, they must be posited through inference to the best explanation in the context of explaining correlations between physical and psychological (neural and experiential) properties. Applied to experiential intentionality, the idea would be that for any experiential property E_i and neural property N_j, such that there is an exceptionless correlation between E_i and N_j, the best explanation of this correlation is that $E_i = N_j$.[123]

One problem with this response is that it suffers from all the problems Block and Stalnaker's view does. In particular, Chalmers and Jackson (2001) have charged, among other things, (a) that correlations between neural and experiential properties are explained at least equally well by the hypothesis that experiential properties merely *supervene nomologically* upon neural properties (say, due to causal laws that connect them) and (b) that reduction must always be *epistemically transparent*, in that it should be clear why it is that a reduced property F is *nothing but* some reducer property G—which means that something about identity claims does call for explanation after all. The debate over these matters is as yet unsettled, and we cannot undertake to discuss it at depth here. In Kriegel 2009 Ch.8, I argue for a compromise position, though one that does call for explanations of identities. In any case, when it comes to naturalization projects, it seems to me that an explanatory, or epistemically transparent, dimension is even more clearly called for. For naturalization projects are first and foremost epistemic projects designed to further our *understanding*, by demystifying otherwise mysterious phenomena. In setting out to naturalize an otherwise mysterious phenomenon, we typically seek to cast it as continuous (and/or integrated) with more familiar phenomena by which we are untroubled. Simply declaring that an otherwise mysterious phenomenon must be identical with some natural, unmysterious phenomenon, because we are antecedently persuaded that naturalism is true, does not advance that cause one bit.[124]

A third response is to concede that adverbialism does not deliver naturalization, and that moreover it is incompatible with *reductive* naturalization, but maintain that it can be conjoined with, and thus does not preclude, a *non-reductive* naturalization of experiential intentionality. The starting point for such non-reductive naturalization would be to find suitable naturalistically unproblematic properties and claim that our adverbial properties nomologically supervene on them. Presumably this nomological supervenience would hold in virtue of certain causal laws that govern the interaction of the relevant naturalistically unproblematic properties with experiential properties. So the adverbialist could conjoin (ATEI) with the thesis that for any determinate E_i, of being intentionally directed F_i-wise, there is a naturalistically kosher property K_i, such that some law of nature dictates that E_i is causally produced by K_i under specified conditions. Since nomological supervenience is itself a naturalistically kosher notion, casting as it does both the supervenient and the subvenient property as integrated into a single causal-mechanistic web of properties, the result would be a naturalistic, though non-reductive, account of E_i. (A particularly intriguing version of this kind of non-reductive adverbialism would invoke higher-order tracking properties as the nomological-supervenience base of the adverbial properties. On this view, a property E_i, of being intentionally directed F_i-wise, supervenes nomologically on the property of being suitably higher-order tracked to track F_i.[125]) This kind of naturalization scheme can be patterned after Chalmers' (1996) "naturalistic dualism" about consciousness. According to Chalmers, dualist views of consciousness are non-naturalist only if they hold that any connection (e.g., correlation) between consciousness and physical properties is purely accidental, or is due to pre-established harmony, or to a god's continuous oversight, or cetera. A dualist view that grounds psycho-physical connections in laws of nature that dictate the causal interaction between physical properties and experiential properties is perfectly naturalistic. It is nonetheless non-reductive, in that it casts the relationship between the experiential and the physical as causal rather than constitutive. Since no physical properties are constitutive of experience, the latter is metaphysically primitive, or fundamental: in addition to the fundamental-level physical properties of spin, charm, etc., one must admit a property of experience. Applied to the present concern, the view would be that exp-intentional properties are fundamental properties that supervene nomologically, but not metaphysically, upon certain naturalistically kosher properties (e.g., higher-order tracking properties).

The problem with this response is, again, that it inherits all the disadvantages of Chalmers' naturalistic dualism. The literature on this is enormous, and often focuses on issues of causal overdetermination (Kim 1989), charging that Chalmers is forced into the position that either consciousness is epiphenomenal or the physical realm is not causally closed (in the sense that some physical events have no physical causes). These concerns would apply to exp-intentional properties, as construed by the non-reductive adverbialist. However, let me raise another, more seldom discussed oddity associated with non-reductivism.[126] This is the fact that while other fundamental properties (spin, charm, etc.) are instantiated only by particulars at the fundamental level of reality, experiential properties (including exp-intentional properties) are also instantiated by non-fundamental entities, namely, mental states and their subjects. If experiential properties were fundamental, they would thus be unique in that all other fundamental properties are instantiated only by *microscopic* particulars, whereas experiential properties are instantiated routinely by *macroscopic* particulars. This oddity makes it uncomfortable to treat the emerging view as genuinely naturalistic, as it introduces something new and deeply unfamiliar into our conception of nature, something that our current conception makes no provision for. We may put the argument as follows:

1. For any property F, if F is fundamental, then there is no particular *a*, such that (i) *a* is macroscopic and (ii) *a* is F;
2. For any property F, if F is experiential, then there *is* a particular *a*, such that (i) *a* is macroscopic and (ii) *a* is F; therefore,
3. For any property F, if F is experiential, then F is not fundamental.

It may be possible to reject Premise 1, by devising some positive account of fundamental properties that would make such rejection plausible, but I am unfamiliar with any attempt.[127] It may also be possible to reject Premise 2, by positing unfamiliar experiential properties that you and I do not instantiate but microscopic particulars do, but this seems overly speculative and unwarranted, and in any case it would not be *those* experiential properties that would underlie experiential intentionality.[128] This strikes me as a major liability for the non-reductive brand of adverbialism under consideration.

Insofar as I am attracted to adverbialism, I am inclined to embed it within something like the following attitude to the naturalization project. First of all, naturalization is indeed of paramount theoretical value—but its value is only instrumental. The non-instrumental end of the philosophical theory of intentionality is to render intentionality intelligible, in some admittedly elusive but characteristically philosophical sense of "intelligible." Naturalization is so valuable because naturalizing a phenomenon is a reliable way of rendering it intelligible. Once one is able to see how something like intentionality could occur in a world devoid of super-natural elements, one acquires the sense of having intellectually domesticated intentionality. So *rendering intelligible* is the final end of inquiry and naturalization is just a means to it. However, while naturalizing intentionality is *one* way to render it intelligible, it need not be the *only* way. Plausibly, naturalizing something renders it intelligible because once a phenomenon is naturalized, it is seen to be continuous with phenomena we are untroubled by. Whereas supernatural phenomena are in some important sense foreign, natural ones are the kind of thing we know. They are *familiar*. It is this familiarity that a phenomenon acquires when it is naturalized, and which accounts for its being rendered intelligible thereby. It is not at all obvious, however, that there is no other way to "familiarize" intentionality. Another way to familiarize intentionality might be to ground all intentionality in a kind of intentionality with which we are acquainted in a first-person way, and which we can recognize and grasp simply by attending to our own stream of consciousness. Experiential intentionality fits this bill: it is a kind of intentionality that is deeply familiar in its own way, namely, in that we encounter it in our personal mental life and can fully grasp it in an entirely pre-theoretic manner. If all other intentionality could be shown to be grounded in this type of already familiar intentionality, that would be a way of familiarizing intentionality, and thus rendering it intelligible, though without naturalizing it. In a sense, where naturalization offers third-person familiarization, grounding in experience offers first-person familiarization. In both cases, though, intentionality is rendered intelligible.

This meta-theoretical attitude to the project of naturalization is palpably radical and bound to be rejected by many. Certainly much more should be said by way of developing it, and applying it to the project of naturalizing intentionality, before we could confidently take it to blunt the force of the objection that adverbialism is damaged by its tension with the project of naturalizing intentionality. It does concede, in any event, the reality of such a tension. This is, by my lights, a significant reason to resist adverbialism.

Conclusions: Comparing the Options

Philosophical *knowledge*, on one view, is always knowledge of conditionals: if you adopt p, then you are committed also to q, at least given background assumption r. The end of philosophical inquiry will arrive when the entire web of conditionals has been mapped out, so that the logical geography of every intellectual issue is fully transparent. At that point, assenting to some of the ultimate antecedents in this web of conditionals, and dissenting from others, would generate commitment to a philosophical system. Commitment to a *global* philosophical system—a *grand* system, in the enlightenment sense—would be constituted by assenting to a *maximal* subset of those ultimate antecedents, where a subset is maximal just in case assenting to any further antecedent would generate an incoherent system.[129] Importantly, at the end of philosophical inquiry, as envisaged here, there are likely to be more than one possible global system. The choice among the several global systems—that is, the choice among the maximal subsets of ultimate antecedents—would not be the province of reason, since reason will have done all it can by the time the logical geography of everything has been mapped out. Rather, the choice would have to be made by *intuition*.[130] Thus just as philosophical *practical* reason is the slave of the philosophical passions, so philosophical *theoretical* reason is the slave of philosophical intuitions.

Why do I belabor so this sketchy conception of philosophical knowledge? Because as I look at the various accounts of experiential intentionality I have examined in this chapter and the last, and contemplate the positive and negative commitments associated with each, I find that my intuition is torn between the package deal offered by higher-order tracking theory and that offered by the adverbial theory. Both strike me as stable positions that present attractive comprehensive accounts of experiential intentionality, but which also come with important liabilities. In order to accommodate the phenomenon of intentional inexistence, the higher-order tracking theory has to deny the possibility of certain conscious experiences that *seem* manifestly possible. Meanwhile, the adverbial theory precludes, or at least puts in question, the (plausible) naturalization of experiential intentionality, at least against the background of certain assumptions that seem hard to deny. At the same time, the higher-order tracking theory not only does not preclude, but probably delivers, such naturalization, while adverbialism ratifies the apparent possibility of conscious experiences exhibiting intentional inexistence.

The perfect account of experiential intentionality, the account I *want*, would both (i) deliver the naturalization of experiential intentionality and (ii) ratify the apparent possibility of exp-intentional states I can conceive of in favorable epistemic circumstances. But neither the higher-order tracking theory nor the adverbial theory does both, as far as I can see. Moreover, the tension between these two desiderata may be principled: the prospects for naturalization require experiential intentionality to involve (constitutively) a relation, but the acceptance of certain experiences endowed with intentional inexistence requires that experiential intentionality *not* involve (constitutively) that relation. If this is right, then I simply cannot have the kind of theory of experiential intentionality that I *want*. Instead, I have to choose between two imperfect accounts. One naturalizes experiential intentionality but at the cost of disbarring certain apparently possible exp-intentional states. The other ratifies the possibility of those exp-intentional states but sacrifices the naturalization of experiential intentionality.

Interestingly, the tension here is between two different *kinds* of virtue a theory of intentionality can display. In the assessment of scientific theories, it is common to distinguish between *empirical* and *theoretical* virtues: the empirical virtues concern accounting for the data; the theoretical virtues concern parsimony, simplicity, unity, clarity, elegance, conservatism, etc. It is natural to think that a similar distinction applies to philosophical theories, but with the role of data being played by pre-theoretic verdicts about what falls in the extension of a certain phenomenon, such that getting the extension right is the empirical virtue (or "quasi-empirical," if we prefer). Since ratifying the possibility of apparently possible exp-intentional states is a matter of getting right the pre-theoretically desirable extension of experiential intentionality, what is at stake here is the (quasi-)*empirical* adequacy of our theory of experiential intentionality. Meanwhile, since delivering naturalization (or not precluding it) is a matter of cohering with a central tenet of an independently desirable theory of the world, what is at stake there is a *theoretical* virtue of our theory of the experiential intentionality.

Enter intuition, and its choice between ratification and naturalization, and so between (quasi-)empirical adequacy and theoretical virtue. All I can report is that, at the end of the day, if I have to choose between thinking of the world I live in, on the one hand, as a place where experiential intentionality is a naturalistic (indeed, physically reducible) property but does not extend as far as it manifestly appears to, or thinking of the world, on the other hand, as a place where experiential intentionality extends as far as it seems to but is non-naturalistic, my intuition leans slightly, hesitantly, cringingly toward the former. That is, my intuition prizes naturalization a tad over ratification. It would be entertaining for me to profess a credence of ~55 percent in the higher-order tracking theory and ~45 percent in the adverbial theory.[131]

Notes

1. Chapter 3 Here and onward, I use "tracking-based accounts" to cover both first-order tracking accounts and higher-order tracking theories.

2. This comes out even more clearly here: "Jimmy is thinking of a three-headed parrot, therefore there is a three-headed parrot that Jimmy is thinking of" is clearly invalid, even though "Jimmy is kicking a three-headed parrot, therefore there is a three-headed parrot that Jimmy is kicking" is valid. Moreover, there is an element of specificity in the conclusion lacking from the premise. This element is taken by some to be essential to intensionality (Moltmann 1997, Zimmerman 2001). Lack of specificity in intensional verbs is claimed to actually support certain inferences not otherwise supported. For example, "Jimmy is kicking a parrot and Johnny is kicking a parrot, therefore Jimmy and Johnny are kicking the same thing" is claimed to be invalid, but "Jimmy is imagining a parrot and Johnny is imagining a parrot, therefore Jimmy and Johnny are imagining the same thing" is claimed to be valid. I am not particularly persuaded by this, personally, but it is plausible that there is some connection between intensionality and lack of specificity.

3. This is sometimes referred to as "truth-preserving," or *salva veritate*, substitution of co-referential terms. However, every valid inference is truth-preserving, so we could as well refer to truth-preserving existential generalization as the other phenomenon. Here I will take for granted the truth-preservation.

4. Some report not to hear this as invalid. If so, the following is certainly invalid: "Tim thinks that the fastest man in Harlem must be faster than the fastest man in Astoria, Tom is the fastest man in Harlem, therefore Tim thinks that Tom must be faster than the fastest man in Astoria." In the text, I go for a usage of "think" that takes names as grammatical objects, rather than one that takes "that" clauses, for mostly esthetic reasons.

5. I should note that there is some controversy over the extensional adequacy of Chisholm's criterion. It is sometimes claimed that verbs of transaction, for example, can occur in contexts in which

they do not support existential generalization. If a minute ago I bought a copy of the *Tractatus* on Amazon, but no single copy in Amazon's storage facility has yet been designated to me, then "I bought a copy of the *Tractatus* on Amazon, therefore there is a copy of the *Tractatus* such that I bought it on Amazon" is invalid (since its premise is true but its conclusion false). The same goes for verbs of creation in progressive contexts: consider "I started building an empire yesterday, therefore there is an empire such that I started building it yesterday" (imagine, if you can, a world where my empire never comes to be). Yet philosophical discussions of intentionality do not regard the properties of buying and building as within the domain of phenomena in need of accounting for by the theory of intentionality. In response, however, it might be claimed that buying and building are in fact covertly psychological, intentional phenomena. If one could show that the motor or bodily actions characteristic of transaction and creation, when performed in the absence of certain intentions or beliefs, say, do not qualify as transaction and creation, and more generally show that there is no way to understand transaction and creation without reference to intentional states, then it would suddenly seem that, despite initial appearances, transaction and creation are in fact within the domain of phenomena in need of accounting for by the theory of intentionality. *Prima facie*, the prospects for such a program strike me as quite plausible.

6. Following Searle (1992), this attribute (or perhaps just one very close to it) is sometimes referred to as "aspectual shape." I am more esthetically pleased by "intentional indifference," for the reasons immediately adduced in the text.

7. We can also run the thought-experiment as involving Tassandra in one possible world and Twin-Tassandra in another, and stipulate that all these conditions apply to them.

8. Prosopagnosia is a condition in which subjects are incapable of perceptually identifying faces, though they are otherwise perceptually unimpaired. Visual agnosia is a condition in which subjects are generally incapable of recognizing objects in their visual field.

9. Note that this argument takes the same form as the argument from experiential contrast for the existence of cognitive experience that was discussed in §1.3.3. Both are arguments from experiential contrast.

10. There would be some debate here on whether the experiential difference is part of the *perceptual* experiential character. In a way, this would come down to whether there are non-sensory, cognitive aspects to perceptual experience as such, as some philosophers assert and others deny.

11. I remind the reader that "knowingly looks at X" means only "looks at X while knowing that one looks at X," and does not mean "looks at X while having full knowledge of what one looks at."

12. And it could be, of course, that my friend Mike is a prankster, and has no twin brother, such that the morning Mike and the evening Mike are in reality one and the same object. As long as the prank succeeds, the experiential situation is the same for me as in the scenario in which Mike does have a twin brother. That experiential situation is the kind of situation Tassandra is in.

13. This does raise the question of what exactly the intentional difference between the two experiences is, what accuracy conditions we can ascribe to the one but not the other; I will return to this question later in this subsection. But the argument that the two experiences have different experiential properties, and those properties are exp-intentional properties, wherefore the two experiences have different exp-intentional properties, does not need a specification of the intentional difference to go through.

14. In particular, insofar as we accept that necessarily co-extensive properties are identical, and that the properties of being Phosphorus and being Hesperus are necessarily co-extensive (because Phosphorus is identical to Hesperus and there is no such thing as contingent identity, so the actually identical is necessarily identical), we must accept that being Phosphorus and being Hesperus are one and the same property.

15. More generally, the thought is that accounting for intentional indifference requires a distinction of the sort Frege (1892) drew between sense and reference. Tracking relations account for reference, but intentional indifference is an aspect of sense (indeed, the reason sense is posited in the first place), and sense is to be accounted for in terms of functional role. This maneuver is clearly articulated by McGinn (1982), but the resulting position probably characterizes all of so-called dual-aspect theories of content (e.g., Field 1977, Block 1986).

16. Two comments. First, it is certainly clear that the distal causes and effects of Phosphorus and Hesperus are the same, since Phosphorus acting on the subject is the same as Hesperus acting on the subject and the subject acting on Phosphorus is the same as the subject acting on Hesperus. So long-armed functional roles, such as are appealed to by Harman (1987), would not help. Second, if functional role cannot bring intentional indifference into the picture, it is unclear how other manners might. Thus, what it is about non-conceptuality and atomism that might make the intentional states endowed with them possessed of intentional indifference is mysterious.

17. I am distinguishing, for present purposes, between *inferential* role and *causal* role. Causal role can certainly be specified without appeal to the notion of content. But inferential role cannot. It is impossible to make sense of the idea that the *sentences* "p" and "if p, then q" entail "q" without first making sense of the fact that the *propositions* <p> and <if p, then q> entail <q>. The propositions are, however, the contents of the sentences. (This presentation of the point is made in terms of propositions for the sake of ease of exposition. I do not actually wish to commit to the existence of propositions, nor to the notion that relations to propositions constitute the contents of sentences.)

18. In addition, we should remember that impure tracking accounts of experiential intentionality were found to be deeply problematic in §2.1.3, insofar as they appear to have no resources to account for the difference between experiential and non-experiential intentionality. Also, we should keep in mind that there is also a neutral tracking account of experiential intentionality, but as argued in §2.1.3 it is even less plausible than the pure and impure tracking accounts.

19. Since intentional indifference is a feature of experiential intentionality, the upshot is that there is a feature of experiential intentionality that neither first- nor higher-order tracking accounts can accommodate.

20. I say so despite realizing that smarter people than me have defended minimalist positions on the scope of experiential character, on which there are relatively few kinds of experiential character and they tend to be low-level. It is quite hard to assess phenomenological positions of this sort, and it becomes harder the more outlandish the position. If someone is willing to argue that while most recognized perceptual experiential characters are real, there is no such thing as olfactory experiential character, it is hard to undermine his or her position from the inside. I am not clear on what sort of argument can be presented against this position, and likewise I find myself hard pressed to present an argument against the view that there is no experiential character to do with identifying an object.

21. This kind of objection is animated, clearly, by a certain deflationary attitude toward phenomenology and experiential character, the kind of attitude that involves hostility toward subtle experiential features, including cognitive-experiential features and high-level perceptual-experiential features. I have not presented a sustained argument against this attitude (the only discussion of relevance being in §1.3.3), but find no *prima facie* plausibility in it, nor any cogent argument for it, so I disregard it in this book. For a sustained argument for the existence of cognitive experience, see Kriegel forthcoming.

22. This depends, of course, on one's view of event individuation. On Kim's (1976) account of events as property exemplifications, there are two distinct properties here. However, it seems to me that Bennett (1988) is exactly right in claiming that Kim's account is better thought of as an account of *facts*, not *events*. Smith's eating a poisoned fish and Smith's eating at Cardiff's westernmost pub are distinct

facts but one and the same event. As far as events are concerned, we should adopt Davidson's (1969) view of them as bare particulars.

23. Moreover, recall that we are interested in all this because it might support a tracking account of experiential intentionality. But if experiential intentionality is just a certain tracking relation, and that tracking relation is observer-dependent, then experiential intentionality is observer-dependent (and not only in the trivial sense that it is instantiated by observers). This would strike many as implausible—even if such an irrealist approach to intentionality is plausible somewhere, surely it is least plausible when it comes to experiential intentionality.

24. Following Bennett (1988), I tend to think of the relevant events as identical (events being Davidsonian bare particulars) and the relevant facts, or states of affairs, as non-identical (they being Kimean property exemplifications). For the explanation presented in the text to go through, then, it would have to be claimed that "eating at Cardiff's westernmost pub" and "eating a poisoned fish" denote facts/states of affairs rather than events (I think of facts as states of affairs that are actual, that obtain). And indeed so they do according to Bennett, since they are imperfect nominals, which Bennett claims pick out facts rather than events.

25. There is some debate within the relevant literature on whether this kind of biconditional must be *a priori*, or could alternatively be allowed to be just necessary. Wright (1988) originally insisted that it must be *a priori*, but see Miscevic 1998 for dissent. None of this should matter for our present purposes, but I will follow the mainstream in assuming that aprioricity is required.

26. By "predicament relevantly similar to Tassandra's," I mean the fact that Tassandra is unaware of the identity of Phosphorus and Hesperus and of when they are visible, is looking at each knowingly in similar circumstances, etc. By "internal states" I mean either mental states of a certain kind, or neurophysiological states, or functional states, or whatever turns out to be the states internal to the subject that distinguishes Tassandra on the two occasions. (I assume that if there are no different states, she could not be said to have two different experiences.)

27. Recall that I am using "is knowingly looking at X" as short for "is looking at X while being aware that it is X."

28. The subject is "relevantly ignorant" in that s/he is unaware that Phosphorus and Hesperus are one and the same.

29. This general approach can also illuminate exactly what the intentional difference between Phosphorescent and Hesperescent experiences is, what accuracy condition can be ascribed to one but not the other—namely, that something appears-to-be-Phosphorus-to-the-relevantly-ignorant-subject-in-normal-conditions and that something appears-to-be-Hesperus-to-the-relevantly-ignorant-subject-in-normal-conditions.

30. The characterization of the relevant responses cannot appeal to intentional and/or experiential properties of the internal response appealed to, on pain of circularity of the resulting account. One option is to characterize them in terms of their functional roles (Shoemaker 1994, 2002), another is in terms of their neurophysiological realizers (Kriegel 2002a, 2009 Ch.3). Both proposals face difficulties returning the right results in a number of cases where intuition instructs of sameness or difference of content. In Kriegel 2009 Ch.3, I discuss these cases in some detail, and develop a fairly specific account of the response-dependent properties that return the right results in all those cases. Unfortunately, those response-dependent properties are defined in terms of internal responses that lack any homogeneity. They are what I call there *conjunctive dispositions*, i.e., properties of being disposed to elicit responses of type R_1 in subjects of type S_1 in circumstances C_1, *and* responses of type R_1 in subjects of type S_2 in circumstances C_2, *and* responses of type R_2 in subjects of type S_1 under circumstances C_3, *and* . . . and so on and so forth. These are, in effect, hodgepodges of responses brought together sheerly for the purpose of generating an account of what conscious experiences track that returns the right results.

I conclude the discussion there by noting that the upshot of using conjunctive dispositions in this way is clearly unsatisfying, but that nonetheless this is superior to all the other options in logical space. This is still my view, but I appreciate that this is a controversial matter.

31. A centered world is an ordered triple of a metaphysically possible world, an individual, and a time. Thus, two centered worlds could be qualitatively indistinguishable in every respect *except* the subject's position (spatial or temporal) in them. Egan (2006) considers that centering features are not properties, on the grounds that properties are associated with functions from uncentered possible worlds to extensions rather than from centered possible worlds to extensions. However, one might also allow centering features to be properties, on the grounds that they are universals (for they are wholly present in more than one place at the same time). To some extent this is a verbal issue, since there is certainly a well-behaved ontologist's technical notion of a property that allows centering features to be properties.

32. The corresponding claim we obtain against the background of familiar assumptions would be this: There is a class of response-dependent properties P and a tracking relation T, such that for any mental state x and subject S, where S is in x, there is a suitable mental state y, where S is in y, such that x has the exp-intentional content it does (and not another) because y bears T to x's bearing T to the member(s) of P that y does bear T to x's bearing T to (and not other members), and x has exp-intentional content (at all) because y bears T to x's bearing T to some member(s) of P (at all).

33. This would be a version of the naturalized self-tracking account that accommodates intentional indifference. Corresponding to it would be the following thesis: There is a class of response-dependent properties P and a tracking relation T, such that for any mental state x, there are states x_1 and x_2 and a relation R, where (i) x_1 is a proper part of x, (ii) x_2 is a proper part of x, and (iii) x_2 bears R to x, such that x has the exp-intentional content it does (rather than another) because x_1 bears T to x_2's bearing T to the member(s) of P that x_1 does bear T to x_2's bearing T to (and not other members), and x has exp-intentional content (at all) because (i)-(iii) hold and x_1 bears T to x_2's bearing T to some member(s) of P (at all).

34. Accordingly, the following bit of reasoning is actually valid: Raheem is thinking of Phosphorus; Phosphorus = Hesperus; therefore, Raheem is thinking of Hesperus. However, this is never a *sound* reasoning, because its first premise is always false: it is never Phosphorus that is being thought of (when thinking is taken to be an exp-intentional state). What is thought of is a certain appearance property of Phosphorus.' (Fittingly, parallel claims apply to tracking. Thus, the following bit of reasoning is valid but unsound: x tracks Phosphorus; Phosphorus = Hesperus; therefore, x tracks Hesperus. It is just that exp-intentional states do not really track concrete particulars, such as Venus. Rather, they track properties of Venus, and more specifically, appearance properties of Venus.) The following is also valid but unsound: Raheem is thinking of something's appearing-to-be-Phosphorus-to-the-relevantly-ignorant-subject-in-normal-conditions; appearing-to-be-Phosphorus-to-the-relevantly-ignorant-subject-in-normal-conditions = appearing-to-be-Hesperus-to-the-relevantly-ignorant-subject-in-normal-conditions; therefore, Raheem is thinking of something's appearing-to-be-Hesperus-to-the-relevantly-ignorant-subject-in-normal-conditions. Here too the unsoundness is due not to invalidity, but to the falsity of a premise—this time the second. For the expressions on each side of the identity sign do not denote the same property. All this is to say that, strictly speaking, on this view, exp-intentional states do not in fact exhibit intentional indifference: they do not exhibit a feature that underwrites substitution failure.

35. At this stage, in saying that only appearance properties can be constituents of content, I mean to exclude non-appearance properties, but not necessarily non-properties, such as concrete particulars. There may be a way to expand the scope of what can figure in exp-intentional content—i.e., what can be a constituent of such content—to particulars, though they would have to be fairly unusual particulars: what we might call *appearance particulars*. I do not have in mind mental particulars that exist "only in the mind," such as sense data (Jackson 1977). Rather, I have in mind non-mental particulars whose

essential, individuating properties are appearance properties (response-dependent properties or centering features). For example, one could posit a particular—call it *Apparent-Phosphorus*$_{Sn,Rk,Cj}$—such that for any particular x, x is *Apparent-Phosphorus*$_{Sn,Rk,Cj}$ iff x has *essentially* the property of being such as to elicit response of type R_k in subjects of type S_n under conditions of type C_j. This would be an appearance particular, and as such could figure in an exp-intentional content. Positing appearance particulars has a cost, insofar as it will lead to ontological explosion. But if it is indeed true that the benefit is a solution to the puzzle of intentional indifference, then as far as I am concerned, the benefit outweighs the costs. Personally, I am not worried by the multiplication of particulars involved in this, since I take the mereological composition of concrete particulars to be response-dependent anyway (Kriegel 2008c).

36. As noted above, I am sympathetic to it. But I am also aware that it comes with important costs, and so am not fully subscribed to it. I am, however, fully subscribed to the idea that (HOTT★) is preferable over (HOTT), though for separate reasons. In Kriegel 2009 Ch.3, I argue that the qualitative character of a conscious experience—what makes it the conscious experience it is—is identical with being suitably tracked to track response-dependent properties. This provides independent support for (HOTT★).

37. Thompson does not use the term "exp-intentional content," of course, but his point can be put in those terms without change of substance. Also, it is perhaps worth mentioning that the experiences I presented were plausibly *cognitive* experiences with a different cognitive exp-intentional content: an experience of Phosphorus and an experience of Hesperus enjoyed by a subject who recognizes Phosphorus and Hesperus but is unaware that they are one and the same. Thompson's cases involve *perceptual* experiences.

38. It is noteworthy that the relevant change need not be in the visual processing, but may have to do with the laws of optics, or some such non-psychological laws.

39. Interestingly, these thought-experiments can be used to produce new scenarios involving intentional indifference. Consider the converse of the El Greco World thought-experiment, with two subjects leading similar lives, but one living in the actual world and another living in a world just like ours except that the laws of nature are sufficiently strange that they produce an El Greco-ed perceptual phenomenology (as Jonathan Simon suggested to me in conversation). Objects in the external world are the same in both worlds, but experiential characters are different. The result is that actual experiences and El Greco-ed experiences bear the right tracking relation to the same property but have different exp-intentional content. A similar story could be told about Doubled experiential character: other things being equal, perceptual experiences of the Meter in Paris and perceptual experiences of half the Meter in Doubled Paris will have different exp-intentional content but both track the property of being one meter long.

40. Note that this nomological possibility of brain-in-vat scenario probably contrasts with Thompson's scenarios, which probably are not nomologically possible.

41. An interesting consequence of this account is that the exp-intentional contents of the envatted brain's experiences is veridical—at least when mine is. Of course, if, when fed sensory stimulation characteristic of a yellow butterfly, the envatted brain is undergoing a pink-elephant-ish experience, then its experience is non-veridical. But normally, it will be veridical.

42. I develop a variant of the argument from intentional inexistence to be discussed below, in a way that focuses on *particulars*, in Kriegel 2007.

43. As we will see momentarily, though, there are connections to be drawn between uninstantiated properties and properties we have reasons to avoid ontological commitment to.

44. I will consider below objections claiming that we cannot.

45. By calling the duplicate "lifelong," I mean to contrast it with a scenario in which a person actually lives in the environment she experiences and only later has her brain envatted. By calling the

duplication "accidental," I mean to contrast it with a scenario in which someone—an evil scientist or demon, for example—intentionally generates the experiential stream enjoyed by the brain. These specifications are intended to rule out (a) claiming that the envatted brain continues to have an exp-intentional state of the type it had pre-envatment because exp-intentional content is determined once and for all at the end of an early "learning" period, and (b) claiming that those exp-intentional contents derive from the contents the scientist or demon envisages when feeding the envatted brain its stimulation.

46. In addition, the relevant experiential character is introspectible, so by the transparency thesis should be exp-intentional.

47. This simple observation is typically overlooked by proponents of "intentional relations." A rare exception is Priest (2005), who recognizes the costs of such talk and explicitly embraces the idea that a property can be instantiated in the absence of an instantiator. Tellingly, Priest's views on intentionality are often dismissed as obscure. Yet his view strikes me as the only stable option for a proponent of those "special" intentional relations.

48. For fuller development of some of the issues that arise in this connection, see Kriegel 2011a.

49. Perhaps it is just my nominalist predispositions, but I have always found such appeals to be in some sense "cheap."

50. Or perhaps as follows: every fact whose constituents exist within space-time can be fully explained by other such facts. This could be more formally put as follows: (ECRC) For any state of affairs S, such that (i) all of S's constituents exist within space-time and (ii) S is explainable, there is a state of affairs S★, such that (i) all of S★'s constituents exist within space-time and (ii) S★ fully explains S.

51. Nonetheless, there may also be causal explanations that violate the explanatory closure of the realm of concreta. When a hallucination of a frightening dragon causes one to run away, the running is a concrete event but its cause is a relation between a concretum and an abstractum, which in a sense involves the abstractum in the causal explanation of a concretum. There are certain moves that can be made by the primitivist here to fend off this worry. But while I doubt they will be successful, I will not pursue the matter here.

52. Some philosophers sometimes speak as though properties *are* functions from possible worlds to extensions. This seems to me to be based on a vaguely irrealist approach to properties, whereby it is thought that a property just is whatever is the best way to model it (or its individuation). On their face, properties seem to be more like ways-things-could-be than like *functions*. Moreover, the case for the existence of properties is much stronger than the case for the existence of merely possible worlds, so it is much more natural to think of appeal to merely possible worlds as having to do with a useful way to *model* properties than with an account of what they *are*.

53. As noted above, it may well be that an experience as of a square triangle is possible, but must be a *cognitive* rather than *perceptual* experience. In that case, the difficulty I have in mind would not arise concerning the putative property of a square triangle. But it is almost certain that it will arise with *some* putative property. As long as there is some predicate we can concoct grammatically, but for which there is no experienceable corresponding putative property, the problem will arise.

54. It may be suggested that the individuation of necessarily uninstantiated properties requires that we broaden our view and individuate properties in terms of functions from worlds in general, possible and impossible, to extensions. But this requires a prior individuation of impossible worlds, and it is not entirely clear how this would go.

55. It is, of course, controversial whether any tracking story about misrepresentation is plausible, even for more standard cases of misrepresentation, involving (say) an experience as of a big cat when in fact one is looking at a small dog on a moonless night.

56. This raises the specter of responding by denying the possibility of Twin-Emorie's Escher triangle experience being the way it is described in the thought-experiment. I will address this momentarily.

57. In line with the first option, an objector might claim that, contrary to appearances, conscious experiences with Escher-triangle-ish experiential character are not about Escher triangles at all, but about whatever they happen to track (or be higher-order tracked to track). Twin-Emorie's experience, for example, tracks whatever state of the vat-controlling machine is responsible for producing Escher-triangle-ish experiences in Twin-Emorie. This objection is misguided, however. In fact, nothing I have said thus far rules out that Twin-Emorie's experience is indeed about the relevant state of the machine. However, that state of the machine certainly does not figure in the *exp-intentional* content of the experience, since even if the experience is about the relevant state of the machine, it is not in virtue of its experiential character that it is. For all I have said here, there may be any number of other contents Twin-Emorie's experience carries. But its *exp-intentional* content has to do with an Escher triangle, and tracking accounts cannot accommodate *that*. This is why the argument from intentional inexistence is an argument against tracking accounts *of experiential intentionality*. The objector could come back and just deny that the experience has an exp-intentional content. This is to claim that the experience is not an exp-intentional state. But we have already argued that it does and is. The objector would have to deny either that the experience is assessable for accuracy in virtue of its Escher-triangle-ish experiential character, or that being assessable for accuracy is sufficient for having intentional content. Both options seem far-fetched to me.

58. If in some metaphysically possible and nomologically impossible world Twin-Emorie can have an experience as of an Escher triangle, the objector could suggest that this is because in that world experiential intentionality is realized by a kind of relation different from the one in which it is realized in the actual world and every nomologically possible world.

59. For the distinction between rebutting and undercutting defeaters, see Pollock 1986.

60. As elsewhere, it seems to me that dropping the reference to the subject is best understood as implicit reference to the normal subject in normal conditions. If so, to say that *p* is conceivable is to say that *p* appears possible to the normal subject under normal conditions.

61. For a compelling defense of this general principle, see Huemer 2001 Ch.5.

62. For relevant discussion of the distinction between ideal and superficial (or *prima facie*) conceivability, see Chalmers 2002. I do not wish to subscribe to Chalmers' positive position, however.

63. Thus, Frege's (1903) set theory seems superficially coherent, but has a hidden incoherence in it, exposed only upon reflection, namely, through Russell's Paradox (Russell 1902). Perhaps something similar is true here.

64. Keep in mind that as we trace the Escher triangle's angle, we do not as yet *know* that it is impossible. So it is not clear why we do not take the extra step of trying to imagine the triangle as a whole, if imagining a triangle as a whole is in general possible.

65. Alternatively, it would have to be denied that conscious thoughts have an exp-intentional content at all—to my mind, an even more extraordinary claim (see §1.3.3, as well as Kriegel forthcoming).

66. Note that colors, being experientially simple properties, do not submit to a compositional analysis that might attempt to account for intentional directedness at nomologically-necessarily uninstantiated properties in terms of tracking simpler properties which combine in a nomologically impossible way to make up the nomologically-necessarily uninstantiated property (e.g., the property of being a three-headed flying bobcat). I will say more about the compositional strategy in §3.5.

67. The view of properties as tropes (Williams 1953) casts them as individual aspects, or logical parts, of concreta, and thus clearly makes room for them inside space-time. The view of properties as universals *in re* (Armstrong 1978) casts universals as existing only in the things that instantiate them, rather than in the Platonic heavens, as universals *ante rem* are supposed to. Since the universals *in re* exist in the particulars that instantiate them, and those particulars exist in space-time, the universals *in re* exist in space-time. Now, there are surely criteria for concreteness and abstractness by which universals *in re*

come out abstract rather than concrete. For example, universals *in re* are wholly present in more than one place at the same time, and may be thought to that extent abstract. But they are also wholly present within space-time, and are to this extent concrete. However, what matters is that the principle of the explanatory closure of the concrete realm is most plausible, it seems to me, when the notion of concreteness at play in it is that which appeals to internality to space-time.

68. Suppose Hailey hallucinates a chimerically colored dragon. Tracking-based accounts explain Hailey's experience's being chimerically-colored-dragon-ish in terms of the experience's being related to the property of being a chimerically colored dragon in the appropriate first- and/or higher-order tracking way. But this is to appeal to an *uninstantiated* property (nothing is a chimerically colored dragon) in the explanation of the experience's *instantiated* properties. This is, of course, constitutive (broadly philosophical) explanation, not causal (broadly scientific) explanation.

69. For more detail on this line of argument, see Kriegel 2011a.

70. I can certainly *conceive* of an abstract entity being added or subtracted from a possible world.

71. In fact, this would apply to any philosopher who (i) denies the existence of metaphysically-necessarily uninstantiated properties and (ii) maintains that the laws of nature are necessary. Some philosophers have argued that nomological necessity entails metaphysical necessity, because the laws of nature are metaphysically necessary (Shoemaker 1998). Others have made the slightly weaker claim that properties *individuate* by their causal role, which, when combined with the principle of nomic subsumption (causation always has to be subsumed under causal laws), yields an individuation of properties by their location within the web of laws making up nature.

72. It might be objected that there are properties that are not actually instantiated but that are nomologically-possibly instantiated, and that those *can* be tracked, which shows that at least *some* conscious experiences as of non-existent objects are possible. However, this is doubly unsatisfying. First, although it is plausible that actually uninstantiated but nomologically-possibly instantiated properties can be tracked by the lights of Dretske's teleo-informational account, it is equally plausible that they *cannot* be tracked by the lights of Fodor's "counterfactual dependence" account (see its second clause in §2.1.1), as well as evolutionary accounts such as Millikan's. Secondly, and more importantly, while denying the ideal conceivability of experiences as of *logically* impossible objects may have *some* merit, it is hard to swallow the notion that there can be no experiences as of *nomologically* impossible objects, which is what this objector would have to do.

73. It is, of course, a vexed matter just what it takes for a phenomenon to be "natural," in the sense of being legitimately appealed to in a naturalization project. But that the notion of the natural is hard to pin down should not mislead us to say that there is nothing to it. When it comes to what is naturalistically kosher, philosophers are typically in the position of Justice Potter Stewart, who opined in *Jacobellis v. Ohio* that pornography is hard to define, but added "I know it when I see it." One way to understand this remark is as follows: the notion of pornography is a prototype notion, and we deem something pornographic just when it is sufficiently relevantly similar to familiar prototypes. The same could be said of the natural(istic): we recognize prototypical cases of what is natural, and deem natural anything sufficiently relevantly similar to the prototypes. The prototypes appear to be causal, mechanistic processes involving physical particulars and governed by laws of nature. Although this would require sustained argumentation, my sense is that no notion of tracking that would be sufficiently relevantly similar to such processes would allow for the tracking of nomologically-necessarily uninstantiated properties, properties not instantiated in any world with the same laws of nature as the actual world.

74. I should note that (HOTT)—the higher-order tracking theory—has a marginal advantage here over (first-order) tracking accounts, in that there is one kind of apparently possible exp-intentional state the former does not, but the latter do, have to rule out. I have in mind the conscious experiences of a recently envatted brain who lived a normal life beforehand. Suppose Emorie is abducted by evil

scientists, who put her in a coma and envat her brain in a way that is subjectively undetectable. According to most tracking accounts, the brain's experiences immediately after this operation still track what they used to track before the operation, but after enough time has passed—say, the time it takes for Dretskean (re-)learning to occur—Emorie's brain starts tracking states of the machine responsible for stimulating the brain. At this point, tracking accounts have to deny the metaphysical possibility of a conscious experience that tracks states of the machine but whose exp-intentional content makes no reference to those states. Within a (HOTT) account, there are two re-learning processes that have to occur: one that brings first-order states to track states of the machine rather than of the external environment, and one that brings second-order states to track state-of-machine-trackers rather than states-of-external-environment-trackers. During the interval when the first re-learning process is completed, but the second one is not, there will be internal states to which (HOTT) *can* ascribe, and tracking accounts *cannot* ascribe, the exp-intentional content that those internal states appear intuitively to have. This window represents a(n admittedly marginal) advantage of (HOTT) over tracking accounts of experiential intentionality.

75. More precisely, they do not bear any relation to what they are about *qua* exp-intentional states. Recall that exp-intentional states may have multiple contents, hence nexp-intentional contents. For all I am arguing right now, for those nexp-intentional contents of exp-intentional states, it may well be that a relation to what figures in the content is required. But for their exp-intentional contents, no relation is constitutively required—though it may be contingently required. Also, I put things in terms of bearing a relation *constitutively*, because there is no reason why, on this account, experiences could not on occasion bear relations to what they are about contingently. Certainly veridical exp-intentional states do. Mandik (2009) argues that intentionality cannot involve a relation to what it is about even contingently, but this stronger demand seems to me neither motivated nor plausible.

76. Two remarks are in order. This view should not be confused with the view, from §2.1.3, that there is an irreducibly experiential tracking that experiential intentionality is identical to. For the primitive experiential relation appealed to here is not a *tracking* relation. Relatedly, primitivism obviously suffers from the fact that the relation it posits between exp-intentional states and the putative properties they are intentionally related to is somewhat mysterious. But I will not focus on this problem here.

77. This is because primitivism explains concrete conscious experience in terms of relations to abstracta, as uninstantiated properties must be construed.

78. This is, presumably, because content is taken to be an entity an intentional state is the intentional state it is in virtue of being related to.

79. For another adverbialist account of experiential intentionality, see Mendelovici 2010. My own adverbial account is patterned on the one proposed originally for sense perception by Ducasse (1942) and Chisholm (1957). In the adverbial account of sense perception, it is shown that although the surface grammar of "Gemroy perceives red" casts perception as a relation between two concrete particulars (Gemroy and a red), there is a way to paraphrase such straightforward perceptual ascriptions into sentences with a completely different grammar, suggesting a completely different metaphysic. It can be paraphrased into "Gemroy perceives redly," which suggests a state of affairs consisting in a single particular instantiating a property and that property instantiating another property.

80. This corresponds to the fact that the former features two nouns and a transitive verb, whereas the latter features one noun, one intransitive verb, and one adverb. In general, adverbs and other grammatical modifiers pick out intrinsic modifications of the properties picked out by the expression they modify.

81. There are two ways to understand the locution "being intentionally directed F-wise." One is in terms of something exhibiting the property of F-wise intentional directedness. Another is in terms of something exhibiting F-wise the property of intentional directedness. The former construes "F-wise" as

qualifying the property instantiated, the latter as qualifying not the property but the instantiating of it. For a variety of reasons we will encounter momentarily, there are advantages to the former understanding, which I will therefore presuppose hereafter.

82. Note that against the background of assumptions we have already encountered a number of times, (ATEI*) leads to the following: There is a determinable (or genus) experiential property E, E = being-intentionally-directed-somehow, such that for any mental state x, x betokens the exp-intentional type that it does (and not another) because x instantiates the determinate (or species) E_i that it does (and not another), and x betokens an exp-intentional type (at all) because x instantiates a determinate (or species of) E (at all).

83. Needless to say, necessarily uninstantiated properties are never veridically experienced, so the conditional is always a counterfactual conditional when it comes to them, as per (b).

84. Thus there is no attempt here to account for the adverbial property in terms of the counterfactual property (or property ascribed through the counterfactual). The order of accounting is the opposite.

85. In this second hearing, then, to say of any state that it is about F is to say that it is appropriately related to F. In the first hearing, by contrast, to say of any state that it is about F is to say that the state is either appropriately related to F or such that it would be thus related to F if it were veridical.

86. A stronger version of this idea would take the form of a revelation account of the relevant adverbial properties, along the lines of revelation accounts of color (Johnston 1992). According to such accounts, the nature of the colors is not to be provided to us by a philosophical theory of color, but is rather directly revealed to us in visual experience. Likewise, one might want to say, the nature of adverbial exp-intentional properties is directly revealed to us in introspective encounter.

87. As stressed in Chapter 2, this is supposed to be fully consistent with the transparency of experience.

88. The accounts could also serve to distinguish experiential states that are intentional from those that are not, in case not all experiential states are (exp-)intentional.

89. Interestingly, if all conscious experiences are exp-intentional, then the property of phenomenal directedness would be co-extensive with the property of being a conscious experience. Whether they would be nonetheless distinct properties, or would turn out to be the same property, is a separate question.

90. This problem did exercise some tracking theorists during the nineteen-eighties, when it was sometimes referred to as the "horizontal disjunction problem."

91. It is Strawson's view that this taking is a cognitive rather than sensory feature, but I suppose someone could hold that the phenomenon Strawson has in mind is in fact wrongly construed as cognitive. Note, in any case, that if taking is a cognitive-experiential feature, and is necessary for experiential intentionality, then it follows that all experiential intentionality is cognitive, at least in the sense that the experiential character of exp-intentional states must have at least one cognitive element. I will discuss this in greater detail in §5.1.

92. I should note that Strawson himself nowhere commits to adverbialism. Rather, this is my own use of the notion of "taking." The notion is present already in Chisholm (1957), for whom the act through which the mind *takes* something to be thus-and-so is the fundamental intentional act, with other intentional acts being elaborations or modifications of a core act of taking. Strawson's notion is not borrowed from Chisholm, however, though there is clearly a close connection between the two.

93. More precisely, Masrour holds that there are several legitimate notions of intentionality, but that one of the most important pertains to directedness at objects. There is also another central notion, that of intentional directedness at objects that are presented as in some way objective or mind-independent, and this kind of intentional directedness experiences exhibit in virtue of a different experiential property,

which he calls *schematic dynamical unity* (Masrour 2008 Ch.3, forthcoming-b). This second kind of intentionality Masrour takes to be the more important of the two, but for our present purposes the first one seems more pertinent, so I will focus on it.

94. This seems to commit the view under consideration to the existence of non-intentional conscious experiences, or at least of experiences that are not exp-intentional. For it involves the idea that before the Gestalt shift there was no unity structure, and one's visual experience was therefore *not* exp-intentional. But another interpretation may be that one's visual experience is exp-intentional even before the Gestalt shift—it is intentionally directed at an externally-situated pattern of black and white splotches—because there was *some* objectual unity involved in the experience even before the shift, albeit of a much impoverished level. Thus the view under consideration is compatible with both the notion that all conscious experiences are exp-intentional and the notion that only some are. Again that question is seen to be orthogonal to our main concern.

95. Interestingly, this view too seems to lead to a characterization of the relevant experiential property as cognitive-experiential. For presumably, the purely sensory aspect of one's visual experience is the same before and after the Gestalt shift, it is just that after the switch the experience also exhibits a richer objectual unity structure than before (or perhaps exhibits the objectual unity structure at all). So this objectual unity structure is different even when the sensory component of the experience is indistinguishable, suggesting that the objectual unity structure is a non-sensory component of the visual experiences' experiential character, and is at least to that extent cognitive.

96. This last sentence does not represent a move Masrour would make, because he is not an adverbialist about experiential intentionality. But the combination of adverbialism about experiential intentionality and the claim that objectual unity structure is the phenomenological signature of intentionality generates the suggestion that objectual unity structure constitutes the property of being intentionally directed some*how*.

97. As Frey (forthcoming: 11) puts it, the elements "that one phenomenally appreciates in an experience are always appreciated as *other*." And more: "[W]hen we phenomenally appreciate the presence of a sensuous element in an experience, we appreciate the sensuous element as being both something other than ourselves and as standing in opposition to ourselves. I call this phenomenal structure, this unitary nexus of self and other in experience, *phenomenal presence* . . . [W]e must be careful to distinguish the predicates '_appreciates *x* as other_' and '_appreciates *x* as (being . . . the) self_' from similar expressions that we have already rejected, e.g. '_appreciates *x* as objective_' or '_appreciates *x* as distally located_.' The appreciation of a sensuous element as other isn't an appreciation of something as belonging to one or more ontological kinds or as possessing one or more intrinsic characteristics . . ." (Frey forthcoming: 11–12). Note two things: first, Frey calls the feature he is concerned with "phenomenal presence," but I will call it "phenomenal foreignness"; secondly, Frey's thesis is restricted, at least here, to the *sensuous* elements of experience, but in my own discussion I lift this restriction and apply the thesis to *cognitive* elements as well.

98. This does *not* mean that it must present the property as *not* being instantiated by the self. The property may be instantiated by both oneself and another—it is just that the experience presents it as instantiated by another. In any case, as Frey notes the relevant notion of self is the notion of an *experiential* self—our interest is not in the *bodily* self, for example.

99. As above, I must release Frey from all explicit affiliation with any things adverbial.

100. A fifth option, which I hesitate to take seriously, would be to construe the property of being intentionally directed some*how* in terms of the transparency of experience. As we saw in §2.1.2, the main motivation for construing conscious experiences as intentional is that they are transparent—in introspecting these experiences, one is only aware of their intentional properties. The transparency thesis is cited most often by philosophers attracted to the idea that all experience is intentional, but it can be

used more generally as a test of a *prima facie* case for the intentionality of any given type of experience. It is natural to think of transparency as a *symptom* of an experience's intentionality: a given type of experience's transparency is an indication of its intentionality. In the present context, it is natural to think that an experience is transparent *because* it instantiates the experiential property of being directed somehow (however we choose to account for that property). But it is certainly coherent to reverse that order of explanation and hold that an experience exhibits the property of being directed somehow because it is transparent, where the "because" is understood constitutively: the experience's being transparent constitutes its being intentionally directed somehow. I hesitate to take this option seriously because, although coherent, it seems unmotivated and counter-intuitive.

101. As for the formulation of the view in terms of intentional types, it would be this: (ATEI★1) Necessarily★, for any mental state x and exp-intentional type I, there is an experiential property E, E = phenomenally presenting-an-other-to-be-F, such that x betokens I iff x is E. This further leads, against the background of familiar assumptions, to the following thesis: There is a determinable (or genus) experiential property E, of phenomenally presenting-an-other-to-be-somewhay, such that for any exp-intentional state x, x betokens the exp-intentional content it does (and not another) because x instantiates the determinate (or species) E_i it does (and not another), and x betokens an exp-intentional type (at all) because x instantiates a determinate (or species of) E (at all).

102. Another choice point for the adverbial theory concerns a choice between two possible views on the ontological assay of the property of being intentionally directed F-wise. One is that being intentionally directed F-wise, although it does not involve (constitutively) bearing a relation to F, does involve (constitutively) bearing a relation to *something else*. The other view is that being intentionally directed F-wise is an altogether non-relational property—an *intrinsic* modification of the intentional state. Call the former *relational adverbialism* and the latter *intrinsic adverbialism*. Both agree that being intentionally directed F-wise does not require bearing a relation to F. And they agree, furthermore, that what it takes for x to be intentionally directed F-wise is for x to have the right experiential character, i.e., that there is an experiential property E, such that instantiating E bestows, or *is*, exp-intentional content. The disagreement is on whether E is a relational or non-relational property of the state that instantiates it. It seems to me that relational adverbialism is in a position to inherit all the disadvantages of more standard relational views without preserving the advantages of adverbialism, so my inclination is to prefer intrinsic adverbialism. (It is also possible to hold that exp-intentional states both bear the relevant relation to distinct entities and that they have the relevant non-relational property. Still, a kind of Euthyphro question would arise: does the experience have its intrinsic property because it bears the right relation to those entities or does it bear its relation to those entities because it instantiates the intrinsic property? If I am right in my suspicion of relational adverbialism, the correct answer is the latter: the state bears the relation it does because it instantiates the intrinsic property it does.)

103. Note well, however: if the premise is to be put this way, the term "some" must not be understood to carry ontological commitment, since the premise is intended to imply avoidance of ontological commitment to the putative property F. So either "some" is not to be construed as meaning the same as "there are," or "there are" is to be construed as ontologically non-committal, as in some non-classical logics.

104. This conclusion relies on an extra premise, common in this sort of argument, to the effect that all exp-intentional states (veridical and non-veridical alike) must be such in virtue of the same thing, and therefore it cannot be the case that some are exp-intentional in virtue of being appropriately related to something and some not.

105. The conclusion of this argument is obviously not exactly the adverbial theory as formulated in (ATEI). But (ATEI) offers the only sensible positive account of experiential intentionality open to someone who accepts the conclusion of the argument. In a way, then, we could reach (ATEI) from Proposition 3 in the argument by adding a simple bridge premise of the form "If 3, then (ATEI)."

106. Some disjunctivists will reject our stipulation, holding that the hallucination cannot be experientially indistinguishable from the veridical experience, although it may *seem* to be (see Fish 2009). That too I find myself unable to take seriously.

107. This problem is traditionally applied to the version of the peculiar entity strategy that appeals to actual concrete mental entities, but it applies equally to the other versions: a veil of abstracta and a veil of non-actualia are just as bad as—perhaps worse than—a veil of actual mental concreta. For relevant discussion, see Kriegel 2011a.

108. For a fuller discussion of these liabilities, see Kriegel 2007.

109. Another concern is that since the compositionality of language is a pre-requisite for its learnability, the adverbial language which the adverbialist recommends we speak would not be learnable. This does not strike me as a major concern. Although the entire set of possible sentences in the adverbial language might be unlearnable, it seems that each individual sentence is learnable, and this is really all the adverbialist needs here.

110. In addition, there may also be a second response to Jackson's argument: to paraphrase "I am thinking about green dragons and purple butterflies" as "I am thinking green-wise and dragon-wise and green-dragon-wise and purple-wise and butterfly-wise and purple-butterfly-wise." This is extremely awkward and inelegant, but that is neither here nor there. What matters is that this new paraphrase is distinct from the corresponding paraphrase of "I am thinking about purple dragons and green butterflies" and yet licenses inferences via something similar to conjunction elimination. In any case, there appears to be, then, a reasonable response to Jackson's objection—reasonable enough, certainly, that (ATEI) could not be pronounced dead on its strength alone. And since the other major reason for doing so—the thought that perception is inherently intentional—has no bite in the present context, I conclude that the adverbial theory of experiential intentionality is perfectly viable.

111. I find it natural to think of such thought-experiments in terms of trans-world identity, with every individual being literally identical to one in the actual world (except for the relevant laptop), but the story can of course be told in terms of world-bound individuals and counterpart relations. We would have to imagine that Twin World has a counterpart of every individual in the actual world except for the relevant laptop, which is not a counterpart of the corresponding Twin-Earthly laptop.

112. This presentation of the objection does presupposes that concrete particulars do not individuate by their properties, but by individual essences—*haecceities*. That is, it presupposes rejection of the "bundle theory" of particulars. For discussion of why this is plausible, see Van Cleve 1985. Of course, if concrete particulars do individuate by their properties, exp-intentional content is certainly exhausted by properties, and the threat of singular content does not even arise.

113. Importantly, the same analysis applies to *cognitive* experiences. If I am consciously thinking that my laptop is silver, the content of my thought is not quite singular, though it is particular: I am thinking about *this particular* laptop, but my counterpart in Twin-World is thinking about *that particular* laptop, where what the thoughts refer to is different, but the thoughts are exp-intentionally type-identical.

114. And in one of the two ways "about" can be used that we saw above, the experiences are *about* different things.

115. Donnellan (1966) argues that in some of their uses, definite descriptions do have different contents when they are about different particulars. More precisely, this is the case with definite descriptions in their "referential" use but not in their "attributive" use. If we accept this claim (and see Kripke 1977 for an argument that the distinction is actually pragmatic and not semantic), we will have to stipulate in the text that we are discussing "the first black US president" in its attributive use.

116. This generalizes to any kind of externalism about exp-intentional content. It is true that adverbialism cannot accommodate any wide aspect exp-intentional content may have, but I deny that it has any such, for the reasons adduced in the main text.

117. A somewhat more "personalized" particularity can be generated by construing the content as attributing particularity in demonstrative manner, as in "there is an x, such that x is F_1, . . ., x is *this* concrete particular, . . ., F_n, and x is silver," where the demonstrative content is understood along the lines of Searle's (1983) token-reflexive approach to indexical content. On this approach, the content of "this particular" is captured by something like the description "the particular at which this very intentional state is directed." Kroon (forthcoming) develops such a token-reflexive approach to the singularity of exp-intentional content.

118. This last inference is perhaps what a disjunctivist about experiential intentionality would deny. I have never been able to appreciate the attraction of disjunctivism, so have nothing particularly insightful to say about why I find such disjunctivism about experiential intentionality implausible.

119. One idea that I think leads us astray on these matters is the assumption that the notion of truth is in some sense more basic than the notion of content, and that we ought to understand the latter in terms of the former. Since Davidson's (1967) work on truth-conditional semantics, this has been orthodoxy. However, intuitively at least, it does seem to put the cart before the horse: "snow is white" is true in English, but of course it might be false in Swahili, or in some language yet to be invented. We assess the sentence for truth only insofar as the sentence *means* something, that is, only insofar as it is contentful. Viewed from this perspective, truth-conditional semantics appears to be part of a long philosophical tradition of reversing the manifest order of explanatory priority to generate what are often exciting but ultimately implausible stories. In this tradition are verificationism ("you might think that a sentence is verifiable because it is meaningful, but really it is the opposite: the sentence is meaningful because it is verifiable"), the use theory of meaning ("you might think that people use words the way they do because of what those words mean, but really it is the opposite: the words mean what they do because of how people use them"), and behaviorism about propositional attitudes ("you might think that people take umbrellas because they believe it will rain, but really it is the opposite: people believe it will rain because they take umbrellas"). There are other instances of this in other areas of philosophy of course, two of which being the regularity theory of causation ("you might think there is regularity between A and B because A causes B, but really it is the opposite: A causes B because there is regularity between them") and the accessibility theory of consciousness ("you might think that conscious states are accessible because they are conscious, but really it is the opposite: they are conscious because they are accessible").

120. This may not be a trivial task, but it is one regarding which the literature already contains some insightful suggestions. As mentioned in §1.3.2, I am particularly fond of Siewert's (1998) suggestion that an experience is assessable for accuracy purely in virtue of its experiential character (and without need of any interpretation). This observation is quite compelling and can help adverbialism meet its burden.

121. In the previous section, I presented a number of accounts of E (as *sui generis* directedness, experiential taking, objectual unity structure, and phenomenal foreignness), but those were non-reductive accounts, in that they did not appeal to non-experiential notions. Compare and contrast higher-order tracking theory, which accounts for experiential intentionality in terms of tracking notions, themselves accounted for in non-experiential terms. This is pressing, because as we saw in §3.3.2, naturalistic credentials are the main reason to simply reject the apparent possibility of experiences exhibiting intentional inexistence (which experiences motivate adverbialism) as *merely* apparent.

122. One central question in this approach is whether naturalization is intrinsically or instrumentally valuable. If naturalization is intrinsically/non-instrumentally valuable, i.e. is valuable as an intellectual end in itself, then no further issue arises, but an argument is needed for the non-instrumentality claim. If naturalization is valuable only as a means to some other intellectual end, then two further questions arise, namely, concerning (i) what the final end is that naturalization is a means to and (ii) whether naturalization is the only means for achieving that end. More on this too below.

123. This response concedes that (ATEI) does not *deliver* naturalization, but denies that it is *incompatible* with naturalization. Note that the application of Block and Stalnaker's (1999) approach to the relevant adverbial properties is not a matter of analogy, but subsumption: the adverbial properties are *experiential* properties, so they fall within the scope of Block and Stalnaker's approach to the reduction of *all* experiential properties.

124. I too am antecedently persuaded of the truth of naturalism. But I recognize that some phenomena do not fit the naturalist mold very comfortably, which is partly why they are philosophically problematic (and interesting). To just insist on the truth of naturalism is not to solve any philosophical problem raised by the problematic phenomena.

125. This would be a kind of non-reductive variant on (HOTT). Since I avowed significant credence for (HOTT) in §2.3, I would be particularly sympathetic to this version of non-reductive adverbialism.

126. This consideration developed out of a conversation with Tim Bayne and Jordi Fernández.

127. Moreover, there are reasons to think that such a positive account is unlikely. Experiential properties occupy a certain typical functional role (probably to do broadly with something like global accessibility to information-processing modules, though see Kriegel 2009 Ch.7 for a more specific account), but microscopic particulars do not (and do not have internal states that) occupy that functional role.

128. This suggestion could be patterned after a kind of panexperientialism or panprotoexperientialism, and in any case a sort of type-F monism, of a form Chalmers is clearly very sympathetic to (see Chalmers 2003). This view is immune to the argument indented in the main text, but as noted, it is suspiciously speculative and, more importantly, it is implausible that exp-intentional properties are of the sort such views posit. Exp-intentional properties are clearly instantiated by macroscopic entities.

129. At least this is what a grand system in the *strict* sense would amount to. Clearly, the grand systems of the enlightenment were not this, though arguably they approximated, or at some level aspired to approximate, this sort of ideal. We may say that they are grand systems in the *loose* sense.

130. I am thinking of intuition, more accurately, as entering the picture after perception has already done its work of ruling out some coherent wholes. Presumably, perception is not going to rule out all coherent wholes but one, wherefore intuition would be called upon to select among those wholes (if only by selecting the disjunction of them all).

131. For comments on a previous draft, I thank David Chalmers and a reader for OUP. This chapter is based on ideas explored in two previous publications (Kriegel 2007, 2008a). Since the appearance of these papers, I have received a lot of valuable commentary, and had many instructive conversations, about the relevant ideas. It is hard for me to remember everybody I had relevant interactions with, but here is a partial list: Stephen Biggs, Ben Blumson, Michael Bruno, David Chalmers, Terry Horgan, Pete Mandik, Farid Masrour, Luca Moretti, Adam Pautz, Susanna Siegel, Jonathan Simon, Alberto Voltolini, Sebastian Watzl.

4

The Nature of Non-Experiential Intentionality
An Interpretivist Theory

Introduction/Abstract

In Chapter 1, I argued that our very conception of intentionality is grounded in our grasp of experiential intentionality. This made it a first priority to develop an account of experiential intentionality, a task I pursued in Chapters 2–3. A comprehensive theory of intentionality would also require, however, an account of non-experiential intentionality. This need not represent a distinctive challenge for anyone not committed to the experiential origin thesis, but it does to someone who is. The challenge can be summarized with the following question: what are the identity and existence conditions of non-experiential intentionality? More precisely:

(NIQ) For any nexp-intentional item x, what makes x the nexp-intentional item it is (rather than another, different nexp-intentional item) and a nexp-intentional item at all (rather than an item devoid of non-experiential intentionality)?[1]

On the assumption that intentional items individuate by their intentional contents, the question becomes:

(NIQ★) For any item x and property F, what would make it the case that F figures in the nexp-intentional content of x?[2]

The general form of the answer is offered by the experiential origin thesis from Chapter 1, articulated first in terms of (EO) and then in terms of (EO★). According to (EO), there is only one way for a non-experiential item to qualify as intentional, namely, by sharing an underlying nature with most exp-intentional states. (EO★) is more lenient, and provides a non-experiential item with two ways of qualifying as intentional: either by sharing an underlying nature with most exp-intentional states, or by bearing the right relation to items that share one (a relation that makes it possible to account for its intentionality in terms of that of those items). Recall that the reason for retreating to (EO★) was the thought that many apparently intentional items do not in fact have the same underlying nature as most encountered exp-intentional states, with the result that (EO) would fail to secure the apparent extension of intentionality (see §1.2.3). In the present chapter, I consider four possible approaches to the nature of the relation cited in (EO★): a "potentialist" approach developed by Searle (§4.1), an "inferentialist" approach developed by Loar and Horgan and collaborators (§4.2), an "eliminativist" approach defended by Strawson and Georgalis (§4.3), and an "interpretivist" approach I will develop below (§4.4), arguing that it fares better with respect to the body of desiderata and adequacy constraints that will emerge from the discussion.[3,4]

4.1. Potentialism

One of the earliest philosophers to stress the centrality of consciousness to intentionality was John Searle. Searle's (1992 Ch.7) main thesis is the *connection principle*: a mental state is intentional only if it is at least *potentially* conscious. According to Searle, genuine intentionality involves the phenomenon of *aspectual shape*—something like what I called (in §3.1) *intentional indifference*—and this phenomenon can be brought into the picture only by consciousness. His reasoning can be summarized as follows. Intentional indifference is the phenomenon that underwrites substitution failure: being intentionally directed at Phosphorus is not the same as being intentionally directed at Hesperus, even though Phosphorus is the same as Hesperus. Brain states' tracking relations to the environment cannot distinguish between Phosphorus and Hesperus, however—only experiential character can.[5] If so, what makes a brain state B, appropriately connected to Venus, about Phosphorus and not Hesperus? The only viable answer is that if B realizes a conscious experience C, then one thing that might make B about Phosphorus and not Hesperus is C's experiential character, which might be Phosphorescent rather than Hesperescent. If B realizes a *non*-experiential state N, then what makes B about Phosphorus and not Hesperus would have to be something like the following counterfactual: if N *were* a conscious experience, it *would* have a Phosphorescent rather than Hesperescent experiential character. The only way the counterfactual can be true, however, is if N is the kind of thing that *could* be conscious, that is, if N is *potentially* conscious. Only if a mental state is potentially conscious, then, can it exhibit aspectual shape (intentional indifference), and thus intentionality.

This argument is problematic in a number of ways.[6] Indeed, my own discussion in §3.2.2, if successful, would undermine it. My present concern is not directly with the argument, however, but with Searle's position on non-experiential intentionality, which we may call *potentialism*. The position inspires the following answer to (NIQ): a nexp-intentional item has the intentional content it does in virtue of potentially having the experiential character it potentially does, and has intentional content at all in virtue of potentially having experiential character at all.[7] More formally:

(Pot) Necessarily★, for any item x and property F, F figures in the nexp-intentional content of x iff the following holds: if x were an exp-intentional state, F would figure in x's exp-intentional content.[8]

If Searle's argument from aspectual shape does not go through, then we do not as yet have an argument for (Pot). But that would not constitute a positive argument *against* (Pot). My main concern in this section is with whether there are positive arguments against (Pot). In the literature, one finds two main worries about it: (a) that (Pot) is unclear and (b) that it gets the extension of intentionality wrong (i.e., returns the wrong results on specific cases). Let us consider these worries in turns.

An immediate difficulty with potentialism is that the notion of "potential" is not particularly clear (Fodor and Lepore 1994). What does it mean to say that a mental state is "potentially" conscious? Ideally, one would want a criterion for non-experiential intentionality whose application is clear and returns unequivocal results on specific cases. Neither seems to be the case with (Pot), given the obscurity of potentiality talk.

One option is to unpack potentiality in modal language, e.g., in terms of psychological possibility (Kriegel 2003a), understood as a specific variety of nomological possibility. Let us say that a world is psychologically possible just in case the psychological laws in it are the same as in the actual world. Then we could suggest that x is potentially conscious iff it is psychologically possible that x is conscious, that is, iff there is a psychologically possible world where *x* is conscious. If we adopt this explication, potentialism becomes the thesis that F figures in *x*'s nexp-intentional content just in case there is a psychologically possible world where F figures in *x*'s *exp*-intentional content. More precisely:

(Pot⁺) Necessarily*, for any item *x* and property F, F figures in the nexp-intentional content of *x* iff there is a possible world W, such that (i) W is psychologically possible, (ii) *x* is an exp-intentional state in W, and (iii) F figures in the exp-intentional content of *x* in W.[9]

This thesis is more explicit, and hopefully captures reasonably faithfully the intuitive idea behind the notion of potential consciousness. However, it also exposes potentialism more straightforwardly to the charge of getting the extension wrong.[10]

The charge is originally due to Davies (1995), who notes that some sub-personal representations posited in cognitive science, such as Marr's (1982) "2.5D sketches," are not even *potentially* conscious (see also Graham et al. 2007). Searle might simply deny the psychological reality of 2.5D sketches, but there are other cases where such a response would be extremely implausible. Dorsal-stream visual states are a case in point (Horgan and Kriegel 2008). Visual processing along the so-called dorsal stream of visual cortex generates representations of the environment that guide on-the-fly action but are not "accessible to consciousness" (Milner and Goodale 1995). Here it is unquestionable that such states do exist, and it would be quite odd to deny that they are intentional, given that they cause behavior in virtue of systematically covarying with states of the environment.[11] Presumably this is why cognitive scientists treat them as contentful.[12] At the same time, they are not potentially conscious in any familiar sense, nor in the sense of being conscious in some psychologically possible world (since for them to be conscious the laws of psychology would have to be different).

One option for Searle might be to insist that dorsal-stream visual states and the like are not intentional, but allow that they are representational in some impoverished sense. Recall that in §2.4, I distinguished two notions of representation, one associated with intentionality and one associated with (first-order) tracking. Searle could suggest that in virtue of their tracking profile, dorsal-stream states qualify as mental representations in the latter sense, and this suffices to do justice to the fact that they are treated as such by cognitive scientists. At the same time, they do not qualify as mental representations in the former sense, and thus do not qualify as intentional—precisely because they are not potentially conscious.

There are two problems with this response. First, there may be reasons to construe dorsal-stream states as intentional and not *merely* representational. In particular, there appears to be cognitive interaction between dorsal-stream visual states and conscious visual experiences occurring in the ventral stream of the visual system: the content of dorsal-stream states appears to sometimes causally affect the content of ventral-stream visual experiences (Jacob and Jeannerod 2003). It would be extremely odd if this were the case despite the latter having intentional content and the former having some other, not-quite-intentional content (a merely informational or tracking content). This is an important reason to take dorsal-stream states to have *intentional* content.

Secondly, even if it were justified to deny dorsal-stream states intentional contents, according them instead related but distinct properties, this would be successful in shielding (Pot$^+$) from the charge of getting the extension wrong, but only at the price of making getting the extension *right* impossible either. To get the extension right or wrong, there needs to be an extension that is taken to be pre-theoretically desirable. In the present context, it is natural to construe the pre-theoretically desirable extension of intentionality as determined by folk-theoretic and cognitive-scientific practice. However, if instances of mental states that folk theory and/or cognitive science treat as intentional can be recast as not-quite-intentional simply because they conflict with one's account of intentionality, then there is no longer a pre-theoretic extension against which one's account can be tested.[13] In that case, (Pot$^+$) avoids the evidence against it by sacrificing the possibility of evidence *for* it.

How bad this is depends on one's view on the importance of getting a pre-theoretic extension right. My view is that this is very important. In the previous chapter, I suggested that getting right the pre-theoretically desirable extension of a phenomenon is a sort of (quasi-)empirical virtue of a philosophical theory.[14] Against this background, defending (Pot$^+$) from getting the extension wrong by making impossible getting the extension right results in (Pot$^+$) having no (quasi-)empirical support.[15] In any case, the notion that an account of intentionality should be able to get the extension right underlies the worry that an account of intentionality that grounds it in experiential intentionality will fail to secure the correct extension of intentionality. Without this emphasis on recovering the extension, that concern evaporates.

For these reasons, I find myself unable to endorse Searle's potentialism, even though I am instinctually sympathetic to it. Since my goal is to recover the pre-theoretic apparent extension of intentionality within a theoretical framework, the fact that potentialism fails to get the extension right makes it overall unappealing.

4.2. Inferentialism

Brian Loar, and (in different combinations) Terry Horgan, George Graham, and John Tienson, assign a special role for experiential intentionality in the theory of intentionality because of a consideration akin to Searle's but slightly different.[16] Consider Quine's (1968) thesis of the inscrutability of reference, according to which there is no fact of the matter as to whether the term "rabbit" refers to rabbits, undetached rabbit parts, rabbit stages, or cetera. Loar and Horgan et al. contend that tracking of such rabbit-like entities is indeed bound to be inscrutable, but that intentional content must ultimately be "scrutable" (Loar 1995, Horgan and Tienson 2002, Horgan and Graham 2009). The only thing that can make it scrutable, they argue, is experiential character. Certainly there are no tracking relations that hold between internal states and rabbits but not between those states and undetached rabbit parts. However, what it is like to have a perceptual or cognitive experience as of rabbits is very different from what it is like to have such an experience as of undetached rabbit parts. Perhaps the purely sensory experiential character of such experiences is the same, but there is also a non-sensory, cognitive experiential character that differs.[17]

As with Searle's argument from aspectual shape, this argument from inscrutability will doubtless face some resistance.[18] But again our concern here is not to evaluate the argument. Our concern is with the positive view of non-experiential intentionality one finds in Loar and Horgan et al., which as it happens is again broadly the same. Given the scrutability consideration, Loar/Horgan et al. could take their view in two directions. One would be to hold that only *experiential* intentionality is scrutable, and all other intentionality is inscrutable. The other direction, the one they take, is to hold that *all* intentionality is scrutable, but that the scrutability of non-experiential intentionality is ultimately grounded in the scrutability of experiential intentionality (Loar 2003, Horgan and Graham 2009). The question is how the grounding works.

One way to approach this question is to look at the reasons for taking *all* intentionality to be scrutable. A central reason is that exp-intentional states interact cognitively with nexp-intentional states within the overall cognitive architecture of the mind, and such interaction requires that we conceive of the two kinds of state as having content of the same general sort. Consider a standard visual episode: a rabbit causes stimulation of the retina; information is then processed through the visual system, producing myriad unconscious visual states, culminating in the formation of a visual experience as of a rabbit; the experience, in conspiracy with a host of background beliefs (e.g., about one's perceptual connection to the environment), produces a perceptual judgment or thought to the effect that one is perceiving a rabbit; this perceptual judgment, in conspiracy with further background beliefs (e.g., about the general structure of the world), leads to the thought that a rabbit is present.[19] In this episode, visual and cognitive experiences interact crucially with unconscious visual states and background beliefs.[20] It is odd to imagine that the conscious experiences involved in this episode have a scrutable and determinate content but the unconscious states have an inscrutable and indeterminate content. It is odd to think that the conscious experiences are engaging with a rabbit, while as far as the unconscious states are concerned, it could be a rabbit, undetached rabbit parts, or rabbit stages.

If this is the reason to think that nexp-intentional states must have scrutable content as well, then one simple move is to claim that the feature in virtue of which they have scrutable content is precisely their cognitive integration with exp-intentional states. The answer to (NIQ) suggested by these reflections is this: what makes a nexp-intentional state have intentional content at all is that it is cognitively connected in the right way, that is, integrated into a cognitive system in which there are some exp-intentional states; what makes it have the specific intentional content it does (rather than another) is that it is cognitively connected to the specific exp-intentional states it is (and not others). Thus:

(Inf) Necessarily*, for any item x and property F, F figures in the nexp-intentional content of x iff there is a mental state y and a property

G, such that (i) G figures in the exp-intentional content of *y*, (ii) *x* is suitably cognitively connected to *y*, and (iii) F is suitably cognitively connected to G.[21]

This does not contain any terms as problematic as "potential." At the same time, talk of cognitive connectedness is not all that clear, especially given its application to both states (vehicles) and contents. One natural suggestion is to understand this notion of cognitive connection in terms of (a) *causal* connection between states/vehicles and (b) corresponding *inferential* connection between the contents of those states/vehicles. This leads to the following formulation:

(Inf⁺) Necessarily★, for any item *x* and property F, F figures in the nexp-intentional content of *x* iff there is a mental state *y* and a property G, such that (i) G figures in the exp-intentional content of *y*, (ii) *x* is suitably causally connected to *y*, and (iii) F is suitably inferentially connected to G.[22]

Call this *inferentialism* about non-experiential intentionality. This is the view of nexp-intentional content that Loar and Horgan et al. appear to hold. Inferentialism, so formulated, fares unquestionably better than potentialism with respect to the theoretical virtue of clarity.[23]

Does inferentialism fare better in terms of getting the extension of intentionality right? It would if it could capture intentional states that are not even potentially conscious. At first glance, it does seem that such states are suitably causally integrated into cognitive systems with exp-intentional states. However, there is no *guarantee* that all such states would indeed be thus integrated. I mentioned above that dorsal visual states probably are, but it is important to appreciate that this is a matter of some empirical controversy.[24] In any case, a creature is certainly possible for whom dorsal-stream processing is thoroughly insulated. In this creature, dorsal-stream processing never makes contact with any executive function or other rational control modules, or with any other conscious experiences or conscious-experience-producing subsystems. The resulting states may be causally connected (backward-lookingly) to earlier stages of visual processing and (forward-lookingly) to motor outputs, but never actually interact with conscious experiences. It may well be that cognitive science would still treat them as contentful states, however, especially if they still controlled motor responses in virtue of covarying with external conditions.[25]

In fact, we can imagine a simple organism whose cognitive system consists entirely of an elementary dorsal-like processing route. There is visual stimulation, dorsal-like processing, and motor response—nothing more. This organism is not conscious, is incapable of undergoing conscious experiences. Inferentialism returns the verdict that this organism's visual states are not intentional. Yet they are indistinguishable from *our* dorsal visual states both intrinsically and in terms of their connections to the environment (and possibly even to other internal states, depending on how the aforementioned empirical controversies are resolved). Arguably, cognitive science would treat this organism's dorsal visual states as it would treat ours, i.e. as intentional. But inferentialism would not.

This is a symptom of a deeper oddity with inferentialism. According to inferentialism, there could be two unconscious token states indistinguishable in terms of their non-relational properties and in terms of their relations to the environment, but with different contents—in case they are suitably connected to different conscious experiences. If one is cognitively connected to a conscious thought that rabbits are cool, whereas the other is cognitively connected to a conscious thought that undetached rabbit parts are cool, then the two will have different intentional contents. More dramatically yet, if one token is not cognitively connected to any conscious experiences, it would lack intentionality altogether, despite being intrinsically and "trackingly" (if you please) indistinguishable from a token state with (scrutable) intentionality.

In the same vein, note that inferentialism would also problematically deny intentional states to certain zombies. We often focus on zombies that are *physically* indistinguishable from us, but in the present context it is more illuminating to consider *functionally* indistinguishable zombies. These creatures may be physically very different from us, but their cognitive system is functionally isomorphic to ours, in the sense that their internal states have the same functional roles as ours, but lack experiential character. It is debatable whether such creatures are genuinely (metaphysically) possible, but widely accepted that they are conceivable, therefore conceptually possible. Their conceptual possibility strikes me as an embarrassment to inferentialism. According to inferentialism, such zombies would lack intentional states. This separates conceptually intentionality from (what at least appears to be) cognition, in a way that is difficult to accept.[26] It is more difficult to accept, certainly, than the conceptual separation of conscious experience from physical realization that zombie scenarios are standardly used to establish.[27]

It is highly questionable, then, whether inferentialism fares meaningfully better than potentialism in terms of getting right the extension of intentionality. Although it can accommodate some impotentially conscious intentional states, it is hard-pressed to accommodate some sub-personal states (e.g., cognitively insulated dorsal states), some states of simple organisms, and some states of zombies, all of which appear to be intentional. Potentialism cannot accommodate those states either, but the worry is that although inferentialism fares better than potentialism, overall it is not all that satisfactory. As in Searle's case, Loar/Horgan et al. could bite those bullets by simply denying that such states are intentional, claiming instead that they are merely representational in a tracking sense. But also as in Searle's case, this would not be all that satisfying, and for the same reasons. Overall, it seems to me that inferentialism does fare better than potentialism with respect to clarity and extension, but not sweepingly so.

It is somewhat disconcerting that neither potentialism nor inferentialism can capture the pre-theoretically desirable extension of intentionality. This may tempt us to downplay the importance of this form of (quasi-)empirical adequacy, stressing instead the theoretical virtues of these accounts. However, following this thought we could be led to a view that maximizes theoretical virtue at the expense of any concern for getting the extension right. The next section considers such a view.

4.3. Eliminativism

Perhaps the starkest such view, found in Strawson (2005, 2008) and Georgalis (2006), is that there simply *is* no non-experiential intentionality.[28] There is no non-experiential item x, such that x has intentional content. Only conscious experiences have intentionality. Thus:

(Elim) Necessarily★, there is no item x and property F, such that F figures in the nexp-intentional content of x.

Call this *eliminativism* about non-experiential intentionality.

This kind of eliminativism is considerably simpler, clearer, and more elegant—thus more theoretically virtuous—than potentialism and inferentialism. It is quite straightforwardly problematic, obviously, inasmuch as it does very poorly on the task of getting the pre-theoretically desirable extension right.[29] As before, however, eliminativism can soften the blow by allowing that some of the items it denies intentional content to are nonetheless representational, in the impoverished sense that they track something (Horst 1996). But also as before, this is not particularly satisfying: it sacrifices the possibility of (quasi-)empirical adequacy to avoid actual inadequacy.

In search of a more satisfying defense of eliminativism on this point, one might argue that, in fact, cognitive science has no need for the notion of intentionality, or for that matter representation. Thus, according to some commentators on connectionism as an approach to cognitive architecture, there is no profit whatsoever in describing connectionist networks as employing "internal representations" (Ramsey 1997). A parallel claim could be made about describing them as involving intentional states. Similar claims have been made about artificial intelligence, embodied cognition, etc. (see, e.g., Brooks 1991). An eliminativist about non-experiential intentionality could co-opt these claims in an attempt to defend the extensional adequacy of eliminativism. However, such claims are still marginal and commitment to them is a major liability: if eliminativism cannot be acceptable unless a relatively radical interpretation of cognitive science is adopted, then eliminativism is not in good shape.[30]

Furthermore, in discussing the possible intentionality of non-experiential items, we have focused on non-conscious mental states, but importantly, in denying intentionality to all non-experiential items, (Elim) must deny intentionality even to non-mental items, such as linguistic expressions, paintings, and traffic signs. This is surprising, given that linguistic expressions, for example, appear to exhibit both intentional inexistence and intentional indifference. This underscores the depth of eliminativism's (quasi-)empirical inadequacy.

Now, a view is possible, of course, according to which there is no intentionality in non-experiential *mental* items, but altogether non-mental items, such as linguistic expressions, do exhibit intentionality. This *semi-eliminativism*, if you will, is more adequate extensionally, of course, but it does face a serious problem in trying to *account* for linguistic intentionality. The problem is that it cannot incorporate the standard account of how linguistic intentionality derives from mental intentionality (whereas potentialism and inferentialism can). The standard account, as developed first by Grice (1957), is that the linguistic content of utterances derives from the mental content of certain complex speaker intentions.[31] Importantly, the intentions Grice appealed to were unconscious intentions—and they had to be, because they were so complex that they could not be reasonably expected to be conscious occurrent intentions.[32] However, our semi-eliminativist denies the existence of such intentions.[33] So she cannot allow linguistic expressions to derive their intentional content from them. She must provide an alternative account of how linguistic intentionality derives from mental intentionality. Indeed, given her rejection of non-experiential mental intentionality, she would require an account that grounds linguistic intentionality directly in experiential intentionality. It is not at all clear how this would work.

It should be noted that it is not immediately obvious how the potentialist or inferentialist could account for linguistic intentionality either, since linguistic expressions are not potentially conscious, nor inferentially connected to conscious experiences. However, Grice's speaker intentions *are* both potentially conscious and inferentially connected to conscious experiences, so the potentialist and the inferentialist could modify their positions so as to account for linguistic intentionality via those intentions. The modified account would be a two-step account, where first the intentionality of non-experiential mental states is accounted for in terms of potential experience or inferential connection to experience, then the intentionality of non-mental items is accounted for in terms of some appropriate relation to the certain non-experiential mental states (e.g., Gricean speaker intentions).

To summarize the discussion thus far, eliminativism gets the extension of intentionality completely wrong, but then potentialism and inferentialism do not get the extension exactly right either, and eliminativism is more theoretically virtuous than both. In the end it is somewhat disappointing that none of the accounts of non-experiential intentionality considered thus far captures the pre-theoretically desirable extension of what it attempts to account for. In the next section, I present an account that I claim succeeds in doing so.

4.4. Interpretivism

Of the three accounts considered thus far, inferentialism gets closest to recovering the pre-theoretically desirable extension of intentionality. Yet even inferentialism leaves out much of what seems to be intentional:

certain cognitively insulated sub-personal states, certain states of certain simple creatures, and certain zombie states. Moreover, it would require modification, or expansion, to recover altogether non-mental intentionality, such as that of linguistic expressions, pictures, and traffic signs. The purpose of the present section is to develop and defend an account that captures just the amount of non-experiential intentionality we are antecedently committed to. I present the account in §4.4.1, develop it in some detail in §4.4.2, and consider possible objections to it in §4.4.3.

4.4.1. Interpretivism about Non-Experiential Intentionality

As my starting point I take Dennett's interpretivist account of intentionality in terms of the "intentional stance." According to Dennett (1971, 1981, 1987), there is a web of intentional concepts, such as of belief and desire, that we can use to produce a rough-and-ready interpretation of conspecifics (and other creatures) in real time and "on the go." When we use this web of intentional concepts, we take a theoretical stance toward our targets of interpretation that involves conceiving of them as intentional systems; this is the "intentional stance." The intentional stance produces a kind of interpretation that is a good enough approximation of the truth to make it useful for everyday commerce, but not good enough that we can take it at face value. If we operated without constraints on the employment of time, energy, and other resources, we could produce a much more accurate theory of conspecifics' behavior, in principle a fully accurate one. But this other interpretation would deploy a web of neurophysiological and broadly physical concepts, not the web of intentional concepts we use in everyday life; it would involve taking the "physical stance." In everyday life, the most cost-beneficial balance between resource expenditure and interpretative accuracy happens to be that provided by the intentional stance.

On this sort of view, it is not so much because certain intentional facts hold that certain interpretations are justified, as that because those interpretations are justified that the intentional facts hold.[34] Thus, for someone to believe that *p* just is for the best exercise of the intentional stance to assign to her the belief that *p*. As Dennett (1981: 72) puts it, "all there is to really and truly believing that *p* is being an intentional system for which *p* occurs as a belief in the best (most predictive) interpretation." Similar remarks can be found in Davidson; consider: "what a fully informed interpreter could know about what a speaker means is all there is to learn; the same goes for what the speaker believes" (Davidson 1986: 315).[35]

As a global theory of all intentionality, this sort of view faces an immediate difficulty, namely, that it leads straightforwardly to infinite regress: an item x can acquire the content C only if there is an item y with content C★, where C★ = <x has C>; but for y to have that content, there would have to be an item z with content C★★, C★★ = <y has C★>; and so on ad infinitum.[36] The only way to stop the regress (without circularity) is to posit a class of privileged intentional states, such that (i) their intentionality is *not* inherited from interpretation and (ii) they have interpretive acts as a subset, wherefrom unprivileged items might inherit their intentionality.

My suggestion is to designate exp-intentional states as that privileged class, with conscious, experiential interpretive acts—what we may call "interpretive experiences" (including cognitive interpretive experiences)—as the requisite subset.[37] The upshot is a picture in which a Dennett-style interpretivism is applied not across the board but only to nexp-intentional items, while a separate account is provided for exp-intentional states, including interpretive experiences. The separate account I would suggest would of course be in terms of higher-order tracking or adverbial modification.

To a first approximation, the resulting answer to (NIQ) would be this: what makes a non-experiential state or item have the intentional content it does, and to have one at all, is that the best exercise of the intentional stance would produce an interpretation according to which that state has the intentional content it does (thus has one at all).[38] We could call this the *experiential-intentional stance* view of non-experiential intentionality, or perhaps less coyly the *ideal interpreter theory* of non-experiential intentionality, but I will refer to it hereafter simply as *interpretivism*. For the view is that something has or is an unconscious belief that p, say, just in case an ideal interpreter would, under ideal conditions, experientially interpret it as having or being a belief that p. Generalized, the view is that an item has some nexp-intentional content just in case an ideal interpreter would, under ideal conditions, experientially interpret that item to have that content. More precisely:

(Int) Necessarily★, for any item x and property F, F figures in the nexp-intentional content of x iff x is such as to produce in ideal interpreters under ideal conditions the response of having an interpretive experience as of F figuring in the intentional content of x.

My *ultimate* position would be an expanded version of this interpretivism that allowed items to qualify as intentional either by being ideally interpreted, as in (Int), or by having an underlying nature in common with most encountered exp-intentional states (as per §1.1.2). More on this in Chapter 5. In the remainder of this subsection, I offer some clarifications of (Int).

First, the locution "such as to produce" admits of at least three readings. On a *manifestational* reading, x is such as to produce y iff x does produce y. On a *dispositional* reading, x is such as to produce y iff x is *disposed* to produce y. On a *categorical* reading, x is such as to produce y iff x has the categorical property that *underlies* the disposition to produce y.[39] In the context of an ideal interpreter theory, the dispositional reading is probably the most appropriate.[40]

Secondly, for now let us understand the ideal interpreter as someone who brings to the task of interpretation no knowledge of any nexp-intentional facts (i.e., no knowledge of any instantiation of a nexp-intentional property), but on the other hand (i) knows all the *non*-intentional facts and all the *exp*-intentional facts, (ii) can draw every valid deductive inference and every justifiable non-deductive inference, and (iii) can avoid drawing any invalid deductive inference and any unjustified non-deductive inference.[41] Thus the ideal interpreter is fully informed and a perfect reasoner, but is parachuted into the world, so to speak, with no knowledge of nexp-intentional facts whatsoever.[42]

Thirdly, let ideal conditions be those under which a subject can perform the cognitive task she is faced with to the best of her abilities. This relativizes ideal conditions to subjects and tasks, as one would expect: conditions C are ideal relative to subject S and task T iff S can perform T maximally competently under C, that is, iff there are no conditions C★, such that S performs T better (more competently) under C★ than under C. What makes performance better or worse (more or less competent) depends, of course, on what the value is by which we judge or evaluate the performance. Typically, the relevant value is accuracy, but in the present context it cannot be, since there are no independent, pre-existing facts for the ideal subject to be accurate about. Instead, we must conceive of the relevant value directly in terms of the subject's broader goals, which we may let be continuous with ours—*eudaimonia*, survival and reproduction, or whatever.[43] Observe that against this background, any condition is ideal relative to the ideal interpreter and the task of interpretation. For our ideal interpreter can perform its task ideally under any conditions.⁴⁴ So the qualifier "in ideal conditions" is strictly speaking redundant.⁴⁵

Finally, in the present context we should construe the response of interpreting x to have an F-content as any mental act in which an F-content is ascribed to something. The "in which" locution here must be read intentionally: a mental act in which an intentional content is ascribed to something is a mental act with an intentional content to the effect that something has some intentional content. In the next subsection, I discuss which kinds of mental act might be such.

With these clarifications in place, we can formulate the ideal interpreter theory more explicitly:

(Int⁺) Necessarily*, for any item x and property F, F figures in the nexp-intentional content of x iff possibly, there are conditions C, an interpreter Å, and a mental act y, such that (i) y has an exp-intentional content to the effect that F figures in the intentional content of x, (ii) Å is an ideal reasoner fully informed of the non-intentional and exp-intentional facts, and (iii) x is disposed to produce y in Å under C.

I will now argue that, of the accounts of non-experiential intentionality discussed here, this is the best.

The most important virtue of interpretivism is that it alone gets the extension of non-experiential intentionality just right. First, dorsal-stream visual states have the response-dependent property appealed to in (Int⁺): the ideal interpreter would ascribe to them the relevant contents, because doing so makes sense of certain behaviors, namely, those that lead cognitive scientists to ascribe content to dorsal states.⁴⁶ This is so even though such states are not even potentially conscious, and even if they are cognitively insulated from conscious experiences. So where potentialism and inferentialism return the wrong results, interpretivism returns the right ones. In addition, the ideal interpreter would ascribe content to some of the internal states of simple creatures and even zombies, certainly to those internal states that are indistinguishable from our intentional states intrinsically and "trackingly." Again, this is because the behavior of these creatures and zombies would be more intelligible if those states are treated as intentional. So interpretivism returns the right results also in the standard cases in which inferentialism returns the wrong ones.⁴⁷ Finally, as we will see in more detail in §4.4.2, interpretivism also manages to assign content to linguistic expressions, where (semi-)eliminativism fails, and moreover manages to do so in a more unified manner than potentialism and inferentialism. In this way, interpretivism is greatly preferable to potentialism, inferentialism, and (semi-)eliminativism along the dimension of getting right the extension of intentionality.[48]

Importantly, there seems to be something principled in the way interpretivism returns the right results in all the above cases (such that this success is likely to repeat itself in possible cases we have not considered). The reason is this: what makes it desirable to count something as falling in the extension of intentionality is non-accidentally related to what makes it the case that interpretivism returns the result that it is a case of intentionality. There are two kinds of fact that make it desirable to count a given unconscious state as intentional: (i) that it is so treated by cognitive science and (ii) that it is so treated by folk theory. Certainly in the former case, but probably also in the latter, what makes it desirable to count the state as intentional is that it is explanatorily beneficial to do so. However, whenever it is explanatorily beneficial to treat a state as intentional, an ideal interpreter would treat that state as intentional, so interpretivism would ratify the state's status as intentional. Thus it is no accident that interpretivism returns the independently desirable results in the above cases, and there is every reason to expect it would do so in other cases. The only way it could fail to return the right results is if there were non-experiential items to which we have independent reasons to ascribe intentionality but for which it is explanatorily useless to do so. In all likelihood, however, there could be no such states: unlike exp-intentional states, we have no first-person acquaintance with nexp-intentional states; our only reason to believe in them is precisely that doing so is theoretically or explanatorily profitable from a third-person perspective.

It is clear, then, that interpretivism is far more (quasi-)empirically virtuous than its competition. Although this is harder to assess, it seems to me that interpretivism is also more *theoretically* virtuous, on the whole, than potentialism and inferentialism. For starters, interpretivism is somewhat more *parsimonious* than them, inasmuch as they are committed to the existence of a response-*independent* kind of non-experiential intentionality, whereas interpretivism is not. It seems also clearer than potentialism—there are no immediately problematic terms in (Int), such as "potential"—and no less clear than inferentialism.[49] Furthermore, I will argue in the next subsection that it offers a more *unified* account of non-experiential intentionality (of both mental and non-mental items). Thus along the dimensions of parsimony, clarity, and unity, interpretivism's overall theoretical adequacy is superior to that of potentialism and inferentialism.[50] Interpretivism does strike me as *less* theoretically virtuous than eliminativism, certainly in terms of parsimony and clarity. But I take it that eliminativism is so (quasi-)empirically *vicious* that interpretivism is all things considered much preferable to it.

I conclude that interpretivism is by far the best account of non-experiential intentionality considered in this chapter. Most crucially, it alone returns the right results on all cases we would pre-theoretically tend to consider instances of intentionality. I am open to the possibility that another account be developed that would be equally good or even better. But until such an account is offered, I am satisfied to adopt interpretivism as my account of non-experiential intentionality. In the next subsection, I want to develop further some of the particulars of interpretivism, and of the version thereof I would be keenest to adopt.

4.4.2. Interpretivism Developed

To repeat, unlike Dennett, I do not offer interpretivism as an account of all intentionality. I offer it only by way of accounting, in terms of experiential intentionality, for the intentionality of items that do not have the same underlying nature as most encountered exp-intentional states. The upshot is that there are three categories of intentional items: (i) encountered exp-intentional states, (ii) items that have the same underlying nature as most encountered exp-intentional states, and (iii) items that can be interpreted as intentional from the experiential-intentional stance. We may say that items from (i) and (ii) have an *underived* intentionality, whereas those from (iii) have merely a *derived* one.[51,52]

To clarify the notion of derived intentionality, let us start by drawing a *prima facie* "meta-distinction" between two ways of drawing a distinction between derived and underived intentionality. Such a distinction can be understood either (a) as a distinction between two different properties or (b) as a distinction between two different ways of instantiating one and the same property.[53] On the first understanding, derivativeness and non-derivativeness are attributes of properties; on the second, of property instantiations. We can flag this by saying that a statement such as:

1. *x* is derivatively intentional and *y* is underivatively intentional

is ambiguous as between:

2. *x* is derivatively-intentional and *y* is underivatively-intentional;
3. *x* is-derivatively intentional and *y* is-underivatively intentional.

In (2), "derivatively" and "underivatively" qualify the predicate "intentional"; in (3), they qualify the copula. In the former case, derivative intentionality and non-derivative intentionality are cast as two different properties; in the latter, as two ways an item could instantiate one and the same property.[54]

It may be, however, that the difference between these two construals is not all that deep and is ultimately a matter of degree more than kind. After all, even if there are two distinct properties, underivative-intentionality and derivative-intentionality, we can define a disjunctive genus, intentionality *simpliciter*, of which they are both species. There would then be a difference between two ways in which some item *x* could instantiate intentionality *simpliciter*: by instantiating the property of underivative-intentionality and by instantiating the property of derivative-intentionality. Conversely, whenever there are two ways to instantiate one and the same property P, there are also two second-order properties: the property of instantiating P one way and the property of instantiating P the other way. So it is hard to draw a sharp distinction between a two-properties construal and a two-instantiations construal. There is nonetheless a substantive issue in the choice between understanding the distinction between derived and underived intentionality as concerning two properties or as concerning two ways of instantiating the same property. It concerns the degree of objective similarity among instances of derived and underived intentionality, and hence the degree of homogeneity within the category of intentionality *simpliciter*.[55] The greater the similarity and homogeneity, the more natural it is to think of them as two different ways of instantiating the same property; the greater the dissimilarity and heterogeneity, as two different properties.

In light of these clarifications, it seems to me most natural to consider the distinction between the intentionality of items that have the same underlying nature as most exp-intentional states, on the one hand, and that of items that are experientially interpretable by an ideal interpreter, on the other hand, as a distinction between two different *properties*. For the objective similarity between the former items and the latter items is relatively small, it seems to me. Thus interpretivism can be thought of as offering an account of the underlying nature of the property of *derived* intentionality, to complement the accounts proposed in Chapters 2 and 3 of the underlying nature of *underived* intentionality. In the remainder of this subsection, I consider the main notions that go to build up the interpetivist account.

I start with clarifications of the very notion of *interpretation*. There are, in fact, several views on the nature of interpretation, and different versions of interpretivism will be defined by the adoption of different views on that matter. In the literature on interpretation, three main theories seem to compete (see Goldman 1989): theory theory, simulation theory, and rationality theory.[56] According to theory theory, intentional ascription is based on something like inference to the best explanation from the behavior (including verbal behavior) of the target of ascription, the kind of inference characteristic of theorizing in general. According to simulation theory, intentional ascription is based on the "off-line" tokening of the very intentional states ascribed, by way of simulation of the target of ascription's internal goings-on.[57] According to rationality theory, intentional ascription is based first and foremost on the application of a principle of charity that casts the target of ascription as a rational agent whose intentional states are by and large justified. In addition to these three "pure" theories, which assume that all intentional ascription is carried out by a single mechanism, there are also "impure" theories that combine two or three of the above mechanisms. Thus if we restrict ourselves to these three possible interpretive mechanisms, there are seven possible views of how interpretation works.[58]

In §1.2.2, I argued that first-person exp-intentional ascription is based on none of these three mechanisms, but on direct observational contact with the intentional state ascribed. However, nexp-intentional ascription, as well as third-person exp-intentional ascription, is likely based on one or more of these mechanisms. For my part, although I cannot argue for this here, it seems to me that a simulation mechanism is particularly plausible for the ascription of exp-intentional states to others (i.e., third-person exp-intentional ascription), while a theory mechanism is more plausible for the ascription of nexp-intentional states (to either oneself or another). Both mechanisms require, however, the assistance of a rationality mechanism, for the reasons discussed in §1.2. The considerations brought up there suggest the following model. Ascriptions of nexp-intentional states, whether first- or third-person, as well as many forms of third-person exp-intentional ascription, proceed in two phases: first, inference to the best explanation (via the theory mechanism) produces a number of possible ascriptions fully consistent with the behavioral data; then, the principle of charity is used (via the rationality mechanism) to pick among them the single ascription that casts the target of interpretation in the most rational light. At the same time, there are certain third-person ascriptions of exp-intentional states that proceed otherwise: first, *simulation* (perhaps assisted by theory) produces a number of possible ascriptions fully consistent with the behavioral data; then, the rationality mechanism again kicks in and picks among them the most charitable one.[59]

Note that the proposed account of how intentional ascription works outside first-person exp-intentional ascription casts acts of interpretation as by and large *cognitive*: interpretive experiences are cognitive experiences (conscious occurrent thoughts). To interpret x as having intentional content featuring F is to *judge* that x has a content featuring F. This does not rule out entirely a role for non-cognitive, perceptual acts of interpretation, however. For such perceptual acts may be relevant to third-person exp-intentional ascription, where perceptually based simulation is operative. Furthermore, perceptual interpretive acts may be relevant to the ascription of intentional content to non-mental items. As mentioned in §1.3.3, Siegel (2006) argues that we can directly perceive meaning, or more generally the semantic properties of text: when I look at English words, but not at Cyrillic ones, I can *see*, and not merely *infer*, what (and that) they mean. This is an alleged example of a perceptual interpretive experience.

Let us turn now to the question of the nature of *ideal conditions*. I said above that a condition C is ideal relative to a subject S and a task T just in case S can, under C, perform T to the best of S's abilities; and also that given this construal, it would seem that any conditions are ideal relative to the ideal interpreter and the task of interpretation. In addition, it may be worth stipulating that the conditions relevant to the formulation of interpretivism are conditions of *forced choice*: the interpreter must either assent to "F figures in the intentional content of x" or dissent from it. Suspending judgment, or being unaware that a judgment is called for, are not an option.

There may be ideal conditions under which there is no *single* best interpretation of some item. Perhaps there are two equally good interpretations, one assigning to x content C_1 and one assigning to it content C_2. In those cases, interpretivism entails that the item's content is indeterminate between C_1 and C_2. But this kind of content indeterminacy is not the corrosive variety threatened by inscrutability worries, as it should be rather infrequent, and to that extent harmless. For there is no reason to suppose that in standard cases there is more than one most explanatorily beneficial interpretation in ideal circumstances. Crucially, since the ideal interpreter knows all the exp-intentional facts, it knows that ordinarily Lizzu consciously thinks of rabbits rather than of undetached rabbit parts, and would therefore interpret Lizzu's relevant nexp-intentional states as intentionally directed at rabbits and not undetached rabbit parts, for the reasons mentioned in the discussion of inferentialism (i.e., that Lizzu's nexp-intentional states interact cognitively with her exp-intentional states).[60]

Having clarified the nature of interpretation and the ideal conditions for it, let us consider the nature of the *ideal interpreter*. I said that an ideal interpreter is one who exercises the intentional stance perfectly under all conditions, but more can be said. For starters, we may construe an interpreter (in general) as any subject capable of entering interpretive states, or performing interpretive acts, that is, acts of mentally ascribing content to something. There are then several options for how to characterize what makes an interpreter ideal. One option is virtue-epistemological: an ideal interpreter is a well-informed interpreter who exhibits (to the highest degree) all the epistemic virtues that bear on the production of interpretive states. Another option is teleofunctionalist: an ideal interpreter is an interpreter whose mechanisms responsible for the production of interpretive states always function exactly as they are supposed to. The best characterization for our present purposes, however, is the one offered above: the ideal interpreter is an epistemic agent parachuted into the world with no knowledge of the facts we are appealing to the interpreter in order to fix, but complete knowledge of all other facts and perfect reasoning capabilities.[61] This, if anyone, is an ideal interpreter.

Note that an ideal interpreter, because ideal, would also assign intentional contents to conscious experiences. It would typically assign to them nexp-intentional contents, but sometimes also exp-intentional contents. Of course, we have *stipulated* that the ideal interpreter knows all the exp-intentional facts. But even if we deprived her of this knowledge, the impoverished interpreter would still be able, on the basis of her knowledge of the non-intentional facts and her perfect reasoning capabilities, to ascribe at least some exp-intentional contents. However, there is still an asymmetry between experiential and non-experiential intentionality on the picture presented here. In the first place, it is natural to suppose, consistently with a robustly realist approach to experiential intentionality, that the ideal interpreter might on occasion assign the *wrong* exp-intentional content to a conscious experience.[62] By contrast, it cannot ascribe the wrong nexp-intentional content, since the facts about nexp-intentional content are *constituted* by its ascription thereof. More importantly, regardless of the possibility of misattribution, there is an asymmetry concerning the direction of (constitutive) explanation: with experiential intentionality, the ideal interpreter assigns content C to item x because x has C; with non-experiential intentionality, item x has content C because the interpreter assigns C to x.[63]

With these clarifications in place, one issue that should be addressed is how interpretivism proposes to account for linguistic intentionality (and other forms of non-mental intentionality). According to interpretivism, cât means cat because an ideal interpreter would take cât to mean cat. That is, an ideal interpreter would assign to cât cat-content. Importantly, however, the *reason* the ideal interpreter would assign to cât cat-content need not be the same reason it assigns cat-content to certain sub-personal states. The reason it assigns cat-content to the relevant sub-personal visual states probably has to do with the states' tracking relations to the (feline) environment and their cognitive connections to other intentional states, notably exp-intentional states with cat-content. The reason it assigns cat-content to cât is probably somewhat different. It *might* have to do with (i) tracking relations between tokens of cât and cats within carefully delineated communities and (ii) the connections of those tokens to conscious thoughts they are systematically used to express.[64] But it might also have to do with the (possibly Gricean) speaker intentions responsible for the production of these tokens. On this latter model, linguistic intentionality is grounded in experiential intentionality in two phases: roughly, first the relevant types of speaker intention inherit their intentional content from exp-intentional states, then linguistic utterances inherit their intentional content from those speaker intentions. This model is somewhat more plausible, or goes deeper, as presumably the community-specific tracking relations exist precisely due to the intentions of speakers. The two models just sketched could also be combined into a third one, wherein the ideal interpreter assigns content to linguistic utterances on the basis of a range of considerations: (i) their community-specific tracking relations to the environment,

(ii) systematic connections to exp-intentional states they are used to express, (iii) systematic connections to the Gricean speaker intentions, and perhaps (iv) some other element(s).

It may be objected that there is a natural way to understand mainstream philosophy of language as wedded to a diametrically opposed approach to linguistic intentionality, one that does not appeal to interpretation and in fact is naturally understood to cast linguistic content as underived. According to direct reference theorists of natural kind terms, for example, the intentional content of the term "water" is exhausted by its referent, the property of being water. What makes it the case that the property of being water exhausts the intentional content of the term "water" is that the right broadly causal relation obtains between the term and the property (Kripke 1972), not any interpretation of the term "water."[65]

However, it seems to me that while there is a reading of direct reference theory—roughly the one just presented—that pits it against interpretivism, there is another reading, at least equally natural, that does not. On this alternative reading, what makes it the case that water exhausts the intentional content of "water" is not the broadly causal relation between water and "water," but rather the fact that speakers *intend* to use "water" to refer to whatever bears the right broadly causal relation to "water." To my mind, this second understanding is much more plausible: "water" is directly referential, whereas (e.g.) "friend" is not, because, and only because, speakers use "water" and "friend" with relevantly different intentions in mind.[66] On this view, once a term is directly referential, its content is exhausted by its referent. But what makes the term directly referential in the first place is not its referent, but the speaker intentions with which it is used![67] This intention-based understanding of linguistic content, including directly referential content, is clearly consistent with the Gricean-interpretivist approach suggested above. Admittedly, the brutely causal reading is not.[68] But the brutely causal reading is, upon reflection, utterly implausible, as it requires that a term be made directly referential not by its users but by its referent.

This interpretivist account of linguistic intentionality can also be readily extended to other forms of non-mental intentionality, such as we find in photographs and traffic signs. On the resulting view, such items have their intentional content due to ideal interpretation, which the ideal interpreter performs, roughly, on the basis of recognizing the exp-intentional states responsible for the items' production, the tracking relations that ensue, and the like materials.[69] The result is an extremely unified account of all derived intentionality: at a reasonable level of abstraction, the story for both non-experiential mental intentionality and myriad forms of non-mental intentionality is the same. This unity boosts the overall theoretical virtue of interpretivism.

Interpretivism about non-experiential intentionality will bring in its train all the hallmarks of the more standard, global type of interpretivism. Most notably, it will lead to content holism and rule out a priori massive error and irrationality—but, of course, only for the domain of non-experiential intentionality. Content holism is the view that contents cannot be assigned to individual items but must be assigned to whole groups of items "at once."[70] This is because creatures' behavior admits of several coherent interpretations in which changes in the assignment of content to one item can be compensated for by changes in the assignment of content to other items—as we saw in some detail in §1.2.[71] This kind of holism strikes me as antecedently plausible where the interpretation of behavior caused by unconscious mental states is concerned. If so, it is an advantage of interpretivism about non-experiential intentionality that it leads to holism about nexp-intentional content.[72] As for the doctrine that massive error and irrationality are a priori impossible, it is based partly on the crucial role of the principle(s) of charity.[73] As Davidson (1974) has shown, the combination of content holism and the employment of the principle of charity tends to undermine the ascription of erroneous and/or irrational contents to other items in the relevant web of non-experiential items, with the result that sweeping error and irrationality are ruled out a priori.

4.4.3. Objections and Replies

The positive case for interpretivism is fairly straightforward, then: it is extensionally adequate and theoretically attractive. Let me end by fending off some possible objections to it.

One possible objection is that interpretivism about non-experiential intentionality would lead to a certain kind of *irrealism* about it. Certainly in Dennett's early writings, interpretivism appears to have a clear irrealist aspect. Of course, "realism" and "irrealism" are essentially contested terms. But one perfectly legitimate view considers a theory to be realist just if it casts its target phenomena as mind- or observer-independent. In the case of intentionality, the claim would have to be that there are ascriber-independent facts of the matter concerning the instantiation of intentional properties. The irrealist would deny this, claiming that either there are no intentional facts or there are such facts but they are ascriber-dependent one and all. By the lights of this test, interpretivism is indeed irrealist, since it construes intentional properties as interpreter-dependent.[74]

My response has two parts. First, although there are certainly ways of delineating the realist/irrealist divide so that interpretivism comes out irrealist, there are also ways of delineating it so that interpretivism comes out realist. Suppose our test for a realist view of certain properties is that it claim that the relevant properties *exist*, or even more demandingly, that they be *instantiated*. Interpretivism is certainly realist by the lights of this test, since the disposition it describes *is* in fact instantiated by some items: persons and their non-experiential states *are* often disposed the way (Int$^+$) requires them to be. (Indeed, since interpretivism casts intentional properties as response-dependent, it may be rightly considered a kind of "response-dependent realism," which is of course a kind of realism.) We need not take a position here on what the best delineation of the realist/irrealist divide is. The point is that on some reasonable delineations interpretivism is realist and on others it is irrealist. So the charge of leading to irrealism may have less weight to it than initially appears.

This may illuminate the elusive role of "real patterns" in interpretivism, which Dennett (1991) takes to underlie its realist component. Although it is not entirely transparent from Dennett's writings exactly what that role is, the idea seems to be that there are certain interpretation-*independent* properties whose presence the ideal interpreter detects when it responds in the relevant ways. After all, there is a question as to why the ideal interpreter would respond with R to x but not y. And the answer must be that there are certain interpretation-independent features exhibited by x but not y that the ideal interpreter detects. These are the "real patterns" that underlie—are perhaps the categorical basis of—something's disposition to elicit interpretation. One intriguing suggestion is that the relevant real patterns are patterns of tracking: when x tracks F, the ideal interpreter detects this, and on this basis interprets x as intentionally directed at F. However, as we saw above, the full story is likely to be more complicated, as the ideal interpreter also appeals to causal connections between x and exp-intentional states, and in some cases to a variety of other materials (e.g., connections to speaker intentions) to fix x's content.[75]

As far as the residual commitment to irrealism is concerned, I am inclined to think that it is quite appropriate, and thus does not reflect negatively on interpretivism. First of all, it is irrealism only about *derived* intentionality, which is not all that surprising, especially when combined with realism about *underived* intentionality.[76] Once realism about *some* kind of intentionality has been secured, there ought to be less of a pressure to secure it for other kinds of intentionality. The strong pre-theoretic intuition is that *some* intentionality is "realistic," not that *all* is. So the combination of realism about underived intentionality and irrealism about derived intentionality should seem quite unproblematic.

This combination is in effect the combination of realism about experiential intentionality (and all intentionality with the same underlying nature) and irrealism about non-experiential intentionality (without the relevant underlying nature). From a certain perspective, this kind of combination, creating an important asymmetry between experiential and non-experiential intentionality, is independently motivated. Consider that when the debate over intentional realism and irrealism was raging in the eighties, all parties to the debate seemed to accept it as a "rule of the game" that unless there is an indispensability argument for intentional properties, we should not believe in them.[77] This approach seems right for intentional properties we have only third-person reasons to believe in, and nexp-intentional properties are such. But exp-intentional properties are not: as we saw in §1.2, one does not typically ascribe to oneself an exp-intentional state in order to explain anything, but rather because one is directly acquainted with it, in some sense, from the first-person perspective. So while dispositional beliefs, Freudian repressed states, and occurrent sub-personal states need to earn their explanatory keep, intentional conscious experiences, such as a visual experience as of butterflies, do not: it is virtually impossible to genuinely doubt their existence. The upshot is that realism about experiential intentionality can be defended in a way that is entirely independent from the way proponents of intentional realism in the eighties tried to defend it, that is, regardless of considerations of explanatory indispensability.[78]

A second and somewhat related objection might be that combining interpretivism about derived intentionality with "industrial-strength" realism about underived intentionality casts the two kinds of intentionality as really very different properties, as we saw in §4.4.2, rather than as two "versions" of the same property, which is how they ought to be cast. This may be deemed an embarrassing consequence.

In response, I deny that the consequence is particularly embarrassing. As we saw in the discussion of the meta-distinction between two ways of construing the derived/underived distinction, the difference between the two construals is a matter of degree rather than kind: the dichotomy between two ways of construing the derived/underived distinction gives way to a spectrum of degrees of similarity/homogeneity. To claim that derived and underived intentionality are two different properties is just to say that the similarity relations between their instances fall toward the heterogeneous end of the spectrum. Given the continuity between the two construals of the derived/underived distinction, even if it were counter-intuitive that derived and underived intentionality are two different properties (and it does not, in fact, seem to me particularly counter-intuitive), this would be at most a minor liability. For since we are dealing with a continuum, there is no dichotomy here between a clearly desirable and a clearly undesirable result.

Another related objection is that, since the ideal interpreter must detect *something* in assigning the contents it does (lest the assignment be arbitrary), whatever the ideal interpreter detects could be appealed to in an alternative, non-interpretivist account of non-experiential intentionality. This is an instance of the general problem dispositionalist accounts face in many areas of philosophy, namely, that they seem to be preempted by alternative accounts that appeal to the categorical bases of the relevant dispositions.

The standard approach to this kind of concern is that whether the account should appeal to the disposition or to its categorical basis depends on the degree of homogeneity we find at the basis. In the present case, whether we should account for non-experiential intentionality in terms of the disposition to elicit interpretive reactions in an ideal interpreter or in terms of what the ideal interpreter detects when issuing its interpretations depends on how homogeneous the class of patterns the interpreter detects is. It is not entirely clear to me what the correct answer to this question is. Certainly, however, the disposition is *more* homogeneous than its categorical basis.[79] As a result, one gets the impression that whatever the ideal interpreter detects becomes relevant to the assignment of nexp-intentional content precisely *because* the ideal interpreter detects it—so that the explanatory primacy lies with the disposition, not with its categorical basis. In any case, for my part I have no strong feelings *against* accounting for non-experiential intentionality rather in terms of that categorical basis, if that is where the balance of evidence ultimately points.

A fourth possible objection is that interpretivism fails to deliver one important feature of an account of non-experiential intentionality, namely, the ability to illuminate the *reason* non-experiential intentionality is grounded in experiential intentionality. It fails to explain what is so special about experiential intentionality that all other intentionality should be grounded in *it*. Thus interpretivism does not illuminate the attraction in the experiential origin thesis.[80]

My response is twofold. First, the account of non-experiential intentionality and the motivation for the experiential origin thesis are, strictly speaking, logically independent. Nothing rules out different combinations of views on the nature of non-experiential intentionality and arguments for the experiential origin thesis, even if some combinations are more natural than others. More importantly, however, the argument I have presented for the experiential origin thesis in Chapter 1 was actually explicitly entangled with consideration of the different ways in which intentional states are ascribed. This suggests a connection between the two after all. Thus interpretivism about non-experiential intentionality does point to a special feature of experiential intentionality, though one that is epistemological in character. I mentioned that interpretivism captures well the fact that when we have antecedent reason to treat some non-experiential item as intentional, the reason is always that doing so is explanatorily useful. I also mentioned that this is not the case with experiential intentionality. This suggests that while non-experiential intentionality is merely a theoretical posit, the reality of experiential intentionality foists itself upon us pre-theoretically, and is to that extent a special kind of intentionality, fit—at least epistemologically—to serve as the source of all other kinds of intentionality.

Conclusion

The aim of this chapter has been to argue for interpretivism about non-experiential intentionality. In this context, I examined four possible accounts of non-experiential intentionality. There are most certainly other possible accounts, but these four cover the main options in the existing literature. One important kind of progress we made through the discussion has been to articulate a body of desiderata and adequacy constraints that should govern the evaluation of any proposed account of non-experiential intentionality. It is useful to think of this body as comprising two main branches, one to do with theoretical virtues and one to do with (quasi-)empirical virtues. The theoretical virtues concern clarity, simplicity, elegance, unity, etc., and certainly appear to discriminate among the different accounts we have considered. The (quasi-)empirical virtues concern the accounts' ability to return the right results, with results counting as "right" when they are independently desirable in virtue of their congruence with the verdicts of folk theory and cognitive-scientific practice. I have argued that the account that fares best with respect to this body of desiderata is interpretivism, the view that non-experiential intentionality occurs when, and only when, an ideal interpreter would consciously interpret an item to have a certain non-experiential-intentional content.[81]

Notes

1. Recall that "nexp-intentional" is our short for "non-experiential-intentional," which means endowed with intentionality but not experiential intentionality. By "intentional item," I do not mean here an item that something is intentionally directed at, but rather something that is itself endowed with intentional directedness.

2. In other words: For any non-experiential item x, such that x has intentional content, what makes it the case (i) that x has the intentional content that it does, and thus is the nexp-intentional state that it is, and (ii) that x has an intentional content at all, and thus is a nexp-intentional state at all?

3. Warning: there will be many biconditionals stated explicitly in this chapter, as in most of the discussion before it. For the most part, however, they can be skipped. The spirit of the view they are supposed to capture the letter of should be understandable independently of them.

4. All these authors are committed to the experiential origin thesis, as we will see later in the chapter, consistently with my observation that only such authors would regard it as a distinctive challenge to develop an account of non-experiential intentionality. Those who reject the thesis could simply apply whatever account they have of experiential intentionality to non-experiential intentionality, or (more likely) conversely.

5. This reasoning is obviously very similar—perhaps the same as—that in the argument from intentional indifference presented in §3.2.1.

6. For some criticisms, see Fodor and Lepore 1994, Davies 1995, Kriegel 2003a, Shani 2008.

7. For a more explicit, and more fleshed out, statement of this kind of view, see Mendelovici 2010 and Smithies Ms.

8. This is really an answer to (NIQ★). The corresponding answer to (NIQ) is something more like the following: For any nexp-intentional state x, x has the intentional content it does (and not another) because x potentially has the exp-intentional content it potentially does (and not another) and x has intentional content (at all) because x potentially has an exp-intentional content (at all). Another, somewhat more interesting formulation might be this: For any non-experiential item x and intentional

content C, x has C iff there is an experiential character E, such that (i) for any conscious experience y, if y has E, then y has C, and (ii) x potentially has E.

9. Accordingly: For any nexp-intentional state x, there is a psychologically possible world W, such that x has in the actual world the intentional content it does (and not another) because x has in W the exp-intentional content it does (and not another), and x has intentional content (at all) because x has in W an exp-intentional content (at all). Or: For any non-experiential item x and intentional content C, x has C iff there is an experiential character E, such that (i) for any conscious experience y, if y has E, then y has C, and (ii) there is a psychologically possible world W, such that x has E in W.

10. In addition, there is the question of how (Pot$^+$) would handle the apparent possibility that a non-experiential state might have one experiential character in one psychologically possible world and another in another. One option is to deny that this is a genuine possibility, but presumably a reason would have to be adduced. Another option is to say that such a state would have indeterminate content, or that it would determinately have multiple contents; here the challenge would be to show that this is acceptable and not so ubiquitous that any state could have just about any content. A third option is to modify (Pot$^+$) and assign to the state the content that goes with the experiential character the state has in the nearest psychologically possible world. I have not thought about this enough, but instinctively, this third option strikes me as the best.

11. The reason it is more unquestionable that these states exist than Marr's 2.5D sketches is that the latter are posited in the context of a computational account of vision, which can be treated as merely instrumental, whereas the former are posited in the context of a neurological account of vision, and such an account is less open to instrumentalist treatment.

12. Perhaps the classic bit of behavior which manifests the causal relevance of dorsal-stream states is brought out in a seminal experiment due to Aglioti et al. (1995). In this experiment, subjects were asked to reach for a coin which was placed within a three-dimensional version of the Titchener illusion. This is the illusion in which a circle appears bigger when surrounded by smaller circles than when surrounded by bigger ones. The experimenters produced a situation where coins were surrounded by differently sized coins and then asked subjects to reach for them. Apparently, subjects did not adjust their grip aperture (measured by the distance between the thumb and the index finger) in response to surrounding coins. That is, their grip apertures were the same for differently surrounded equisized coins. This suggests that, at some point in the visual processing, some representations of the coins' size are formed that are not infected by the Titchener illusion, and moreover, that it is these representations that guide the reaching and grasping behavior. The going hypothesis is that they are dorsal-stream visual representations (Milner and Goodale 1995).

13. I frame things in term of folk *theory*, rather than folk *psychology*, because not only nexp-intentional *psychological* states are included among the nexp-intentional items we are interested in. There are also paintings, poems, and road signs, which the folk may have intuitions about, though not as part of their psychological theory.

14. One reason to treat this particular test—consistency with folk theory and scientific practice—as (quasi-)empirical is that it is a familiar thought in philosophical methodology that in the same sense in which empirical theories face the tribunal of experience, philosophical theories face the tribunal of intuition and of existing scientific practice. A philosophical theory does not make contact with any other sorts of data. The only data for philosophical theorizing are judgments produced either "intuitively" or on the basis of "our best theory of the world." In any case, this particular test is distinguishable from tests that clearly pertain to the theoretical virtues of simplicity, unity, clarity, etc.

15. This is not to say that it does not have support at all—it still has *theoretical* virtues. But its (quasi-)empirical adequacy is sacrificed. Of course, this is done in order to shield (Pot$^+$) from being seen as not only lacking (quasi-)empirical adequacy but also acquiring (quasi-)empirical inadequacy, which

is certainly worse. So overall the move of casting certain (pre-theoretically) contentful states as merely representational and not intentional may be good for (Pot⁺). But in a way, this attests to a certain weakness of (Pot⁺): its inability to positively acquire (quasi-)empirical adequacy.

16. See Loar 2003; Horgan and Tienson 2002; Horgan, Tienson, and Graham 2004; Graham, Horgan, and Tienson 2007; Horgan and Graham 2009. Below, I will refer to the view that arises from the latter group of writings as the view of Horgan et al., because although there are different combinations of authorship here, Horgan is the only author involved in all of them. I should note that Horgan et al. do not quite commit in writing to the truth of the view I am going to ascribe to them. They consider it the best of a few options, all of which they might be comfortable with. At the same time, in conversation both Terry Horgan and George Graham have professed a strong leaning in that direction.

17. It is an interesting question what the relationship is between the phenomenon of aspectual shape and the phenomenon of scrutability. Prior to serious reflection, the view strikes me as coherent that some mental states succeed, on the one hand, in being intentionally directed at Venus as Phosphorus rather than as Hesperus, but fail, on the other hand, to be directed at Venus as Phosphorus rather than as undetached Phosphorus parts. (Perhaps this is because metaphysical freaks such as undetached object parts escape subjects' discriminatory powers in a way "non-freaky" necessarily coincident objects may not. But perhaps not.) It also seems possible to appreciate the coherence of the view that some mental states fail, on the one hand, to be intentionally directed at Venus as Phosphorus rather than Hesperus, but succeed, on the other hand, in being directed at it as Phosphorus or Hesperus rather than as undetached Phosphorus or Hesperus parts. (Perhaps that is because the "un-naturalness" of undetached Venus parts makes them ineligible referents—and perhaps not.) If these views are indeed coherent, then scrutability and aspectual shape are different phenomena. If, however, it turns out that these views are incoherent, then deep down scrutability and aspectual shape are probably one and the same phenomenon.

18. For me, the main problem with this argument is that it presupposes that there is no other way to assign determinate, scrutable content to mental states (experiential or not) other than by appeal to experiential character. This is not at all obvious. For example, it is sometimes claimed that the property of being a rabbit is more *natural* than the property of being an undetached rabbit part, and that in virtue of its naturalness, it functions as a sort of reference-magnet for the relevant intentional states (Lewis 1984). Personally, I am suspicious of the notion of naturalness, and of reference-magnetism in general. But it does seem to me difficult to rule out the possibility of a content-determination mechanism that does not appeal to experiential character. Loar and Horgan et al. could insist that until an actual mechanism of content-determination is offered and shown to be viable, we should assent to his argument. However, there is something unsatisfying about this. Certainly many proponents of broadly teleological views of intentionality are unlikely to be impressed by the argument, claiming that their solution to the so-called problem of functional indeterminacy (Dretske 1986, Neander 1995, Papineau 1998) also provides a solution to the problem of referential inscrutability.

19. There is a question as to what those background beliefs are. It is natural to understand them as "dispositional beliefs," but as mentioned in §1.2.3, I am skeptical of the existence of dispositional beliefs, instead embracing the existence of dispositions to believe. So "background beliefs" should be understood to denote (a subset of) dispositions to believe. Speaking of dispositions to believe would make the sentence too inelegant to write down, though more accurately expressive of what I really believe.

20. Recall that by "cognitive experiences" I mean conscious experiences with a proprietary non-sensory experiential character. Revisit §1.3.3 (as well as Kriegel forthcoming) for details.

21. There may be some advantage in requiring cognitive connection of a number of states rather than one. The result would be the following (admittedly less elegant) formulation: Necessarily★, for any item x and property F, F figures in the nexp-intentional content of x iff there are mental states $y_1, \ldots, y_n$ and properties $G_1, \ldots, G_n$, such that (i) for any i, G_i figures in the exp-intentional content of y_i,

(ii) x is suitably cognitively connected to $y_1, \ldots, y_n$, and (iii) F is suitably cognitively connected to G_1, $\ldots, G_n$. The corresponding claim obtained against the assumption of individuation by content would be something like this: For any nexp-intentional state x, x has the intentional content it does (and not another) because x is suitably cognitively connected to the exp-intentional states that it is (and not to others) and x has intentional content (at all) because x is suitably cognitively connected to exp-intentional states (at all).

22. Here too, there may be advantage in requiring cognitive connection of a number of states rather than one. The result would be the following (admittedly less elegant) formulation: Necessarily*, for any item x and property F, F figures in the nexp-intentional content of x iff there are mental states $y_1, \ldots, y_n$ and properties $G_1, \ldots, G_n$, such that (i) for any i, G_i figures in the exp-intentional content of y_i, (ii) x is suitably causally connected to $y_1, \ldots, y_n$, and (iii) F is suitably inferentially connected to $G_1, \ldots, G_n$.

23. There is some question concerning the application of inferential relations to properties rather than, say, propositions. But it is natural to understand this in terms of necessitation relations (for deductive inference) or probabilification relations (for non-deductive inference) among properties: F is inferentially related to G just in case the instantiation of F necessitates or probabilifies the instantiation of G (or vice versa).

24. Milner and Goodale (1995) themselves originally argued that the two streams are functionally insulated from each other, though the consensus has since been moving in the opposite direction.

25. Loar and Horgan et al. could respond that even in this scenario it is the case that dorsal-stream states *belong to the same cognitive system* as some conscious experiences. The variant presented in the next paragraph takes this possibility into consideration, however. In the relevant sense of "cognitive system," moreover, it may well be the case that such cognitive insulation would amount to constituting different cognitive systems.

26. I say "what appears to be cognition" because it might be claimed that a system could be functionally isomorphic with a cognitive system but not be itself a cognitive system, perhaps precisely because qualifying as a cognitive system requires the capacity to undergo conscious experiences.

27. I focus on *conceptual* separation because, as noted, it is debatable whether such zombies are more than just *conceptually* possible. If such zombies are not metaphysically possible, then they do not force on the inferentialist a metaphysical separation of intentionality and cognition. Some philosophers may wish to deny even the conceptual possibility of such zombies, but I think this is *prima facie* implausible (though I am open to being convinced).

28. Something like eliminativism may also propounded, though in quite a subtler version, by Horst (1996).

29. The problem is exacerbated relative to potentialism and inferentialism not only in scope but also in depth. The scope of the problem is worse because eliminativism fails to accommodate not only the cases potentialism and inferentialism fail to, but any other case of a non-experiential item naturally treated as contentful in cognitive science. The depth of the problem concerns the fact that eliminativism fails to get right not only the extension as we antecedently conceive of it by deference to cognitive science, but also the extension as we antecedently conceive of it by deference to folk theory. For there are cases of non-experiential items that everyday practice and intuition treat as contentful, such as paintings and traffic signs. This exacerbates the problem by doing violence not only to the picture of intentionality that emerges from scientific research but also to the folk conception of it.

30. Furthermore, as noted in the previous footnote, eliminativism returns the results that seem wrong not only by cognitive science's lights but also by folk theory's. In response to this last challenge, it might be suggested (and was suggested to me by Georgalis in personal communication) that folk-psychological commitments to what intentional states there are may simply be false—just as some

commitments of folk physics are false (e.g., that weight is intrinsic to the weighty). This, however, is not the same as getting the pre-theoretically desirable extension right—it is rather to argue against a premium on getting right the pre-theoretically desirable extension.

31. See also Cummins 1979, 1989 Ch.1, Schiffer 1982, and Dretske 1988 Ch.3.

32. The relevant intention involves something like intending (i) to produce a certain response in one's audience, (ii) that the audience recognize this first intention, and (iii) that (i) will be based on (ii). This intention is a little too complex to hope that its propositional content be present before the mind. The problem for the semi-eliminativist is that a less complex intention would arguably not be rich enough to ground linguistic content.

33. Here I am assuming that intentions cannot exist as non-intentional states. Thus if there are no non-conscious intentional states, then there are no non-conscious intentions. This strikes me as obviously true: if someone says "I intend," and when we ask "*what* do you intend?," she answers "nothing, I just intend," then this person does not understand what the word "intend" means. Thus it is conceptually necessary for intentions to have intentional content.

34. There are parts of the Dennett corpus that present a more realist face (Dennett 1991). But let us set aside this more realist strand for now. The matter will be taken up again in §4.4.3.

35. I should say that I do not wish to enter an exegetical debate over whether these statements are representative of Dennett's and/or Davidson's considered overall account of intentionality or content. My interest is in the view itself, not in whether it is correctly attributable to Dennett and/or Davidson.

36. This is only an impressionistic sketch of the problem. For a fuller and more accurate paper-length development of it, see Kriegel 2010. It is possible, of course, to avoid the problem simply by advancing a non-reductive (or "non-constitutive") version of such a Dennett-style account of intentionality (see Child 1994 Ch.1). But the kind of view I want to offer as an account of *non-experiential* intentionality is reductive, so I focus in this discussion on the reductive version.

37. Two possible liberalizations of this general strategy are possible. One is to allow in the privileged group not only exp-intentional states, but also nexp-intentional items that have the same underlying nature as exp-intentional states. The other is to allow some of the relevant interpretations to be non-experiential but require that, when they are not, then as noted above, they must have their own (interpretive) content only in virtue of being interpreted by some second-order interpretation, and that second-order interpretation would itself be either experiential or interpreted by a third-order interpretive state, and so on. Ultimately, this regress of interpretations would have to end with a conscious, experiential interpretive act. Both liberalizations are possible but not in fact necessary, for reasons that will emerge later on.

38. I mention something like this account as an option in passing in Kriegel 2003a and Kriegel 2010 and expand on it somewhat, in a more endorsing mode, in Kriegel 2007.

39. For example, if we say that a vase V is such as to break, we could mean one of three things: (a) V breaks; (b) V is disposed to break; (c) V is made of a kind of material that disposes a thing to break.

40. The dispositional reading is preferable because there *exists* no ideal interpreter, as construed here. So (Int) would be plausible only if it did not require *actual* responses on an ideal interpreter's part, but only counterfactual ones. At the same time, I think this would not matter much to the case for its superiority over the alternative accounts of non-experiential intentionality, at least insofar as that superiority holds even if we adopt the categorical reading.

41. This may have to be further tweaked in several ways. First, it may be necessary to require that the ideal interpreter possess all the relevant intentional concepts, though we could also simply expect that, given its other abilities, it might simply be in a position to acquire them once "parachuted" into the world. Secondly, there is no reason to restrict the ideal interpreter's inferential acumen to *first-person* inference. More plausibly, it should be allowed to be perfect at sub-personal cognitive processing as well. Some people cannot hear "inference" as applying to such processes, so to accommodate their hearing,

we could explicitly mention sub-personal processing in the construal of the ideal interpreter. Here, I simply allow "inference" to cover both personal and sub-personal varieties. Thirdly, given that facts described as intentional may turn out to be reducible to facts describable in non-intentional terms, we should modify the characterization of the ideal interpreter by making explicit reference to the description under which the ideal interpreter knows the facts it does (which is one way of thinking of what propositions are). Finally, what counts as a justifiable non-deductive inference is open to debate, but one should just plug here one's favorite view of the matter. For example, if one holds that all non-deductive inferences are to the best explanation and that the best explanation is always and everywhere that which maximizes unification, then one should construe the ideal interpreter as a being who infers the truth of the most unifying explanation of any non-intentional facts (in addition to making every valid deductive inference from those facts).

42. There are also ways to construe the ideal interpreter so that it is more continuous with real-life interpreters. For example, we might propose the following two-step elucidation: an interpreter who makes an ideal interpretation at t is an ideal interpreter at t; an ideal interpreter *simpliciter* is someone who is an ideal interpreter at t for any t.

43. What our "goals" are in the relevant sense will clearly depend on the theoretical perspective taken. Different versions of interpretivism can be formulated by assuming different perspectives. In the present context, the perspective that takes survival and reproduction as most central strikes me as the most congenial. Assuming it, we obtain the following: conditions C are ideal relative to subject S and task T iff S's performance of T under C maximizes S's survival and reproduction prospects (that is, iff there are no conditions C★, such that S's performance of T under C★ enhances S's survival and reproduction prospects more than S's performance of T under C).

44. It may be worried that since the ideal interpreter is defined in terms of the *capacity* to draw inferences, and capacities can be inhibited, that there are some sub-ideal conditions for the ideal interpreter's execution of its interpretive function, namely, the conditions under which the relevant capacity is in fact inhibited. If so, we would need to specify in the biconditional that the interpreter's response is elicited in other conditions, conditions under which the interpreter's capacity to draw inferences is not inhibited.

45. It is an interesting question whether the point applies to any ideal X-er theory. The answer is that it depends on how the ideal X-er is construed in each case.

46. These are the behaviors mentioned in Endnote 12 above (see Aglioti et al. 1995).

47. I should stress that it seems to me that there should be a way to develop inferentialism and interpretivism in such a way that they would turn out to be compatible with each other; or perhaps I should say, it should be possible to develop an account of non-experiential intentionality that would be both inferentialist and interpretivist. This would require that the inferential role be specified in a normative way and where part of the normativity would be based on the fact that the inferential connections would be specified so as to maximize the rationality of the creature to whom the intentional states are ascribed (as per the intentional stance).

48. Another, related interesting feature of interpretivism is that it can make sense of attribution of intentional states to collectives, whereas the other three views cannot. We routinely say that such-and-such committee believes that p, such-and-such firm decides to do so-and-so, and such-and-such ethnicity values this and that. Such ascriptions may be merely metaphorical, in which case they do not need to be made sense of by an account of intentionality. But in case such ascriptions are literal, it would be nice to be able to account for them. Clearly, the collectives' beliefs are not potentially conscious in the relevant sense, since the collectives do not have *conscious* beliefs, nor are inferentially connected to conscious experiences in the relevant sense, since the collectives do not *have* conscious experiences. However, the collectives *are* ideally consciously interpretable as believing what they do, insofar as this helps explain their behavior.

49. Admittedly, (Int⁺) is quite complicated as a whole, but each individual element in it is fairly clear.

50. Another central dimension for the assessment of comparative theoretical virtue is that of conservatism, but it does not seem to apply here at all, as there is no reigning theory of non-experiential intentionality that the four accounts considered here are considering are attempting to displace and are supposed to revise as minimally as possible. Rather, they attempt to be the first reigning theory on the matter. So there is nothing for them to conserve.

51. The intentionality of items from both (ii) and (iii) is grounded in that of items from (i), but that of items from (ii) has the same metaphysical nature as that of items from (i), whereas that of items from (iii) has a different metaphysical nature and may be said to be derivative upon that of items from (i) and perhaps (ii).

52. The distinction between derived and underived intentionality is common in the literature, though I have no desire to commit to any particular conception of the distinction. It should also be noted that there are different ways of putting essentially the same distinction: Haugeland (1980) speaks of "original intentionality" instead of underived intentionality; Block (1986) speaks of "autonomous intentionality"; Searle (1992 Ch.7) of "intrinsic intentionality"; Haugeland (2002) again of "authentic intentionality." Interestingly, Dennett's own interpretivism, even though it is intended as an account of all intentionality, can also been seen as only an account of derived intentionality, since he denies that there is any kind of underived or "original" intentionality (Dennett 1990).

53. For a related discussion, see Horst 1996 Ch.3. Horst argues that there is "conceptually derivative" intentionality and "causally derivative" intentionality. The former involves a distinct property, the latter a distinct way of acquiring or coming to instantiate the same old property.

54. Compare the meta-distinction between the intrinsic/extrinsic distinction, as a distinction between two different kinds of property, and the intrinsically/extrinsically distinction, as a distinction between two different ways of having the same property (Figdor 2008). By the same token, the present meta-distinction is effectively between the derivative/non-derivative distinction and the derivatively/non-derivatively distinction.

55. Some philosophers would put this in terms of the "naturalness" of the property of intentionality *simpliciter*. As I am disenamored of the relevant notion of naturalness (for reasons that should not concern us here), I do not do so myself.

56. Rationality theory should not be confused with the interpretivism as I construed here—their subject matters are not even the same. The latter is an account of what intentionality is (in terms of interpretation). The former is an account of how interpretation works (in terms of principles of charity).

57. What "off-line" means exactly in this context is not particularly clear to me from the literature.

58. These are: theory; simulation; rationality; theory + simulation; simulation + rationality; theory + rationality; theory + simulation + rationality.

59. Everything I said about the mechanics of ascription through the rationality mechanism in §1.2 would apply here (though I did not use that term there).

60. This may raise the suspicion that interpretivism collapses to inferentialism: the ideal interpreter is simply figuring out the facts that inferentialists appeal to in ascribing intentional content to nexp-intentional states. That this suspicion is misplaced can be seen immediately from the fact that interpretivism and inferentialism are extensionally different, the former being more liberal in its ascription of intentional content: as we saw in §4.4.1, it ascribes intentionality to states of zombies, whereas inferentialism does not.

61. Importantly, since we are appealing to the interpreter to fix the nexp-intentional facts, we can grant it complete knowledge not only of the non-intentional facts, but also of the exp-intentional facts.

62. Indeed, it might assign no exp-intentional content to a conscious experience that has one or fail to assign an exp-intentional content to an experience that lacks one. Importantly, even if it turns out that there does exist an ideal interpreter, and that s/he never makes a mistake in attributing exp-intentional content, the truth of the resulting biconditional could only be *a posteriori*. By contrast, the biconditional is true a priori when it comes to the ascription of nexp-intentional content. Interestingly (Wright 1992) takes this difference in epistemic status to define the distinction between a realist view of some phenomenon and an anti-realist view. So by his lights in any case the view presented here is realist about exp-intentional content and anti-realist about nexp-intentional content. More on the realism/anti-realism divide below.

63. Note that (Int$^+$) is an equivalence thesis that leaves open what the direction of explanation is. However, (Int$^+$) is an account of non-experiential intentionality, not account of nexp-intentional ascription. This is what gives it its direction of explanation.

64. The relevant communities must be carefully delineated because even though the tracking relations between tokens of c$\hat{\ }$a$\hat{\ }$t and cats obtain within the English-speaking world, they do not obtain outside it.

65. It is possible, of course, to deny that water exhausts the content of "water," holding instead that the content of "water" is crucially and constitutively associated with a description of water, say as the actual watery stuff. It is quite possible that such descriptive theories of reference are more readily integrated into an interpretivist framework. But it is surely a liability of interpretivism if it is inconsistent with direct-reference treatments of linguistic intentionality across the board, so that its plausibility is beholden to the vicissitudes of a descriptivist theory of linguistic content.

66. Obviously, if speakers used "water" to refer to whatever in their actual environment is the dominant causal source of dispositions to apply the term "water," be it water, twin-water, or any other superficially similar substance, as per some descriptivist theories of reference, then "water" would not be directly referential. And that is also why friend is indeed not directly referential, but rather refers to anything that satisfies the "superficial" description associated with friendship.

67. Moreover, the Davidsonian case for interpretivism, sketched in §1.2.1, applies straightforwardly to linguistic intentionality, since as we saw there, normative principles of charity are needed to ascribe meaning to linguistic utterances.

68. By the "brutely causal" reading I mean the reading according to which a term's referent is determined by its causal relations rather than by its users' intention to use it to refer to whatever it bears those causal relations to.

69. As for other forms of non-experiential intentionality, the interpretivist may need to offer further potential materials. However, it may be possible to apply a broadly Gricean approach to some or all forms of non-mental intentionality, not only to linguistic intentionality. Thus, it has recently been argued that the Gricean account applies just as well to pictures (Abell 2005, Blumson 2006). Note that this would take care of the grounding of the intentionality of paintings, photographs, etc., as well as the intentionality of traffic signs and other forms of symbols that combine linguistic and pictorial representations. If there are forms of non-mental intentionality that are neither linguistic nor pictorial, nor based in stipulative conventions (which are also, and more straightforwardly, grounded in intentions), then the interpretivist might need to either show that they too can be grounded in Gricean intentions, or else provide an altogether new kind of material for the ideal interpreter to appeal to in its content-bestowing conscious interpretations.

70. The temporal language here is metaphorical. The literal sense is logical, and pertains to the lack of logical priority (just as simultaneity consists in the lack of temporal priority).

71. For example, a student who shows up in the wrong room on the day of the exam may be interpreted either as (i) believing that the exam is in (what is in fact) the wrong room and desiring to

take the exam or (ii) believing that the exam is in (what is in fact) the right room and desiring not to take the exam.

72. Interestingly, this may vindicate Bourget's (2010) claim, which we encountered in §2.1, that atomistic content is distinctive of experiential intentionality. The claim that all non-experiential intentionality is holistic does not entail that no experiential intentionality is non-holistic, but that latter claim is independently plausible, and together they would vindicate Bourget's claim.

73. For example, if your interlocutor points at your new laptop and says "congratulations on your new capsicum," it is possible to interpret her as either (i) desiring to congratulate you on a new pepper and believing that the word "capsicum" means pepper or (ii) desiring to congratulate you on a new laptop and believing that the word "capsicum" means laptop; but a competent interpreter would always opt for the second interpretation, even though both accommodate the data equally well, because (presumably) she would employ the principle of charity.

74. This leads to non-experiential intentionality being mind-dependent, and not only in the trivial sense that they are instantiated by/in minds: interpretivism construes nexp-intentional facts as interpreter-dependent, and since the interpreters are minds, interpretivism implies that intentional properties are mind-dependent. Thus, on this view, whether a creature is in an intentional state, such as believing that *p*, depends not only on how things are with the creature, but also on how things are with the interpreter. Clearly, this is quite a strong form of irrealism.

75. In the case of non-experiential mental states, speaker intentions are irrelevant of course, but still, there too it seems most plausible to suppose that the real patterns concern some abstraction from a mental state's overall long-armed causal role, i.e., its broadly causal (including tracking) relations to distal as well as proximal causes and effects. (For the notion of a "long-armed" causal role, see Harman 1987.)

76. And indeed we *are* realists about experiential intentionality, since the adverbial and higher-order tracking theories thereof are both realist. As long as we are realists about experiential intentionality, the emerging overall view of intentionality combines realism about experiential intentionality with (limited) irrealism about all other intentionality, which is not all that embarrassing.

77. That is, unless the citation of intentional properties can be shown to be explanatorily indispensable for a complete theory of the world, we would be unjustified in positing them. The parties to the debate differed in their assessment of who won, of course, but they all agreed on this rule of the game.

78. It may, of course, turn out that intentional properties are dispensable, say because they are relational and only non-relational properties are explanatorily relevant to psychology (Stich 1978, 1983). But even if this is not the case, the very approach of ontological commitment by explanatory indispensability leaves the door open to an irrealist gloss (of a pragmatist variety) that observational encounter does not. For more on this, see Kriegel 2011b.

79. This is so because, as we noted, the ideal interpreter would probably appeal to several different materials: what the state tracks, what it other states it is cognitively connected with, etc. The variety of materials constitutes the relevant heterogeneity.

80. With Searle's potentialism and Loar/Horgan et al.'s inferentialism, we have not only an account of non-experiential intentionality, but also a story about the special feature of experiential intentionality that gives it its special place in the theory of intentionality: respectively, aspectual shape and scrutability of content. It is not clear, according to the objector, just what it is, according to interpretivism, that makes experiential intentionality so special.

81. For comments on a previous draft, I am indebted to David Chalmers, Nicholas Georgalis, George Graham, Michelle Montague, David Pitt, and especially Tim Bayne. For very helpful conversations, I would like to thank Allan Hazlett, Terry Horgan, and Amie Thomasson. I also benefited from

presenting material from the paper at the 2009 Pacific APA and a conference that summer at the University of Bern, and would like to thank the audience there, in particular Ben Blumson, Josh Glasgow, Philippe Keller, Rae Langton, Sebastian Leuggers, Eduard Marbach, Michelle Montague, Carolina Sartorio, Gianfranco Soldati, and Galen Strawson. The bulk of the first draft of this chapter was written during a research fellowship at the University of Sydney, to which I am greatly indebted.

5

Toward a General Theory of Intentionality

Introduction/Abstract

A "general theory of intentionality" is one that tells us, for any intentional item whatsoever, what makes it an intentional item at all (rather than a non-intentional item) and what makes it the intentional item it is (rather than a different intentional item). That is, it is a theory that specifies the identity and existence conditions of all intentionality. Following the formulation of similar questions in Chapters 2 and 4, we can formulate the organizing question of a general theory of intentionality thus:

> (IQ) For any intentional item x, what makes x the intentional item it is and an intentional item at all?

On the assumption that the intentional content of an intentional state is what makes it the intentional state it is, and an intentional state at all, the question becomes this:

> (IQ★) For any intentional item x and property F, what would make it the case that F figures in the intentional content of x?

This chapter combines the results of the previous chapters to produce possible answers to this question.

A framework for a general theory of intentionality is provided by the experiential origin thesis, in particular in its formulation as (EO★) in §1.2.3. According to it, there are two ways for an item to qualify as intentional (fall under our concept of intentionality). One is to share an underlying nature with most encountered exp-intentional states. The other is to bear the right relation to an item that shares (or items that share) an underlying nature with most encountered exp-intentional states, the kind of relation in virtue of which the intentionality of the item that bears it can be derived from the intentionality of the item(s) to which it is borne. More precisely, recall:

(EO★) There is a relation R and a nature N, such that (i) most encountered exp-intentional states have N and (ii) for any item x, x qualifies as intentional iff either (a) x has N, or (b) there is an item y, such that (b-i) y has N and (b-ii) x bears R to y.

The variables that call for an account here are N and R: the underlying nature N of encountered exp-intentional states and the relation R that derivatively intentional items bear to non-derivatively intentional items. Chapters 2–3 effectively explored different views on N, while Chapter 4 considered different views on R.

In Chapters 2–3, I focused on three main accounts of the underlying nature of experiential intentionality (the tracking account, higher-order tracking theory, and adverbial theory), and touched in passing on a fourth (primitivism).[1] In Chapter 4, I discussed four possible accounts of the kind of relation an item must bear to items that have that underlying nature in order to qualify as derivatively intentional (potentialism, inferentialism, eliminativism, and interpretivism). Restricting ourselves to just these options, we obtain a matrix of sixteen possible general theories of intentionality to choose among.[2]

In the course of the previous chapters, I have made my own preferences clear. Among accounts of N (the underlying nature of experiential intentionality), I find the higher-order tracking and adverbial theories most plausible (with the former slightly more plausible than the latter). Among accounts of R (the relation underlying intentionality-derivation, if you will), I find interpretivism most plausible. As a result, I am tempted by two kinds of general theory of intentionality: (i) the combination of higher-order tracking theory and interpretivism, and (ii) the combination of adverbialism and interpretivism. Since I find the higher-order tracking theory slightly more plausible than the adverbial theory, I naturally have a slight preference for the first combination over the second.

In any case, this chapter is devoted to the explicit statement of both of these general theories, as well as of some of their main philosophical implications. In §5.1, I discuss the combination of adverbialism plus interpretivism, and in §5.2, the combination of higher-order tracking theory plus interpretivism. Before starting, I should warn the reader that this chapter is even more replete with precise formulations of various biconditionals. As before, it is not necessary to read them in order to follow the discussion, though in some sense they are more essential to this chapter's mandate than previously.

5.1. Adverbialism plus Interpretivism

The first general theory of intentionality is obtained by combining (ATEI) from Chapter 3 and (Int) from Chapter 4, that is, adverbialism about N and interpretivism about R.[3]

According to adverbialism, there is a certain adverbial experiential property, of being-intentionally-directed-somehow, that constitutes the underlying nature of experiential intentionality in general. This property is shared, certainly, by not only *most* but *all* encountered exp-intentional states. In addition, however, it is shared by *un*encountered exp-intentional states, that is, by exp-intentional states the normal subject has not encountered during the formation of her conception of aboutness. (Thus, although my first gustatory experience as of snake meat came well after my conception of aboutness had been formed, that experience did exhibit, according to adverbialism, the property of being-intentionally-directed-somehow.) Therefore, unencountered exp-intentional states qualify as intentional through Clause (a) in (EO★): they share an underlying nature with most encountered exp-intentional states.

Since both encountered and unencountered exp-intentional states qualify as intentional through Clause (a), we can say that *all* exp-intentional states do. The next question is whether *only* exp-intentional states do, that is, whether any nexp-intentional states might as well. The answer seems to be that only exp-intentional states do. In order to qualify through Clause (a), a nexp-intentional state would have to exhibit the intrinsic (adverbial) experiential property of being-intentionally-directed-somehow. But being non-experiential, nexp-intentional states cannot be expected to exhibit *any* experiential property, adverbial or not.[4] Thus adverbialism about the underlying nature of most encountered exp-intentional states leads to the view that *all and only* exp-intentional states have that nature. Therefore, all and only exp-intentional states boast non-derivative intentionality. All other intentional items must qualify as intentional only derivatively, that is, in virtue of bearing R to exp-intentional states.

To complete a *general* theory of intentionality, then, we would need an account of the relation R in virtue of which nexp-intentional states qualify as intentional. This is provided by interpretivism, according to which a nexp-intentional item is intentional in virtue of being such as to produce an interpretive experience as of its being intentional in ideal interpreters under ideal conditions. Combining adverbialism about the underlying nature of encountered exp-intentional states with interpretivism about nexp-intentional states generates a view according to which an item qualifies as intentional in one of the two following ways: either (a) it exhibits the adverbial experiential property of being intentionally-directed-somehow, or (b) it is such as to elicit in ideal subjects under ideal conditions an interpretation of it as intentional. That is:

> Necessarily★, for any item x, x qualifies as intentional iff either (a) there is an experiential property E, E = being-intentionally-directed-somehow, such that x is E, or (b) x is such as to produce in ideal interpreters under ideal conditions the response of having an interpretive experience as of x being intentional.

Note, however, that this thesis addresses only the *existence conditions* of intentionality—what makes an item an intentional item at all. It does not remark on what makes the item the specific kind of intentional item it is—what the *identity* conditions of intentionality are. To that extent, it does not provide a full answer to (IQ) or (IQ★). However, it can be easily generalized to do so, since adverbialism and interpretivism do remark on what makes an item the specific kind of intentional item it is, not only on what makes it an intentional item at all. The result would be that there are two ways for an item to qualify as having a certain kind of content: (a) by having the corresponding adverbial experiential property, or (b) by being ideally interpreted as having that kind of content. More precisely:

> (GT1) Necessarily★, for any item x and putative property F, x qualifies as having an intentional content that features F iff either (a) there is an experiential property E, E = being-intentionally-directed-F-wise, such that x is E, or (b) x is such as to produce in ideal interpreters under ideal conditions the response of having an interpretive experience as of x having an intentional content that features F.[5]

This is truly a general theory of intentionality: of any intentional item, it says what makes it the intentional item it is and an intentional item at all.

In Chapters 3 and 4, I also offered more fully spelled out formulations of adverbialism and interpretivism. Most conspicuously, (Int⁺) spelled out interpretivism by specifying more fully what is involved in being such as to produce the relevant interpretive response.[6] This can be profitably plugged into the above to generate a more spelled out formulation:

> (GT1⁺) Necessarily★, for any item x and putative property F, x qualifies as having an intentional content that features F iff either (a) there is an experiential property E, E = being-intentionally-directed-F-wise, such that x is E, or (b) possibly, there are conditions C, an interpreter Å, and a mental act y, such that (i) y has an exp-intentional content to the effect that F figures in the intentional content of x, (ii) Å is an ideal reasoner fully informed of the non-intentional and exp-intentional facts, and (iii) x is disposed to produce y in Å under C.[7]

This is obtained by basically adopting all the specifications and clarifications I have offered in §4.4 for the central terms in (Int).

Further clarifications of interpretivism are possible in light of the adoption of adverbialism about underived intentionality. That is, in light of Part (a) of the thesis, the adverbialist part, we can get more explicit on what is involved in Part (b), the interpretivist part. For on the adverbialist view, having an interpretive experience as of F figuring in the intentional content of x is a matter of being in a mental state with an experiential character that involves the feeling of being directed at x's having an F-content, a feeling which is here understood along adverbialist lines. That is, having an interpretive experience as of F figuring in the intentional content of x is a matter of having an experience that exhibits the adverbial property of being intentionally directed F-figures-in-the-content-of-x-wise. This leads to the following formulation:

> (GT1⁺⁺) Necessarily★, for any item x and putative property F, x qualifies as having an intentional content that features F iff either (a) there is an experiential property E, E = being-intentionally-directed-F-wise, such that x is E, or (b) possibly, there are conditions C, an interpreter Å, a mental act y, and an experiential property E★, E★ = being-intentionally-directed-F-figures-in-the-content-of-x-wise, such that (i) y is E★, (ii) Å is an ideal reasoner fully informed of the non-intentional and exp-intentional facts, and (iii) x is disposed to produce y in Å under C.[8]

Further specifications and clarifications of the interpretivist component are surely possible, but here I will rest content with the above.

There are also possible further specifications of the adverbialist component. As we saw in §3.4, there are different views on the nature of the generic feeling as of aboutness or directedness—what I have called the "phenomenological signature of intentionality." I mentioned four possible views: the phenomenological signature as *sui generis* phenomenal directedness (Loar 2003), as experiential taking (Strawson 2008), as objectual unity structure (Masrour 2008 Ch.2), and—my personal favorite—as phenomenal foreignness (Frey forthcoming). If we embed in (GT1^{++}) the explicit formulation in §3.4 of the version of adverbialism that appeals to phenomenal foreignness,[9] for example, we obtain:

(GT1^{++1}) Necessarily★, for any item x and putative property F, x qualifies as having an intentional content that features F iff either (a) there is an experiential property E, E = phenomenally presenting-an-other-to-be-F, such that x is E, or (b) possibly, there are conditions C, an interpreter Å, a mental act y, and an experiential property E★, E★ = phenomenally presenting-an-other-to-present-an-other-to-be-F, such that (i) y is E★, (ii) Å is an ideal reasoner fully informed of the non-intentional and exp-intentional facts, and (iii) x is disposed to produce y in Å under C.[10]

We can generate (GT1^{++2}), (GT1^{++3}), and so forth by embedding reference to other views of the phenomenological signature of intentionality.

The picture of intentionality we are offered here is this. There is the generic feeling as of being about something, which is the property of being intentionally directed somehow. This is the most primary and most basic intentional property, in that it is the most general determinable (or genus) of underived intentionality. It has many determinates (or species), which are intentional properties as well: being intentionally directed chocolate-wise, being intentionally directed dragon-wise. A subset of these determinates (species) comprises a group of intentional properties we may describe as the properties of being intentionally directed interpretation-wise—e.g., the property of being intentionally directed F-figures-in-the-content-of-x-wise. There are then properties of being disposed to elicit mental states that exhibit this kind of interpretation-wise intentional directedness, and those dispositional properties too are intentional properties.[11] There are no other intentional properties.

On this picture, intentionality is originally injected into the world when a certain type of experiential character makes its appearance, namely, the character of being intentionally directed some*how*. It is the fact that some mental states exhibit the experiential property with the requisite phenomenological signature that brings in its train the dimension of intentionality. The appearance of phenomenal foreignness, or experiential taking, or objectual unity structure, or *sui generis* intentional directedness, or whatever the relevant experiential property actually is, injects intentional content into an otherwise content-less, non-intentional reality. Once intentionality has been thus injected into the world, however, it can be "passed along," via experiential interpretive acts, to things that do not have the relevant experiential property.

It is clear from this picture, I think, why the adverbial account is naturally developed as non-reductive. If what injects intentionality into the world is a certain kind of adverbial experiential character, and not any broadly physical relation to worldly entities, then it is most natural to suppose that the relevant adverbial experiential character itself is a non-physical property (even if it is a property *of* physical particulars). As noted in §3.5, though, it is *coherent* to maintain that the relevant experiential character is constituted by a physical property after all, due (say) to some brute identity holding between the former and the latter.

Interestingly, this picture involves a kind of *intellectualism* about intentionality. For the experiential feature that injects intentionality into the world is most naturally understood as a cognitive rather than sensory experiential feature. This is appreciated most easily when we consider Masrour's objectual unity structure, as exemplified in the visual experience of R.C. James' Dalmatian. Most first-time observers of the image fail to see the Dalmatian at first but then undergo a Gestalt shift—a felt, experientially distinctive Gestalt shift—whereupon they become aware of the canine object. According to Masrour, the visual experience is (in one central sense) non-intentional prior to this Gestalt shift and acquires an intentional dimension only after the shift. Yet it is fairly clear that the *sensory*-experiential properties of the experience are the same before and after the shift: the same distribution of black spots against a white background is sensed pre- and post-shift. What is different, experientially, is thus non-sensory. This non-sensory experiential feature may be built into the perceptual phenomenology or be altogether post-perceptual, but either way, insofar as it is non-sensory it is a cognitive-experiential feature in at least a minimal sense. To that extent, the experiential Gestalt shift is a cognitive experience. The upshot is that if objectual unity structure is the phenomenological signature of intentionality, then it turns out that it is a kind of cognitive-experiential character that injects intentionality into the world. In the absence of cognitive experience, there would be no aboutness.[12]

I said that this intellectualist aspect is most easily appreciated when we consider the objectual-unity-structure version of adverbialism. But it can be brought out also with the phenomenal-foreignness, experiential-taking, and *sui-generis*-phenomenal-directedness versions. We can certainly envisage creatures who, due to the lack of certain cognitive capacities, undergo conscious experiences sensorily indistinguishable from ours but lacking the element of phenomenal foreignness. Ditto, it seems to me, for the putative elements of experiential taking and *sui generis* phenomenal directedness.[13]

This intellectualism about underived intentionality has implications for derived intentionality as well. Since there would be no derived intentionality if there was no underived intentionality, and there would be no underived intentionality if there was no cognitive experience, there would be no derived intentionality if there was no cognitive experience. Furthermore, on some highly plausible versions of interpretivism, the very derivation of derived intentionality, if you will, depends upon a (further) type of cognitive experience. The versions I have in mind construe all conscious interpretation as cognitive-experiential, that is, as a matter of conscious judgments about content.[14] This would allow us to argue as follows: 1) Interpretivism entails that all nexp-intentional content is ultimately grounded in the exp-intentional content of interpretive experiences; 2) The exp-intentional content of all interpretive experiences is ultimately grounded in, or perhaps identical to, the experiential character of interpretive experiences; 3) The experiential character of all interpretive experiences is a cognitive-experiential character; therefore, 4) Interpretivism entails that all non-experiential content is ultimately grounded in a cognitive-experiential character. The most controversial premise in this argument is the third: it is not easy to say anything definitive about the nature of the experiential character of interpretive experiences.[15] But if one holds that all interpretive experiential characters must have a cognitive-experiential component, then it would certainly follow that the experiential character of conscious interpretive acts—interpretive experiences—is always cognitive-experiential.

A less surprising implication of the adverbialism-cum-interpretivism picture of intentionality is a strong kind of content *internalism*. In its purest form, content internalism is the view that every intentional property is a non-relational property of its bearer:

(PI) For any item x and property P, if P is an intentional property of x, then P is a non-relational property of x.

This pure internalism can be made less pure by weakening the claim made about intentional properties or by limiting the scope of intentional properties the claim is made about. Let me discuss a number of relevant examples (some of which will become relevant only in the next section).

It is possible to weaken (PI) by requiring intentional properties not quite to be non-relational properties, but to be intrinsic properties, or perhaps just "locally supervenient" properties. It is sometimes thought that some intrinsic properties are relational (namely, when a instantiates F in virtue of a bearing a relation to a proper part of a, as in, e.g., my property of having a hand). So being a non-relational property is more demanding than being an intrinsic property, and the pure internalism above is more demanding than the following weakened internalism:

(WI1) For any item x and property P, if P is an intentional property of x, then P is an intrinsic property of x.

It is also plausible that some extrinsic properties supervene on intrinsic properties (e.g., the property of being no less of a perfect sphere than any other figure supervenes on the property of being a perfect sphere). So being an intrinsic property is more demanding than being a property that supervenes on intrinsic properties, i.e., a *locally supervenient* property. The following version of internalism is thus even weaker:

(WI2) For any item x and property P, if P is an intentional property of x, then P is a locally supervenient property of x.[16]

Another, quite common weakening focuses not on the properties of mental states themselves, but of the subjects who are in them.[17] Arguably, it is possible for a mental state's intentional properties to fail to supervene on the intrinsic properties of that state and yet manage to supervene on the intrinsic properties of the state's subject. If so, a yet weaker version of internalism would state that mental states' intentional properties locally supervene on these states' subjects' properties. More precisely:

(WI3) For any mental state *x* and property P, if P is an intentional property of *x*, then there is a subject S, such that (i) S is in *x* and (ii) S's property of being in a state that instantiates P is a locally supervenient property of S.[18]

These are the main ways of retreating from pure internalism by making weaker claims.

More pertinently for our present purposes, one can also retreat from pure internalism by limiting its application, that is, by excluding certain intentional properties from its scope. The most interesting version of this, in the present context, would limit internalism to *underived* intentional properties:

(LI1) For any item *x* and property P, if P is a non-derivatively intentional property of *x*, then P is a non-relational property of *x*.

This is the interesting version, because it is an obvious consequence of (GT1). Since (GT1) implies that all non-derivatively intentional properties are exp-intentional, and adverbialism construes exp-intentional properties as non-relational, it follows that all non-derivatively intentional properties are non-relational. Thus according to (GT1), Oscar and Twin-Oscar's conscious water thoughts (their water-ish cognitive experiences) are intentionally type-identical.[19]

Some restrictions of the scope of internalism give up the spirit of the internalist outlook on content. For example, philosophers impressed by externalism about proper names and natural kind terms, and correspondingly about individual concepts and natural kind concepts, might nonetheless accept an internalism restricted to all mental states whose constituents are not individual or natural kind concepts.[20] This would be a major concession for the internalist to make. By contrast, the restriction of internalism to non-derivatively intentional properties is different. Even though it concedes that externalism may be true of some derivatively intentional properties, it paints a picture of intentionality on which the only reason there is any intentional content in the world in the first place is that certain non-relational properties constitute intentional contents. Thus it is only once water-ish experiences such as Oscar's and Twin-Oscar's introduce the relevant non-relational intentional properties into the world that some further items can acquire an intentional dimension which may be partly determined by factors outside those items.

It might be thought that if all non-derivatively intentional content is internalistic, or "narrow," then the content that derives from it would have to be narrow as well, with the result that there is no wide content at all.[21] On the one hand, I am not altogether hostile to the consequence, as I personally take the intuitive evidence for externalism to be weak. On the other hand, I am not persuaded that it is a consequence of internalism about underived intentionality that internalism is true of all intentionality. Partly this depends on what we require from a content to count as narrow. If indeed we require that having the content be a non-relational property of the contentful, then the thought is misguided. In fact, on the picture suggested by (GT1), all derivatively intentional items have their content in virtue of relational properties, namely, the relevant interpretation-dependent properties, which involve relations to ideal interpreters.[22] Moreover, as noted in §4.4, the ideal interpreter is likely to assign content to derivatively intentional items on the basis of, among other things, what those items track. So externalistic factors could, in principle, enter the ideal interpreter's considerations in determining the content of derivatively intentional items, with the result that some intrinsically indistinguishable items would have different intentional contents. Thus there is no reason why wide content could not derive from narrow content.

This, then, is the first general theory of intentionality suggested by the previous chapters—a combination of adverbialism about experiential intentionality and interpretivism about non-experiential intentionality, set against the experiential origin thesis. This general theory is strongly internalist and importantly intellectualist. It portrays the source of intentionality as a kind of non-relational cognitive-experiential character. Tracking and the like broadly causal relations are according to it altogether irrelevant to intentionality, except perhaps causally (rather than constitutively). It is an adverbial experiential modification of some of our mental states that injects intentionality into the world.

I find this skeletal general theory of intentionality quite intriguing, and as argued in Chapter 3, also reasonably plausible, mostly because of its ability to respect the appearances of experiential intentionality (which intentional experiences appear possible). But as also noted in Chapter 3, this picture sits uncomfortably with the objective of naturalizing intentionality. It may render intentionality intelligible by casting it as grounded in something each of us is familiar with from personal acquaintance, but it does not quite render it intelligible through a demystification of its place in nature. This consideration, which is admittedly in some sense more ideologically driven than evidence-driven, is what gives me pause in contemplating the overall attraction of this approach to intentionality. In the next section, I consider an alternative skeletal general theory of intentionality that I find slightly more attractive, all things considered.

5.2. Higher-Order Tracking Theory plus Interpretivism

The second general theory of intentionality suggested by earlier chapters retains interpretivism about R, the relation underlying derived intentionality, but combines it with the higher-order tracking theory of N, the underlying nature of underived intentionality.

According to higher-order tracking theory, recall, an item is exp-intentional just in case it is suitably tracked to track something.[23] As with the adverbial theory, this identifies an underlying nature of the intentionality exhibited by most encountered exp-intentional states that is in fact exhibited by *all* encountered exp-intentional states, indeed all exp-intentional states (encountered or not). By the lights of (EO★), then, all exp-intentional states have underived intentionality. For they all have the same underlying nature as most encountered exp-intentional states, namely, being suitably tracked to track something.

With adverbialism, it was clear not only that *all* exp-intentional states have the same underlying nature as most encountered exp-intentional states, but also that *only* exp-intentional states do—that no nexp-intentional state has the relevant adverbial experiential property. This is less clear with higher-order tracking theory. It is less clear, that is, that there are no nexp-intentional items that are suitably tracked to track something. For all we know, there might be some non-experiential sub-personal states that are suitably tracked to track features in the environment.[24] If there are such, then by the lights of (EO★), these sub-personal states would have underived intentionality as well, despite being non-experiential. Pending the discovery that there really are such non-experiential states, however, we may proceed on the assumption that *only* exp-intentional states are suitably tracked to track, hence are endowed with underived intentionality.[25]

On the assumption, then, that not only *all* but also *only* exp-intentional states qualify as intentional because they are suitably tracked to track something, all nexp-intentional states must qualify as intentional because they bear the right relation R to exp-intentional states. The right relation, according to interpretivism, is that of ideal interpretability. The upshot is a picture where an item can qualify as intentional in one of two ways: either (a) it is suitably tracked to track something, or (b) it is such as to elicit in ideal interpreters under ideal conditions an interpretive experience of it as intentional. That is:

> Necessarily★, for any item x, x qualifies as intentional iff either (a) there is a tracking relation T and a suitable mental state y, such that y bears T to x's bearing T to something, or (b) x is such as to produce in ideal interpreters under ideal conditions the response of having an interpretive experience as of x being intentional.

As in §5.1, this thesis fails to remark on the *identity* conditions of intentionality (what makes an intentional item the specific kind of intentional item it is), but can be generalized to do so. The result would be that there are two ways for an item to qualify as being intentionally directed at some specific property: (a) by being tracked to track that property, or (b) by being ideally interpretable as being intentionally directed at that property. More precisely:

> (GT2) Necessarily★, for any item x and property F, x qualifies as having an intentional content that features F iff either (a) there is a tracking relation T and a suitable mental state y, such that y bears T to x's bearing T to F, or (b) x is such as to produce in ideal interpreters under ideal conditions the response of having an interpretive experience as of x having an intentional content that features F.

This is the general theory of intentionality one obtains by combining (HOTT) from Chapter 2, (Int) from Chapter 4, and (EO★) from Chapter 1. If we plug into it (Int⁺) rather than (Int), we obtain this more explicit thesis:

> (GT2⁺) Necessarily★, for any item x and property F, x qualifies as having an intentional content that features F iff either (a) there is a tracking relation T and a suitable mental state y, such that y bears T to x's bearing T to F, or (b) possibly, there are conditions C,

an interpreter Å, and a mental act z, such that (i) z has an exp-intentional content to the effect that F figures in the intentional content of x, (ii) Å is an ideal reasoner fully informed of the non-intentional and exp-intentional facts, and (iii) x is disposed to produce z in Å under C.

The basic idea, in any case, is that F figures in the content of x either (a) if x is tracked to track F, when x is non-derivatively intentional, or (b) if x is ideally interpretable as featuring F in its content, when x is derivatively intentional.

An interesting question arises concerning the unpacking of the interpretivist component of (GT2$^+$) in light of its (HOTT) component. Notice that the interpretivist component describes the interpretive state z as the state with an exp-intentional content to the effect that F figures in the intentional content of x. The question is how to understand this kind of interpretive state within the (HOTT) framework. The problem is that since x's having F in its content is *constituted* by the interpretive state's attribution of F to x's content, there is not a prior fact concerning x's having F in its content for the interpretive state to (be tracked to) track. This problem does not arise within the adverbialist framework, because the content of the interpretive state is not understood in terms of any relation to independent facts, but rather in terms of adverbial modification of the interpretive state's experiential character. It does arise within the (HOTT) framework, because something must be tracked (or rather be tracked to be tracked) for the interpretive state to have its content.

The right approach to this problem is to seek some fact D, distinct from the fact of x's having F in its content, such that it is plausible that an interpreted state x having F in its content is constituted by D being tracked to be tracked by the interpretive state z. Recall that in §4.4.3, I mentioned Dennett's "real patterns" as interpretation-independent facts underlying the disposition to elicit the relevant interpretive responses. It is natural to suppose that D is whatever interpretation-independent "real pattern" this is. So the fact of x's having F in its (derived) content may be thought of as constituted by z's being higher-order tracked to track those "real patterns."

In §4.4.3, I suggested more specifically that the real patterns are facts about the long-armed causal role of a mental state, including facts about what it tracks. If so, we may think of the fact of x's having F in its (derived) content as constituted by z's being higher-order tracked to track a subset of x's broadly causal relations, including x's tracking of F. The emerging picture of interpretation is quite complex, involving as it does three orders of tracking, but it is also quite pleasing, insofar as with a certain oversimplification, it can be seen to unify the overall account of intentionality under the notion of higher-order tracking. The simplification is to disregard the aspects of x's long-armed causal role that do not concern x's tracking of F and focus on the tracking dimension of its causal role exclusively.[26] If we do adopt this (HOTT) gloss on interpretation, the result is an account of derived intentionality in terms of third-order tracking. This complements nicely the account of underived intentionality in terms of second-order tracking. The ensuing general theory of intentionality may be formulated more precisely thus:

> ($GT2^{++}$) Necessarily★, there is a tracking relation T, such that for any item x and property F, x qualifies as having an intentional content that features F iff either (a) there is a suitable mental state y, such that y bears T to x's bearing T to F, or (b) possibly, there are conditions C, an interpreter Å, and mental acts z and w, such that (i) w bears T to z's bearing T to x's bearing T to F, (ii) Å is an ideal reasoner fully informed of the non-intentional and exp-intentional facts, and (iii) x is disposed to produce z and w in Å under C.

There is a certain beauty in this kind of general theory of intentionality, due to the cohesion of the all-encompassing tracking-based account. But there is also a significant degree of plausibility. For my part, I have greater credence in ($GT2^{++}$) than in any other general theory of intentionality specified at the same level of abstraction. This is just a result of (i) my credence in (HOTT) being higher than in any other account of experiential intentionality at the same level of abstraction, and (ii) my credence in the account of interpretive experience in terms of three orders of tracking being no lower than my credence in any other account of interpretive experience at the same level of abstraction.

At a lower level of abstraction, however, I indicated in Chapter 2 my preference for a specific version of (HOTT), namely, the self-tracking version. This was formulated initially—in (STA)—in terms of conscious experiences tracking themselves to track external features, and later—in

244   THE SOURCES OF INTENTIONALITY

(NSTA)—in terms of a more complex structure involving parts of experiences bearing various tracking and representation-transmission relations.[27] Although the combination of (STA), (Int), and (EO★) generates a version of (GT2), let us present it here as a *third* general theory of intentionality:

> (GT3) Necessarily★, for any item x and property F, x qualifies as having an intentional content that features F iff either (a) there is a tracking relation T, such that x bears T to x's own bearing of T to F, or (b) x is such as to produce in ideal interpreters under ideal conditions the response of having an interpretive experience as of F figuring in the intentional content of x.[28]

And let us present the combination of (NSTA), (Int), and (EO★) as generating a *fourth* general theory of intentionality:

> (GT4) Necessarily★, for any item x and property F, x qualifies as having an intentional content that features F iff either (a) there are states x_1 and x_2, a tracking relation T, and a representation-transmission relation R, such that (i) x_1 is a proper part of x, (ii) x_2 is a proper part of x, (iii) x_1 bears T to x_2's bearing T to F, and (iv) x_2 bears R to x, or (b) x is such as to produce in ideal interpreters under ideal conditions the response of having an interpretive experience as of F figuring in the intentional content of x.

The more fully explicit formulation of this fourth general theory would be obtained by combining (NSTA) with (Int$^+$) rather than (Int), and adopting the resulting picture of what an interpretive experience is:

> (GT4^{++}) Necessarily★, there is a tracking relation T, such that for any item x and property F, x qualifies as having an intentional content that features F iff either (a) there are states x_1 and x_2, and a representation-transmission relation R, such that (i) x_1 is a proper part of x, (ii) x_2 is a proper part of x, (iii) x_1 bears T to x_2's bearing T to F, and (iv) x_2 bears R to x, or (b) possibly, there are conditions C, an interpreter Å, and mental states $y, y_1,$ and y_2, such that (i) y_1 is a proper part of y, (ii) y_2 is a proper part of y, (iii) y_1 bears T to y_2's bearing T to x's bearing T to F, (iv) y_2 bears R to y, (v) Å is an ideal reasoner fully informed of the non-intentional and exp-intentional facts, and (vi) x is disposed to produce $y, y_1,$ and y_2 in Å under C.

Here too, I can report a credence in (GT4^{++}) higher than in any other general theory of intentionality at the same level of abstraction." (GT4^{++}) itself admits of several versions, corresponding to different accounts of the tracking relation T, and as noted in §2.1.1, my own tendency would be to adopt a teleo-informational version.[30]

This kind of general theory of intentionality is more conservative than the kind examined in §5.1, insofar as it appeals centrally to the kind of tracking relation that more mainstream accounts of intentionality have focused on in the past few decades. Nonetheless, it represents a major departure from such mainstream accounts. According to it, the reason there is intentionality in the world in the first place is that a certain kind of sophisticated higher-order tracking (or perhaps self-tracking) exists. It is with the appearance of such higher-order tracking that intentionality gets injected into the world originally. What introduces intentional content into an otherwise contentless, non-intentional reality is the fact that some mental states are suitably higher-order tracked to track environmental features. Once injected into the world, intentionality gets "passed around" through a subset of possible suitably higher-order tracked trackers, namely, those that are suitably higher-order tracked to track the right patterns.[31]

This picture of intentionality is not as inherently intellectualist and internalist as that from §5.1. How intellectualist it is will depend on whether one takes higher-order tracking to be "intellectual." Clearly, such higher-order tracking is not sensory in any mundane sense. But at least on analogy with the Lockean tradition of understanding introspection in terms of an "inner sense," such higher-order tracking may be understood as "quasi-sensory," in the sense that higher-order trackers are products of quasi-sensory monitoring mechanisms.[32] These mechanisms would be "quasi-sensory" in that their operation would be analogous to the operation of familiar sensory mechanisms (e.g., in employing information-processing procedures that require, or implicate, the operation of specialized transducers).[33] So a significantly non-intellectualist version of (GT2-4) is quite plausible. However, the quasi-sensory view of higher-order tracking is controversial, and denying that anything higher-order in the cognitive system is ever significantly analogous to sensory mechanisms might be viable.[34] Such a position would lead one to hold that experiential intentionality, hence underived intentionality, requires considerable intellectual sophistication, namely, the kind of intellectual sophistication involved in a system engaging in higher-order tracking.

This would introduce a strongly intellectualist dimension into (GT2-4). For my part, I am more tempted by the non-intellectualist take on higher-order tracking, as it aligns better with the notion, stressed in Chapter 1, that introspective encounter involves observational contact with the encountered.[35]

As for internalism, (GT2-4) have no special affinity to it. In fact, any tracking-based approach to intentionality has a much more natural affinity to content externalism, since trackers individuate sensitively to what they track.[36] Thus, if an internal state in Oscar tracks water, whereas an otherwise indistinguishable internal state in Twin-Oscar tracks twin-water, and twin-water is not water, then Oscar's and Twin-Oscar's internal states are type-different trackers. Since they are type-different trackers, any higher-order internal states that tracked *them* would be tracking different things, and would therefore be themselves type-different trackers (this time type-different higher-order trackers). This despite any intrinsic indistinguishability they might enjoy. It would seem, then, that the standard reasons to embrace content externalism apply to the higher-order tracking theory of experiential/underived intentionality.[37]

There are some options for resisting externalism here, but most are not special to higher-order tracking theory. For example, one might hold that twin-water is a kind of water, in that water is simply multiply realized, with H_2O and XYZ being different realizers.[38] This might, on certain views, cast H_2O-trackers as type-identical with XYZ-trackers, and therefore H_2O-tracker-trackers as type-identical with XYZ-tracker-trackers.

More interestingly, and continuously with an idea suggested in §3.2.2, one might hold that the properties tracked by exp-intentional states are always response-dependent properties (or centering features), and that this leads to some sort of internalism. Recall that in response to the argument from "intentional indifference," I proposed a variant on (HOTT), (HOTT*), according to which exp-intentional states are tracked to track response-dependent properties exclusively.[39] This view entails, I have argued elsewhere (Kriegel 2008b), that exp-intentional contents supervene on the intrinsic properties of the subject. This is because response-dependent properties are non-twin-earthable, in that whenever two mental states are intentionally directed at two different response-dependent properties, there must also be internal differences in those mental states' subjects (since response-dependent properties can differ only if the subjective responses they are defined in terms of differ).[40]

In §5.1, I mentioned a pure form of internalism, as well as a number of weakened or limited internalisms. One way to both weaken the internalist thesis and limit its scope would be to superimpose (WI3) and (LI1), that is, claim that all underived-intentional properties of mental states supervene upon the intrinsic properties of these states' subjects.[41] More precisely:

(LWI) For any state x, subject S, and property P, if (i) P is a non-derivatively intentional property of x and (ii) S is in x, then x's being P supervenes on the intrinsic properties of S.[42]

If we accept the argument that intentional states directed at response-dependent properties can (type-)differ only when there is some internal (type-)difference in the subjects' responses, we must accept that the variant on (GT2) that incorporates (HOTT★) rather than (HOTT) entails (LWI).[43] That variant would be formulated as follows:

(GT2★) Necessarily★, for any item x and property F, x qualifies as having an intentional content that features F iff either (a) it is the case that (i) F is a response-dependent property and (ii) there is a tracking relation T and a suitable mental state y, such that y bears T to x's bearing T to F, or (b) x is such as to produce in ideal interpreters under ideal conditions the response of having an interpretive experience as of x having an intentional content that features F.[44,45]

My claim, then, is that (GT2★) entails (LWI), and (LWI) is a meaningful form of internalism.

Naturally, the same would apply to the correspondingly modified versions of (GT3) and (GT4). For example, in §3.2.2 we also formulated a starred variant of (NSTA), which would integrate as follows into a starred version of (GT4):[46]

(GT4★) Necessarily★, for any item x and property F, x qualifies as having an intentional content that features F iff either (a) there are states x_1 and x_2, a tracking relation T, and a representation-transmission relation R, such that (i) x_1 is a proper part of x, (ii) x_2 is a proper part of x, (iii) x_1 bears T to x_2's bearing T to F, and (iv) F is a response-dependent property, and (v) x_2 bears R to x, or (b) x is such as to produce in ideal interpreters under ideal conditions the response of having an interpretive experience as of F figuring in the intentional content of x.[47]

This too entails (LWI), for the same reasons.

I conclude that while a higher-order tracking theory of underived intentionality has more natural affinity to content externalism, there are (reasonably well-motivated) ways to develop it in a broadly internalist direction. Accordingly, general theories of intentionality founded on a higher-order tracking theory of underived intentionality *can* involve a limited and weakened but nonetheless quite important form of content internalism. The main motivation for the internalist versions of those general theories of intentionality can be summed up very simply: since such theories would be better positioned to handle the phenomenon of intentional indifference, for the reasons discussed in §3.2.2, there is reason to adopt them over their externalist counterparts.

Putting together all the specific views on different matters I have argued for, we would obtain a general theory of intentionality that combines (i) the experiential origin thesis in its (EO★) version, (ii) interpretivism about derived intentionality, (iii) higher-order tracking theory of underived intentionality, (iv) a naturalized self-tracking construal of higher-order tracking, (v) an internalist twist that appeals to response-dependent properties only in underived-intentional content, and (vi) a teleo-informational take on the tracking relation. The result is this:

> (GT4★$^{++1}$) Necessarily★, for any item x and property F, x qualifies as having an intentional content that features F iff either (a) there are states x_1 and x_2, and a representation-transmission relation R, such that (i) x_1 is a proper part of x, (ii) x_2 is a proper part of x, (iii) x_1 has the function of nomically depending upon x_2's having the function of nomically depending upon F, (iv) F is a response-dependent property, and (v) x_2 bears R to x, or (b) possibly, there are conditions C, an interpreter Å, and mental states y, y_1, and y_2, such that (i) y_1 is a proper part of y, (ii) y_2 is a proper part of y, (iii) y_1 has the function of nomically depending upon y_2's having the function of nomically depending upon x's having the function of nomically depending upon F, (iv) y_2 bears R to y, (v) Å is an ideal reasoner fully informed of the non-intentional and exp-intentional facts, and (vi) x is disposed to produce y, y_1, and y_2 in Å under C.

This thesis is a version of (GT2), and my preferred version at the relevant level of abstraction.[48]

This concludes my discussion of the second general theory of intentionality suggested by the previous chapters—a combination of higher-order tracking theory about experiential intentionality and interpretivism about non-experiential intentionality, set against the experiential origin thesis. The result is a higher-order tracking theory of underived intentionality combined with an interpretivist theory of derived intentionality. This general theory is profitably developed in an internalist direction, though could perfectly well be developed as externalist as well, and is open to development as either intellectualist or non-intellectualist.[49]

There are certain liabilities associated with this approach to intentionality, most notably its inability—discussed in §3.3—to accommodate certain apparently possible conscious experiences (e.g., as of impossible objects). But the attractions of the approach seem to me to outweigh its disattractions. A major attraction, for me at least, is that the approach manages to ground all intentionality in experiential intentionality without giving up impressive advances made in naturalist work on intentionality since the seventies. It retains the notion that tracking relations are the building blocks of intentionality, and with it the promise of naturalizing intentionality, while at the same time rectifying what I consider to be a major blindspot in the mainstream naturalist tradition, by placing experiential intentionality at the heart of the theory of intentionality.

In doing so, this approach to intentionality combines the thought that intentionality is originally injected into the world when the right kind of experiential character makes its appearance, *and* the thought that it is originally injected into the world with the appearance of the right kind of tracking-based relation. It is just that according to this view there is a remarkably complex tracking-based relation involved in the right kind of experiential character. In fact, the complex tracking-based relation *constitutes*, or perhaps is *identical* to, the relevant type of experiential character.[50] Thus on this picture both experience and tracking function as the source of intentionality.

Notes

1. Primitivism, recall, is the view that intentionality is constituted by a primitive, irreducibly experiential relations to properties.

2. They are: (1) a tracking account of N plus potentialism about R; (2) a tracking account of N plus inferentialism about R; (3) a tracking account of N plus eliminativism about R; (4) a tracking

account of N plus interpretivism about R; (5) a higher-order tracking theory of N plus potentialism about R; (6) a higher-order tracking theory of N plus inferentialism about R; (7) a higher-order tracking theory of N plus eliminativism about R; (8) a higher-order tracking theory of N plus interpretivism about R; (9) an adverbial theory of N plus potentialism about R; (10) an adverbial theory of N plus inferentialism about R; (11) an adverbial theory of N plus eliminativism about R; (12) an adverbial theory of N plus interpretivism about R; (13) primitivism about N plus potentialism about R; (14) primitivism about N plus inferentialism about R; (15) primitivism about N plus eliminativism about R; (16) primitivism about N plus interpretivism about R. Some of these combinations will be more natural than others. Consistently with the argumentation in Chapters 2–4, I will focus here on the two combinations that strike me as most plausible, namely, (8) and (12).

3. I remind the reader that (ATEI) and (Int) are the following theses: (ATEI) Necessarily★, for any mental state x and putative property F, there is an experiential property E, E = being-intentionally-directed-F-wise, such that F figures in x's exp-intentional content iff x is E; (Int) Necessarily★, for any item x and property F, F figures in the nexp-intentional content of x iff x is such as to produce in ideal interpreters under ideal conditions the response of having an interpretive experience as of F figuring in the intentional content of x.

4. One might modify the adverbialism of Chapter 3 to make the adverbial property a-experiential, that is, make it have non-experiential realization in addition to the experiential ones. However, it is not clear to make what kind of non-experiential property might realize being-intentionally-directed-somehow.

5. Recall that we have also offered a formulation of adverbialism in terms of intentional types (rather than contents), namely, (ATEI★). If we formulated the thesis in the text in those terms, we would obtain something like the following: Necessarily★, for any item x and intentional type I, x qualifies as a token of I iff either (a) there is an experiential property E, E = being-intentionally-directed-F-wise, such that x is E, or (b) x is such as to produce in ideal interpreters under ideal conditions the response of having an interpretive experience as of x betokening I.

6. Recall: (Int⁺) Necessarily★, for any item x and property F, F figures in the nexp-intentional content of x iff possibly, there are conditions C, an interpreter Å, and a mental act y, such that (i) y has an exp-intentional content to the effect that F figures in the intentional content of x, (ii) Å is an ideal reasoner fully informed of the non-intentional and exp-intentional facts, and (iii) x is disposed to produce y in Å under C.

7. As before, the thesis could also be stated in terms of intentional types: Necessarily★, for any item x and intentional type I, x qualifies as a token of I iff either (a) there is an experiential property E, E = being-intentionally-directed-F-wise, such that x is E, or (b) possibly, there are conditions C, an interpreter Å, and a mental act y, such that (i) y has an exp-intentional content to the effect that x betokens I, (ii) Å is an ideal reasoner fully informed of the non-intentional and exp-intentional facts, and (iii) x is disposed to produce y in Å under C.

8. Again, this could be stated in terms of intentional types, rather than intentional contents, as well.

9. This was (ATEI1): Necessarily★, for any mental state x and putative property F, there is an experiential property E, E = phenomenally-presenting-an-other-to-be-F, such that F figures in x's exp-intentional content iff x is E.

10. We can also embed the phenomenal-foreignness view into (GT1) to obtain a simpler (though less explicit and determinate) statement of the view: (GT1') Necessarily★, for any item x and putative property F, x qualifies as having an intentional content that features F iff either (a) there is an experiential property E, E = phenomenally-presenting-an-other-to-be-F, such that x is E, or (b) x is such as to produce in ideal interpreters under ideal conditions the response of having an interpretive experience

as of *x* having an intentional content that features F. Also, as before the view can also be stated in terms of intentional types rather than intentional contents.

11. These are the derived-intentional properties.

12. This may raise the objection that certain animals and human neonates may be robbed of intentionality, and more generally the worry that the account is *too* intellectualist. There are some reasonable approaches to this objection, familiar from discussions of animal consciousness. I have nothing especially original to say here, except perhaps to note that I am open to the possibility that intentionality is rarer in nature than we have been accustomed to suppose (though representation, in the impoverished sense, might be nearly ubiquitous). For a fuller presentation of my position on animal consciousness, see Kriegel 2009 Ch.5.

13. I am certainly tempted to think of phenomenal foreignness as a cognitive-experiential property, though Frey is not (personal communication). By contrast, Strawson confirmed (in conversation) that he does think of experiential taking as a kind of cognitive experience. I have not had the opportunity to discuss the matter with Loar, whom I have never met.

14. Obviously, any version according to which conscious interpretive acts are all conscious *judgments* would qualify. But so would views according to which some such acts are perceptions whose relevant (interpretive) experiential character involves essentially cognitive-experiential features. This seems to me a plausible way to understand perceptual interpretive acts. For example, suppose I just *see* that my friend is smelling something funny, say by seeing a particular facial contortion of my friend's. In this case, my visual experience ascribes to my friend an intentional state, namely, an olfactory experience as of a foul odor. But observe that such a perceptual interpretive act involves seeing that my friend is smelling something funny *by* seeing a facial contortion. Arguably, the experiential character of seeing the facial contortion exhausts the purely sensory component of the overall's experience's experiential character. What one sees *by* seeing the facial contortion, the experiential component that goes beyond seeing the contortion, is a kind of non-sensory phenomenology.

15. An involved phenomenological analysis may excavate interesting aspects of this experiential character, but short of engaging in such analysis, there is not much to do beyond point out the intentional commonality interpretive phenomenology underlies.

16. This could be made more explicit, as follows: For any item x and property P, if P is an intentional property of x, then there are properties $Q_1, \ldots, Q_n$, such that (i) $Q_1, \ldots, Q_n$ are intrinsic properties of x and (ii) x's being P supervenes on x's being $Q_1, \ldots, Q_n$.

17. It is not clear whether this weakening can make sense for intentional properties of non-mental items in addition to mental states. Part of the question concerns the exact ontological relation between subjects and their states, and the ontological nature of "items" that may qualify as intentional.

18. Another, somewhat more explicit formulation might be: For any mental state x and property P, if P is an intentional property of x, then there is a subject a S and properties $Q_1, \ldots, Q_n$, such that (i) S is in x, (ii) S is $Q_1, \ldots, Q_n$, (iii) x's being P supervenes on S's being $Q_1, \ldots, Q_n$, and (iv) $Q_1, \ldots, Q_n$ are intrinsic properties of S. This requires that the supervenience relation apply intelligibly not only to properties, but also to property instantiations, and moreover to property instantiations where the instantiator is not the same.

19. Both their experiences have a water-ish adverbial experiential property—both are thinking water(y)-wise. Likewise for Oscar and Twin-Oscar's water-ish perceptual experiences, emotional experiences, etc. And more generally, all non-derivatively intentional properties of Oscar and Twin-Oscar are the same where their experiential characters (determined purely internalistically) are the same.

20. I use the term "individual concept" to denote the constituent of a mental state expressed by a proper name that is a constituent of a sentence.

21. I follow common practice in calling content as it is conceived by the internalist "narrow" and as it is conceived by the externalist "wide."

22. It is sometimes said that such dispositional properties are in fact intrinsic, because they do not require actual relations, only dispositions to bear relations. I have no objection to regarding the relevant intentional properties as intrinsic on this ground, but it is still significant that grasping what the property is would require grasping certain relations the bearer of the property must bear in order to instantiate the property. There is something about the spirit of internalism that would be lost here. Note also that there is quite a lively debate among metaphysicians as to whether there are extrinsic dispositions (see, e.g., McKitrick 2003), and depending on how that debate is resolved it may become an open question as to whether the dispositional properties that constitute derived-intentional properties are intrinsic or not.

23. More specifically, (HOTT) was the following thesis: Necessarily★, there is a tracking relation T, such that for any mental state x and property F, F figures in x's exp-intentional content iff there is a suitable mental state y, such that y bears T to x's bearing T to F.

24. For that matter, this could be the case with Freudian suppressed mental states and tacit or dispositional states, if such there be.

25. The assumption can be justified by something like what cognitive scientists call the *null hypothesis*: the methodological principle that until one finds evidence for a certain phenomenon, one's theory assumes that the phenomenon does not exist. In any case, the assumption makes underived intentionality as conceived by this second general theory of intentionality co-extensive with it as conceived by the first general theory examined in §5.1. Nonetheless, the two theories differ in what it is they take to be the underlying nature of underived intentionality.

26. The simplification could be developed either as essentially expository or as substantive, that is, in earnest. For my part, I am more inclined in the expository direction: I cannot avow great confidence in this (HOTT) take on interpretation, though it does serve to illustrate what I take to be the right approach to the issue of updating the interpretivist component of (GT2) in light of (GT2)'s higher-order tracking component. (The right approach is to seek the real patterns that the ideal interpreter detects in fixing the content of interpretive states.)

27. More specifically, recall: (STA) Necessarily★, there is a tracking relation T, such that for any mental state x and property F, F figures in x's exp-intentional content iff x bears T to x's own bearing of T to F; (NSTA) Necessarily★, there is a tracking relation T and a representation-transmission relation R, such that for any mental state x and property F, F figures in x's exp-intentional content iff there are states x_1 and x_2, such that (i) x_1 is a proper part of x, (ii) x_2 is a proper part of x, (iii) x_1 bears T to x_2's bearing T to F, and (iv) x_2 bears R to x.

28. Once we incorporate the spelled-out version of interpretivism, (Int⁺), and a self-tracking account of interpretive experience, we obtain the following: (GT3⁺⁺) Necessarily★, there is a tracking relation T, such that for any item x and property F, x qualifies as having an intentional content that features F iff either (a) x bears T to x's own bearing of T to F, or (b) possibly, there are conditions C, an interpreter Å, and a mental act y, such that (i) y bears T to y's own bearing of T to x's bearing of T to F, (ii) Å is an ideal reasoner fully informed of the non-intentional facts, and (iii) x is disposed to produce y in Å under C. Obviously, since as noted in §2.2.1 my credence in (STA) is greater than in (eHOT), my credence in (GT3⁺⁺) is greater than in the kind of general theory of intentionality we would obtain by combining (eHOTT) with (Int⁺).

29. This is just a result of my credence in (NSTA) being greater than my credence in any other account of experiential intentionality at the same level of abstraction and my credence in the employed higher-order tracking account of interpretation being no lower than my credence in any competing accounts. Nonetheless, and obviously, that credence is lower than my credence in some general theories

of intentionality of higher levels of abstraction, including of course any genus of account of which ($GT4^{++}$) is a species, including, naturally, (GT2) and (GT4).

30. This would be: ($GT4^{++1}$) Necessarily★, for any item x and property F, x qualifies as having an intentional content that features F iff either (a) there are states x_1 and x_2, and a representation-transmission relation R, such that (i) x_1 is a proper part of x, (ii) x_2 is a proper part of x, (iii) x_1 has the function of nomically depending upon x_2's having the function of nomically depending upon F, and (iv) x_2 bears R to x, or (b) possibly, there are conditions C, an interpreter Å, and mental states y, y_1, and y_2, such that (i) y_1 is a proper part of y, (ii) y_2 is a proper part of y, (iii) y_1 has the function of nomically depending upon y_2's having the function of nomically depending upon x's having the function of nomically depending upon F, (iv) y_2 bears R to y, (v) Å is an ideal reasoner fully informed of the non-intentional and exp-intentional facts, and (vi) x is disposed to produce y, y_1, and y_2 in Å under C. Again I can report a credence in ($GT4^{++1}$) higher than in any other account of experiential intentionality at the same level of specificity.

31. Although this cannot be stated in the *de dicto* mode without circularity, we can say, in a *de re* mode, that these are the "real patterns" an ideal interpreter would detect when interpreting something to have a certain intentional content.

32. Perhaps Locke's (1690) best-known statement to that effect is that "Consciousness is the perception of what passes in a man's own mind" (*ECHU* 2.1.19). For a fuller discussion of Locke's take on this matter, including an argument that Locke should be considered a sort of self-representational theorist of consciousness, see Coventry and Kriegel 2008.

33. In Kriegel 2009 Ch.4, I consider a number of options for understanding "quasi-sensory" (or rather, there, "quasi-perceptual").

34. Several authors have argued that higher-order representation, whether in introspection or in non-introspective forms of self-awareness, is always intellectual and consists in thinking rather than quasi-sensing. See, *inter alia*, Rosenthal 1986, 1993, Siewert 1998 Ch.6, Carruthers 2000 Chs.8–9.

35. This is not to say that the higher-order tracking must be one and the same as the introspecting. In fact, it is much more natural to suppose that it is not, since it is a component of the experience introspected rather than the act of introspecting. However, for a more complicated take on the relationship between introspecting and higher-order tracking, see the account I develop in Kriegel 2009 Ch.5.

36. That is, trackers individuate in such a way that when the tracked is different, so is the tracker. Thus difference in tracked is sufficient for difference in tracker, as we saw in §3.2.1 and §3.3.1.

37. There is perhaps a way in which a higher-order tracking theory is more internalist in spirit than a first-order tracking theory, namely, insofar as higher-order tracking is more internal, in some intuitive sense, to the subject than first-order tracking. Nonetheless, since one of the relata of higher-order tracking is not just the first-order tracker, but the first-order tracking relation itself, this relatum does individuate partly in terms of what happens outside the subject's organism.

38. Something like this is suggested by Johnston (1997), who argues that water is not a natural kind but a manifest kind and is therefore not necessarily H_2O. It might also possible to accept that water is a natural kind, but then offer an account of natural kinds and natural kind terms that makes XYZ come out a different kind of water. Something like this is suggested by Mellor (1977) and Zemach (1977). It is less clear that the same treatment can be given to all apparently natural kinds we encounter with the naked eye. For example, it is harder to see how the treatment could be extended to gold and fool's gold. It seems less intuitively plausible to say that gold is multiply realizable both as the atomic element number 79 and as whatever the underlying nature of fool's gold (but note that Mellor addresses this).

39. More precisely, recall: (HOTT★) Necessarily★, there is a tracking relation T, such that for any mental state x and property F, F figures in x's exp-intentional content iff (i) F is response-dependent and (ii) there is a suitable mental state y, such that y bears T to x's bearing T to F.

40. Since exp-intentional contents supervene on the subject's intrinsic properties, having the relevant exp-intentional states is a locally supervenient property of the subject. Therefore, a restriction of (WI3) from the previous section to exp-intentional contents would apply to them. Thus there is at least *a* kind of weakened internalism that (HOTT★) would entail. As we will see momentarily, the relevant kind of internalism would be generated by the superimposition of (WI3) and (LI1).

41. This further weakens the thesis, because while whenever S is in x, any properties of x that are intrinsic are also, or are associated with properties that are also, intrinsic properties of S, the converse does not hold: there might be extrinsic properties of x that are intrinsic properties (or are associated with intrinsic properties) of S. For example, suppose x is F in virtue of being related in some way to a mental state y, such that y does not overlap x but y is another mental state of S. Then x's being F is an extrinsic property of x but an intrinsic property (or is associated with an intrinsic property) of S.

42. This means that the intrinsic properties of the subject fix the underived-intentional content of her mental states. A more spelled out formulation of the thesis would be: For any item x, subject S, and property P, if (i) P is an underived-intentional property of x and (ii) S is in x, then there are properties $G_1, \ldots, G_n$, such that (i) $G_1, \ldots, G_n$ are intrinsic properties of S and (ii) x's being P supervenes on S's being $G_1, \ldots, G_n$. This is obtained by superposition of (WI2) and (LI1) from the previous section, plus a further weakening to local supervenience on properties of the subject. (Recall: (WI2) For any item x and property P, if P is an intentional property of x, then P is a locally supervenient property of x; (LI1) For any item x and property P, if P is a derived-intentional property of x, then P is a non-relational property of x.) This limits internalism to derived-intentional properties, then weakens it to require that such properties be not quite non-relational but simply locally supervenient, and moreover only locally supervenient on the subject.

43. For a much more patient development of the argument than offered here, see Kriegel 2008b.

44. Recall, though, that the focus in this formulation on response-dependent properties is somewhat arbitrary and provisional, insofar as we could also advert to centering features, in case they turn out to fill the theoretical role of response-dependent properties better (see §3.2.2).

45. As for the variant on the more worked out (GT2^{++}), it would be this: (GT2★$^{++}$) Necessarily★, there is a tracking relation T, such that for any item x and property F, x qualifies as having an intentional content that features F iff either (a) it is the case that (i) F is a response-dependent property and (ii) there is a suitable mental state y, such that y bears T to x's bearing T to F, or (b) possibly, there are conditions C, an interpreter Å, and mental acts z and w, such that (i) w bears T to z's bearing T to x's bearing T to F, (ii) Å is an ideal reasoner fully informed of the non-intentional and exp-intentional facts, and (iii) x is disposed to produce z and w in Å under C.

46. The starred version here was, recall, the following: (NSTA★) Necessarily★, there is a tracking relation T and a representation-transmission relation R, such that for any mental state x and property F, F figures in x's exp-intentional content iff there are states x_1 and x_2, such that (i) x_1 is a proper part of x, (ii) x_2 is a proper part of x, (iii) F is response-dependent, (iv) x_1 bears T to x_2's bearing T to F, and (v) x_2 bears R to x.

47. I am skipping here the formulation of the result of integrating (NSTA★) into (GT3), (GT3$^+$), (GT3^{++}), and (GT4$^+$), on the assumption the reader is already biconditionaled out. It may nonetheless be worthwhile to formulate (GT4★$^{++}$): Necessarily★, there is a tracking relation T, such that for any item x and property F, x qualifies as having an intentional content that features F iff either (a) there are states x_1 and x_2, and a representation-transmission relation R, such that (i) x_1 is a proper part of x, (ii) x_2 is a proper part of x, (iii) x_1 bears T to x_2's bearing T to F, (iv) F is a response-dependent property, and (v) x_2 bears R to x, or (b) possibly, there are conditions C, an interpreter Å, and mental states y, y_1, and y_2, such that (i) y_1 is a proper part of y, (ii) y_2 is a proper part of y, (iii) y_1 bears T to y_2's bearing T to x's bearing T to F, (iv) y_2 bears R to y, (v) Å is an ideal reasoner fully informed of the non-intentional and

exp-intentional facts, and (vi) x is disposed to produce y, y_1, and y_2 in Å under C. The good news is that this leaves only one more biconditional in this book.

48. Needless to say, while my confidence in this thesis is higher than in any other general theory of intentionality at the same level of specificity, my confidence in it is not high, since it requires all of the individual components to come out right.

49. As should be clear from the discussion above, my own preference would be for a development in internalist and non-intellectualist directions.

50. Or, at the very least, it is necessarily common and peculiar to mental states with that experiential character.

References

Abell, C. 2005. "Pictorial Implicature." *Journal of Aesthetics and Art Criticism* 63: 55–66.

Aglioti, S., J.F.X. DeSouza, and M.A. Goodale 1995. "Size-contrast illusions deceive the eye but not the hand." *Current Biology* 5: 679–685.

Armstrong, D.M. 1962. *Bodily Sensations*. London: Routledge and Kegan Paul.

———. 1968. *A Materialist Theory of the Mind*. London: Routledge.

———. 1978. *Nominalism and Realism: Universals and Scientific Realism*, Vol. 1. Cambridge: Cambridge University Press.

———. 1997. *A World of States of Affairs*. Cambridge: Cambridge University Press.

Audi, R. 1994. "Dispositional Beliefs and Dispositions to Believe." *Noûs* 28: 419–434.

Baars, B.J. 1988. *A Cognitive Theory of Consciousness*. Cambridge: Cambridge University Press.

Bayne, T. and M. Montague 2011. *Cognitive Phenomenology*. Oxford: Oxford University Press.

Bennett, J.F. 1988. *Events and Their Names*. Oxford: Oxford University Press.

Bird, A. 2007. *Nature's Metaphysics: Laws and Properties*. Oxford: Oxford University Press.

Block, N.J. 1986. "Advertisement for a Semantics for Psychology." *Midwest Studies in Philosophy* 10: 615–677.

———. 1990. "Inverted Earth." *Philosophical Perspective* 4: 52–79.

———. 1995. "On a Confusion about the Function of Consciousness." *Behavioral and Brain Sciences* 18: 227–247. Reprinted in Block et al. 1997.

———. 1996. "Mental Paint and Mental Latex." *Philosophical Issues* 7: 19–50.

———. 2007. "Consciousness, Accessibility, and the Mesh between Psychology and Neuroscience." *Behavioural and Brain Sciences* 30: 481–499.

Block, N.J., O. Flanagan, and G. Güzeldere (eds.), 1997. *The Nature of Consciousness: Philosophical Debates*. Cambridge MA: MIT Press.

Block, N.J. and R. Stalnaker 1999. "Conceptual Analysis, Dualism, and the Explanatory Gap." *Philosophical Review* 108: 1–46.

Blumson, B. 2006. *Resemblance and Representation*. PhD Dissertation, Australian National University.

Bourget, D. 2010. "Consciousness is Underived Intentionality." *Noûs* 44: 32–58.

Bradley, F.H. 1893. *Appearance and Reality: A Metaphysical Essay*. New York: Macmillan.

Brandl, J. 2009. "Intentionality, Information, and Experience." In A. Hieke and H. Leitgeb (eds.), *Reduction: Between the Mind and the Brain*. Frankfurt: Ontos Verlag.

Brandom, R.B. 1994a. *Making It Explicit*. Cambridge MA: Harvard University Press.

———. 1994b. "Reasoning and Representing." In M. Michael and J. O'Leary-Hawthorne (eds.), *Philosophy in Mind*. Dordrecht: Kluwer.

Brooks, R. 1991. "Intelligence without Representation." *Artificial Intelligence* 47: 139–159.

Buras, T. 2009. "An Argument against Causal Theories of Mental Content." *American Philosophical Quarterly* 46: 117–130.

Byrne, D. 1997. "Some Like It HOT: Consciousness and Higher Order Thoughts." *Philosophical Studies* 86: 103–129.

Carruthers, P. 2000. *Phenomenal Consciousness*. Cambridge: Cambridge University Press.

Caston, V. 2002. "Aristotle on Consciousness." *Mind* 111: 751–815.

Chalmers, D.J. 1995. "Facing up to the Problem of Consciousness." *Journal of Consciousness Studies* 2: 200–219.

———. 1996. *The Conscious Mind*. Oxford and New York: Oxford University Press.

———. 2002. "Does Conceivability Entail Possibility?" In T. Gendler and J. Hawthorne (eds.), *Conceivability and Possibility*. Oxford and New York: Oxford University Press.

———. 2003. "Consciousness and Its Place in Nature." In S. Stich and F. Warfield (eds.), *Blackwell Guide to the Philosophy of Mind*. Oxford: Blackwell.

———. 2004. "The Representational Character of Experience." In B. Leiter (ed.), *The Future for Philosophy*. Oxford: Oxford University Press.

———. Forthcoming. "The Nature of Epistemic Space." In A. Egan and B. Weatherson (eds.), *Epistemic Modality*. Oxford and New York: Oxford University Press.

Chalmers, D.J. and F.C. Jackson 2001. "Conceptual Analysis and Reductive Explanation." *Philosophical Review* 110: 315–361.

Child, W. 1994. *Causality, Interpretation, and the Mind*. Oxford: Oxford University Press.

Chisholm, R. 1957. *Perceiving: A Philosophical Study*. Ithaca, NY: Cornell University Press.

Chudnoff, E. Forthcoming-a. "Intellectual Gestalts." In U. Kriegel and T. Horgan (eds.), *The Phenomenal Intentionality Research Program*. Oxford and New York: Oxford University Press.

———. Forthcoming-b. "What Intuitions Are Like." *Philosophy and Phenomenological Research*.

Churchland, P.M. 2005. "Chimerical Colors: Some Phenomenological Predictions from Cognitive Neuroscience." *Philosophical Psychology* 18: 527–560.

Colyvan, M. 2001. *The Indispensability of Mathematics*. Oxford and New York: Oxford University Press.

Coventry, A. and U. Kriegel 2008. "Locke on Consciousness." *History of Philosophy Quarterly* 25 (2008): 221–242.

Crane, T. 2001. *Elements of Mind*. Oxford: Oxford University Press.
Cummins, R. 1979. "Intention, Meaning, and Truth Conditions." *Philosophical Studies* 35: 345–360.
———. 1989. *Meaning and Mental Representation*. Cambridge MA: MIT Press.
Davidson, D. 1963. "Actions, Reasons, and Causes." *Journal of Philosophy* 60: 685–700.
———. 1967. "Truth and Meaning." *Synthese* 17: 304–323.
———. 1969. "The Individuation of Events." In N. Rescher (ed.), *Essays in Honor of Carl G. Hempel*. Dordrecht: Reidel.
———. 1970. "Mental Events." In L. Foster and J.W. Swanson (eds.), *Experience and Theory*. London: Duckworth.
———. 1974. "On the Very Idea of a Conceptual Scheme." *Proceedings and Addresses of the American Philosophical Association* 47: 5–20.
———. 1986. "A Coherence Theory of Truth and Knowledge." In E. Lepore (ed.), *Truth and Interpretation: Perspectives on the Philosophy of Donald Davidson*. Oxford: Blackwell.
———. 1987. "Knowing One's Own Mind." *Proceedings and Addresses of the American Philosophical Association* 61: 441–458.
Davies, M. 1995. "Consciousness and the Varieties of Aboutness." In C. Macdonald and G. Macdonald (eds.), *Connectionism: Debates on Psychological Explanation (Vol. II)*. Oxford: Blackwell.
———. 1997. "Externalism and Experience." In Block et al. 1997.
Dennett, D.C. 1971. "Intentional Systems." *Journal of Philosophy* 68: 87–106.
———. 1981. "True Believers." In A.F. Heath (ed.), *Scientific Explanation*. Oxford: Oxford University Press. Reprinted in Dennett 1987.
———. 1987. *The Intentional Stance*. Cambridge MA: MIT Press.
———. 1990. "The Myth of Original Intentionality." In K.A. Mohyeldin Said, W.H. Newton-Smith, R. Viale, and K.V. Wilkes (eds.), *Modeling the Mind*. Oxford: Oxford UP.
———. 1991. "Real Patterns." *Journal of Philosophy* 88: 27–51.
DeRose, K. 1995. "Solving the Skeptical Problem." *Philosophical Review* 104: 1–52.
Donnellan, K.S. 1966. "Reference and Definite Descriptions." *Philosophical Review* 77: 281–304.
Dretske, F.I. 1971. "Conclusive Reasons." *Australasian Journal of Philosophy* 49: 1–22.
———. 1980. "The Intentionality of Cognitive States." *Midwest Studies in Philosophy* 5: 281–294.
———. 1981. *Knowledge and the Flow of Information*. Oxford: Blackwell.
———. 1986. "Misrepresentation." In R. Bogdan (ed.), *Belief*. Oxford: Oxford University Press.
———. 1988. *Explaining Behavior*. Cambridge MA: MIT Press.
———. 1995. *Naturalizing the Mind*. Cambridge MA: MIT Press.

———. 1996. "Phenomenal Externalism." *Philosophical Issues* 7: 143–159.

———. 2006. "Perception without Awareness." In T.S. Gendler and J. Hawthorne (eds.), *Perceptual Experience*. Oxford: Oxford University Press.

Ducasse, C.J. 1942. "Moore's Refutation of Idealism." In P.A. Schlipp (ed.), *The Philosophy of G.E. Moore*. La Salle IL: Open Court.

Egan, A. 2006. "Appearance Properties?" *Noûs* 40: 495–521.

Evans, G. 1982. *The Varieties of Reference* (edited by J. McDowell). Oxford: Oxford University Press.

Farkas, K. 2008. "Phenomenal Intentionality without Compromise." *The Monist* 91: 273–293.

Field, H. 1977. "Logic, Meaning, and Conceptual Role." *Journal of Philosophy* 74: 379–409.

———. 1994. "Deflationist Views about Meaning and Content." *Mind* 103: 249–285.

Figdor, C. 2008. "Intrinsically/Extrinsically." *Journal of Philosophy* 105: 691–718.

Fine, K. 2001. "The Question of Realism." *Philosophers' Imprint* 1: 1–30.

Fish, W. 2009. *Perception, Hallucination, and Illusion*. Oxford: Oxford University Press.

Fodor, J.A. 1975. *The Language of Thought*. Cambridge MA: Harvard University Press.

———. 1983. *The Modularity of Mind*. Cambridge MA: MIT Press.

———. 1990. *A Theory of Content and Other Essays*. Cambridge MA: MIT Press.

Fodor, J.A. and E. Lepore 1992. *Holism: A Shopper's Guide*. Oxford: Blackwell.

———. 1993. "Is Intentional Ascription Intrinsically Normative?" In B. Dahlbom (ed.), *Dennett and his Critics*. Oxford: Blackwell.

———. 1994. "What Is the Connection Principle?" *Philosophy and Phenomenological Research* 54: 837–845.

Frege, G. 1892. "On Sense and Reference." Reprinted in P. Geach and M. Black (eds.), *Translations from the Philosophical Writings of Gottlob Frege*. Oxford: Blackwell, 1960.

———. 1903. *The Basic Laws of Arithmetic*. Translated by M. Furth. Berkeley: University of California Press, 1964.

Frey, C. Forthcoming. "Phenomenal Presence." In T. Horgan and U. Kriegel (eds.), *The Phenomenal Intentionality Research Program*. Oxford and New York: Oxford University Press.

Gelman, S.A. and E.M. Markman 1986. "Categories and Induction in Young Children." *Cognition* 23: 183–209.

Georgalis, N. 2006. *The Primacy of the Subjective*. Cambridge MA: MIT Press.

Gerken, M. 2008. "Is There a Simple Argument for Higher-Order Representation Theories of Awareness Consciousness?" *Erkenntnis* 69: 243–259.

Goldman, A.I. 1983. "Review of *Philosophical Explanations*." *Philosophical Review* 92: 81–88.

———. 1989. "Interpretation Psychologized." *Mind and Language* 4: 161–185.

———. 1993. "The Psychology of Folk Psychology." *Behavioral and Brain Sciences* 16: 15–28.
Graham, G., T. Horgan, and J. Tienson 2007. "Consciousness and Intentionality." In M. Velmans and S. Schneider (eds.), *Blackwell Companion to Consciousness*. Malden MA: Blackwell.
Grice, H.P. 1957. "Meaning." *Philosophical Review* 66: 377–388.
———. 1969. "Utterer's Meaning and Intention." *Philosophical Review* 68: 147–177.
Harman, G. 1987. "(Non-Solipsistic) Conceptual Role Semantics." In E. Lepore (ed.), *New Directions in Semantics*. London: Academic Press.
———. 1990. "The Intrinsic Quality of Experience." *Philosophical Perspectives* 4: 31–52.
Haugeland, J. 1980. "Programs, Causal Powers, and Intentionality." *Behavioral and Brain Sciences* 3: 432–433.
———. 2002. "Authentic Intentionality." In M. Scheutz (ed.), *Computationalism: New Directions*. Cambridge MA: MIT Press.
Hellie, B. 2007. "Higher-Order Intentionality and Higher-Order Acquaintance." *Philosophical Studies* 134: 289–324.
Horgan, T. and G. Graham 2009. "Phenomenal Intentionality and Content Determinacy." In R. Schantz (ed.), *Prospects for Meaning*. Amsterdam: de Gruyter.
Horgan, T. and U. Kriegel 2007. "Phenomenal Epistemology: What Is Consciousness That We Should Know It So Well?" *Philosophical Issues* 17: 123–144.
———. 2008. "Phenomenal Intentionality Meets the Extended Mind." *Monist* 91: 347–373.
Horgan, T. and M. Potrč. 2010. "The Epistemic Role of Morphological Content." *Acta Analytica* 25: 155–173.
Horgan, T. and J. Tienson 2002. "The Intentionality of Phenomenology and the Phenomenology of Intentionality." In D.J. Chalmers (ed.), *Philosophy of Mind: Classical and Contemporary Readings*. Oxford and New York: Oxford University Press.
Horgan, T., J. Tienson, and G. Graham 2003. "The phenomenology of first-person agency." In S. Walter and H.D. Heckmann (eds.), *Physicalism and Mental Causation*. Exeter: Imprint Academic.
———. 2004. "Phenomenal Intentionality and the Brain in a Vat." In R. Schantz (ed.), *The Externalist Challenge: New Studies on Cognition and Intentionality*. Amsterdam: de Gruyter.
Horgan, T. and M.C. Timmons 2008. "Prolegomena to a future phenomenology of morals." *Phenomenology and the Cognitive Sciences* 7: 115–131.
Horst, S.W. 1996. *Symbols, Computation, and Intentionality*. Berkeley and Los Angeles: University of California Press.

Huemer, M. 2001. *Skepticism and the Veil of Perception.* Lanham MD: Rowman and Littlefield.

———. 2007. "Epistemic Possibility." *Synthese* 156: 119–142.

Jackson, F.C. 1977. *Perception: A Representative Theory.* Cambridge: Cambridge University Press.

Jacob, P. and M. Jeannerod 2003. *Ways of Seeing: The Scope and Limits of Visual Cognition.* Oxford: Oxford University Press.

Johnston, M. 1989. "Dispositional Theories of Value." *Proceedings of Aristotelian Society* 63: 139–174.

———. 1992. "How to Speak of the Colors." *Philosophical Studies* 68: 221–263.

———. 1997. "Manifest Kinds." *Journal of Philosophy* 94: 564–583.

Kelly, S.D. 2004. "On Seeing Things in Merleau-Ponty." In T. Carmon (ed.) *Cambridge Companion to Merleau-Ponty.* Cambridge: Cambridge University Press.

Kim, J. 1976. "Events as Property Exemplifications." In M. Brand and D. Walton (eds.), *Action Theory.* Dordrecht: Reidel.

———. 1977. "Perception and Reference without Causality." *Journal of Philosophy* 74: 606–620.

———. 1989. "The Myth of Nonreductive Materialism." *Proceedings and Addresses of the American Philosophical Association* 63: 31–47.

Klausen, S.H. 2008. "The Phenomenology of Propositional Attitudes." *Phenomenology and the Cognitive Sciences* 7: 445–462.

Klein, M. 1981. "Context and Memory." In L.T. Benjamin Jr. and K.D. Lowman (Eds.), *Activities Handbook for the Teaching of Psychology.* Washington DC: American Psychological Association.

Kobes, B.W. 1995. "Telic Higher-Order Thoughts and Moore's Paradox." *Philosophical Perspectives* 9: 291–312.

Kriegel, U. 2002a. "Phenomenal Content." *Erkenntnis* 57: 175–198.

———. 2002b. "PANIC Theory and the Prospects for a Representational Theory of Phenomenal Consciousness." *Philosophical Psychology* 15: 55–64.

———. 2003a. "Is Intentionality Dependent upon Consciousness?" *Philosophical Studies* 116: 271–307.

———. 2003b. "Consciousness as Sensory Quality and as Implicit Self-Awareness." *Phenomenology and the Cognitive Sciences* 2: 1–26.

———. 2003c. "Consciousness as Intransitive Self-Consciousness: Two Views and an Argument." *Canadian Journal of Philosophy* 33: 103–132.

———. 2005. "Naturalizing Subjective Character." *Philosophy and Phenomenological Research* 71: 23–57.

———. 2007. "Intentional Inexistence and Phenomenal Intentionality." *Philosophical Perspectives* 21: 307–340.

———. 2008a. "The Dispensability of (Merely) Intentional Objects." *Philosophical Studies* 141: 79–95.
———. 2008b. "Real Narrow Content." *Mind and Language* 23: 304–328.
———. 2008c. "Composition as a Secondary Quality." *Pacific Philosophical Quarterly* 89: 359–383.
———. 2009. *Subjective Consciousness: A Self-Representational Theory*. Oxford: Oxford University Press.
———. 2010. "Interpretation: Its Scope and Limits." In A. Hazlett (ed.), *New Waves in Metaphysics*. London: Palgrave-MacMillan.
———. 2011a. "The Veil of Abstracta." *Philosophical Issues* 21.
———. 2011b. "Personal-Level Representation." *Protosociology* 28.
———. Forthcoming. "Cognitive Phenomenology: From Analysis to Argument."
———. Ms. "Two Notions of Mental Representation."
Kriegel, U. and T. Horgan, forthcoming. "The Phenomenal Intentionality Research Program." In T. Horgan and U. Kriegel (eds.), *The Phenomenal Intentionality Research Program*. Oxford and New York: Oxford University Press.
Kripke, S. 1972. "Naming and Necessity." In D. Davidson and G. Harman (eds.), *Semantics of Natural Language*. Dordrecht: Reidel.
———. 1977. "Speaker's Reference and Semantic Reference." *Midwest Studies in Philosophy* 2: 255–276.
Kroon, F. Forthcoming. "Phenomenal Intentionality and the Role of Intentional Objects." In T. Horgan and U. Kriegel (eds.), *The Phenomenal Intentionality Research Program*. Oxford and New York: Oxford University Press.
Lesson, S.B. Ms. "Why Transparency Is Not For-Me."
Levine, J. 1983. "Materialism and Qualia: The Explanatory Gap." *Pacific Philosophical Quarterly* 64: 354–361.
———. 2001. *Purple Haze: The Puzzle of Consciousness*. Oxford and New York: Oxford University Press.
———. 2003. "Experience and Representation." In Q. Smith and A. Jokic (eds.), *Consciousness: New Philosophical Perspectives*. New York: Oxford University Press.
———. 2006. "Awareness and (Self-)Representation." In U. Kriegel and K. Williford (eds.), *Self-Representational Approaches to Consciousness*. Cambridge MA: MIT Press.
Lewis, D.K. 1983. "New Work for the Theory of Universals." *Australasian Journal of Philosophy* 61: 343–377.
———. 1984. "Putnam's Paradox." *Australasian Journal of Philosophy* 62: 221–236.
Loar, B. 1987. "Subjective Intentionality." *Philosophical Topics* 15: 89–124.
———. 1995. "Reference from the First-Person Perspective." *Philosophical Issues* 6: 53–72.

———. 2003. "Phenomenal Intentionality as the Basis for Mental Content." In M. Hahn and B. Ramberg (eds.), *Reflections and Replies: Essays on the Philosophy of Tyler Burge*. Cambridge MA: MIT Press.

Locke, J. 1690. *An Essay Concerning Human Understanding*, ed. P.H. Nidditch. Oxford: Oxford University Press, 1975.

Lombard, L.B. 1986. *Events: A Metaphysical Study*. London: Routledge and Kegan Paul.

Lopes, D.M.M. 2000. "What Is It Like to See with Your Ears? The Representational Theory of Mind." *Philosophical and Phenomenological Research* 60: 439–453.

Lycan, W.G. 1996. *Consciousness and Experience*. Cambridge MA: MIT Press.

———. 2001. "The Case for Phenomenal Externalism." *Philosophical Perspectives* 15: 17–35.

———. 2008. "Phenomenal Intentionalities." *American Philosophical Quarterly* 45: 233–252.

Lurz, R.W. 2006. "Conscious Beliefs and Desires: A Same-Order Approach." In U. Kriegel and K.W. Williford (eds.), *Self-Representational Approaches to Consciousness*. Cambridge MA: MIT Press.

McGinn, C. 1977. "Charity, Interpretation, and Belief." *Journal of Philosophy* 74: 521–535.

———. 1982. "The Structure of Content." In A. Woodfield (ed.), *Thought and Object*, Oxford: Oxford University Press.

———. 1988. "Consciousness and Content." *Proceedings of the British Academy* 76: 219–239. Reprinted in Block et al. 1997.

———. 1989. *Mental Content*. Oxford: Blackwell.

McKitrick, J. 2003. "A Case for Extrinsic Dispositions." *Australasian Journal of Philosophy* 81: 155–174.

Mackie, J.L. 1975. "Problems of Intentionality." In E. Pivčevič (ed.), *Phenomenology and Philosophical Understanding*. Cambridge: Cambridge University Press.

Maloney, J.C. 1994. "Content: Covariation, Control, and Cotingency." *Synthese* 100: 241–290.

Mandik, P. 2009. "Beware of the Unicorn." *Journal of Consciousness Studies* 16: 5–36.

Manfredi, P.A. 1993. "Tacit Beliefs and Other Doxastic Attitudes." *Philosophia* 22: 95–117.

Mangan, B. 2001. "Sensation's Ghost: The Non-Sensory Fringe of Consciousness." *Psyche* 7.

Marr, D. 1982. *Vision*. San Francisco: WH Freeman Publishers.

Masrour, F. 2008. *Structuralism: In Defense of a Kantian Account of Perceptual Experience*. PhD Dissertation, University of Arizona.

———. Forthcoming-a. "Is Perceptual Phenomenology Thin?" *Philosophy and Phenomenological Research*.

———. Forthcoming-b. "Phenomenal Objectivity and Phenomenal Intentionality: In Defense of a Kantian Account." In T. Horgan and U. Kriegel (eds.), *The Phenomenal Intentionality Research Program*. Oxford and New York: Oxford University Press.

Mellor, D.H. 1977. "Natural Kinds." *British Journal for the Philosophy of Science* 28: 299–312.

Mendelovici, A. 2010. *Mental Representation and Closely Conflated Topics*. PhD Dissertation, Princeton University.

Menzies, P. and H. Price 1998. "Causation as a Secondary Quality." *British Journal for the Philosophy of Science* 44: 187–203.

Merleau-Ponty, M. 1944. *Phenomenology of Perception*. Translated by C. Smith. London: Routledge and Kegan Paul, 1962.

Millikan, R.G. 1984. *Language, Thought, and Other Biological Categories*. Cambridge MA: MIT Press.

———. 1993. *White Queen Psychology and Other Essays for Alice*. Cambridge MA: MIT Press.

Milner, A.D. and M.A. Goodale 1995. *The Visual Brain in Action*. Oxford: Oxford University Press.

Miscevic, N. 1998. "The Aposteriority of Response-Dependence." *The Monist* 81: 69–84.

Moltmann, F. 1997. "Intensional Verbs and Quantifiers." *Natural Language Semantics* 5: 1–52.

———. 2008. "Intensional Verbs and Their Intentional Objects." *Natural Language Semantics* 16: 239–270.

Montague, M. 2010. "Recent Work on Intentionality." *Analysis* 70: 765–782.

———. 2011. "The Phenomenology of Particularity." In Bayne and Montague 2011.

Moore, G.E. 1953. "Propositions." In his *Some Main Problems of Philosophy*. Oxford: Routledge.

Neander, K. 1995. "Misrepresenting and Malfunctioning." *Philosophical Studies* 79: 109–141.

———. 1998. "The Division of Phenomenal Labor: A Problem for Representational Theories of Consciousness." *Philosophical Perspectives* 12: 411–434.

Noë, A. 2004. *Action in Perception*. Cambridge MA: MIT Press.

Nozick, R. 1981. *Philosophical Explanations*. Cambridge MA: Harvard University Press.

Papineau, D. 1984. "Representation and Explanation." *Philosophy of Science* 51: 550–572.

———. 1998. "Teleosemantics and Indeterminacy." *Australasian Journal of Philosophy* 76: 1–14.

Parsons, T. 1980. *Nonexistent Objects*. New Haven CT: Yale University Press.

Pautz, A. 2008. "The Interdependence of Intentionality and Phenomenology." *The Monist* 91: 250–272.

———. 2010. "Do Theories of Consciousness Rest on a Mistake?" *Philosophical Issues* 20: 333–367.

Peacocke, C. 1983. *Sense and Content*. Oxford: Clarendon.

———. 1992. *A Study of Concepts*. Cambridge, MA: MIT Press.

———. 1998. "Conscious Attitudes, Attention, and Self-Knowledge." In C. Wright, B.C. Smith, and C. Macdonald (eds.), *Knowing Our Own Minds*. Oxford: Oxford University Press.

———. 2004. "The Phenomenology of Cognition; or *What Is It Like to Think That P?*," *Philosophy and Phenomenological Research* 69: 1–36.

Pollock, J. 1986. *Contemporary Theories of Knowledge*. Towota NJ: Rowman and Littlefield.

Priest, G. 2005. *Towards Non-Being: The Logic and Metaphysics of Intentionality*. Oxford: Oxford University Press.

Putnam, H. 1967. "The Nature of Mental States." Originally published as "Psychological Predicates," in W.H. Capitan and D.D. Merrill (eds.), *Art, Mind, and Religion*. Reprinted in D.M. Rosenthal (ed.), The Nature of Mind. Oxford: Oxford University Press.

———. 1981. *Reason, Truth, and History*. Cambridge: Cambridge University Press.

Quine, W.V.O. 1948. "On What There Is." *Review of Metaphysics* 2: 21–38.

———. 1953. "Mr. Strawson's Logical Theory." *Mind* 62: 433–451.

———. 1956. "Quantifiers and Propositional Attitudes." *Journal of Philosophy* 53: 177–187.

———. 1960. *Word and Object*. Cambridge MA: MIT Press.

———. 1968. "Ontological Relativity." *Journal of Philosophy* 65: 185–212.

———. 1975. "Mind and Verbal Dispositions." In S. Guttenplan (ed.), *Mind and Language*. Oxford: Clarendon.

Ramsey, W. 1997. "Do Connectionist Representations Earn Their Explanatory Keep?" *Mind and Language* 12: 34–66.

Rosch, E.H. 1973. "Natural Categories." *Cognitive Psychology* 4: 328–350.

———. 1975. "Cognitive Representations of Semantic Categories." *Journal of Experimental Psychology* 104: 192–233.

Rosenthal, D.M. 1986. "Two Concepts of Consciousness." *Philosophical Studies* 94: 329–359.

———. 1990. "A Theory of Consciousness." ZiF Technical Report 40, Bielfield, Germany. Reprinted in Block et al. 1997.

———. 1993. "Thinking That One Thinks." In M. Davies and G.W. Humphreys (eds.), *Consciousness: Psychological and Philosophical Essays*. Oxford: Blackwell.

———. 2002. "Explaining Consciousness." In D.J. Chalmers (ed.), *Philosophy of Mind*. Oxford and New York: Oxford University Press.

———. 2004. "Varieties of Higher-Order Theory." In. R.J. Gennaro (ed.), *Higher-Order Theories of Consciousness: An Anthology*. Amsterdam and Philadelphia: John Benjamins.
———. 2005. *Mind and Consciousness*. Oxford: Oxford University Press.
Roush, S. 2005. *Tracking Truth*. Oxford: Oxford University Press.
Russell, B. 1902. "Letter to Frege." In J. van Heijenoort (ed.), *From Frege to Gödel*. Cambridge MA: Harvard University Press, 1967.
———. 1910. "Knowledge by Acquaintance and Knowledge by Description." *Proceedings of the Aristotelian Society* 11: 108–128.
Salmon, N. 1988. "Nonexistence." *Noûs* 32: 277–319.
Schaffer, J. 2004. "Two Conceptions of Sparse Properties." *Pacific Philosophical Quarterly* 85: 92–102.
Schiffer, S. 1982. "Intention Based Semantics." *Notre Dame Journal of Formal Logic* 23: 119–159.
Seager, W. 1999. *Theories of Consciousness*. London: Routledge.
Searle, J.R. 1983. *Intentionality*. Cambridge: Cambridge University Press.
———. 1990. "Consciousness, Explanatory Inversion and Cognitive Science." *Behavioral and Brain Sciences* 13: 585–642.
———. 1991. "Consciousness, Unconsciousness, and Intentionality." *Philosophical Issues* 1: 45–66.
———. 1992. *The Rediscovery of Mind*. Cambridge MA: MIT Press.
Shagrir, O. 2001. "Content, Computation, and Externalism." *Mind* 110: 369–400.
Shani, I. 2008. "Against Consciousness Chauvinism." *The Monist* 91: 294–323.
Shoemaker, S. 1994. "Phenomenal Character." *Noûs* 28: 21–38.
———. 1998. "Causal and Metaphysical Necessity." *Pacific Philosophical Quarterly* 79: 59–77.
———. 2002. "Introspection and Phenomenal Character." In D.J. Chalmers (ed.), *Philosophy of Mind*. Oxford and New York: Oxford University Press.
Siegel, S. 2005. "The Contents of Perception." *Stanford Encyclopedia of Philosophy*.
———. 2006. "Which Properties Are Represented in Perception?" In T. Gendler Szabo and J. Hawthorne (eds.), *Perceptual Experience*. Oxford and New York: Oxford University Press.
Siewert, C.P. 1998. *The Significance of Consciousness*. Princeton NJ: Princeton University Press.
———. 2011. "Phenomenal Thought." In Bayne and Montague 2011.
Smithies, D. Ms. "The Mental Lives of Zombies."
Stampe D. 1977. "Towards a Causal Theory of Linguistic Representation." *Midwest Studies in Philosophy* 2: 42–63.
Stich, S. 1978. "Autonomous Psychology and the Belief-Desire Thesis." *The Monist* 61: 573–591.

———. 1983. *From Folk Psychology to Cognitive Science*. Cambridge MA: MIT Press.
Strawson, G. 1994. *Mental Reality*. Cambridge MA: MIT Press.
———. 2005. "Intentionality and Experience: Terminological Preliminaries." In D.W. Smith and A. Thomasson (eds.), *Phenomenology and Philosophy of Mind*. Oxford and New York: Oxford University Press.
———. 2008. "Real Intentionality 3: Why Intentionality Entails Consciousness." In his *Real Materialism and Other Essays*. Oxford: Oxford University Press.
Tennant, N. 2009. "Cognitive Phenomenology, Semantic Qualia, and Luminous Knowledge." In P. Greenough and D. Pritchard (eds.), *Williamson on Knowledge*. Oxford: Oxford University Press.
Thau, M. 2002. *Consciousness and Cognition*. Oxford: Oxford University Press.
Thomasson, A. 2008. "Phenomenal Consciousness and the Phenomenal World." *The Monist* 91: 191–214.
Thompson, B. 2010. "The Spatial Content of Experience." *Philosophy and Phenomenological Research* 81: 146–184.
Travis, C. 2004. "The Silence of the Senses." *Mind* 113: 57–94.
Twardowski, K. 1894. *On the Content and Object of Presentations*. Translated by R. Grossmann. The Hague: Martinus Nijhoff, 1977.
Tye, M. 1995. *Ten Problems of Consciousness*. Cambridge MA: MIT Press.
———. 1997. "A Representational Theory of Pains and Their Phenomenal Character." In Block et al. 1997.
———. 2000. *Consciousness, Color, and Content*. Cambridge MA: MIT Press.
Van Cleve, J. 1985. "Three Versions of the Bundle Theory." *Philosophical Studies* 47: 95–107.
Weiskrantz, L. 1986. *Blindsight: A Case Study and Implication*. Oxford: Oxford University Press.
Wilberg, J.R. 2009. *Phenomenal Consciousness and Higher-Order Thought*. PhD Dissertation, University of Essex.
———. 2010. "Consciousness and False HOTs." *Philosophical Psychology* 23: 617–638.
Williams, D. 1953. "The Elements of Being: I." *Review of Metaphysics* 7: 3–18.
Wright, C. 1988. "Moral Values, Projection and Secondary Qualities." *Proceedings of Aristotelian Society* 62: 1–26.
———. 1992. *Truth and Objectivity*. Cambridge MA: Harvard University Press.
Whyte, J. 1990. "Success Semantics." *Analysis* 50: 149–157.
Zemach, E. 1976. "Putnam's Theory on the Reference of Substance Terms." *Journal of Philosophy* 73: 116–127.
Zimmerman, T.E. 2001. "Unspecificity and Intensionality." In C. Féry and W. Sternefeld (ed.), *Audiatur Vox Sapentiae*. Berlin: Akademie Verlag.

Index

adverbial
  theory 7–8, 125, 150, 153, 159, 161, 171–173, 185–186, 226, 230, 240, 250
  property 154–156, 165–167, 183, 188, 231–233, 240, 250–251
adverbialism 153, 155, 159, 161–163, 165–1671, 182–188, 230–234, 236, 238–240, 250
  see also adverbial theory
anchoring instance 7, 10, 14, 16–24, 26, 34, 37–40, 42–43, 52, 54–55, 61
Armstrong, D.M. 47, 53, 64, 121, 139, 141–142, 147, 180, 224
ascription, intentional 4, 24, 26–37, 39, 41, 43, 55–60, 182, 204–205, 208–211, 215, 217, 223–225
aspectual shape 174, 190–191, 194, 220, 226
  see also intensionality

Bayne, T. 63, 188, 226
Bennett, J.F. 96, 175–176
Block, N.J. 46, 60, 62–63, 66, 79, 167, 175, 188
Blumson, B. 62, 124, 188, 225, 227
brain in vat 101–103, 107–108, 123–124, 127, 137–139, 161, 178–179, 181–182
Bourget, D. 66, 75, 113, 257, 226
Brandom, R.B. 131, 165

Chalmers, D.J. 62–63, 66, 74, 77, 112, 114, 124, 151, 167–169, 180, 188, 226
charity, principle(s) of 26–29, 32, 34–35, 57–60, 208–209, 213, 224–226
Chisholm, R. 125–126, 161, 173, 183
Chudnoff, E. 48, 61, 65
conditions
  accuracy 47, 137, 140, 166, 174, 176
  ideal 7, 202–204, 209–210, 223, 232, 241, 244, 247, 250
  normal 53, 111, 135, 176–177, 180
content
  (in)determinate 156, 195, 209–210, 219–221
  experiential-intentional 23, 67–68, 80–82, 93–95, 97–100, 102–103, 109, 115, 121–123, 127–128, 130, 135–140, 143, 146, 150–154, 156, 158–160, 163–164, 177–180, 182, 185–187, 191–192, 196, 199, 204, 210–211, 218–219, 225, 233, 236, 246, 250, 252–254
  intentional (in general) 4, 7, 35, 48–51, 65, 67, 110, 113–114, 124, 131, 151–153, 161, 164–165, 175, 182, 186–187, 193–195, 197, 199–200, 202, 204–205, 209–213, 216, 220, 222, 225–226, 229, 232–239, 241–248, 250–254
  non-conceptual 75, 112–114
  non-experiential-intentional 182, 189, 191–196, 198, 202–204, 211, 213–214, 218, 220–222, 224–225, 236, 250
  representational 70–78, 80, 111–117, 220
  see also intentionality

Davidson, D. 27–29, 56–57, 62, 176, 187, 201–202, 213, 222, 225
Davies, M. 115, 192, 218
Dennett, D.C. 28, 55, 57, 201–202, 206, 213–214, 222, 224
Dretske, F. 39, 70–71, 73, 75, 80–81, 89, 96–97, 110–113, 115–116, 122, 124, 132, 143, 149, 181–182, 220, 222

experience
  cognitive 30, 45, 48–50, 57, 59, 63, 65, 75–76, 93, 113, 127, 129, 139, 146, 156, 174–175, 178–179, 183–184, 186, 194–195, 202, 209, 220, 235–236, 238–239, 251
  perceptual 4, 23, 33, 39, 47, 50, 58, 61, 64, 75–76, 93, 137–139, 146, 157, 174–175, 178–179, 194–195, 209, 235, 251
  sensory 45, 47, 50, 59, 63, 75, 118, 128–129, 183–184, 194, 220, 235, 251,
experiential character 6–7, 30–31, 44–51, 59, 62–65, 73–81, 84–87, 89–91, 93, 102, 104, 112–119, 123–124, 128–129, 132, 137, 140, 146, 156–157, 160, 164, 174–175, 178–180, 183–185, 187, 190–191, 194, 219–220, 233, 235–236, 239, 242, 249, 251
externalism 116, 186, 238–239, 246, 248

Field, H. 131, 165, 175
Fodor, J. 55, 72, 76, 80, 96, 105, 111, 124, 143–144, 149, 181, 191, 218

Georgalis, N. 62–63, 190, 221, 226
Goldman, A.I. 63, 65, 110, 208
Graham, G. 65, 192, 194–195, 220, 226
Grice, H.P. 62, 106, 124, 199–200, 211–212, 225

hallucination 139–140, 147–148, 154, 160, 179, 181, 186
  see also intentional inexistence
Harman, G. 39, 78, 175, 226
higher-order theory (of consciousness) 83–85, 87, 90–91, 93, 104, 117–120
higher-order thought 117
  see also higher-order theory
higher-order tracking see tracking, higher-order
higher-order tracking theory see tracking, higher-order
Horgan, T. 45–46, 55, 59, 61, 63, 65, 110, 137, 188, 190, 192, 194–196, 198, 220–221, 226

Intensional(ity) 60, 105, 125–126, 132–133, 173
  see also intentional indifference
intentional indifference 125–128, 131–138, 174–175, 177–178, 190–191, 199, 218, 246, 248
intentional inexistence 125–127, 137–140, 143–144, 147, 149–152, 159, 161, 172, 178–180, 187, 199
intentionality
  concept(ion) of 7, 9–10, 19–25, 34, 37–38, 41–43, 50–51, 54, 61, 67, 100, 189, 229
  derived/derivative 113, 206–208, 213, 215, 236, 243, 248–249
  experiential 6–9, 21, 23, 25, 29, 31, 37, 43–47, 49–51, 54, 56, 62–64, 67–69, 80–84, 87, 90–95, 97, 99–100, 103, 109–110, 116–117, 119–122, 125, 127–128, 130–131, 133, 137–138, 140, 143–144, 147, 149–151, 153, 156, 159–161, 166–168, 170–173, 175–176, 180, 182–184, 186–187, 189, 192, 194–195, 206, 211, 215, 217–218, 226, 230–231, 239, 245–246, 249, 252–253

linguistic 62, 199–200, 211–212, 225
naturalizing 3, 4, 69, 113, 166–167, 170–171, 239, 249
non-experiential 6–8, 29, 37, 51, 56, 82, 175, 189, 191, 194–196, 198–202, 204–206, 211, 213, 215–218, 222–226, 239
original 6, 224
  see also intentionality, underived/non-derivative
phenomenal 45, 62
  see also intentionality, experiential
phenomenological signature of 156, 158, 184, 234–236
pictorial 62
underived/non-derivative 113, 206–208, 215–216, 224, 231, 233–234, 236, 239–240, 243, 245–246, 248–249, 252
internalism 236–239, 246–249, 251–255
interpretation 27–28, 32, 41, 47, 56, 58, 60, 187, 201–203, 208–210, 212–214, 222–226, 232, 234, 236, 239, 242–243, 252
interpretivism 7–8, 189–190, 200–206, 208–209, 211–218, 223–226, 230–234, 236, 239–240, 242, 248–250, 252

Jackson, F.C. 66, 160–162, 167, 177, 186
Johnston, M. 134, 183, 253

Kim, J. 54, 62, 169, 175
Kripke, S. 19, 54, 110, 186, 212

LePore, E. 55, 76, 191, 218
Levine, J. 45, 77, 86, 118–119
Loar, B. 45, 62, 156, 190, 194–196, 198, 220–221, 226, 234, 251
Lycan, W.G. 65, 115–118

McGinn, C. 60, 62, 64, 111, 130, 175
Masrour, F. 66, 118, 124, 129, 157, 183–184, 188, 234–235
Mendelovici, A. 63, 65, 66, 182, 218
Millikan, R.G. 72–73, 80, 111–112, 181
misrepresentation 3–4, 72, 88–90, 92–93, 111, 115, 118–119, 122, 143, 179
Montague, M. 55, 66, 110, 164, 226–227

Papineau, D. 73, 111, 220
Pautz, A. 63, 77, 151, 188

Peacocke, C. 15, 63, 65, 79
phenomenal character *see* experiential character
phenomenology
   cognitive *see* experience, cognitive
   perceptual *see* experience, perceptual
   sensory *see* experience, sensory
property
   dispositional 77–78, 116, 154, 203, 234, 252
   intrinsic 163, 185, 224, 231, 237, 246–247, 251–252, 254
   non-relational 185, 197, 226, 237–239, 254
   relational 96, 153, 163, 185, 237, 239
   response-dependent 204, 246–247, 254
Putnam, H. 70, 101, 107

Quine, W.V.O. 60, 105, 124, 194

representation
   higher-order 84, 86–95, 102, 104, 109, 117–120, 253
   mental 69–74, 79–80, 82–83, 86–87, 96, 98, 102, 104–111, 115–116, 122–123, 143, 192–193
   self- *see* self-representationalism
representationalism 74–82, 87, 90–91, 103–104, 113–116, 119
Rosenthal, D. 40, 85, 88–89, 117–118, 124, 253

Searle, J. 56, 62, 124, 131, 174, 187, 190–192, 194, 198, 224, 226

self-representationalism 84–85, 87, 97–98, 103, 117–119, 122, 253
Siegel, S. 41, 47, 61, 64, 188, 209
Siewert, C.P. 46, 63–66, 129, 187, 253
Strawson, G. 49, 63, 65, 156, 183, 190, 198, 227, 234, 251

teleo-informational 72, 80–81, 99, 123, 142–143, 181, 245, 248
thesis
   experiential origin 7–10, 21–23, 38, 42–43, 50–51, 55, 69, 100, 102–103, 133, 189, 217–218, 229, 239, 248–249
   transparency 79, 91, 115, 120, 130, 179, 184
   see also experience, transparency of
tracking 3–7, 23, 68–74, 78–84, 87, 89–99, 100–104, 106–112, 115–117, 119–125, 127–128, 130–135, 137–138, 140, 142–144, 146–151, 156, 160, 166, 173, 175–183, 187, 190, 192–194, 197–199, 204, 211–212, 214, 225–226, 230, 239, 244–246, 249, 253
   higher-order 7–8, 67–68, 92, 94–95, 97, 100, 102, 104, 108–109, 120–121, 124–125, 127–128, 131–132, 135–136, 138, 143–144, 150–151, 154, 166, 168–169, 171–173, 175, 180–181, 187, 202, 226, 230, 240, 242–246, 248–250, 252–253

zombies 197–198, 204, 221, 224